DISCRIMINATION, EQUALITY AND THE LAW

This monograph explores some of the conceptual questions which underpin the legal disputes which arise in relation to equality and discrimination. Among these are questions about the meaning of 'equality' as a legal concept and its relationship to the principle of non-discrimination; symmetrical and asymmetrical approaches to equality/non-discrimination; the role of comparators in discrimination/equality analysis; the selection of protected characteristics and the proper sphere of statutory and constitutional protections, and the scope for and regulation of potential conflicts between protected grounds. The author engages with domestic, EU and ECtHR case law as well as with wider international approaches.

Volume 19 in the series Human Rights Law in Perspective

Human Rights Law in Perspective

General Editor: Colin Harvey
Professor of Human Rights Law
School of Law

Queen's University Belfast

The language of human rights figures prominently in legal and political debates at the national, regional and international levels. In the UK the Human Rights Act 1998 has generated considerable interest in the law of human rights. It will continue to provoke much debate in the legal community and the search for original insights and new materials will intensify.

The aim of this series is to provide a forum for scholarly reflection on all aspects of the law of human rights. The series will encourage work which engages with the theoretical, comparative and international dimensions of human rights law. The primary aim is to publish over time books which offer an insight into human rights law in its contextual setting. The objective is to promote an understanding of the nature and impact of human rights law. The series is inclusive, in the sense that all perspectives in legal scholarship are welcome. It will incorporate the work of new and established scholars.

Human Rights Law in Perspective is not confined to consideration of the UK. It will strive to reflect comparative, regional and international perspectives. Work which focuses on human rights law in other states will therefore be included in this series. The intention is to offer an inclusive intellectual home for significant scholarly contributions to human rights law.

Recent titles in this series

Transitional Justice from Below:
Grassroots Activism and the Struggle for Change
Edited by Kieran McEvoy and Lorna McGregor

Making Rights Real: The Human Rights Act in its First Decade
Ian Leigh and Roger Masterman

Children's Socio-Economic Rights, Democracy and the Courts
Aoife Nolan

Rights in Divided Societies
Edited by Colin Harvey and Alexander Schwartz

Health and Human Rights
Thérèse Murphy

For the complete list of titles in this series, see 'Human Rights Law in Perspective' link at www.hartpub.co.uk/books/series.asp

Discrimination, Equality and the Law

Aileen McColgan

·HART·
PUBLISHING

OXFORD AND PORTLAND, OREGON
2016

Published in the United Kingdom by Hart Publishing Ltd
16C Worcester Place, Oxford, OX1 2JW
Telephone: +44 (0)1865 517530
Fax: +44 (0)1865 510710
E-mail: mail@hartpub.co.uk
Website: http://www.hartpub.co.uk

Published in North America (US and Canada) by
Hart Publishing
c/o International Specialized Book Services
920 NE 58th Avenue, Suite 300
Portland, OR 97213-3786
USA
Tel: +1 503 287 3093 or toll-free: (1) 800 944 6190
Fax: +1 503 280 8832
E-mail: orders@isbs.com
Website: http://www.isbs.com

Hart Publishing is an imprint of Bloomsbury Publishing plc.

British Library Cataloguing in Publication Data
Data Available

ISBN: 978-1-50990-499-0

Typeset by Hope Services, Abingdon
Printed and bound in Great Britain by
TJ International Ltd, Padstow, Cornwall

Acknowledgements

This book is the outrageously tardy product of a sabbatical I enjoyed at the School of Law, King's College London in early 2005. The application for that sabbatical stated with some confidence that the book in respect of which it was sought was likely to be completed six months after the sabbatical ended (that is, December 2005). In the event I spent the sabbatical reading rather than writing and it took eight years longer than anticipated to get to the point at which (in December 2013) I have turned to these acknowledgements.

My first thanks, then, to those at the School of Law (latterly the Dickson Poon School of Law) for their patience. The same is true of the publishers who were assured every six months for the last five years or so that the book was virtually finished. Its eventual completion was as great a surprise to me as it was no doubt to series editor Colin Harvey and to Richard and the others at Hart.

My thanks also to those who contributed by commenting on various drafts of different chapters: Ulele Burnham, Joanne Conaghan, Maleiha Malik and Colm O'Cinneide. Many others have helped in conversation and debate to shape my thinking on the themes I consider in the book, amongst them (again alphabetically arranged) my daughters Caoimhe and Rionach Downing and my friends and colleagues Judy Fudge, Sarah Hannett, Ronan McCrea, Christopher McCrudden, Karon Monaghan and John Tasioulas.

Finally, the book is dedicated to the memory of my beloved parents, Sam and Eithne, who in showing us always the value of fairness managed to make feminists of all of their offspring.

Contents

Table of Cases

INTERNATIONAL JURISDICTIONS

Inter-American Court of Human Rights

NATIONAL JURISDICTIONS

United Kingdom

Australia

Canada

European Union - Commission Decisions

European Union - Court of Justice

Alphabetical order

Numerical order

France

Ireland, Republic of

Mauritius

Pakistan

South Africa

United States of America

Table of Legislation

United Kingdom

Statutory Instruments

Canada

European Union

Treaties

Directives

1

'Equality', 'Discrimination' and the Law: an Introduction

THE LAST DECADE or so has seen extraordinary changes in the landscape of equality/discrimination law in the UK. Not only have the grounds to which statutory protection applies extended beyond race, sex and disability to include sexual orientation, religion and belief, and age, but the patchwork of legislative provisions has been transformed into a relatively coherent legal framework (in Great Britain) by the Equality Act 2010. The implementation of the Human Rights Act 1998, in October 2000, opened the door to equality/discrimination challenges beyond the boundaries of the sometimes rigid framework of anti-discrimination statutes. And perhaps most radical of all, the enactment of what have come to be known as the 'public sector equality duties' has begun to transform the landscape by including equality considerations as mandatory factors which must be taken into account by public authorities in all their decisions.[1]

This book is directed towards a largely UK readership, though I hope it will also be of interest to others. It is a book primarily for lawyers, whether academics, practitioners or students. It is not a textbook or a practitioners' manual and does not set out to detail domestic statutory provisions, or those of a more international flavour. It seeks, rather, to address deeper questions concerning the proper shape and development of equality/discrimination law.

The questions that I attempt to address in this book are those which have come to interest me during the course of a quarter century's involvement in the area. My first exposure was as an undergraduate law student. The House of Lords' decision in *Hayward v Cammell Laird (No 2)*,[2] in which a canteen cook won the right to equal pay with her male comparators – male painters, thermal insulation engineers and joiners – was one of the cases, much dreaded by students, decided in the period immediately preceding my final exams. What I remember about that particular decision, however, was that my delight in their Lordships' requirement for equality in relation to each contractual term relating to pay, rather than 'in the round', outweighed my irritation in having (yet) another case to memorise.

---

[1] As well as by non-public bodies performing public functions in relation to those functions.
[2] *Hayward v Cammell Laird (No 2)* [1988] AC 894.

During my LLM studies in Edinburgh, the formal aspect of which seemed to consist largely in gazing in bewilderment at the equations in Joseph Raz's *Authority of Law,* I fell into a women's reading group run by Beverley Brown as a result of which I replaced my sex-and-shopping reading material with Mary Daly and Germaine Greer. There followed a job writing about labour law where I was allowed to pursue an increasing interest in sex discrimination/equal pay which in turn led me to academia. Finding myself teaching criminal law, my first real ventures into academic writing concerned the legal treatment of women who killed abusive men, and of women who complained of sexual assault.[3] Criminal law gave way to labour law and I began to write about equal pay and sex discrimination law, then about (broadly) employment-related discrimination more generally.

My interest in these areas as aspects of labour law was balanced by broader concerns about equality in the context of public and human rights litigation. The latter began in a theoretical way with the writing of a sceptical book about the likely impact of the Human Rights Act 1998 on women and gender equality.[4] Shortly after this book was completed I began to practise as a barrister, as a result of which my macro-level scepticism about both the common law and the Human Rights Act became tempered, at least at the micro level, by the recognition that there were aspects of both that were useful additions to the lawyer's tool kit.[5] With the amendment of the discrimination statutes expressly to regulate discrimination by public authorities,[6] and the implementation of the public sector equality duties, the statutory regime (now consolidated, if not radically simplified), common law and human rights arguments have begun to come together in a much more coherent way than was previously the case.

Now seems the time to attempt to engage with some of the difficult questions thrown up by the competing demands of those with different interests in the outcomes of arguments about equality/discrimination. What groups or individuals, for example, are the proper subject of our concern when we talk about 'equality' or 'discrimination'?. Ought we to be striving for a society which is blind to differences of race, gender or sexual orientation? Whatever the answer to the previous questions, do they similarly apply to disability? to age? to religious or other beliefs, or to their absence? to appearance? to gluttony? to wealth? to cleverness? to the ability or inclination to keep one's nose to the grindstone?

If the answer is not that society should be blind to these, or some of these, or to other, differences, to what extent can such differences be respected without

---

[3] A McColgan, 'In Defence of Battered Women who Kill' (1993) 13 *Oxford Journal of Legal Studies* 508–29, 'Common Law and the Relevance of Sexual History Evidence' (1996) 16 *Oxford Journal of Legal Studies* 275–307.

[4] A McColgan, Women under the Law; the False Promise of Human Rights (Harlow: Longman, 1999).

[5] See Sedley J (as he then was), 'Human Rights: A Twenty-First Century Agenda' [1995] *Public Law* 386, 388.

[6] First by the implementation of the Race Relations (Amendment) Act 2000 then with the amendment of the Disability Discrimination Act 1995 and finally the Sex Discrimination Act 1975.

running the danger of reifying and/or perpetuating that which might otherwise be minor and/or transient? What balance is to be struck between avoiding the demand for assimilation and driving people into bunkers which reflect, if at all, only limited aspects of their multifaceted individuality? When is difference good? When is it bad? When is it to be respected and when merely tolerated? When, by recognising difference, do we make it real? Do we ever have to accommodate difference where, in so doing, we allow the disadvantaged to be further disadvantaged in the pursuit of some other kind of equality? Do we have to allow those who insist on their difference to subject others to disadvantage in pursuit of that difference? And does the answer to this question and the previous one depend on whether the person or group whose difference is being insisted on is him/her/itself disadvantaged?

What do we mean by 'disadvantage'? What factors, by reference to which people may be identified, should be excluded from consideration when it comes to the distribution of advantages in the context of work, for example, night clubbing or flat sharing? Ought these factors always to be ignored? Or should we be striving to treat equally on the basis of these or other characteristics? If so, what does treating equally mean? Are the answers to each of these questions the same for each of these factors? And are they the same as the factors which should be disallowed from consideration, or otherwise subjected to 'equal' treatment, in the context of education, access to healthcare or the policing function of the state?

These and other questions are the subject of the chapters that follow. Some can be regarded as legal questions in the sense that legal analysis will generate answers to them, whether firm or tentative, within particular legal systems. Some of those answers will be considered over the course of this book, the legal systems to which reference will be made being those currently applicable in Britain as well as, to greater or lesser extents, Canada, the US and South Africa. But many of these questions are most interestingly addressed in the realm of the 'ought' rather than the 'is', because their answers may most fruitfully be determined by matters other than the particular choice of words legislators or adjudicators have selected or compromised on, often when considering issues of more immediate concern to the decision makers.

STRUCTURE OF THE BOOK

The 'ought', then, is what I am primarily interested in, and it is the 'ought' which drives the selection of the comparative material discussed in the book, which is organised as follows. In this chapter I make a very brief sketch of the legal framework which operates in Britain. This sketch serves to anchor what follows but does not purport to do more than nod towards some of the complex legal issues which arise in connection with that framework. As above, this is not the book to read to discover the detail of British discrimination law. The main purpose of this chapter is to introduce some of the recent debates about the underpinning purpose of anti-discrimination law and the scope and target of equality-related concerns.

In Chapter 2 I outline the role of 'grounds' or 'protected characteristics' in the current legal approach to discrimination, and begin to consider which such grounds/characteristics ought to be protected from discrimination. In doing this I discuss the various approaches taken to grounds in the US, Canada and the jurisprudence of the European Court of Human Rights. Part of the purpose of this chapter is to challenge the general tendency which those with a concern for equality might have to favour expansion of the list of protected characteristics. There are, in my view, strong reasons of principle, as well as pragmatism, to confine fairly narrowly those characteristics which are provided with relatively comprehensive protection from discrimination and to focus on the correlation between identification with those grounds and disadvantage across multiple spheres of life. In discussing these reasons, I introduce what is a core theme of this book: the tensions which result from treating religion and belief, in particular, as synonymous with characteristics such as ethnicity or sexual orientation, for example, in the legal regulation of discrimination.

In Chapter 3 I explore what I call 'symmetrical' and 'asymmetrical' approaches to discrimination, that is, conceptualisations of discrimination which are, respectively, generally compatible with and hostile to 'positive' discrimination. Domestic law has historically been suspicious of any approach which takes race, sex or other protected characteristic into account, preferring an ideal of justice blindfolded. While there are obvious attractions in a refusal to take into account characteristics which are generally irrelevant to 'merit', the demand for symmetry generally starts from the position that the current system rewards 'merit' (defined other than by reference to characteristics such as sex, race, sexual orientation, etc), and that any significant shift requires justification. If it is understood, however, not only that starting points are not equal, but also that notions of 'merit' are themselves open to challenge, and that many of those who are currently advantaged are the beneficiaries of systems which reward other than on the basis of any objectively defensible concept of 'merit', that perspective may shift. In Chapter 3 I try to show not only that the traditional British demand for symmetry is unusual both across common law jurisdictions and within Europe, but also that it is not to be preferred as a matter of principle over asymmetric approaches such as those adopted elsewhere. The chapter also touches on the recent shifts in the domestic approach, in particular in relation to claims arising under Article 14 of the European Convention on Human Rights (ECHR) and in connection with the public sector equality duty (PSED) considered below.

In Chapter 4 I consider the comparative approach to discrimination (that is, its conceptualisation largely in terms of differential treatment accorded to similarly situated individuals). I discuss the shortcomings of this approach and the extent to which it continues to exercise its traditional stranglehold on domestic analyses of discrimination. I consider the approach taken by the Court of Justice of the European Union (CJEU – formerly ECJ) and the European Court of Human Rights (ECtHR) and by Canada's Supreme Court. I then consider developments in the jurisprudence of the ECHR which, I suggest, indicate the possibility of a radical, non-comparative approach to discrimination/equality being developed by that Court. Though progress in this direction by the ECtHR is patchy, I conclude by discussing a number of domestic decisions which indicate that the seed sown by that Court may have taken root here.

In Chapter 5 I consider some of the possible conflicts which arise *within* equality, that is, as a result of the various different grounds upon which discrimination is regulated. In particular, I consider the recent case law concerning claims made by religious individuals and collectives from exemptions from the generally applicable prohibitions on discrimination, and the extent to which individuals' adherence to discriminatory views should be permitted to justify discrimination against them. Among the cases I consider are the recent decisions of the ECtHR in the *Ladele* and *McFarlane* cases,[7] in *ASLEF v UK* and in *Redfearn v UK*. [8] I conclude that the treatment of religion/belief as a characteristic similar to ethnicity, gender etc for the purposes of a broad prohibition on discrimination gives rise to significant difficulties and is not required by the ECHR.

In Chapter 6 I discuss the relationship and tensions between equality and multiculturalism. My starting point is a concern with what Ayelet Shachar calls the 'paradox of multicultural vulnerability', in which attempts to protect what are seen as minority interests end up sacrificing the rights and interests of some within minority groups.[9] Having considered some of the competing positions on the relationship between gender equality, in particular, and the recognition of cultural and/or religious practices, I turn to consider the question of Muslim family law. By looking with some care at the issues that arise in relation to the application in the UK of such law, I seek to challenge the easy assumptions that are often made about the best interests of minority (specifically, in this context, Muslim) women.

Chapter 7 is a brief concluding chapter in which I seek to draw together some of the themes arising elsewhere in the book and suggest how discrimination/equality law might best develop. What emerges from the book, I hope, is a way of thinking about equality/discrimination law which can provide a starting point from which some of the many other questions which arise in this context may be contemplated.

---

[7] *Eweida & Ors v UK* (2013) 57 EHRR 213.
[8] *ASLEF v UK* (2007) 45 EHRR 793 and *Redfearn v UK* (2012) 33 BHRC 713.
[9] A Shachar, 'On Citizenship and Multicultural Vulnerability' (2000) 28 *Political Theory* 64, 65.

THE LEGAL FRAMEWORK

The Equality Act 2010

Before turning to consider questions such as the relationship between equality and discrimination, or the values which legal regulation of discrimination might serve to defend, it is important briefly to outline the domestic legal framework. 2010–11 saw the replacement, in Britain, of a thicket of legislative provisions dealing with discrimination on various grounds and in a variety of contexts with a single Equality Act 2010, which gathers together the great majority of detailed domestic statutory provisions regulating discrimination into a single (albeit very lengthy) Act. (Its provisions remain to be interpreted and applied in compliance with the relevant provisions of EU law and the ECHR.)

The Equality Act, whose provisions were largely implemented in October 2010 and April 2011, was predominantly concerned with consolidation but included a number of substantive changes, some of which are considered below. Its basic scheme (what I shall refer to as the 'negative prohibitions'), consists in (i) definitions of what are now called 'protected characteristics'; (ii) definitions of types of discrimination (and harassment) and (iii) prohibitions on various types of discrimination, on the basis of particular characteristics, in specific contexts.

Without venturing beyond the broadest of sketches, the characteristics protected by the Equality Act are age, disability, gender reassignment, marriage and civil partnership, pregnancy and maternity, race, religion or belief, sex and sexual orientation. These characteristics are not identically treated (protection from disability discrimination and discrimination connected with gender reassignment and marriage/civil partnership is asymmetrical whereas the other protected characteristics are subject to symmetrical protection, for example; the definitions of discrimination applicable to disability are more numerous than those applicable to the other protected characteristics; direct discrimination is capable of justification only when it relates to age and the PSED does not apply in relation to marriage or civil partnership). Notwithstanding these important differences, the Equality Act's approach is characterised by a broad similarity of treatment across the protected characteristics.

As to the meaning of 'discrimination', the Act generally regulates *direct* discrimination (less favourable treatment *because of* a protected characteristic); *indirect* discrimination (unjustified application of a provision, criterion or practice the *effect* of which is disproportionately to disadvantage members of groups defined by reference to a protected characteristic); *victimisation* (*un*favourable treatment because of an allegation or complaint of discrimination); and *harassment* (unwanted conduct connected with a protected characteristic the purpose or effect of which is to violate dignity or create an 'intimidating, hostile, degrading, humiliating or offensive environment' for the person complaining of it). In addition, disability discrimination encompasses failures to make reasonable adjustments and unjustified *un*favourable treatment of a disabled persons 'because of something arising in consequence of' the person's disability.[10]

Turning, finally, to (iii) above, the Equality Act regulates discrimination in the context of work, education, membership of associations, access to goods, services and facilities, including housing, and the exercise of public functions generally.[11] Neither the Act, nor the many statutory provisions it replaced, imposes a general prohibition on discrimination on the basis of the 'protected characteristics'. But of increasing significance is the imposition by the Act, as by its predecessor provisions on race, sex and disability, of the PSED.

In its unified form, the PSED requires (s 149) that public authorities (and those exercising public functions, in the exercise of those functions[12]) must have 'due regard' to a number of *statutory needs*. These needs are (broadly) the need to *eliminate unlawful discrimination* and the needs to *advance equality of opportunity* and to *foster good relations* between persons defined by reference to protected characteristics. The PSED is significant for a number of reasons. Without at this stage delving too far into the principles established by the courts in relation to the previous PSEDs, it is worth mentioning that the duty applies to *all* of the functions of a public authority; that the measure of *due* regard is context specific; and that the PSED is not satisfied by the paying of 'due regard' only to questions of the potential disparate impact a policy or decision might have on groups of people defined by reference to relevant 'protected characteristics', but also requires that such regard be paid to the positive needs to 'advance equality of opportunity' and to 'foster good relations' between such groups.

Paying due regard to the need to advance equality of opportunity requires, in turn, that due regard be paid to the needs to *remove or minimise disadvantages* associated with relevant protected characteristics; to *take steps to meet particular needs* associated with relevant protected characteristics; and to *encourage participation* in public life or other activity by those in groups defined by reference to relevant protected characteristics whose participation is disproportionately low. The latter requires that 'due regard' be paid to the need to tackle prejudice, and promote understanding.[13]

The PSED is a qualitatively different type of provision than those which prohibit discrimination, even discrimination by public authorities. While the first limb of the PSED could be seen instrumentally as a means by which public authorities can avoid subsequent breaches of the prohibitions on discrimination,[14] this cannot be said of the other aspects of the duty. The statutory needs to promote equality and foster good relations between those defined by reference to the various protected grounds are not limited by the material scope of the

[10] Equality Act 2010, ss 13, 19, 27, 26, 21 and 15 respectively.
[11] Equality Act 2010, pts 3–7.
[12] All functions in the case of public authorities, public functions in the case of others (s149(2)).
[13] Section 149 Equality Act 2010.
[14] In particular in the form of indirect discrimination which can be avoided by *ex ante* consideration of the impact of decisions and whether or not any disparity in impact can be justified.

anti-discrimination provisions and have implications, accordingly, for many reaches of life in respect of which public authorities have influence. It is a matter of real concern, then, that the continued existence of the PSED is under threat by a government which has proven rather less than enthusiastic about the policy challenges which have been presented by the legal implementation of the equality mainstreaming principle.

EU Law

Also of great significance in the domestic context is EU law, in particular Article 157 of the Treaty on the Functioning of the European Union (TFEU)[15] and the Race, Gender and Employment Equality Directives.[16] Domestic law cannot be considered in isolation from these provisions, and they in turn are interpreted by the CJEU as the manifestation of a 'general principle' of non-discrimination in EU law, deriving from international law and the constitutional traditions of Member States,[17] and now articulated in Article 21 of the EU Charter of Rights. EU equality provisions have been responsible for securing, in domestic law, protection against discrimination on grounds of pregnancy and gender reassignment,[18] to name but a few examples, and for removing statutory caps on compensation in discrimination claims.[19] The potential for future change to domestic equality/discrimination law as a result of EU development, whether legislative or judicially driven, cannot be overestimated, not least in view of the adoption of the EU Charter of Rights and the prospective accession to the ECHR of the EU. Whereas the Human Rights Act 1998, further considered below, provides for robust judicial interpretation and for declarations of incompatibility where domestic legislation is, respectively, in tension, or frankly incompatible, with Convention rights, but not (in the case of primary legislation) allowing for judicial 'strike down',[20] all domestic law is vulnerable to judicial override to the extent of its incompatibility with EU law.

[15] Formerly Article 141 TEC, Article 119 Treaty of Rome.

[16] Directives 2000/43 (the Race Directive); 2000/73 (Employment Equality Directive), 2004/113/EC (the Gender Goods and Services Directive) and 2006/54/EC (the Recast Gender Directive).

[17] See for example Cases C-144/04 *Mangold v Helm* [2005] ECR I-9981, paras 75–76; C-555/0 *Kücükdeveci v Swedex GmbH & Co KG* [2010] ECR I-365, para 50; C-297/10 *Hennings v Eisenbahn-Bundesamt* and C-298/10 *Land Berlin v Mai* [2012] IRLR 83, paras 46–47. What began in cases C-117/75 and C-16/77 *Ruckdeschel & Ors* [1977] ECR 1753, para 7 as the requirement that 'similar situations should not be treated differently unless differentiation is objectively justified' (*per* AG Bot in *Kücükdeveci*, para 79, citing also Cases C-201/85 and C-202/85 *Klensch & Ors* [1986] ECR 3477, para 9, and C-442/00 *Rodrìguez Caballero* [2002] ECR I-11915, para 32) was capable in Case C-303/06 *Coleman v Attridge Law* [2008] ELR I-146 of underpinning a sophisticated analysis which applied the principle of non-discrimination on grounds of disability to treatment afforded a worker by reason of her son's disability.

[18] Respectively Cases C-32/93 *Webb v EMO (Air Cargo) Ltd (UK)* [1994] ECR I-3567 and C-13/94 *P v S & Cornwall* [1996] ECR I-2143.

[19] Case C-271/91 *Marshall v Southampton and West Hampshire AHA* [1993] ECR I-4367.

[20] This is a relatively crude characterisation of the Act's approach (see s 6) but suffices for most practical purposes.

Human Rights Act 1998/Article 14

Legal concepts of discrimination and equality are also of practical significance in the application of the Human Rights Act 1998, which gives partial effect in domestic law to the Articles of the European Convention on Human Rights scheduled thereto. Among those Articles is Article 14, which provides that:

> The enjoyment of the rights and freedoms set forth in this Convention shall be secured without discrimination on any ground such as sex, race, colour, language, religion, political or other opinion, national or social origin, association with a national minority, property, birth or other status.

This provision, applying as it does to numerous enumerated and unenumerated grounds,[21] can operate more flexibly than is typical for detailed statutory provisions such as are found in the Equality Act's prohibitions on discrimination. That is not to say that Article 14 is invariably – or even typically – interpreted free from the kind of formalism which has typified the approach of the domestic courts to the Equality Act's predecessor provisions. The early Human Rights Act jurisprudence straitjacketed Article 14 with multiple and overlapping requirements to be met before public authorities were called upon to justify differential, or differently impacting, treatment.[22] One example was a demand that claimants establish that they had been treated differently than a relevantly similar 'comparator' was or would have been treated. I shall consider the role of comparators in this and other contexts in Chapter 4. Suffice to say here, however, that recent case law, both domestic and that of the ECtHR, suggests a more flexible approach.[23]

In 2002 in a case involving challenges under Articles 2, 3, 5 and 14 ECHR to the death in police custody of a Roma youth who had been referred to even in official materials as 'the Gypsy',[24] dissenting Judge Bonello launched an excoriating attack on the failure of the Court

> in over fifty years of pertinacious judicial scrutiny [to find] . . . one single instance of violation of the right to life (art 2) or the right not to be subjected to torture or other degrading or inhuman treatment or punishment (art 3) induced by the race, colour or place of origin of the victim.[25]

The case was brought by the relatives of a child who had been wrongfully detained, had his skull fractured and timely medical assistance denied him by the police, and had died. The Court found breaches of Articles 2, 3 and 5 but,

---

[21] Adopting the Canadian terminology. The grounds protected by Art 14 are considered in Chapter 2.

[22] See in particular the decision of the Court of Appeal in *Wandsworth London Borough Council v Michalak* [2003] 1 WLR 617, 20 subsequently disapproved by the House of Lords in *Carson v SSWP* [2006] 1 AC 173.

[23] See, for example, *A & Ors v Home Secretary* [2005] 2 AC 68 (the *Belmarsh* case).

[24] *Anguelova v Bulgaria* (2002) 38 EHRR 31.

[25] ibid, para 2.

despite evidence that the law enforcement system in Bulgaria was systematically racist,[26] had demanded, and found there to be lacking, 'proof "beyond reasonable doubt" ' of race discrimination as a condition of finding that Article 14 had been breached.[27] Judge Bonello protested that:

> Frequently and regularly the Court acknowledges that members of vulnerable minorities are deprived of life or subjected to appalling treatment in violation of art 3; but not once has the Court found that this happens to be linked to their ethnicity. Kurds, coloureds, Islamics, Roma and others are again and again killed, tortured or maimed, but the Court is not persuaded that their race, colour, nationality or place of origin has anything to do with it. Misfortunes punctually visit disadvantaged minority groups, but only as the result of well-disposed coincidence.[28]

By 2008 the Grand Chamber of the Court had, in *DH v Czech Republic*,[29] expressly recognised for the first time that Article 14 prohibited indirect as well as direct discrimination.[30] This provided the possibility of successful challenges to institutionalised practices which, though likely the result of direct racial hostility and/or stereotyping, would be difficult to establish as such. The Court further ruled that, where the applicant established disparate impact (whether by reference to statistical evidence or otherwise), the burden of proof passed to the state to show that disparity was the result of objective factors unrelated to the protected ground. This took the sting from the Court's failure in *DH* itself to find that the de facto segregation of Roma children in 'special schools' involved direct discrimination, particularly in view of the Court's additional ruling that no difference in treatment which was based (as the treatment here was accepted as being based) exclusively or to a decisive extent on a person's ethnic origin was capable of being objectively justified in a contemporary democratic society built on the principles of pluralism and respect for different cultures, so as to escape censure under Article 14.[31] Further, and discussed in Chapter 4 below, the ECtHR has begun to draw in its Article 14 analysis on the jurisprudence of specialist bodies such as (in relation to violence against women) the Committee on the Elimination of Discrimination against Women.

The Common Law

Prior to the implementation of the Human Rights Act 1998 the common law formed the only remaining part of the tool kit if the discrimination under challenge fell within neither the statutory framework nor the scope of EU law. The

---

[26] See the discussion of this in the partly dissenting judgment of Judge Bonello.
[27] Above n 24, para 166.
[28] See also *Nachova v Bulgaria* (2006) 42 EHRR 43, paras 148–57.
[29] *DH v Czech Republic* (2008) 47 EHRR 3.
[30] Though this was arguably the effect of *Thlimmenos v Greece* (2001) 31 EHRR 15.
[31] Citing *Timishev v Russia* [2005] ECHR 55762/00, para 58.

historical approach of the common law to discrimination left much to be desired however, the judiciary itself being responsible for doctrines such as coverture by which 'the very being or legal existence of the wife is suspended during the marriage or at least incorporated and consolidated into that of the husband under whose wing, protection and cover she performs everything',[32] and otherwise displaying a marked lack of concern with discrimination on grounds now protected by statute and international law. Thus in *Roberts v Hopwood* (1925) public employers' attempts to pay men and women equally were struck down as the pursuit of 'some eccentric principles of socialistic philanthropy'.[33] And in *Short v Poole* (1926), which formed the basis for development of *Wednesbury* review,[34] Warrington LJ suggested that it would be ultra vires, because 'so clearly founded on alien and irrelevant grounds', for a public authority to dismiss a teacher 'because she had red hair, or for some equally frivolous and foolish reason', but upheld the decision to dismiss the claimant, a teacher, because she was a married woman.[35]

In *Scala Ballroom (Wolverhampton) Ltd v Ratcliffe* (1958) the English Court of Appeal upheld the legality of a bar on non-white entrants to the ballroom as 'a course which [the company was] entitled to adopt in [its] own business interests'.[36] Some progress had been made by 1972 when, in *Cumings & Ors v Birkenhead Corporation*, Lord Denning insisted that a rule allocating school places according to hair 'or, for that matter', skin colour 'would be so unreasonable, so capricious, so irrelevant to any proper system of education that it would be *ultra vires* altogether, and this court would strike it down at once'.[37] But those comments were made in a judgment upholding the refusal of an education authority to consider children who had attended Roman Catholic primary school for placement at non-Roman Catholic secondary schools. In *Schlegel v Corcoran* (1942) an Irish court had classified as reasonable a refusal to transfer rooms to a Jewish dentist on the grounds that the practice 'may, under Mr Gross, develop a Jewish complexion . . . such an anticipation is not groundless in a locality with a number of Jewish residents'.[38] And religious discrimination in testamentary dispositions was accepted as 'not . . . contrary to public policy' in *Re Lysaght* (1966), in which the High Court upheld the validity of a legacy to fund training of people who were British born and neither Jewish nor Roman Catholics,[39] and in *Blathwayt v Baron Cawley* (1976), in which the House of

---

[32] Blackstone, *Commentaries on the Laws of England* (1765–69) (Book 1, Ch 15) 442.
[33] *Roberts v Hopwood* [1925] AC 578.
[34] *Associated Provincial Picture Houses v Wednesbury* [1948] 1 KB 223.
[35] *Short v Poole* [1926] Ch 66.
[36] *Scala Ballroom (Wolverhampton) Ltd v Ratcliffe* [1958] 1 WLR 1057.
[37] *Cumings & Ors v Birkenhead Corporation* [1972] Ch 12.
[38] *Schlegel v Corcoran* (1942) IR 19. See further Conor Gearty, 'The Internal and External "Other" in the Union Legal Order: Racism, Religious Intolerance and Xenophobia in Europe' in P Alston, M Bustelo and J Heenan (eds), *The EU and Human Rights* (Oxford: Oxford University Press, 1999) 327, 341.
[39] *In re Lysaght* [1966] Ch 191.

Lords upheld a testamentary condition excluding those who were or became Roman Catholic.[40]

General disinterest on the part of the common law in discrimination appears only to have been encouraged by the implementation of the statutory prohibitions: whereas, in 1966, Lord Denning (again) had suggested that the refusal of the Field Club to issue training licences to women 'may well be said to be arbitrary and capricious', women being perfectly capable of training horses,[41] the House of Lords ruled in 1983 that sex discrimination was unlawful only if prohibited by the Sex Discrimination Act 1975.[42] And in 1996 the domestic courts upheld a ban on gays in the military against challenge on the public law ground of irrationality. In *R v Ministry of Defence ex p Smith* Simon Brown J (as he then was) remarked in the Divisional Court on the lack of evidence put before him to justify the ' "blanket, non-discretionary, specific", "status based" ban' but had ' "albeit with hesitation and regret" ', decided that it was not so irrational as to fail the *Wednesbury* test which requires the court to be satisfied that the administrative action at issue 'is beyond the range of responses open to a reasonable decision-maker'.[43] The Court of Appeal upheld his decision, the then Master of the Rolls Sir Thomas Bingham ruling that 'The threshold of irrationality is a high one. It was not crossed in this case'.[44]

The fact that much discrimination is widely regarded as acceptable, even common-sensical, at least until it is legally prohibited,[45] is why irrationality review at common law has been of very limited utility in challenging discrimination. But, as Sir Stephen Sedley remarked in his 1995 Paul Sieghart Memorial Lecture, 'The two most self-evident truths of life on this planet are after all that the earth is flat and that the sun goes round it'.[46]

In 1999, the Privy Council ruled in *Matadeen v Pointu* that 'treating like cases alike and unlike cases differently is a general axiom of rational behaviour'.[47] The Board went on, however, to question whether the 'axiom' was justiciable, Lord Hoffmann suggesting that 'the very banality of the principle [of equality] must suggest a doubt as to whether merely to state it can provide an answer' to whether discriminatory treatment was irrational (and therefore unlawful as a matter of public law).

---

[40] *Blathwayt v Baron Caw* [1976] AC 419.

[41] *Nagle v Feilden* [1966] 2 QB 633, although he did suggest that a different approach might be appropriate in relation to 'an unsuitable occupation for a woman, like that of a jockey or speedway-rider'.

[42] *Amin v Entry Clearance Officer, Bombay* [1983] 2 AC 818. See, similarly, *Bernstein v IAT & Anor* [1988] Imm AR 449.

[43] *R v Ministry of Defence ex p Smith* [1996] QB 517, 522, as summarised by Sir Thomas Bingham MR in the Court of Appeal, and at 541.

[44] ibid, 558.

[45] And often even after this – see, for example, the blustering dissent of Shaw LJ in *Coleman v Skyrail Oceanic Ltd (t/a Goodmos Tours)* [1981] ICR 864.

[46] S Sedley, 'Human Rights: A Twenty-First Century Agenda' [1995] *Public Law* 386, 386.

[47] *Matadeen v Pointu* [1999] 1 AC 98.

Of course persons should be uniformly treated, unless there is some valid reason to treat them differently. But what counts as a valid reason for treating them differently? And, perhaps more important, who is to decide whether the reason is valid or not? Must it always be the courts? . . . The fact that equality of treatment is a general principle of rational behaviour does not entail that it should necessarily be a justiciable principle.[48]

Matadeen was relied upon by the defendant in *Gurung v Ministry of Defence* to argue that the courts ought not to intervene in a case in which race discrimination was alleged.[49] McCombe J drew a distinction between the ground upon which discrimination was alleged in *Matadeen* (whether or not students in Mauritius had studied an oriental language) and that at issue in *Gurung* (skin colour). Referring to an extra-judicial speech by Lord Steyn,[50] in which his Lordship declared that the common law 'principle of equality' provided 'comprehensive[. . .] protect[ion]' against discrimination on 'irrational' grounds including 'race, colour, belief [and] gender', McCombe J declared that 'Th[e *Matadeen*] decision obviously leaves intact the common law principle of equality of which Lord Steyn spoke in his lecture'. In view of the fact that Mauritius's Constitution expressly prohibited race discrimination 'it can hardly have been thought that [such] discrimination might not be properly justiciable'. Such discrimination was 'irrational and inconsistent with the principle of equality that is the cornerstone of our law'.

The following year the Court of Appeal in *ABCIFER* rejected an argument, based on *Matadeen*, that a distinction drawn between categories of British citizens on the basis of their place of birth contravened the 'common law principle of equality'.[51] According to Dyson LJ, for the Court, the Privy Council in *Matadeen* was concerned with the application of *Wednesbury* to alleged discrimination, rather than with 'propounding' a 'free-standing principle of equality in English domestic law'. The common law challenge to the discrimination at issue in *ABCIFER* failed but a subsequent challenge under the Race Relations Act 1976, which included a complaint relating to the failure to comply with the PSED imposed by the Act, succeeded.[52] It may be that the scope for common law arguments about equality has reduced with the creation and development of the PSEDs (now PSED), and the implementation of the Human Rights Act 1998, and that any future common law developments of substance will take place only, if at all, as a result of amendment or repeal of the statutory provisions.

---

[48] ibid, 109.
[49] *Gurung v Ministry of Defence* [2002] EWHC 2463 (Admin).
[50] Now at (2002) 18 *European Human Rights Law Review* 723.
[51] *R (ABCIFER) v Secretary of State for Defence* [2003] QB 1397.
[52] *R (Elias) v Secretary of State for Defence* [2006] 1 WLR 3213.

'EQUALITY' AND 'DISCRIMINATION'

The sections above are intended only to provide a very broad outline of the legal contexts most relevant to the domestic framework in which legal determination of what might broadly be termed equality questions (what is meant by 'discrimination'?; who is protected from it and in relation to what types of decision?; can generally unlawful discrimination be justified, or does a relevant exception apply?, and so on) may take place. Next I want to get rid of some possible misconceptions relating to terminology.

It has become increasingly common to refer to domestic and EU provisions regulating discrimination in the workplace and elsewhere under the rubric 'equality' law, 'equality' appearing to have more positive connotations than 'discrimination' (or, more accurately, 'anti-discrimination'). The PSED is so called, for example, because it goes beyond prohibiting unlawful discrimination to require public authorities to pay 'due regard' to the need to take positive steps (though not necessarily actually to take such steps). But while discussion of 'equality' as distinct from 'non-discrimination' can be of some use in connoting such positive obligations to *do*, as distinct from to *desist*, referring to 'equality' in this context is replete with difficulties resulting from the 'contested and changing' meaning of the term.[53]

The concept of equality has been regarded by some as providing an underpinning or purpose to our prohibitions on discrimination. The need for such underpinnings results from the disputed meaning of 'discrimination' itself. I stated above that 'direct discrimination' is defined by the Equality Act as less favourable treatment *because* of a protected characteristic. The Act also provides (s 23) that 'On a comparison of cases for the purposes of [deciding whether there has been such *less* favourable treatment] there must be no material difference between the circumstances relating to each case'. Once we go beyond a bare prohibition on such discrimination, and assuming that we can agree what is a 'material difference' in any particular case, it becomes necessary to ground our responses to questions such as 'when is it discriminatory to treat differently situated persons similarly?',[54] or 'when may we treat persons differently because of a protected characteristic?'[55] in a concept other than that of 'discrimination' (or 'non-discrimination') itself.

One candidate might be 'equality'. A formal, Aristotelian approach would answer the questions posed with the observation that, just as 'likes should be treated alike', so 'unlikes' should be treated differently 'in proportion to their unlikeness', with the result that a factor which causes two otherwise 'like' cases

---

[53]   J Fudge, 'Substantive Equality, the Supreme Court of Canada, and the Limits to Redistribution' (2007) 23 *South African Journal on Human Rights* 235, 236.

[54]   This being the substance of indirect discrimination, subject to the question of justification.

[55]   ie, when is positive discrimination/positive action (see Chapter 3) lawful/justifiable, also when is direct discrimination permissible?

to be 'unlike' both permits and requires differential treatment.[56] But, on this approach, everything hangs on the recognition of 'like'. In *Powell v Pennsylvania* (1888), for example, in which the US Supreme Court rejected an equal protection challenge to the differential treatment of vendors of butter and margarine, Harlan J declared for the Court that:

> The statute places under the same restrictions, and subjects to like penalties and burdens, all who manufacture, or sell, or offer for sale, or keep in possession to sell, the articles embraced by its prohibitions; thus recognizing and preserving the principle of equality among those engaged in the same business.[57]

As Tussman and tenBroek pointed out, if 'like' means 'simply "similar in the possession of the classifying trait" . . . any classification whatsoever would be reasonable by this test . . . a law applying to red-haired makers of margarine would satisfy the requirements of equality'.[58] McIntyre J, for the majority of Canada's Supreme Court in *Andrews v Law Society of British Columbia* (1989), further noted that the 'like cases alike' test 'applied literally . . . could be used to justify the Nuremberg laws of Adolf Hitler'.[59]

Peter Westen claimed in 1982 that the idea of treating like alike was vacuous because it did not contain any basis on which to determine 'likeness', and that 'equality is entirely "Circular" . . . an empty vessel with no substantive moral content of its own . . .'.[60] The idea of formal equality can be rescued in part, as Marc Gold has suggested, by requiring that 'legislative distinctions must be relevant to the purposes of the law'. Coupled with (as in the US) 'constitutional principles that impose limits on the purposes of legislation', this would at least avoid the Nuremberg problem.[61] But such an approach is really directed at the type of general equality clause which is found in the Fourteenth Amendment to the US Constitution, as distinct from the characteristic-specific protection afforded by, for example, section 15 of Canada's Charter of Rights,[62] or Article 14 of the European Convention on Human Rights.[63]

Like the concept of 'non-discrimination' itself, therefore, such ruminations on the application of 'equality' do not progress the search for answers very far.[64] Illustrative of the difficulties in which the focus on 'equality', as distinct from 'discrimination', can result is the voluminous philosophical literature on 'luck

---

[56] *Ethica Nicomachea* V.3 1131a–b (W Ross trans, 1925).

[57] *Powell v Pennsylvania* (1888) 127 US 678.

[58] J Tussman and J tenBroek, 'The Equal Protection of the Laws' (1949) 37 *California Law Review* 341, 345.

[59] *Andrews v Law Society of British Columbia* [1989] 1 SCR 143, 166.

[60] P Westen, 'The Empty Idea of Equality' (1982) 95 *Harvard Law Review* 537, 547, footnotes omitted.

[61] M Gold, 'The Canadian Concept of Equality' (1996) 46 *University of Toronto Law Journal* 349, 352.

[62] Further discussed below and in Chapters 2 and 3.

[63] This is further discussed in Chapter 3.

[64] This is the point made by Lord Hoffmann in *Matadeen* and later in *Carson*, and by Dyson LJ in *ABCIFER*, above.

egalitarianism'. As Samuel Scheffler explains it, the 'central idea [of luck egalitarianism] is that inequalities in the advantages that people enjoy are acceptable if they derive from the choices that people have voluntarily made, but that inequalities deriving from unchosen features of people's circumstances are unjust'.[65] Luck egalitarianism is an example of an attempt, in relation to questions of distributional justice, to answer the question 'what cases are "like"?', 'unlikeness' being confined, as much as possible, to questions of choice.

Luck egalitarianism at first glance occupies progressive clothing inasmuch as its advocates are concerned not merely with equality of *treatment* but with equality of *outcome* or, more specifically, the question when and to what extent inequalities of outcome may be considered justifiable. This is an important distinction: as Aesop observed, providing milk to the stork and the fox in identical shallow dishes serves the fox alone, while serving it in identical long and narrow-necked jars allows only the stork to drink. And allowing only those with high school diplomas to work in more attractive jobs served, in 1960s America, to close such jobs to African American workers many of whom were the product of segregated schooling.[66] The preoccupation with outcomes is shared by thinkers including Amaryta Sen, Iris Marion Young and Martha Nussbaum, whose work on capabilities attempts to apply equality thinking to the reality of unequal starting points and differential needs. Closer inspection of luck egalitarianism, however, exposes it as a market-orientated philosophy which seeks to reconcile reliance on the market with the demands of social justice and which serves to distract attention from the reasons why real people find themselves in radically different social and economic positions.

Luck egalitarianism focuses primarily on the distribution of material resources to the neglect, as Elizabeth Anderson pointed out, of

> the much broader agendas of actual egalitarian political movements . . . the freedom [of gay and lesbian people] to appear in public as who they are, without shame or fear of violence, the right to get married and enjoy benefits of marriage, to adopt and retain custody of children' [, the inclusion and demarginalisation of disabled people and an end to the] . . . demeaning stereotypes that cast them as stupid, incompetent, and pathetic.[67]

It is, further, as Anderson went on to complain, preoccupied with the extent of redistributive obligations towards 'beach bums, the lazy and irresponsible, people who can't manage to entertain themselves with simple pleasures, religious fanatics [and the] stupid, talentless, and bitter',[68] the literature significantly con-

---

[65] S Scheffler, 'What is Egalitarianism?' (2003) 31(1) *Philosophy & Public Affairs* 5–39, 5. Scheffler characterises Dworkin as a 'luck egalitarian', a classification disputed by R Dworkin in 'Equality, Luck and Hierarchy' (2003) 31 *Philosophy & Public Affairs* 190.

[66] *Griggs v Power Duke Co* 401 US 424 (1971). The requirement for high school diplomas as a condition of access to any but the least attractive jobs replaced an overt ban on African American workers in those jobs.

[67] E Anderson, 'What is the Point of Equality?' (1999) 109 *Ethics* 109 287–337, 288.

[68] ibid, discussing R Dworkin, 'What Is Equality? Part 2: Equality of Resources' (1981) 10 *Philosophy and Public Affairs* 283, 288; Philippe Van Parijs, 'Why Surfers Should Be Fed: The Liberal

cerned with the extent to which an egalitarian society is obliged to pander to the preferences of those with tastes (cultivated or unwanted) for plovers' eggs or pre-phylloxera claret[69] and generating suggestions such as that of Phillipe Van Parijs that

> to fairly implement the equal right to get married, when male partners are scarce, every woman should be given an equal tradable share in the pool of eligible bachelors and have to bid for whole partnership rights, thus implementing a transfer of wealth from successful brides to compensate the losers in love.[70]

Luck egalitarianism equates those whose disadvantage in terms of satisfaction of material wants is connected with their disability, ethnicity, class position or care for dependents, for example,[71] with those who are 'disadvantaged' by their bone idleness, taste for champagne and caviar (the satisfaction of which is resource intensive) or assumption that the world owes them a living. These concerns provoked Anderson to ask whether 'If much recent academic work defending equality had been secretly penned by conservatives . . . the results [would] be any more embarrassing for egalitarians?'[72]

The challenge to the focus of luck egalitarians on resource distribution does not derive from an absence of concern about such distribution. Rather, as Iris Marion Young points out, much inequality in distribution

> is attributable neither to individual preferences and choices nor to luck or accident [but is caused by] . . . social institutions, their rules and relations, and the decisions others make within them that affect the lives of the individuals compared. . . People similarly positioned in social structures frequently experience multiple forms of exclusion, unequal burdens or costs deriving from institutional organization, rules, or decisions, and the cumulative consequences of each.[73]

Young suggests that, in theorising justice, we should not concentrate simply on distribution as such but that we should have regard to *patterns* of resource distribution according to social group, disparities which are not in *themselves* unjust but which, when present 'along several parameters', may *indicate*

Case for an Unconditional Basic Income' (1991) 20 *Philosophy and Public Affairs* 101–31; GA Cohen, 'On the Currency of Egalitarian Justice' (1989) 99 *Ethics* 906–44; R Arneson, 'Equality and Equality of Opportunity for Welfare' in L Pojman and R Westmoreland (eds), *Equality: Selected Readings* (New York: Oxford University Press, 1997) 229–41; T Nagel, 'The Policy of Preference' in *Mortal Questions* (Cambridge: Cambridge University Press, 1979) 91–105. See also R Dworkin, *Sovereign Virtue: The Theory and Practice of Equality* (Cambridge, MA: Harvard University Press, 2000).

[69] See for example R Dworkin 'What Is Equality? Part 1' (1981) 10 *Philosophy and Public Affairs* 185–246, 229; *A Matter of Principle* (Oxford: Oxford University Press, 1985) 206–08; and Cohen (n 68) 922 ff.

[70] Van Parijs (n 68) 287–88, citing *Real Freedom for All* (Oxford: Clarendon Press, 1995) 127.

[71] See Anderson (n 67) 300.

[72] See Anderson (n 67) 287; also Matt Matravers, 'Responsibility, Luck and the "Equality of What?" Debate' (2002) 50 *Political Studies* 558–72 for interesting discussions of the debates.

[73] IM Young, 'Equality of Whom? Social Groups and Judgments of Injustice' (2001) 9 *Journal of Political Philosophy* 1, 8. See also IM Young, *Justice and the Politics of Difference* (Princeton: Princeton University Press, 1990).

injustice.[74] 'Ultimately [however] the judgments of injustice . . . are not about the distributive patterns . . . [but about] generalized social *processes* which restrict the opportunities of some people to develop their capacities or access benefits while they enhance those of others'.[75]

Anne Phillips argues that the focus of luck egalitarians of individual preferences is wrong because it 'encourage[s] us to think that our chance talents and aspirations really do explain how and where we end up'.[76] While she concedes that differences between two individuals may be explicable by questions of choice, it is 'inherently suspicious to attribute systematic differences in outcome to the different mind-sets of different groups'.[77] A commitment to egalitarianism does not sit comfortably, for example, with assertions made by economists such as Gary Becker that women earned less in the 1960s not because they were herded into 'female' jobs, the skills associated with those jobs being systematically undervalued, and were consigned (as they were at the time) to 'female' rates pegged below the lowest male rate of pay, but rather because 'women spend less time in the labour force than men, and therefore have less incentive to invest in market skills' and because they 'chose' to acquire less labour-market-related types of skill than those acquired by men.[78]

Becker suggested in the 1960s that 'A woman wants her investment to be useful both as a housewife and as a participant in the labour force'[79] and that 'Married women . . . allocate less energy to each hour of work than married men . . . [and] seek occupations and jobs that are less effort intensive'.[80] Thirty years later, Stephen Rhodes claimed that gender wage gaps might be attributable in part to men's 'relatively greater interest in obtaining high pay or in taking a leadership role' and women's allegedly greater interest in 'convenient hours, or rewarding interpersonal aspects of the job – relations with co-workers and supervisors, the opportunity to help others, and the like',[81] while Mathys and Pincus claimed that women's actual wages were supplemented by the 'intrinsic compensation' of 'job security and safety issues . . . The pleasant, sanitised working conditions in many office settings . . . friendships and sociability . . . jobs that allow for social interaction . . . scheduling flexibility . . . job status . . . "cause" or "calling"'.[82] Leaving aside the fact that commentators such as

---

[74] Young (n 73) 16, emphasis in original.

[75] ibid, emphasis in original.

[76] A Phillips, 'Defending Equality of Outcome' (2004) 12 *Journal of Political Philosophy* 1–19, 15.

[77] ibid.

[78] G Becker, 'Investment in Human Capital: A Theoretical Analysis' (1962) 70(5)(II) *Journal of Political Economy* 9, 38. See generally on this issue A McColgan, *Pay Equity: Just Wages for Women* (Oxford: Clarendon Press, 1996) Chapter 6.

[79] Becker (n 78) 39.

[80] ibid, 52. For a more recent articulation of this approach see C Hakim, *Key Issues in Women's Work: Female Heterogeneity and the Polarisation of Women's Employment* (London: Athlone Press, 1996) 69.

[81] S Rhodes, *Incomparable Worth: Pay Equity Meets the Market* (New York: Cambridge University Press, 1993) 14.

[82] N Mathys and L Pincus, 'Is Pay Equity Equitable? A Perspective That Looks Beyond Pay' (1993) 44 *Labor Law Journal* 351, 352–53.

Mathys and Pincus tend to overlook the exposure to disease, excrement and violence associated with 'clean' jobs such as nursing, and overlook also the discriminatory practices which contribute to occupational segregation and pay differentials even between men and women engaged in similar work,[83] the focus on choices 'begs too many questions', as Anne Phillips puts it 'about why the members of one group might have ended up with a radically different set of preferences to another; and overlooks much we already know about the different conditions under which their choices were made'.[84]

The danger is that, by de-coupling the notion of (in)equality from the actual circumstances of people's lives,[85] we can end up attributing responsibility to those in positions of disadvantage for the fact of that disadvantage. Not everything is attributable either to 'luck' or to individual responsibility, and characterising social structures which generate inequalities as being questions of 'luck', even if it does result in a suggestion of redistribution, removes the focus from the question about how those social structures are created and maintained, by whom and in whose interests. This in turns means that redistribution in favour of the disadvantaged can be characterised as acts of beneficence which can be withheld by the benefactors and/or confined to beneficiaries deemed morally 'worthy'.

The foregoing discussions highlight the slipperiness of the concept of equality when it is considered abstracted from the social context in which inequalities occur. There is little to be gained, and much to be lost, from contemplating questions of equality by reference to lazy surfers,[86] those with tastes for expensive photography,[87] or desert islands and clamshells.[88] A focus on the eradication of the *causes* of disadvantage – the inequalities in life chances generated by social structures – is likely to pose a more radical challenge to those inequalities than a concern with redistribution of those material resources whose distribution is accepted as being the result of 'luck'. And a focus on the causes of disadvantage may focus attention as much on *discrimination* as on *inequality*, as much on the purpose, history and context of differential treatment as on the mere fact of such treatment, much less of disparities in resource distribution between individuals.

---

[83] *The Guardian* reported on 8 March 2011 that the hourly pay gaps between men and women were as high as 29% in the case of financial managers and chartered secretaries, 23% for healthcare practice managers, 26% for office managers, 37% for 'physicists, geologists and meteorologists', 29% for doctors, 24% for 'solicitors and lawyers, judges and coroners', 29% for musicians and 42% for brokers ('International women's day: the pay gap between men and women for your job'), www.guardian.co.uk/news/datablog/2011/mar/08/international-womens-day-pay-gap.

[84] Phillips (n 76) 15. See also Matthew Seligmann, 'Luck, Leverage, and Equality: A Bargaining Problem for Luck Egalitarians' (2007) 35 *Philosophy and Public Affairs* 266–92.

[85] *cf* Pete Wylie, 'Story of the Blues, Part Two' on 'people who talk about revolution and the class struggle without referring explicitly to everyday life . . .'.

[86] Van Parijs (n 68).

[87] See Cohen (n 68).

[88] See Dworkin, *Sovereign Virtue* (n 68) 140 ff.

'Formal' and 'Substantive' Equality

Many of those troubled by the search for meaning in what threatens to be an 'empty concept' of equality[89] have resorted to a concept of 'substantive equality', which is further discussed below.[90] It is interesting at this juncture to note, however, that the search for the underpinnings of the anti-discrimination principle referred to at 22 above has progressed in the opposite direction also. Thus has it been suggested, in the EU context, that 'the principle of non-discrimination helps to fill [the] vacuum' created by the failure of 'equality' as a concept to provide any 'internal guidance as to the relevance of particular characteristics of individuals or groups . . . [Non-discrimination] is the hidden value'.[91] In the US, too, suggested normative underpinnings for the 'equal treatment' required by the Equal Protection Clause of the Fourteenth Amendment to the US Constitution have included anti-discrimination, the debate then focusing on whether this was best understood as an 'anti-classification' or an 'anti-subordination' principle.[92] These debates are further considered in Chapter 3. Briefly, however, 'anti-classification' is the 'anti-discrimination' version of the 'like cases alike' or 'formal' approach to equality,[93] while 'anti-subordination' has much more in common with 'substantive' equality.

Writing in 2001, Sandra Fredman suggested that prohibitions on direct discrimination on specified grounds 'have traditionally been founded and legitimated on grounds that they further the liberal goals of state neutrality, individualism, and the promotion of autonomy', neutrality being 'expressed first and foremost through the notion of formal equality before the law' and 'Beyond that . . . through a focus on fairness as consistency, drawn from the well-worn maxim that likes should be treated alike'.[94] This maxim expresses the core of the formal approach to equality. For Fredman, the focus on individual-

---

[89] See Westen (n 60).

[90] Elisa Holmes, by contrast ('Anti-Discrimination Rights Without Equality' (2005) 68 *Modern Law Review* 175–94) suggests that 'anti-discrimination rights are not equal treatment norms [as] . . . they prohibit different treatment only on some grounds', further that such rights are only negligibly connected with the instrumental pursuit of equality.

[91] C Barnard, 'The Principle of Equality in the Community Context' (1998) 57(2) *Cambridge Law Journal* 532, 563.

[92] See, famously, Owen M Fiss, 'Groups and the Equal Protection Clause' (1976) 5 *Philosophy & Public Affairs* 107, 157, considered in Chapter 3, Michael C Dorf, 'A Partial Defense of an Anti-Discrimination Principle' (2002) *Cornell Law Faculty Publications* Paper 116, http://scholarship. law.cornell.edu/cgi/viewcontent.cgi?article=1115&context=facpub, 3. Writing in the 1970s, Fiss rejected anti-discrimination, which he saw as concerned with classification, in favour of 'anti-subordination'. As discussed in Chapter 3, however, this equation of anti-discrimination with anti-classification is by no means a given, and it is equally plausible to suggest that a principle of anti-discrimination can be interpreted as concerned with challenging subordination (or, more broadly, disadvantage).

[93] Albeit (in the US case) that different standards of justification are required in respect of unequal treatment according to the ground of classification (see further Suzanne Goldberg, 'Equality without Tiers' (2003–04) 77 *Southern California Law Review* 481.

[94] S Fredman, 'Equality: A New Generation?' (2001) *Acta Juridica* 214, 223.

ism characterises as the 'chief mischief of discrimination . . . that a person is subjected to detriment because she is attributed with stereotypical qualities based on a denigratory notion of her group membership'[95] rather than being treated on the basis of her 'individual merits and regardless of her group membership' while 'Autonomy is . . . furthered by freeing her to make her own choices as to her view of the good life'.[96]

For Fredman, formal equality (the principle that like cases should be treated alike) permits 'leveling down'[97] and 'ignores the extent to which such neutrality reinforces dominant values or existing distributions of power. . . The apparent commitment to neutrality can therefore be seen to mask an insistence on a particular set of values, based on those of the dominant culture'.[98] Thus, for example, demanding that women who wish to advance in the workplace conform to the prevailing workplace practices ignores the fact that many such practices (the availability to work long and/or 'flexible' hours, to be able to socialise after hours and/or to travel at short notice, all of which require freedom from hands-on caring responsibilities) may conform to formal equality but presume a male worker and block women's progress. And insisting on a school uniform which prohibits the wearing of trousers by adolescent girls, or of head coverings by pupils, will disadvantage Muslim girls as well as Muslim, Sikh and Jewish boys, while preserving formal equality of treatment for all.

Evadné Grant points out that 'Fundamental to the critique of formal equality is its inability to address the historical disadvantage suffered by those subject to discrimination and to recognise that the effect of differential treatment may in fact be heightened as a result'.[99] The requirement to treat 'like cases alike' frequently translates into a blanket prohibition on taking particular personal characteristics (race, for example, or gender) into account. But the result of this prohibition may be to prevent measures being adopted which could undo the effects of past disadvantage. If, for example, state-sponsored apartheid has resulted in a situation in which 20 per cent of the people (who just happen to be white) own 98 per cent of a country's wealth, requiring that future treatment be colour blind will serve to perpetuate, rather than address, that fact.

This was not lost on the architects of the new South Africa. That country's Constitution not only guarantees equality before the law and the right to equal protection of the law,[100] but specifically provides that 'To promote the achievement of equality, legislative and other measures designed to protect or advance persons, or categories of persons, disadvantaged by unfair discrimination may

---

[95] ibid, 223–24.

[96] ibid, 224.

[97] Famously, the outcome of the decision of the ECtHR in *Abdulaziz v UK* (1985) 7 EHRR 471, in which immigration rules which discriminated on grounds of sex were challenged, was that the favourable treatment was withdrawn from men rather than extended to women.

[98] Fredman (n 94) 224–25.

[99] E Grant, 'Dignity and Equality' (2007) 7 *Human Rights Law Review* 299–329, 320.

[100] S 9(1).

be taken',[101] and prohibits only *unfair* discrimination.[102] Grant further contrasts the approach taken by South Africa's Supreme Court to that country's constitutional anti-discrimination provisions, quoting Ackerman J's suggestion in *National Coalition for Gay and Lesbian Equality v Minister of Home Affairs* (2000)[103] that

> the more vulnerable the group adversely affected by the discrimination, the more likely the discrimination will be held to be unfair. Vulnerability in turn depends to a very significant extent on past patterns of disadvantage, stereotyping and the like. This is why an enquiry into past disadvantage is so important.[104]

In a later article Fredman distinguished 'formal' from 'substantive' equality, suggesting that 'distributive justice plays a central role' in the latter which 'means, in turn, that equality requires more than restraint from the state. In addition, it calls for a duty upon the state to take positive measures to promote equality, including, where appropriate, allocation of resources'.[105] Whether the 'objective' of 'substantive equality' is seen as 'equality of opportunity' or 'equality of results', positive measures are required (in the first case to assist 'Those who lack the requisite qualifications as a result of past discrimination . . . [and] women with child-care responsibilities' for example, in the second to 'enlarg[e] the cake').[106] Fredman went on to identify four 'specific . . . aims' of substantive equality as 'break[ing] the cycle of disadvantage associated with out-groups'; 'promot[ing] respect for the equal dignity and worth of all, thereby redressing stigma, stereotyping, humiliation and violence because of membership of an out-group'; 'positive[ly] affirm[ing] and celebrati[ng] . . . identity within community'; and 'facilitat[ing] full participation in society'.[107] 'Unlike formal equality, which . . . is suspicious of all classification, a substantive equality analysis would only be suspicious of groups who are excluded because of, or in spite of, their especial vulnerability'.[108]

Nicholas Smith attacks the terminological distinction employed by Fredman and others[109] between 'formal' and 'substantive' equality,[110] suggesting that the distinctions at issue concern policy rather than 'form' as against 'substance' and that '"substantive" just means "real", or whatever an author happens to prefer as the solution to the cluster of social issues we usually discuss under the rubric

---

[101] Section 9(2).

[102] Section 9(3) and (4).

[103] *National Coalition for Gay and Lesbian Equality v Minister of Home Affairs*, 2000 (2) SA 1.

[104] Paragraph 44, cited by Grant (n 99) 320.

[105] S Fredman, 'Providing Equality: Substantive Equality and The Positive Duty to Provide' (2005) 21 *South African Journal on Human Rights* 163, 163.

[106] ibid, 167.

[107] ibid.

[108] ibid, 170.

[109] Specifically C Barnard and B Hepple, 'Substantive Equality' (2000) 59(3) *Cambridge Law Journal* 562–85.

[110] N Smith, 'A Critique of Recent Approaches to Discrimination Law' (2007) *New Zealand Law Review* 499.

of "equality" '.[111] The point has a certain rhetorical appeal but to the extent that it leaves us with a formal approach to equality it robs us of the tools to do much more than to require that red-haired manufacturers of margarine be treated without distinction by legislation applicable to red-haired manufacturers of margarine, or 'non-Aryans' without distinction by laws forbidding persons falling under this description from access to the civil service. It is an underpinning premise of the book that the concept of equality must be a substantive, rather than a formal, one if it is to do any significant work in combating discrimination. But the question which remains concerns the nature of the values to which 'substantive' equality requires recourse.[112]

Dignity and Equality

One value which makes a regular appearance in discussions of substantive equality is dignity. Fredman's mention of dignity in connection with the 'specific aims' of substantive equality is mentioned above. There is little doubt that among the foundations and core purposes of human rights generally is the protection of human dignity.[113] But as David Feldman and others have pointed out, the meaning of dignity is 'difficult to pin down'.[114] Nicholas Smith, for example, argues that ' "dignity" is something that is attributed to people because of something else' and that ' "dignity" cannot replace " 'rationality' (or any other core human attribute) as a foundation for equality, because rationality is (a candidate for) the foundation of human dignity . . .'.[115] For Smith (citing Feldman) respect for human dignity 'in general is an even more abstract notion than "equality"':[116]

> The law will not be made any clearer by attempts to give content to the right not to be discriminated against by explaining that upholding 'equality' means respecting our 'dignity'. It is possible to say that distinctions made by the law (in the case of government discrimination) that treat people with less than equal concern and respect ignore 'human dignity'; but one still has to work out when the law does or does not treat a person with equal consideration. It will sometimes be clear that it does not, but there

---

[111] ibid, 507.

[112] See also Fudge (n 53).

[113] See also the discussion of Advocate General Maduro in *Coleman v Attridge Law* (17) paras 8–14. The Advocate General suggested at para 8 that the 'values underlying equality' were 'human dignity and personal autonomy', and derived from this the propositions (para 9) that the protected characteristics 'are characteristics which should not play any role in any assessment as to whether it is right or not to treat someone less favourably' and (para 12) (because 'One way of undermining the dignity and autonomy of people who belong to a certain group is to target not them, but third persons who are closely associated with them and do not themselves belong to the group', '[a] robust conception of equality entails that these subtler forms of discrimination should also be caught by anti-discrimination legislation'.

[114] D Feldman, 'Human Dignity as a Legal Value: Part 1' (1999) *Public Law* 682, 682.

[115] Smith (n 110) 514.

[116] ibid, 522.

will be hard cases. Difficulties will arise because 'equality' is a moral concept – moral argument is required to apply it. That argument is about the best understanding of equal concern for persons, not about some other value. Rephrasing that as a duty (or an element of a duty) to respect each person's inherent worth does not make equality's meaning any more concrete or give it the content it was lacking.[117]

Smith accepts that 'There is nothing wrong with using the placeholder "dignity" as a summary of what is considered special about human beings. One should not, however, expect it to denote something previously overlooked that will explain what it means to discriminate against someone'.[118] And Feldman suggests that 'dignity is a quality characteristic of human beings, so that an individual cannot have a right to it'.[119] But 'An umbrella of rights may be justified in preventing interference with . . . general human dignity (i.e. dignity attributable to people "by virtue of their membership of the human species")', and 'some rights seem to have a particularly prominent role in upholding human dignity. These include . . . the right to be free of discriminatory treatment . . . Discrimination on the basis of status, etc., is . . . a major assault on dignity'.[120]

Most commentators would agree with Feldman that the protection of human dignity (however defined) is a central aim of human rights generally, though the relationship between such dignity and the concept of equality is contested. Dignity has played a significant role in the judicial application of section 15(1) of Canada's Charter of Rights, which provides that:

> Every individual is equal before and under the law and has the right to the equal protection and equal benefit of the law without discrimination and, in particular, without discrimination based on race, national or ethnic origin, colour, religion, sex, age or mental or physical disability.[121]

In *Law v Canada* (1999) Canada's Supreme Court, after a period of judicial disagreement as to the interpretation of section 15, unanimously defined its purpose as

> to prevent the violation of essential human dignity and freedom through the imposition of disadvantage, stereotyping, or political or social prejudice, and to promote a society in which all persons enjoy equal recognition at law as human beings or as members of Canadian society, equally capable and equally deserving of concern, respect and consideration.[122]

Having stated that 'the equality guarantee in s.15(1) is concerned with the realization of personal autonomy and self-determination', and that human dignity 'means that an individual or group feels self-respect and self-worth', 'is concerned with physical and psychological integrity and empowerment [and] . . . is

---

[117] ibid, 523.

[118] ibid, 523–24.

[119] Feldman (n 114) 689.

[120] ibid, 695.

[121] Section 15(2), which specifically permits positive action, is considered in Chapter 3.

[122] *Law v Canada* [1991] 1 SCR 497, para 51.

harmed by unfair treatment premised upon personal traits or circumstances which do not relate to individual needs, capacities, or merits', Iacobucci J went on to rule, for a unanimous Court in *Law*, that such dignity 'does not relate to the status or position of an individual in society *per se*, but rather concerns the manner in which a person legitimately feels when confronted with a particular law',[123] thus firmly embracing a subjective approach to the concept.

The Court in *Law* adopted a three-part approach to section 15 which asked (i) whether the law, programme or activity created a distinction, on purpose or in effect, between the claimant and his or her comparators; (ii) if so, whether such differential treatment was based on enumerated or analogous grounds; and (iii) if so, whether the purpose or effect of the law, programme or activity in question was discriminatory in

> imposing a burden upon or withholding a benefit from the claimant in a manner which reflects the stereotypical application of presumed group or personal character-istics, or . . . otherwise ha[ving] the effect of perpetuating or promoting the view that the individual is less capable or worthy of recognition or value as a human being or as a member of Canadian society, equally deserving of concern, respect, and considera-tion.[124]

In determining whether the impugned distinction had the effect of 'demeaning [the claimant's] dignity', Iacobucci J drew particular attention to 'four . . . fac-tors . . . although . . . there are undoubtedly others, and not all four factors will necessarily be relevant in every case'.[125] These were

> 1) the social disadvantage of the group represented by the claimant; 2) the correspond-ence between legislative distinctions and the actual need, capacity or circumstances of the claimant; 3) the ameliorative purpose or effects of the impugned legislation on a more disadvantage group; and 4) the nature of the claimant's interest.

Denise Reaume suggested in 2003 that Canada's Supreme Court was 'on the right track in latching onto dignity as the substantive concept informing equal-ity rights'.[126] Hers was a relatively isolated voice, however. Donna Greschner, for example, argued that ' "human dignity" underlies the entire Charter, and there-fore cannot be used to differentiate equality rights from other Charter rights', further that 'dignity is inherently malleable [and]. . . becomes an assertion, not an analysis. . . [and] casting discrimination in the language of dignity is too loaded. From the claimants' perspective, they must prove that a distinction vio-lates their dignity, which is a bit unseemly . . .'.[127] And for Sophie Moreau, who ascribes great significance to the concept of dignity in explaining the unfairness which is, on her analysis, central to 'discrimination', the 'subjective conception

---

[123] ibid, para 53.
[124] He further stressed the comparative nature of equality: ibid, paras 56–58.
[125] ibid, para 62.
[126] D Reaume, 'Dignity and Discrimination' (2002–03) 63 *Louisiana Law Review* 645, 646.
[127] D Greschner, 'Does *Law* Advance the Cause of Equality?' (2001) 27 *Queen's Law Journal* 299, 312–13.

of dignity', which is concerned with the diminution of 'individuals' feelings of self-worth',[128] is insufficient to 'render that treatment unfair'.[129] Moreau argues that discrimination is best understood as 'depriving some of a benefit available to others, in circumstances where this treatment is unfair to them',[130] with treatment being 'unfair' where it fails to respect the 'abstract . . . ideal of respect for the equal dignity of all'. 'Dignity' is in turn understood in Kantian terms as the

> unchanging, supreme value that inheres in every human being.. the idea of a human being's 'unconditional and incomparable worth'. . . [131] Because this worth is unconditional – that is to say, is independent of the individual's circumstances or the extent to which she is actually shown respect by others – it cannot be diminished by others' disregard for it. So even if an individual is marginalized or stigmatized in her society, this cannot diminish her dignity in the objective sense we are considering.[132] She always has a claim to concern and respect for her intrinsic worth. And because all individuals have this same intrinsic worth, all are entitled to an equal degree of concern and respect.[133]

Having accepted that the 'objective conception of dignity does not have sufficient content to explain the precise nature of the wrongs that are done to individuals who are not treated with equal concern and respect [or to] . . . tell us what kinds of treatment fail to show proper consideration for that worth',[134] Moreau goes on to outline four 'more specific conceptions of the wrong of unequal treatment'. Leaving aside the 'subjective' concept of dignity found wanting above, Moreau suggests that 'unequal treatment wrongs individuals when: (i) it is based on prejudice or stereotyping; (ii) it perpetuates oppressive power relationships; [or] (iii) it leaves some individuals without access to basic goods'. In these conceptions of wrongful discrimination, 'the particular features of certain forms of unequal treatment . . . drive the analysis and provide the explanation of why the treatment is wrong'.[135]

---

[128] SR Moreau, 'The Wrongs of Unequal Treatment' (2004) 54 *University of Toronto Law Review* 291, 297.

[129] ibid, 313.

[130] ibid, 292.

[131] ibid, 294–95 citing I Kant (JW Ellington trans), *Grounding for the Metaphysics of Morals; with, On a Supposed Right to Lie Because of Philanthropic Concerns*, 3rd edn (Indianapolis: Hackett, 1993) s II, 436.

[132] See similarly Smith (n 110) 517–19.

[133] Moreau (n 128) 295, noting that 'the term "equal" does very little independent work here. That is, Dworkin's ideal is really an ideal of "concern and respect," based on an assumption of the supreme worth of each human being: it is an ideal that pertains to the relationship between the government and the citizen in question, not one that depends on any comparison between citizens . . .' and referring to Joseph Raz's suggestion that Dworkin's abstract ideal of equal concern and respect 'is not, then, really an ideal of equality at all; and that any account of the wrongs of unequal treatment that purports to flesh out this ideal will not be an account of equality' (citing J Raz, *The Morality of Freedom* (Oxford: Clarendon Press, 1986) 220–21.

[134] ibid, 296.

[135] ibid, 296.

For Moreau, then, the test in *Law v Canada*

> must . . . be answered by appeal to some other substantive conception of what makes unequal treatment into a wrong against the individual . . . [the courts] must appeal, for instance, to the fact that the differential treatment was based upon stereotyping and prejudice; to the fact that it perpetuates oppressive or to the fact that it leaves the claimant without access to power relations; basic goods.[136]

It 'ultimately relies upon conceptions of the wrong that are not explicitly discussed in this case itself and have not subsequently received explicit discussion because the *Law* test obscures the fact that they must be invoked'.[137]

The difficulties associated with a dignity-driven approach are not limited to those outlined above. Lucy Vickers suggests that 'founding the concept of equality on dignity . . . creates room to provide broader recognition for differences rather than mere tolerance . . . equality and dignity . . . can involve recognition of the uniqueness of individuals, and their distinctiveness'[138] and an 'acknowledg[ment] that inequality arises not just in socio-economic terms, but in more cultural and symbolic terms too'. But:[139]

> [U]sing dignity and recognition as bases for legal protection can lead to the reifying of difference as between groups . . . a focus on recognition as the aim of equality with regard to religion and belief in particular is likely to increase the risk . . . of viewing religious groupings as having solid boundaries and single identities, rather than consisting of a range of complementary as well as competing voices . . . a focus on dignity and recognition involves an inherent tension between valuing the universal equality of different people, and valuing their uniqueness, and their unique characteristics. In effect, there exists some tension between equality based on universal humanity and the recognition of individual identity as of value.[140]

And Judy Fudge, who commented that Iacobucci J's characterisation in *Law* of the four contextual factors 'as guidelines' did not prevent subsequent courts from 'treat[ing] them as elements in a test to determine whether equality rights have been violated',[141] was also highly critical of the role of dignity in the *Law* analysis of section 15 of the Charter, suggesting that the Supreme Court's 'decision to view equality through a dignity lens, when combined with how it sees its institutional role, functions to limit substantive equality's redistributive potential'.[142] While

---

[136] ibid, 319.

[137] ibid, 320.

[138] L Vickers, 'Promoting Equality or Fostering Resentment? The Public Sector Equality Duty and Religion and Belief' (2011) 31(1) *Legal Studies* 135–58, 149, citing N Fraser, 'From Redistribution to Recognition? Dilemmas of Justice in a 'Post-Socialist' Age' (1995) 212(1) *New Left Review* 68; C Taylor *Multiculturalism and 'The Politics of Recognition'* (Princeton: Princeton University Press, 1992).

[139] ibid.

[140] ibid, 149–50.

[141] Fudge (n 53) 241, citing B Ryder, CC Faria and E Lawrence 'What's Law Good for?: An Empirical Overview of Charter Equality Decisions' (2004) 24 *Supreme Court Law Review* (2d) 103.

[142] ibid, 235.

dignity does not necessarily limit substantive equality to identity-based recognition issues [and] . . . can capture the notion of status-based subordination and capture redistributive elements. . . [t]he effect of interpreting equality through the lens of dignity [with an 'emphasis [on] self-worth and integrity' and a 'downplay[ing of] material and systemic factors'] has been to focus on discrimination and to narrow the ambit of substantive equality . . . Most equality claims fail because the claimant cannot establish discrimination, which involves an affront to one's dignity.[143]

Emily Grabham suggests that Iacobucci J's reference in *Law* to ' "human dignity" being harmed by marginalization' was accompanied by a downplaying of 'the effects of social and economic status',[144] and that

the concept may not say enough about real social inequality to be strategically useful in attaining substantive equality . . . current representations of social inequality in terms of systemic and interlocking discrimination undermine the potency of such an inherently individualistic concept. 'Human dignity', furthermore, has no coherent internal dynamic: it is analogous to the 'empty' concept of equality identified by Peter Westen being fundamentally a 'shell concept' open to diverse, but usually majoritarian interpretations that do not challenge the status quo. If, for example, same-sex couples remain disenfranchised and economically disadvantaged by tax codes (especially, in the UK context, inheritance tax provisions) and spousal support legislation, this may not be a violation of their human dignity because they are still 'respected' as individuals.[145]

Grabham worried that a 'narrow reading' of 'human dignity' might exclude from its scope 'material factors . . . Put another way, one could conceivably be dignified *and* materially disadvantaged'.[146] And while

[i]f endowed with an appreciation of material inequalities and the effects of marginalisation, [the concept of human dignity] might yet be a useful elaboration of the substantive equality test under section 15(1) . . . with a narrow reading, the Supreme Court may be dragging equality back into the mythical world of neutrality, 'merit', 'individualism' and 'family values'.[147]

Grabham's fears were realised in *Gosselin v Quebec (Attorney General)* in which the 'human dignity' approach was employed to defeat a section 15 challenge by young social security claimants to provincial rules which limited to one-third of the subsistence level paid to older claimants the benefits payable to those aged under 30, unless they participated in one of three particular education or work experience programmes which together had capacity for just over a third of the relevant claimants.[148] The Supreme Court ruled, by a slim

---

[143] ibid, 241, citing S Martin, 'Balancing Individual Rights to Equality and Social Goals' (2001) 80 *The Canadian Bar Review* 299.

[144] E Grabham, '*Law v Canada*: New Directions for Equality Under the Canadian Charter?' (2002) 22 *Oxford Journal of Legal Studies* 641, 654.

[145] ibid, 654.

[146] ibid, 654–55.

[147] ibid, 655–56.

[148] *Gosselin v Quebec (Attorney General)* [2002] 4 SCR 429. *cf* Conseil Constitutionnel decision no 94-359 DC *Loi relative à la diversité de l'habitat* 19 Janvier 1995 Actualité Juridique le droit administratif 1995, 455, cited by Feldman (n 114) 699–700, fn 46.

majority, that the scheme did not treat the claimant as less worthy than older welfare recipients. Under-30s did not, as a group, suffer from pre-existing disadvantage or stigmatisation and there was a rational fit between the legislative approach and the actual circumstances of younger welfare recipients who, as a group, needed exactly the kind of education and training promoted by the scheme. The legislator could act on the basis of informed general assumptions which corresponded, albeit imperfectly, to the actual circumstances of the affected group as long as they were not based on arbitrary or demeaning stereotypes.

The majority in *Gosselin* expressed the view that a reasonable person in the claimant's position would take into account the fact that the scheme was aimed at ameliorating the situation of welfare recipients under 30 in determining whether it treated her and her peers as less worthy of respect and consideration than older recipients, and concluded that it did not. Madam Justice L'Heureux-Dubé took a different view:

131 . . . The reasonable claimant would have been informed of the legislature's intention to help young people enter the marketplace. She would have been informed that those 30 and over have more difficulty changing careers, and that those under 30 run serious social and personal risks if they do not enter the job market in a timely manner. She would have been told that the long-term goal of the legislative scheme was to affirm her dignity.

132 . . . Even if she wished to participate in training programs, [the reasonable claimant] would have found that there were intervals between the completion of one program and the starting of another, during which the amount of her social assistance benefit would have plunged. The reasonable claimant would have made daily life choices in the face of an imminent and severe threat of poverty. The reasonable claimant would likely have suffered malnourishment. She might have turned to prostitution and crime to make ends meet. The reasonable claimant would have perceived that as a result of her deep poverty, she had been excluded from full participation in Canadian society. She would have perceived that her right to dignity was infringed as a sole consequence of being under 30 years of age, a factor over which, at any given moment, she had no control. While individuals may be able to strive to overcome the detriment imposed by merit-based distinctions, Ms. Gosselin was powerless to alter the single personal characteristic that the government's scheme made determinative for her level of benefits.

133 The reasonable claimant would have suffered, as Ms. Gosselin manifestly did suffer, from discrimination as a result of the impugned legislative distinction. I see no other conclusion but that Ms. Gosselin would have reasonably felt that she was being less valued as a member of society than people 30 and over and that she was being treated as less deserving of respect.

For Reaume, the violation of dignity in *Gosselin* was not simply (as Bastarche J recorded) the economic hardship, but also that 'the assumption that anyone under thirty should live with his or her parents if unable to find work . . . suggests that nothing of any significance is lost by remaining under parental authority until one reaches the age of thirty [and] . . . foregoing any aspiration of an independent life. . . retaining a child-like status'.[149]

By 2008 the Supreme Court had had cause to reconsider *Law v Canada*, suggesting in *R v Kapp* that *Law* had 'made an important contribution to our understanding of the conceptual underpinnings of substantive equality' but that 'difficulties [had] arisen from the attempt in *Law* to employ human dignity *as a legal test*'.[150] Confirming that 'human dignity is an essential value underlying the s. 15 equality guarantee' and that 'the protection of all of the rights guaranteed by the *Charter* has as its lodestar the promotion of human dignity', McLachlin CJ referred to the 'abstract and subjective' nature of the concept of human dignity, and suggested that 'even with the guidance of the four contextual factors, [it could] only become confusing and difficult to apply [and] . . . has also proven to be an *additional* burden on equality claimants, rather than the philosophical enhancement it was intended to be'.[151] The Chief Justice went on to stress the four factors set out by the Court in *Law* as guidelines and to emphasise that they 'should not be read literally as if they were legislative dispositions, but as a way of focussing on the central concern of s. 15 . . . combatting discrimination, defined in terms of perpetuating disadvantage and stereotyping'.[152]

More recently, in *Withler v Canada (Attorney General)* (2011), Canada's Supreme Court omitted any reference to dignity in its section 15 analysis,[153] ruling that the question whether differential treatment was discriminatory turned on the claimant's ability to show 'discriminatory impact in terms of prejudicing or stereotyping'.[154] The first could be done 'by showing that the impugned law, in purpose or effect, perpetuates prejudice or disadvantage to members of a group on the basis of personal characteristics within s. 15(1)', the second 'by showing that the disadvantage imposed by the law is based on a stereotype that does not correspond to the actual circumstances and characteristics of the claimant or claimant group'.[155] It would usually, but not invariably, be the case that 'such stereotyping result[ed] in perpetuation of prejudice and disadvantage', it being 'conceivable that a group that has not historically experienced disadvantage may find itself the subject of conduct that, if permitted to continue, would create a discriminatory impact on members of the group'.[156]

The concept of dignity may have fallen out of favour in the equality analysis of Canadian courts but it remains a feature in the jurisprudence of South Africa's Constitution, section 9 of which prohibits 'unfair' discrimination on grounds 'including race, gender, sex, pregnancy, marital status, ethnic or social

---

[149] Reaume (n 126) 693–94.
[150] *R v Kapp* [2008] 2 SCR 483, paras 20–21.
[151] ibid, paras 21–22.
[152] ibid, paras 23–24.
[153] *Withler v Canada (Attorney General)* [2011] 1 SCR 396.
[154] ibid, para 34.
[155] ibid, paras 35–36.
[156] ibid, para 36.

origin, colour, sexual orientation, age, disability, religion, conscience, belief, culture, language and birth'. In the leading case of *Harksen v Lane NO* (1998)[157] the Court set out 'the stages of enquiry which become necessary where an attack is made on a provision in reliance' on section 9. The first is concerned with determining whether there has been differential treatment which is not irrational (irrational distinctions breaching the provision). Once a rational distinction has been identified the first question is whether the distinction amounts to *discrimination*, the second whether any such discrimination is *unfair*. Distinctions drawn on the grounds listed in section 9 are discriminatory, and are further presumed to be unfair.[158] Distinctions 'based on attributes and characteristics which have the potential to impair the fundamental human dignity of persons as human beings or to affect them adversely in a comparably serious manner' will also be discriminatory, the burden being placed on the claimant to establish unfairness 'primarily' by reference to 'the impact of the discrimination on the complainant and others in his or her situation'.[159] The *Harksen* Court further ruled that factors to be considered, from an objective perspective, in determining unfairness included:

(a) the position of the complainants in society and whether they have suffered in the past from patterns of disadvantage, whether the discrimination in the case under consideration is on a specified ground or not;

(b) the nature of the provision or power and the purpose sought to be achieved by it. If its purpose is manifestly not directed, in the first instance, at impairing the complainants in the manner indicated above, but is aimed at achieving a worthy and important societal goal, such as, for example, the furthering of equality for all, this purpose may, depending on the facts of the particular case, have a significant bearing on the question whether complainants have in fact suffered the impairment in question . . .

(c) with due regard to (a) and (b) above, and any other relevant factors, the extent to which the discrimination has affected the rights or interests of complainants and whether it has led to an impairment of their fundamental human dignity or constitutes an impairment of a comparably serious nature.[160]

The Constitutional Court went on to make clear that these factors, designed to 'assist in giving 'precision and elaboration' to the constitutional test of unfairness' were not 'a closed list. Others may emerge as our equality jurisprudence continues to develop. In any event it is the cumulative effect of these factors that

---

[157] *Harksen v Lane NO* 1998 (1) SA 300 (CC). The case concerned the application of the interim Constitution but the approach is equally applicable to s 9 of the final Constitution. See also *President of the Republic of South Africa v Hugo* (CCT 11/96) 1997 SA 4 1 (CC), [1998] 1 LRC 662.

[158] *Harksen* (n 157) para 54, referring to s 9(5). Note that even 'unfair' discrimination may be saved by the Constitution's general limitation clause: see, for example *Poswa v MEC for Economic Affairs* 2001 (6) BCLR 545 (CC).

[159] *Harksen* (n 157) para 50.

[160] ibid, para 50.

must be examined and in respect of which a determination must be made as to whether the discrimination is unfair'.

Evadné Grant suggests that the dignity-driven approach of South Africa's Constitutional Court, and of German constitutional law,[161] 'is rooted in a rich tradition which is capable of underpinning an approach to equality which avoids excessive individualism and fully recognises the interplay between individual and community needs'.[162] She distinguishes between objective and subjective approaches to dignity,[163] that is, between the Stoical/Jewish/Christian idea that 'Because all men had reason, they were all equal and worthy of respect', and the classical Roman view of dignity as relating to status or reputation. Grant concludes from the South African constitutional jurisprudence relating to 'capital and corporal punishment, privacy, defamation [and] socio-economic rights', as well as equality,[164] that, while the Constitutional Court 'has declined to provide a precise definition' of human dignity, the concept which emerges emphasises the ' "value and worth" of every person'[165] in the sense of 'a common humanity and entitlement of each person to basic respect', and recognises that 'human dignity, freedom and equality, the foundational values of our society, are denied those who have no food, clothing or shelter'.[166]

For Grant, 'The focus on dignity results in emphasis being placed simultaneously on context, impact and the point of view of the affected persons. Such focus is in fact the guarantor of substantive as opposed to formal equality'.[167] She further suggests that 'The malleability of the concept is limited by the requirement to consider specific contextual factors that provide the basis for the assessment of the impairment of dignity and give content to the concept'.[168] In response to those who 'have objected in particular to the prominent role played by personal feelings of affront in the analysis of unfair discrimination',[169] Grant argues that (i) 'the conception of dignity revealed in South Africa's jurisprudence is not confined to individual self-worth'[170] but is also concerned to

---

[161] See, for example, Chava Schwebel, 'Welfare Rights in Canadian and German Constitutional Law' (2011) 12 German Law Journal 1901–40.

[162] Grant (n 9) 299. See also Saras Jagwanth, 'Affirmative Action in a Transformative Context: The South African Experience' (2003–04) 36 Connecticut Law Review 725.

[163] Grant (n 99) 304.

[164] Respectively S v Makwanyane 1995 (3) SA 391 (CC) and S v Williams 1995 (7) BCLR 861 (CC); Bernstein v Bester 1996 (4) BCLR 449 (CC) and National Coalition for Gay and Lesbian Equality v Minister of Justice 1999 (1) SA 6 (CC); 1998 (12) BCLR 1517 (CC) (privacy); Khumalov Holomisa 2002 (5) SA 401 (CC) (defamation); Government of the Republic of South Africa v Grootboom 2001 (1) SA 46 (CC) paras 38 and 41 (socio-economic rights).

[165] Grant (n 99) 331, citing Makwanyane.

[166] ibid, 312, citing Yacoob J in Government of the Republic of South Africa v Grootboom 2001 (1) SA 46 (CC) para 29.

[167] ibid, 318–19.

[168] ibid, 319.

[169] ibid, 325, citing C Albertyn and B Goldblatt, 'Facing the Challenge of Transformation: Difficulties in the Development of an Indigenous Jurisprudence of Equality' (1998) 14 South African Journal on Human Rights 248, 272.

[170] ibid, 326, citing in particular the decision in Khumalo v Holomisa 2002 (5) SA 401 (CC) in which the Court ruled that 'The value of human dignity in our Constitution is not only concerned

'ensur[e] that individuals are not forced to live in deprived material and social conditions'; (ii) 'the individual is to be seen, not as isolated and detached but in the context of both group-membership (or more often memberships) and membership of the broader society'; and (iii)

> analysis of the cases shows little support for the conclusion that the Constitutional Court is concerned merely with individual affront . . . While in some cases personal affront does play an important role, such as in the sexual orientation cases, the context in which this is considered is that of group membership and the need to build a new society that values diversity and difference. Conversely . . . where measures have clearly been designed to pursue a transformative agenda, that has been emphasised and personal affront downplayed.[171]

Alternative Conceptions of Equality

It appears from *Withler* that the Canadian courts have opted, for the present at least, to focus on 'prejudice and disadvantage' as the primary markers of 'discrimination' for the purposes of section 15. A number of alternative suggestions have been made as to the underpinning and/or purpose of anti-discrimination/equality law. Hugh Collins has suggested that, 'in so far as anti-discrimination laws deviate from' a focus on direct discrimination (that is, from simply prohibiting differential treatment on listed grounds), 'it is clear that the social problem is regarded as one involving structural or systematic disadvantage[172] for protected groups', and that such laws are better characterised as seeking to address problems of social exclusion.[173] In Collins's view, 'social inclusion provides a more determinate criterion for the composition of protected groups' than the equal treatment principle;[174] allows an asymmetrical approach to groups advantaged and disadvantaged by reference to criteria such as sex and age;[175] avoids questions such as 'whether the group is classified by unalterable genetics,

---

with an individual's sense of self-worth, but constitutes an affirmation of the worth of human beings in our society. It includes the intrinsic worth of human beings shared by all people as well as the individual reputation of each person built upon his or her own individual achievements' para 27.

[171] ibid, 327. Smith (n 110) 517–19, also distinguishes between subjective and objective approaches to dignity, citing G Huscroft, 'Discrimination, Dignity, and the Limits of Equality' (2000) 9 *Otago Law Review* 697 at 705 to suggest that the subjective approach favoured by Canada's Supreme Court 'facilitates a substantial reduction of the protection the right [not to be discriminated against] might otherwise afford'.

[172] Understood as 'patterns of disadvantage' produced by 'certain permanent arrangements, practices, institutions, and social structures', para 26.

[173] H Collins, 'Discrimination, Equality and Social Inclusion'(2003) 66 *Modern Law Review* 16, 26. See also 'Social Inclusion: A Better Approach to Equality Issues?' (2004–05) 14 *Transnational Law and Contemporary Problems* 897–918. Collins appears, on Bamforth's approach (N Bamforth, 'Conceptions of Anti-Discrimination Law' (2004) 24 *Oxford Journal of Legal Studies* 693–716, 704–07) to be concerned with social goals rather than justificatory principles of anti-discrimination law but his analysis would appear to be equally applicable to the latter.

[174] Collins, 'Discrimination, Equality and Social Inclusion' (n 173) 27.

[175] ibid, 36.

socially constructed qualities, or legally imposed characteristics'[176] or 'whether the group is regarded with disrespect'[177] and 'concentrates on remedying the position of those who fail to achieve the essential elements of well-being' while eschewing any 'broader ambition of securing more generally a more egalitarian society'.[178]

Colm O'Cinneide acknowledges the temptation to abandon equality as an underpinning principle of anti-discrimination law. Conceptualising such law as

> designed to remove obstacles to the enjoyment of basic human entitlements, [or] to combat attempts to deny human dignity, or to express contempt towards particular groups[179] . . . can explain why particular types of discrimination directed against particular social groups are singled-out for particularly intense forms of legal regulation and attract particular moral abhorrence [and] cuts through much of the confusion generated by the linking of equality and anti-discrimination law to fuzzy and contested concepts of equality. Eliminating disadvantage that constitutes a denial of dignity or basic entitlements can readily be shown to be more important than ensuring exact sameness of treatment for all.[180]

O'Cinneide suggests, however, that 'equality and anti-discrimination legal norms address a complex variety of different types of harm or demeaning treatment'[181] and that 'Attempts to define a single underlying targeted wrong, such as attacks upon human "dignity", the expression of "contempt", group "stereotyping", the denial of autonomy or other basic human entitlements, and so on, tend to be either under-inclusive or excessively vague', and in any event are themselves entangled with 'ideals of equality of respect and equal worth, even if these concepts are relatively inchoate'. For O'Cinneide, 'the basic perception that human dignity is offended by discriminatory treatment stems from a normative attachment to an ideal of the equality of status of human beings' and, while 'Equality and anti-discrimination law may be structured around the prevention of certain types of denial of dignity. . . its ultimate *raison d'etre* is as a tool to help achieve some form of social transformation, as part of the unfolding logic of a commitment to an ideal of equality of status':

> Equality and anti-discrimination norms can therefore be seen as complex construct of different elements: they are designed to prevent certain types of denial of human dignity rather than to guarantee 'equality of opportunity' *per se,* but their use is also

---

[176]   ibid, 27.

[177]   ibid, 28.

[178]   Collins, 'Social Inclusion' (n 173) 914.

[179]   C O'Cinneide, 'Fumbling Towards Coherence: The Slow Evolution of Equality and Anti-Discrimination Law in Britain' (2006) 57 *Northern Ireland Law Quarterly* 57, 60, citing Bamforth (n 173) 713–15; J Gardner, 'Liberals and Unlawful Discrimination' (1989) 9 *Oxford Journal of Legal Studies* 1; C MacKinnon, 'Sex Equality: On Difference and Domination' in *Toward a Feminist Theory of the State* (Cambridge, MA: Harvard University Press, 1989) 215; D Reaume, 'Comparing Theories of Sex Discrimination: The Role of Comparison' (2005) 25 *Oxford Journal of Legal Studies* 547–64, and 'Discrimination and Dignity' (n 126).

[180]   O'Cinneide (n 179) 60.

[181]   ibid, 60, citing Moreau, (n 128).

directly or indirectly intended to alter social structures to secure greater equality of respect or status for disadvantaged groups. They are also often 'packaged' within a wider range of measures directed towards the elimination or amelioration of group disadvantage: anti-discrimination legislation is regularly accompanied by alterations in police practice, housing and family policies, and other forms of provision of public services.[182]

O'Cinneide's approach echoes those of Samuel Scheffler and Elizabeth Anderson. The former suggests that equality is properly understood, as a 'social and political ideal' which 'emphasizes the irrelevance of individual differences for fundamental social and political purposes',[183] 'a moral ideal governing the relations in which people stand to one another . . . opposed not to luck but to oppression, to heritable hierarchies of social status, to ideas of caste, to class privilege and the rigid stratification of classes, and to the undemocratic distribution of power'.[184] For Anderson, the 'equal moral worth of persons' is measured in terms not of 'virtue or talent' but of intrinsic human value, an approach which eschews the possibility of 'natural slaves, plebeians, or aristocrats'[185] and insists that 'Diversities in socially ascribed identities, distinct roles in the division of labor, or differences in personal traits, whether these be neutral biological and psychological differences, valuable talents and virtues, or unfortunate disabilities and infirmities, never justify' oppression, which she defines as the 'dominat[ion], exploit[ation], marginali[sation], demean[ing] and inflict[ion of] violence' by some groups of people upon others.[186]

O'Cinneide suggests that Collins's focus on social inclusion fails to challenge the norms into which the socially excluded are to be included and thus 'to capture the potential transformative effect of equality law' which, although 'perhaps more often an aspiration than a reality . . . remains a potential outcome, and a key element of what equality norms aspire to achieve',[187] pointing to the 'Superficially successful inclusion . . . of women in the workplace', coupled as it has been with 'the persistent failure of corporate culture to accommodate carer responsibilities, the burdens of pregnancy and alternative working methods' as inconsistent 'with the transformative ambitions of equality norms'.[188] The rather peremptory tone of Collins's suggestion that 'parents with young children who do not work and are not supported financially by a partner in work *should not be permitted to follow the social norm of taking responsibility for childcare to the extent of excluding themselves from the labour market*' (emphasis added) is not significantly softened by the statement that employer practices must shift to accommodate part-time work in order to permit the inclusion of

---

[182] ibid, 61–62.
[183] Scheffler (n 65) 17.
[184] ibid, 21–22.
[185] Citing J Rawls, 'Kantian Constructivism in Moral Theory' (1980) 77 *Journal of Philosophy* 515–72, 525.
[186] Anderson (n 67) 312–13.
[187] O'Cinneide (n 179) 62–63.
[188] ibid, 63.

such parents in the labour market given Collins's insistence that 'the aim is not equal or fair opportunity, but the elimination of rules that have an exclusionary effect'.[189] This being the case, a model based on social inclusion would appear to permit the occupational segregation of part-time workers into traditionally female and relatively underpaid jobs, and the continued social subordination of women and others.

Collins might also be criticised for his failure to limit the categories of the socially excluded who might benefit from anti-discrimination/equality norms. While his criterion: 'whether the group is one that in practice has been dispro-portionately socially excluded compared with the population as a whole'[190] may usefully protect single parents, women and (at least in relation to employment recruitment) those aged over 55 and under 22,[191] it appears also to offer protec-tion to other (sometimes) socially excluded categories of person such as paedo-philes or white supremacists. This issue is further considered in Chapter 2.

My intention above has been simply to flag some of the ongoing debates. The choice of model for the conceptualisation of equality/discrimination is a nor-mative rather than an analytical exercise: which approach fits best with the work that equality analysis should and can perform? My own preference is for a substantive rather than a formal approach, as indicated above. I have a pro-found mistrust for the preoccupations of luck egalitarians who, it seems to me, fail to grasp the way in which the opportunities of many are circumscribed by the functional equivalents of wires in the bird cage used by Marilyn Frye to explain sexual and racial oppression:

> The cage makes the bird entirely unfree to fly. If one studies the causes of this impris-onment by looking at one wire at a time, however, it appears puzzling. How does a wire only a couple of centimeters wide prevent a bird's flight? One wire at a time, we can neither describe nor explain the inhibition of the bird's flight. Only a large number of wires arranged in a specific way and connected to one another to enclose the bird and reinforce one another's rigidity can explain why the bird is unable to fly freely.[192]

I am not convinced by dignity-driven analysis for the reasons put forward by Fudge, Grabham, Greschner and Moreau,[193] though the concept of dignity is far from irrelevant to those of human rights, equality and non-discrimination, as

---

[189] Collins (n 173) 31. Collins's argument that the statutory discrimination legislation *in fact* 'must be understood as pursuing a distributive aim . . . as well as upholding the ideal of respect for the dignity of individuals or equal worth' (27) is also open to doubt in view of the fact that, at least at the time of his writing, it depended very heavily on relatively marginal departures from the sym-metrical 'equal treatment' approach of the legislation (28).

[190] ibid, 27.

[191] ibid, 28.

[192] M Frye, *Oppression: The Politics of Reality* (Trumansburg, NY: The Crossing Press, 1983) cited by IM Young in RM Post (ed), The Origins and Fate of Antisubordination Theory: A Symposium on Owen Fiss's 'Groups and the Equal Protection Clause' (2002) Article 9, 8 (www. bepress.com/ils/iss2/art9).

[193] Their operation illustrated by the decision of Canada's Supreme Court in *Gosselin*, above.

David Feldman rightly points out. Nor, in my view, is the goal of social inclusion ambitious enough to underpin any adequate commitment, in particular, to gender equality. More appealing is the focus of thinkers including Anderson, Scheffler and O'Cinneide on oppression. In the chapters which follow, an underpinning theme in the exploration of the law relating to equality/discrimination is its potential to challenge oppression. It is, however, always worth bearing in mind that, as Lucy Vickers has pointed out, different analyses of equality may be suited to different protected grounds. Vickers cites Nancy Fraser's suggestion 'that class inequality is best understood in terms of redistribution, and sexual orientation inequality best understood in terms of recognition'.[194] Christopher McCrudden, too, has suggested, in relation to English public law, that

> there is no one legal meaning of equality or discrimination applicable in the different circumstances . . . there is no consistency in the circumstances in which weaker or stronger conceptions of equality and discrimination currently apply . . . equality in English public law is . . . essentially pluralistic in its sources, in its origins, in its meanings, in its application, and in its functions.[195]

As I will elaborate in Chapter 7, the conclusions drawn throughout the book's substantive chapters as to the proper conceptualisation of discrimination/equality law are not intended to displace any general rationality-based preference for equal treatment such as is found, for example, in the regulation by the US Constitution's Equal Treatment Clause of non-suspect classifications.[196]

---

[194]   Vickers (n 138) 152, citing Fraser (n 138) 68.
[195]   C McCrudden, 'Equality and Non-Discrimination', in D Feldman (ed), *English Public Law* (Oxford: Oxford University Press, 2004) 582.
[196]   See further Chapter 2.

2

Defining the Protected Characteristics

INTRODUCTION

MUCH OF THIS chapter is concerned with the grounds or characteristics in relation to which discrimination should be regulated/ equality pursued. I will consider the development, implications and shortcomings of the grounds-based approach before turning to discuss, on the assumption that such an approach is to prevail, the grounds in respect of which discrimination ought to be regulated. Elsewhere I consider whether, in respect of those characteristics which are protected, a 'one size fits all' approach of the kind exemplified by the Equality Act 2010 is the best approach, and whether protection ought to be symmetrical or targeted towards those disadvantaged by reference to the particular protected characteristic.

In Britain at present the Equality Act lists as 'protected characteristics' age, disability, gender reassignment, marriage and civil partnership, pregnancy and maternity, race, religion or belief, sex and sexual orientation. In Northern Ireland, membership of the Irish Traveller community is expressly covered by law as is political belief. The list of grounds protected by law varies across states. Belgium, for example, protects against discrimination on the basis of characteristics including birth, wealth/income, actual or future state of health, physical characteristics, genetic characteristics, social origin, social position and trade union conviction.[1] But a ground-based approach to discrimination is common across most jurisdictions, whether the legal approach to discrimination is found in broad, constitutional-level prohibitions on discrimination or in detailed statutory provisions such as the Equality Act 2010 or its ground-particular predecessors (the Race Relations Act 1976, Disability Discrimination Act 1995 etc).

---

[1] I Chopin and T Uyen Do, 'Developing Anti-Discrimination Law in Europe' (November 2011, European Network of Legal Experts in the Non-discrimination Field), www.non-discrimination. net/content/media/Comparitive%20EN%202011.pdf.

THE US EQUAL PROTECTION CLAUSE:
THE ROOTS OF THE GROUND-BASED APPROACH

A grounds-based approach to discrimination typically requires, as a core element of the wrong, a link between the imposition of a burden or denial of a benefit, on the one hand, and one or more personal characteristics of the individual who complains of discrimination. Unfavourable, even differential, treatment alone is not a basis for complaint unless the differentiation is directly based upon or (in cases of indirect discrimination) associated with a protected characteristic. Thus, for example, whereas the US constitutional equality provision (the Equal Treatment Clause of the Fourteenth Amendment (1868)) provides merely that 'No State shall . . . deny to any person within its jurisdiction the equal protection of the laws', that provision was originally interpreted to prohibit only race discrimination.

The Fourteenth Amendment had been adopted as one of a number of reconstruction amendments in the wake of the civil war, with the Equal Protection Clause being designed to reverse the decision in *Dred Scott v Sandford* (1857), in which the Supreme Court ruled that citizenship and its benefits were unavailable to African-American descendants of slaves.[2] In the *Slaughter-House Cases* (1873), in which the application of the Equal Protection Clause was first considered, the US Supreme Court considered a challenge by New Orleans butchers to an attempt to reserve the entitlement to slaughter livestock to a single corporation.[3] The butchers sought to rely on the Equal Protection Clause of the Fourteenth Amendment and on the Thirteenth Amendment, which prohibited involuntary servitude. Justice Miller, who gave the judgment of the Court, declared that:

> No questions so farreaching and pervading in their consequences, so profoundly interesting to the people of this country, and so important in their bearing upon the relations of the United States, and of the several States to each other and to the citizens of the States and of the United States, have been before this court during the official life of any of its present members.

He went on to state that the 'pervading purpose' of both Amendments was 'the freedom of the slave race, the security and firm establishment of that freedom, and the protection of the newly-made freeman and citizen from the oppressions of those who had formerly exercised unlimited dominion over him', and continued: 'We do not say that no one else but the negro can share in this protection. Both the language and spirit of these articles are to have their fair and just weight in any question of construction'. Justice Miller then recited the historical underpinnings of the Fourteenth Amendment in the *Dred Scott* decision of Equal Protection Clause which 'while it met the condemnation of some of the

---

[2] *Dred Scott v Sandford* 60 US 393 (1857).
[3] *Slaughter-House Cases* 83 US 36, 81 (1873).

ablest statesmen and constitutional lawyers of the country, had never been over-ruled', and went on to consider the meaning to be accorded to the Equal Protection Clause itself:

> In the light of the history of these amendments, and the pervading purpose of them, which we have already discussed, it is not difficult to give a meaning to this clause. The existence of laws in the States where the newly emancipated negroes resided, which discriminated with gross injustice and hardship against them as a class, was the evil to be remedied by this clause, and by it such laws are forbidden.
>
> If, however, the States did not conform their laws to its requirements, then by the fifth section of the article of amendment Congress was authorized to enforce it by suitable legislation. We doubt very much whether any action of a State not directed by way of discrimination against the negroes as a class, or on account of their race, will ever be held to come within the purview of this provision. It is so clearly a provision for that race and that emergency, that a strong case would be necessary for its application to any other. . .

The decision in the *Slaughter-House Cases* was to have far-reaching effects on the legal approach to the regulation of discrimination, placing the question of grounds centre stage. This is further considered below. But the grounds subject to protection under the Equal Protection Clause were to expand very considerably over time. The dissenters in the *Slaughter-House Cases* had favoured an interpretation of the Equal Protection Clause which would have subjected all classifications to judicial review.[4] In *Railroad Co v Richmond* (1877) the Supreme Court dismissed an equal protection challenge to legislation directed at a particular railroad, not on the basis that it did not fall within the equal protection clause, but because the distinction drawn was reasonable.[5] And in *Missouri v Lewis* (1879) the Court, in denying a Fourteenth Amendment challenge to distinctions drawn between different regions of a State, nevertheless affirmed that the effect of the Equal Protection Clause was that 'no person or class of persons shall be denied the same protection of the laws which is enjoyed by other persons or other classes in the same place and under like circumstances'.[6] In *Yick Wo v Hopkins* (1886) the Fourteenth Amendment was applied to discrimination against ethnically Chinese laundry operators which was motivated by 'hostility to the race and nationality to which the petitioners belong, and which, in the eye of the law, is not justified'.[7] And in 1897 the Court declared, in a challenge to legislation requiring railroad companies to pay the legal costs of those successfully suing them, that, while 'generally true' that states had the power of classification,

> it is equally true that such classification cannot be made arbitrarily. The state may not say that all white men shall be subjected to the payment of the attorney's fees of par-

---

[4] See RS Kay, 'The Equal Protection Clause in the Supreme Court: 1873–1903' (1980) 29 *Buffalo Law Review* 667, 676–77.

[5] *Railroad Co v Richmond* 96 US 521 (1877) discussed by Kay, ibid, 683–84.

[6] *Missouri v Lewis* 101 US 22, 31 (1879). See also *Hayes v Missouri* 120 US 68, 71 (1887).

[7] *Yick Wo v Hopkins* 118 US 356, 374 (1886).

ties successfully suing them, and all black men not. It may not say that all men beyond a certain age shall be alone thus subjected, or all men possessed of a certain wealth. These are distinctions which do not furnish any proper basis for the attempted classification. That must always rest upon some difference which bears a reasonable and just relation to the act in respect to which the classification is proposed, and can never be made arbitrarily, and without any such basis.[8]

Equal protection clause challenges continued to be brought to a wide variety of classifications (different categories of sugar and molasses refiners, of utility providers, of women employees, of insurance companies).[9] The approach taken by the Supreme Court in the early part of the twentieth century was to strike down classifications which the Court regarded as 'purely arbitrary, oppressive or capricious'; 'unreasonable or arbitrary'; 'actually and palpably unreasonable and arbitrary'.[10] Under this standard of review the Court upheld distinctions drawn between unnaturalised foreign born residents and others as regards rights to hold firearms and kill wild game[11] though it struck down distinctions between citizens and non-citizens as regards the right to earn a living;[12] between railroad companies and others as regards liability to pay the costs of litigation of those who successfully litigated against them;[13] between farmers and others as regards the criminalisation of combinations in restraint of trade;[14] and between striking workers and others as regards tortious liability.[15] Stephen Siegel, taking issue with Justice Oliver Wendell Holmes's oft-cited comment in *Buck v Bell* (1927) that the Equal Protection Clause was 'the usual last resort of constitutional arguments',[16] reported that:

> Between 1897 . . . and 1937 [the *Lochner* era] . . . the Supreme Court voided forty-six laws on equal protection grounds . . . approximately one-fifth of the total number of

---

[8] *Gulf, C&SFR Co v Ellis* 165 US 150 (1897).

[9] *American Sugar Refining Co v Louisiana* 179 US 89 (1990), *Arkansas Natural Gas Co. v Railroad Commission* 261 US 379 (1923), *Radice v New York* 264 US 292 (1924), *Orient Insurance v Lake Erie & Western RR Co* 175 US 348 (1899). See also *Moore v Missouri* 159 US 673 (1895) (classification of prisoners on the basis of number of previous offences); *Petit v Minnesota* 177 US 164 (1900) (different types of employment); *Williams v Fears* 179 US 270 (1900) (different categories of employment agents), *Bain Peanut Co v Pinson* 282 US 499 (1931) (distinctions between incorporated and unincorporated individuals) and *Tigner v Texas* 310 US 141 (1940) (combinations of farmers and others).

[10] *American Sugar Refining, Arkansas Natural Gas Co, Radice* (n 9).

[11] *Patsone v Pennsylvania* 238 US 138 (1914).

[12] *Truax v Raich* 239 US 33, 43 (1915).

[13] *Gulf, Colorado & Santa Fe Rail Road v Ellis* 165 US 150 (1897). *cf Atchison, Topeka & Santa Fe Rail Road v Matthews* 174 US 96 (1899).

[14] *Connolly v Union Sewer Pipe Co* 184 US 540, 570 (1902).

[15] *Truax v Corrigan* 257 US 312, 333–34 (1921). For discussion of these cases see Kay (n 4). In *Adkins v Children's Hospital of DC* 261 US 525 (1923), one of the *Lochner*-era assaults by the Supreme Court on protective legislation, the Court struck down minimum wage provisions applicable to women in part on the basis that 'we cannot accept the doctrine that women of mature age, *sui juris,* require or may be subjected to restrictions upon their liberty of contract which could not lawfully be imposed in the case of men under similar circumstances'. *Adkins* was overruled in *West Coast Hotel Co v Parrish* 300 US 379 (1937).

[16] *Buck v Bell* 274 US 200 (1927).

decisions in which the Lochner era Court voided governmental action on Fourteenth Amendment grounds . . . the frequency of equal protection invalidations increased as the Lochner era progressed, reflecting the overall ebb and flow of Lochner-era judicial activism. . . During the 1920s, the Court relied on equal protection seventeen times. . . equal protection invalidations were most frequent in the three years just around the Buck decision. Only nine Lochner-era equal protection invalidations involved racial or alienage discrimination despite that being the original focus of the Equal Protection Clause. Most of the cases, thirty-seven in all, involved economic regulation.[17]

It is difficult to resist the temptation to point out the irony of a constitutional equality provision being utilised to strike down legislation designed to limit the wage exploitation of the most vulnerable (women) workers. The *Lochner* era of judicial activism resulted in a threat by President Roosevelt that he would pack the Supreme Court with nine additional judges in order to block the approach taken by the Court against his New Deal attempts to implement minimum wage and other protective legislation. In *US v Carolene Products Co* (1938), which concerned the constitutionality of federal legislation prohibiting skimmed milk to which additional fat (other than milk fat) had been added from being transported between States, the Court toed the required, non-interventionist line by ruling that the legislation was 'presumptively constitutional' and that it passed muster as long as it was 'rationally related' to a 'legitimate' government interest.[18] In embracing the 'rational review' standard, however, the Court left room for more rigorous justification requirements where the constitutional stakes were higher in the famous 'footnote four' of Justice Stone's opinion in which he suggested that:

> There may be narrower scope for operation of the presumption of constitutionality when legislation appears on its face to be within a specific prohibition of the Constitution . . . It is unnecessary to consider now whether legislation which restricts those political processes which can ordinarily be expected to bring about repeal of undesirable legislation, is to be subjected to more exacting judicial scrutiny . . . Nor need we enquire whether similar considerations enter into the review of statutes directed at particular religious . . . or national . . . or racial minorities . . . whether prejudice against discrete and insular minorities may be a special condition, which tends seriously to curtail the operation of those political processes ordinarily to be relied upon to protect minorities, and which may call for a correspondingly more searching judicial inquiry.[19]

---

[17] SA Siegel, 'Justice Holmes, *Buck v. Bell*, and the History of Equal Protection' (2005) 90 *Minnesota Law Review* 106, 131–33.

[18] *US v Carolene Products Co* 304 US 144 (1938). The challenge was brought under the Fifth Amendment's Due Process Clause which (*Boiling v Sharpe* 347 US 497, 499 (1954)) applies to Federal legislation the same standards as the Equal Treatment Clause of the Fourteenth Amendment applies to state measures. The rational review standard had its roots in *McCulloch v Maryland* 17 US 316 (1819). For critique of the *US Carolene* decision see BA Ackerman, 'Beyond Carolene Products' (1985) 98 *Harvard Law Review* 713. Ackerman suggests, at 723–24, that 'discreteness and insularity . . . will normally be a source of great bargaining advantage, not disadvantage, for a group engaged in pluralist American politics', suggesting that diffuse 'groups' suffer significantly more disadvantage than 'discrete and insular' ones.

[19] ibid, 152.

Equally ironically, in *Korematsu v US* (1944), the first case in which the Court categorised race as a 'suspect classification' in respect of which Justice Stone's heightened review (subsequently termed 'strict scrutiny') was required, the Court ruled that the test was satisfied in the internment of persons of Japanese ethnic origin.[20] In *Oyama v California* a different conclusion was reached in a case involving discrimination on grounds of citizenship in relation to land ownership.[21] The discrimination in that case occurred precisely because the claimant was of Japanese ethnicity, but in *Graham v Richardson* (1971) the Court accepted the broad proposition that alienage was a suspect classification subject to strict scrutiny.

I return below to the basis for according strict scrutiny.[22] Here it is sufficient to point out that, since the mid 1970s, race and nationality discrimination have attracted strict scrutiny under the equal protection clause with alienage attracting different levels of protection according to the context and illegitimacy and gender subsequently having attracted 'intermediate scrutiny', which requires that discrimination on these grounds must further an important government interest in a way that is substantially related to that interest.[23] In addition, classifications which impinge on fundamental constitutional rights (such as procreation, interstate movement and religious freedom) attract strict scrutiny.[24] All other grounds of discrimination ('classification') are subject to 'rational review' which asks only whether a governmental action is 'rationally related' to a 'legitimate' government interest, whether or not the 'legitimate interest' identified by the court is the aim actually pursued by the government.[25]

The application of rational review alone to discrimination on grounds of (say) sexual orientation does not mean that all such discrimination is constitutional. In *Romer v Evans* (1996) the Supreme Court ruled both that discrimination on grounds of sexual orientation attracted this standard of review and also that an amendment to Colorado's constitution to prohibit any legislative, executive, or judicial action to recognise gay men or lesbian women as a protected class for the purposes of anti-discrimination legislation breached the Equal Protection Clause of the Fourteenth Amendment.[26] According to the majority of the Court (*per* Kennedy J): 'the amendment imposes a special disability upon those persons alone. Homosexuals are forbidden the safeguards that others

---

[20] *Korematsu v US* 323 US 214 (1944).

[21] *Oyama v California* 322 US 633 (1948).

[22] *Graham v Richardson* 403 US 365 (1971).

[23] *Craig v Boren* 429 US 190 (1976) (sex); *Reed v Campbell* 476 US 852 (1986) (illegitimacy).

[24] See, for example, *San Antonio Independent School District v Rodriguez* 411 US 1, 33–34 (1973), *Plyer v Doe* 457 US 202, 232 (1982) *per* Blackmun J concurring. On procreation and religion respectively see, respectively, *Skinner v Oklahoma* 316 US 535 (1942) and *Nguyen v Nguyen* 882 SW2d 176 177 fn 2 (1994) (Mo Ct App) and see AB Gendelman, 'Equal Protection Clause, the Free Exercise Clause and Religion-Based Preemptory Challenges, The Comment' (1996) 63 *University of Chicago Law Review* 1639, 1652.

[25] For a critique of the jurisprudence see S Goldberg, 'Equality without Tiers' (2003–04) 77 *Southern California Law Review* 481–527.

[26] *Romer v Evans* 517 US 620 (1996).

enjoy or may seek without constraint' and 'Its sheer breadth is so discontinuous with the reasons offered for it that the amendment seems inexplicable by anything but animus toward the class that it affects; it lacks a rational relationship to legitimate state interests'.

Having said this, had Colerado exercised more subtlety in discriminating on grounds of sexual orientation a different outcome might have resulted. It is difficult to escape the conclusion that the freedom accorded the Boy Scouts in *Boy Scouts of America v Dale* (2000) to exclude gays from membership (this on the basis of First Amendment arguments about freedom of expression) would not have been accorded the organisation had sexual orientation been regarded as a suspect classification.[27] While the issue there was whether the State could, consistent with the First Amendment, prohibit discrimination on grounds of sexual orientation by the Boy Scouts (such a body not being directly subject to the Constitution), the absence of significant constitutional protection against sexual orientation discrimination is likely to have had an impact on judicial analyses of the competing interests at stake. Thus, for example, the outcome in *Dale* can be contrasted with that in *Roberts v United States Jaycees* (1984), in which the state interest in prohibiting sex discrimination trumped the interests of a junior chamber of commerce in freedom of association,[28] and in *Railway Mail Association v Corsi* (1945), in which the state's interest in prohibiting race discrimination trumped, inter alia, a trade union's asserted entitlement under the due process clause of the Fourteenth Amendment to select its members and manage its own affairs.[29] Justice Frankfurter, concurring in the latter case, went so far as to state that:

> Elaborately to argue against this contention is to dignify a claim devoid of constitutional substance. Of course a State may leave abstention from such discriminations to the conscience of individuals. On the other hand, a State may choose to put its authority behind one of the cherished aims of American feeling by forbidding indulgence in racial or religious prejudice to another's hurt. To use the Fourteenth Amendment as a sword against such State power would stultify that Amendment. Certainly the insistence by individuals on their private prejudices as to race, color or creed, in relations like those now before us, ought not to have a higher constitutional sanction than the determination of a State to extend the area of non-discrimination beyond that which the Constitution itself exacts.[30]

---

[27] *Boy Scouts of America v Dale* 530 US 640 (2000). See also *Hurley v Irish-American Gay, Lesbian & Bisexual Group of Boston* 515 US 557 (1995).

[28] *Roberts v United States Jaycees* 468 US 609 (1984). See DO Linder, 'Freedom of Association after *Roberts v United States Jaycees*' (1984) 82 *Michigan Law Review* 1878; DP Gearey, 'New Protections after *Boy Scouts of America v. Dale*: A Private University's First Amendment Right to Pursue Diversity' (2004) 71 *University of Chicago Law Review* 1583.

[29] *Railway Mail Association v Corsi* 326 US 88 (1945).

[30] ibid, 98. See also *Runyon v McCrary* 427 US 160, 167–68 (1976); *Bob Jones University v United States* 461 US 574 (1983); JA Bogdanski, 'Section 1981 and the Thirteenth Amendment after *Runyon v. McCrary*. On the Doorsteps of Discriminatory Private Clubs' (1977) 29 *Stanford Law Review* 747. *Runyon* was narrowly interpreted, though not overruled, by the Supreme Court in *Patterson v McLean Credit Union* 491 US 164 (1989) so as to apply only to the making of contracts and not

The difficulty with the US Court's approach to grounds other than those protected by strict or intermediate scrutiny is that scant protection is afforded by rational review. The problem which can arise where many enumerated (and unenumerated) grounds are protected is that the level of that protection is similarly attenuated by the sheer number of grounds covered. Article 14 of the European Convention, for example, regulates discrimination on grounds including (but not limited to) 'political or other opinion . . . social origin . . . property, birth or other status', its protections having been applied, inter alia, to discrimination on grounds of membership of a particular trade union, military status, ownership of non-residential and residential buildings and of large and small parcels of land.[31] In the *Belgian Linguistics Case*, in which the ECtHR first considered the application of Article 14, it required only the differential treatment complained of was in pursuit of a legitimate aim and had a 'reasonable relationship of proportionality' with the aim sought to be realised.[32] Over time that Court has in fact recognised an increasing number of grounds as requiring more in the way of justification where differential treatment is based upon them. Thus discrimination on grounds including sex, religion, legitimacy, nationality or sexual orientation requires 'very weighty reasons' by way of justification[33] and the Court has recently gone so far to state that 'no difference in treatment which is based exclusively or to a decisive extent on a person's ethnic origin is capable of being objectively justified'.[34] The recognition of these 'super grounds' is, however, itself a matter for judicial discretion and, short of a finding that a particular ground is already the subject of enhanced protection, there is no clear way of drawing the line.[35] The same is true of the question whether any

(there) to racial harassment during the existence of a contract. Congress stepped in with the Civil Rights Act 1991 to overrule *Patterson*. See also CW Schmidt, '*Doe v. Kamehameha*: Section 1981 and the Future of Racial Preferences in Private Schools' (2007) 42 *Harvard Civil Rights-Civil Liberties Law Review* 557.

[31] Respectively, *National Union of Belgian Police v Belgium* (1979) 1 EHRR 578; *Engel v Netherlands* (1976) 1 EHRR 647; *Spadea & Scalebrino v Italy* (1995) 21 EHRR 482 and *Chassagnou v France* (1999) 7 BHRC 151.

[32] Relating to certain aspects of the laws on the use of languages in education in Belgium *(Belgian Linguistics) (No 2)* (1968) 1 EHRR 252, para 10.

[33] *Abdulaziz, Cabales and Balkandali v United Kingdom* (1985) 7 EHRR 471 (sex); *Hoffmann v Austria* (1993) 17 EHRR 293 (religion); *Mazurek v France* (2006) 42 EHRR 9 (legitimacy); *Gaygusuz v Austria* (1996) 23 EHRR 365 (nationality) and *L & V v Austria* (2003) 36 EHRR 55 (sexual orientation).

[34] *Timishev v Russia* (2007) 44 EHRR 37, para 58 and see *DH v Czech Republic* (2008) 47 EHRR 3 in which this approach was applied to race discrimination characterised by the Court as indirect in nature.

[35] In *R (Carson) v Secretary of State for Work & Pensions* [2006] 1 AC 173 Lord Hoffmann suggested that 'there is usually no difficulty about deciding whether one is dealing with a case in which the right to respect for the individuality of a human being is at stake or merely a question of general social policy' (para 17) though he acknowledged also that 'There may be borderline cases in which it is not easy to allocate the ground of discrimination to one category or the other and, as I have observed, there are shifts in the values of society on these matters. *Ghaidan v Godin-Mendoza* [2004] 2 AC 557 recognised that discrimination on grounds of sexual orientation was now firmly in the first category. Discrimination on grounds of old age may be a contemporary example of a borderline case'.

unenumerated ground is recognised at all for the purposes of Article 14 or, in Canada, section 15 of the Charter.

The basis on which grounds are differentiated by particular courts is considered below. The point here being made is that more is not necessarily better, as breadth of protection can serve to undermine depth. It also gives rise, as we see in Chapter 5, to potential conflicts between grounds which are not readily resolvable in the absence of clearly articulated hierarchies of protection, or at least of clearly articulated principles of the reasons for which protection from discrimination is accorded, and of the boundaries of that protection.

The question which has arisen in the US context is, all classifications being in principle subject to challenge, whether the ground at issue is entitled to an enhanced level of protection. The list of grounds attracting enhanced Constitutional protection has not changed since the mid to late 1970s and notable among the absentees are age,[36] mental disability[37] and sexual orientation.[38] What is less clear is the basis on which enhanced protection is accorded or denied. Suzanne Goldberg points out that the Supreme Court 'did not articulate detailed indicia for discerning which classifications should [be regarded as suspect] . . . until the early 1970s' when, in *San Antonio Independent School District v Rodriguez* (1973), it set out the 'traditional indicia of suspectness'.[39] In a case concerning a challenge based on wealth (or, rather, the lack thereof) Justice Powell, who delivered the opinion of the Court, stated that:

> The system of alleged discrimination and the class it defines have none of the traditional indicia of suspectness: the class is not saddled with such disabilities, or subjected to such a history of purposeful unequal treatment, or relegated to such a position of political powerlessness as to command extraordinary protection from the majoritarian political process.[40]

In the same year, in *Frontiero v Richardson*,[41] Justice Brennan suggested that strict scrutiny ought to apply to sex discrimination, in part because gender was, like race, an 'immutable' and unchosen characteristic which in his view was irrelevant to the purpose of the federal law at issue. He also made reference to the long history of sex discrimination in the US and the fact that the Equal Pay Act of 1963, the Civil Rights Act of 1964 and Equal Rights Amendment (then

[36] *Massachusetts Board of Retirement v Murgia* 427 US 307 (1976).
[37] *City of Cleburne v Cleburne Living Center Inc* 473 US 432 (1985).
[38] In *Rowland v Mad River Social District* 470 US 1009, 1010 (1985) Justice Brennan, in dissent, had stated that homosexuals comprised a 'significant and insular minority of this country's population'. In *Romer v Evans* 517 US 620 (1996), the Court ruled that sexual orientation attracted only rational review, but went on to rule that the legislative measure there under challenge breached that Equal Protection Clause. Poverty is also unprotected: *James v Valtierra* 402 US 137 (1971) and *San Antonio Independent School District v Rodriguez* 411 US 1 (1973), though *cf Shapiro v Thompson* 394 US 618 (1969) in which the Court had struck down a requirement that welfare recipients reside in a State for a year before they became eligible for assistance, suggesting that poverty was a protected ground.
[39] *San Antonio Independent School District v Rodriguez* (n 38). See Goldberg (n 25) 485.
[40] *San Antonio Independent School District v Rodriguez* (n 38) 28.
[41] *Frontiero v Richardson* 411 US 677 (1973).

awaiting ratification from the States[42]) already made it clear that classification on grounds of sex was 'inherently invidious'. Goldberg remarks that the indicia of suspectness 'as developed over time, aimed to identify characteristics that "are so seldom relevant to the achievement of any legitimate state interest that laws grounded in such considerations are deemed to reflect prejudice and antipathy"'.[43]

The approach to suspectness has to some extent slipped its moorings in footnote four, neither women nor African Americans (the latter the target of the Clause when it was included within the Constitution) actually comprising 'discrete and insular' minorities.[44] It is also clear that *classification*, rather than *disadvantage*, triggers that standard of review, this contrary to the implication of footnote four that the protection of the Equal Treatment Clause applied only to those *disadvantaged* by their class status.[45] Having said this, these and other criteria have been deployed to police the boundaries of suspect classes. In *Kimel v Florida Board of Regents* (2000),[46] for example, the Supreme Court excluded age discrimination from enhanced protection on the basis, in part, that 'Old age . . . does not define a discrete and insular minority'.[47] And while the Supreme Court has never in terms demanded immutability as a requirement for 'strict scrutiny',[48] it has regularly emphasised immutability in ascribing protection to a class. In *Sugarman v Dougall* (1973), for example, which concerned discrimination against non-citizens, Justice Rehnquist argued that the Court should deem suspect only those classifications based on 'status . . . which cannot be altered by an individual'.[49] In *Parham v Hughes* (1979) the Court emphasised immutability in listing the grounds discrimination on the basis of which would give rise to

---

[42] That ratification was never forthcoming.

[43] Goldberg (n 25) 502, quoting *Cleburne* (n 37) 440. See also *Fullilove v Klutznick* 448 US 448 (1980). See also Michael Gentitjes, 'The Equal Protection Clause and Immutability: the Chaos of Suspect Classification' (2010) 40 *University of Memphis Law Review* 507–53.

[44] This did not, however, prevent the Supreme Court, in *Kimel v Florida Board of Regents* 528 US 62 (2000), from excluding age discrimination from enhanced protection on the basis, in part, that 'Old age . . . does not define a discrete and insular minority'. For a critique of the 'discrete and insular minority' test see Ackerman (n 18); L Brilmayer, 'Carolene, Conflicts, and the Fate of the "Insider-Outsider"' (1986) 134 *University of Pennsylvania Law Review* 1291, 1294.

[45] See *Regents of the University of California v Bakke* 438 US 265 (1978) in which the Supreme Court, by a majority, rejected the university's argument that white men, of whom the claimant was one, had no need for protection against race-based discrimination (there in relation to entrance criteria intended to benefit candidates of minority ethnicity).

[46] *Kimel v Florida Board of Regents* 528 US 62 (2000).

[47] For critique of the demand for discreteness and insularity see Ackerman (n 18) 724 and 741–42. Ackerman suggests that, while this demand was understandable at the time of the *Carolene* decision in light of the recent history of the Nuremburg laws which 'served to recall, in the starkest way, the grim process by which black Americans had been stripped of their civil rights in the aftermath of Reconstruction [in part] . . . by virtue of their discreteness and insularity . . . After a generation of renewed struggle for civil rights, however, it no longer follows that the discreteness or insularity of a group will continue to serve as a decisive disadvantage in the ongoing process of pluralist bargaining'.

[48] And see the dissents from Justices Brennan and Marshall in *Rowland v Mad River Local School District* 470 US 1009 (1985).

[49] *Sugarman v Dougall* 413 US 634 (1973).

strict scrutiny.[50] And in *Plyler v Doe* (1982) the Court ruled that children whose status was undocumented did not form a protected group since 'undocumented status is not irrelevant to any proper legislative goal. Nor is undocumented status an absolutely immutable characteristic since it is the product of conscious, indeed unlawful, action'.[51]

Commentators differ as to the correct interpretation of the case law on suspect grounds and, accordingly, on how those grounds might be extended.[52] The immutability argument was at one stage deployed by those seeking to have sexual orientation included within the suspect grounds. In *Watkins v US Army* (1989), in which the Court of Appeals for the Ninth Circuit ruled, by a majority, that the military was estopped from refusing to re-enlist a soldier on the grounds that he was gay, Norris J concurred on a strict scrutiny approach, stating that immutability 'may describe those traits that are so central to a person's identity that it would be abhorrent for government to penalize a person for refusing to change them'.[53] In *Jantz v Muci* (1991) the District Court of Kansas accepted that sexual orientation was immutable on the basis that it could be changed 'only . . . at a prohibitive cost'.[54] And in *Equality Foundation of Greater Cincinnati, Inc v City of Cincinnati* (1994), the District Court of Ohio applied strict scrutiny to sexual orientation on the basis that it was 'beyond the control of the individual'.[55]

Both the *Jantz* and the *Equality Foundation* cases were reversed on appeal,[56] however, and the immutability approach 'proved to be friendly fire, precisely because of the volatile state of the scientific arguments concerning sexual orientation. Generally, the courts have rejected the immutability claim outright'.[57] In

---

[50] *Parham v Hughes* 441 US 347, 351 (1979). In addition to race the Court listed national origin (*Oyama v California*, 332 US 633 (1948)); alienage (*Graham v Richardson* 403 US 365 (1971)); illegitimacy (*Gomez v Perez*, 409 US 535 (1973)) and gender (*Reed v Reed*, 404 US 71 (1971)). See also *Bowen v Gilliard* 483 US 587, 602–03 (1987). cf *San Antonio School District v Rodriguez* (n 38) in which the Court, *per* Justice Powell, listed as 'the traditional indicia of suspectness' that a class is 'saddled with such disabilities, or subjected to such a history of purposeful unequal treatment, or relegated to such a position of political powerlessness as to command extraordinary protection from the majoritarian political process'. And see *Cleburne* (n 37) in which (see especially 440–41) irrelevance to legislative aim was emphasised as pointing to suspect classification and doubt cast (fn 10) on immutability as a requirement. Note also that alienage, accepted as a suspect ground in *Graham v Richardson* 403 US 365 (1971) is not immutable.

[51] *Plyler v Doe* 457 US 202 (1982). The Court went on to rule that the denial of education to such children was unconstitutional on the basis that it was irrational.

[52] See, for example, S Gilreath, 'Of Fruit Flies and Men: Rethinking Immutability in Equal Protection Analysis – with a View toward a Constitutional Moral Imperative' Wake Forest University Legal Studies Research Paper Series April 2006; M Perry, 'Modern Equal Protection: A Conceptualization and Appraisal' (1979) 79 *Columbia Law Review* 1023.

[53] *Watkins v US Army* 875 F2d 699, 726 (1989) (para 109).

[54] *Jantz v Muci* 759 F Supp 1543, 1548 (D Kan 1991).

[55] *Equality Foundation of Greater Cincinnati, Inc v City of Cincinnati* 860 F Supp 417, 437 (SD Ohio 1994).

[56] 976 F2d 623 (10th Cir 1992); 128 F3d 289 (6th Cir 1997).

[57] Gilreath (n 52) 12. See also E Arriola, 'Sexual Identity and the Constitution: Homosexual Persons as a Discrete and Insular Minority' (1992) 14 *Women's Rights Law Reporter* 263 and for a review of recent State Supreme Court decisions on sexual orientation see M Helfand, 'The Usual

the 1990 *High Tech Gays* case, for example, the Court of Appeals for the Ninth Circuit rejected a challenge to sexual orientation discrimination in security vetting by the Department of Defense on the basis that 'Homosexuality is not an immutable characteristic; it is behavioral and hence is fundamentally different from traits such as race, gender, or alienage, which define already existing suspect and quasi-suspect classes'.[58] In *Woodward v US* (1989) the Federal Court of Appeals upheld the discharge of a naval officer on the basis of his sexual orientation on similar grounds.[59] And more recently 'the immutability factor continues to animate judicial decisions, serving as a focal point in the ongoing litigations over state statutory schemes prohibiting same-sex marriage'[60] though, as Helfand points out, 'Scholars and courts alike regularly demonstrate a basic uncertainty as to whether an immutable trait is a trait that has not been chosen, a trait that cannot be changed, or a trait that an individual should not be forced to change'.[61]

Canada: 'Enumerated' and 'Analogous' Grounds

The US Equal Protection Clause is on one end of the chronological spectrum of constitutional equality provisions. South Africa's constitutional equality clause is on the other. Section 9 of South Africa's Constitutional Bill of Rights (1996), which is discussed elsewhere, protects against unfair discrimination on (s 9(3)) 'one or more grounds, including race, gender, sex, pregnancy, marital status, ethnic or social origin, colour, sexual orientation, age, disability, religion, conscience, belief, culture, language and birth'. It goes on to state (s 9(5)) that 'Discrimination on one or more of the grounds listed in subsection (3) is unfair unless it is established that the discrimination is fair'. Canada's Charter of Rights 1982 also contains an open list of grounds. Having declared that 'Every individual is equal before and under the law', section 15(1) goes on to provide that each individual 'has the right to the equal protection and equal benefit of the law without discrimination' and, in particular, without discrimination based on race, national or ethnic origin, colour, religion, sex, age or mental or physical disability'.

Suspect Classifications: Criminals, Aliens and the Future of Same Sex Marriage' (2009–10) 12 *University of Pennsylvania Journal of Constitutional Law* 1, 3–5.

[58] *High Tech Gays v Def Indus Sec Clearance Office* 895 F2d 563, 573 (9th Cir 1990).

[59] *Woodward v US* 871 F2d 1068, 1076 (Fed Cir 1989), para 45. See also *Equality Foundation of Greater Cincinnati, Inc, v City of Cincinnati* 128 F3d 289 (6th Cir 1997), overruling the decision of the lower court at 860 F Supp 417, 437 (SD Ohio 1994). See also *Dean v District of Columbia* 653 A2d 307, 330 (DC 1995); *Andersen v King County* 138 P3d 963, 974 (Wash 2006).

[60] Helfand (n 57) 4–5, citing, inter alia, *In re Marriage Cases* 183 P3d 384 (2008) 442–43, 452; *Kerrigan v Comm'r of Pub Health* 957 A2d 407 (2008) 438 and *Varnum v Brien* (2009) 763 NW2d 862, 886–87.

[61] ibid, 5, footnotes omitted.

Equality *before* the law is a relatively thin concept, held by British Columbia's Supreme Court in the pre-Charter case of *R v Gonzales* (1962)[62] to be consistent with a provision of the Indian Act which prohibited Indians (but not others) from being intoxicated whilst off reserve, as long as all those to whom the law applied (Indians) were treated equally. The legislative provision there at issue was section 1(b) of Canada's 1960 Bill of Rights which protects from 'discrimination by reason of race, national origin, colour, religion or sex . . . the right of the individual to equality before the law and the protection of the law'. Canada's judges for the most part embraced the 'frozen concept theory' in applying the Bill of Rights, continuing to regard as acceptable for the purposes of the Bill that which was acceptable prior to its enactment.[63] In 1969, in *R v Drybones*,[64] the Supreme Court ruled that the intoxication provisions of the Indian Act were inconsistent with section 1(b) but in 1974, in *Robinson Attorney General v Lavell, Issac v Bedard*,[65] the same Court ruled that section 1(b) was not breached by provisions of the Indian Act which stripped Indian women, but not Indian men, of their Indian status when they married non-Indian spouses.

The history of section 1(b) was significantly responsible for the breadth of drafting evident in section 15 of the Charter, the original version of that provision (which provided only for equality before the law and equal protection of the law) being amended to include the right to equality *under* and the equal *benefit* of the law.[66] Canada's and South Africa's provisions are regarded by equality enthusiasts as among the most progressive in the world. Canada's prohibitions on discrimination apply to any ground not expressly included in section 15(1) but deemed 'analogous' to those listed.[67] Just as the notion of immutability has been significant in the inclusion of grounds regarded as 'suspect' for the purposes of the US Equal Protection Clause, so too it has featured in the Canadian jurisprudence in the determination whether a ground is 'analogous' for the purposes of section 15.[68] The determination of whether or not a ground is 'analogous' to those listed in section 15 turned, in the early Charter

---

[62] *R v Gonzales* (1962) 37 CR 56. The case was decided under section 1(b) of Canada's Bill of Rights which protects from 'discrimination by reason of race, national origin, colour, religion or sex . . . the right of the individual to equality before the law and the protection of the law'.

[63] *Robertson and Rosetanni v R* [1963] SCR 651, *Gonzales* (1962) 37 WWR 257 BC, *Smythe v R* [1971] SCR 680, *Miller & Cockriell v R* [1977] 2 SCR 680.

[64] *R v Drybones* [1970] SCR 282.

[65] *Robinson Attorney General v Lavell, Issac v Bedard* [1974] SCR 1349.

[66] Peter Hogg suggests (*Constitutional Law of Canada* (Scarborough, Ontario: Thomson Canada Limited, 2003) 1087) that 'The words "and under" were intended to abrogate a suggestion by Ritchie J in the *Lavell* case that judicial review on equality grounds did not extend to the substance of the law but only to the way in which it was administered'.

[67] *Andrews v Law Society of British Columbia* [1989] 1 SCR 143. Recognised 'analogous grounds' also include citizenship and status as an aboriginal Canadian living on or off an aboriginal reserve, but not employment or military status, place or duration of residence or conviction of a serious offence.

[68] In *Andrews v Law Society of British Columbia* [1989] 1 SCR 143, the first s 15 decision, the Supreme Court accepted that the provision applied 'at least' to analogous grounds (see in particular the judgment of Wilson J) but subsequently it has become apparent that *only* 'analogous' grounds are included.

case law, on whether it concerned the personal characteristics of persons in a group which has been subjected to historical disadvantage, stereotyping and prejudice.[69] One of the questions which has been asked is whether the group constitutes a 'discrete and insular minority'.[70] In the mid 1990s, in a group of cases known as the '1995 Trilogy',[71] the analysis shifted, a majority of the Court in *Miron* suggesting that the analogous grounds could not be restricted to historically disadvantaged groups if the Charter was to retain future relevance and that the inclusion of sex as an enumerated ground indicated that discrete insularity was not a requirement.[72] In *Corbiere v Canada (Minister of Indian and Northern Affairs)*,[73] a majority of the Supreme Court suggested that the grounds listed in section 15 had in common the fact 'that they often serve as the basis for stereotypical decisions made not on the basis of merit but on the basis of a personal characteristic that is immutable or changeable only at unacceptable cost to personal identity'. The Court went on to rule that actual or 'constructive' immutability was the central characteristic from which resulted 'discrete and insular minorit[ies]' and patterns of historical discrimination, the 'immutable or constructively immutable personal characteristics . . . too often hav[ing] served as illegitimate and demeaning proxies for merit-based decision making'.[74]

For L'Heureux-Dubé J, the question whether a ground was analogous to those enumerated by section 15 turned rather on whether its recognition 'would further the purposes of s. 15(1)', namely:

> To prevent the violation of essential human dignity and freedom through the imposition of disadvantage, stereotyping, or political or social prejudice, and to promote a society in which all persons enjoy equal recognition at law as human beings or as members of Canadian society, equally capable and equally deserving of concern, respect and consideration.[75]

[69] *Andrews*, ibid; *R v Turpin* [1989] 1 SCR 1296.

[70] *Turpin*, ibid, *per* Wilson J who was, however, at pains to state that the question of insularity was 'one of the analytical tools which are of assistance in determining whether the interest advanced by a particular claimant is the kind of interest s. 15 of the *Charter* is designed to protect', and was 'not an end in itself'. Also relevant in her view was the 'search for indicia of discrimination such as stereotyping, historical disadvantage or vulnerability to political and social prejudice'. It was clear from the decision in *Turpin* that the Court's articulation of the 'discrete and insular minority' concept was not intended to straitjacket the protection of s 15.

[71] *Thibaudeau v Canada* [1995] 2 SCR 627; *Egan v Canada* [1995] 2 SCR 513 and *Miron v Trudel* [1995] 2 SCR 418.

[72] Wilson J in *Andrews* had stressed her view that s 15 protection might not be limited to analogous grounds and stated that 'the range of discrete and insular minorities has changed and will continue to change with changing political and social circumstances . . . It can be anticipated that the discrete and insular minorities of tomorrow will include groups not recognised as such today. It is consistent with the constitutional status of s. 15 that it be interpreted with sufficient flexibility to ensure the "unremitting protection" of equality rights in the years to come'.

[73] *Corbiere v Canada (Minister of Indian and Northern Affairs)* [1999] 2 SCR 203.

[74] ibid, para 13 *per* McLachlin and Bastarche JJ, with whom Lamer CJ and Cory and Major JJ agreed.

[75] ibid, para 59, citing *Law v Canada* [1991] SCR 497, para 51. At para 125 she stated that 'To the extent that their reasons suggest a departure from the approach to defining analogous grounds taken in *Andrews, Turpin, Egan, Miron*, and *Law*, I must respectfully disagree with their analysis'. Gonthier, Iacobucci and Binnie JJ agreed. The impact of the different approaches was evident in

She accepted, however, that among the 'contextual factors . . . recognized in the case law' as germane to this question were 'the fundamental nature of the characteristic: whether from the perspective of a reasonable person in the position of the claimant, it is important to their identity, personhood, or belonging', and that immutability in the sense indicated by the majority was a factor, though 'none of the above indicators are necessary for the recognition of an analogous ground or combination of grounds'.[76] Further, the identification of protected grounds

> must . . . be flexible enough to adapt to stereotyping, prejudice, or denials of human dignity and worth that might occur in specific ways for specific groups of people, to recognize that personal characteristics may overlap or intersect (such as race, band membership, and place of residence in this case), and to reflect changing social phenomena or new or different forms of stereotyping or prejudice . . .[77]

The less than absolute approach to immutability which characterises the decisions of the Canadian Supreme Court has permitted the recognition of unenumerated grounds including status as an Aboriginal band member living off-reserve, sexual orientation and marital status[78] within the protection of section 15, and avoided entanglement in sterile and (at least currently) unwinnable arguments about the extent to which, for example, sexual preference is the product of nature or nurture, or religion (which is in any event an enumerated ground) a question of choice.[79] But any reference to immutability, actual or 'constructive', threatens to play into the essentialist trap. It is clear now that gender and, indeed, sex at all but chromosomal level, are capable of transformation. While such alteration is sufficiently difficult to satisfy any requirement of 'constructive' immutability, it is not clear that the characteristic of immutability (constructive or otherwise) ought to be a factor on the basis of which protection from discrimination is rationed.

CHOOSING GROUNDS: AVOIDING ESSENTIALISM

In the domestic and EU law context, prohibitions on discrimination apply to cases in which the protected factor relates to a person other than the complain-

---

Dunmore v Ontario (Attorney General) [2001] 3 SCR 1016 in which she alone found that status as agricultural workers was, in the particular circumstances of the case, an analogous ground (while making no general finding about 'occupational status' (paras 165–70).

[76] Above n 73, paras 60–61.

[77] At para 10 the majority expressly disagreed with the implication by L'Heureux-Dube J that the question whether a ground was protected could vary with the context. For critique of the non-contextual approach adopted by the majority see E Grabham, '*Law v Canada*: New Directions for Equality Under the Canadian Charter?' (2002) 22 *Oxford Journal of Legal Studies* 641.

[78] See, respectively, *Corbiere v Canada (Minister of Indian and Northern Affairs)* [1999] 2 SCR 203, *Vriend v Alberta* [1998] 1 SCR 493 and *Nova Scotia (Attorney General) v Walsh* [2002] 4 SCR 325, though this was conceded by the Crown.

[79] Though subsequent decisions in which mutability played a significant part in the denial of protection include *Baier v Alberta* [2007] 2 SCR 673 (employment status).

ant (as in *Coleman v Attridge Law*, in which a woman complained that she had been discriminated against because of her son's disability[80]). They also apply to cases where the discrimination results from a mistaken attribution of racial status, religious belief or sexual orientation, etc, to the person discriminated against.[81] This being the case, it is not apparent why protection should be accorded only in relation to grounds which can in any sense be described as 'immutable', constructively or otherwise. The relative permanence of character-istics such as sex is likely to explain how they become associated with entrenched disadvantage, ie, because it is impossible or very difficult to avoid the societal prejudice etc directed at the characteristic by altering the characteristic. But if irrational or unfair prejudice is directed at a characteristic which can easily be altered, it seems no answer to the problem that the recipient of the prejudicial treatment should so alter (or disguise) that characteristic.

Is discrimination directed, on racial grounds, at a mixed race person who could 'pass' as white,[82] but presents himself in a way which he regards as truer to his sense of self, any less harmful because he could, by his behaviour, avoid it? The answer to this question cannot lie in any 'truth' about the individual's ethnicity, given that a dark-skinned person of European Mediterranean origin might find himself in a similar position of victimhood should he dress in a way which marked him out as 'Black'. Racial categories are, as Lucius Outlaw remarks, 'fundamentally social in nature'.[83] At the beginning of the twentieth century, the US was absorbed with the question whether the Poles, Irish, Jews and Armenians were 'white' enough to be worthy of citizenship.[84] And Ruth Fletcher, discussing the intersection between race and the regulation of abortion in the Irish State, points out that

> race is something that may well be represented in terms of skin colour, but it is not reducible to this colour. 'Whiteness' and 'Blackness' are two ends of the race continuum

---

[80] Case C-303/06 [1998] ECR I-00621.

[81] See the Explanatory Notes to the Equality Bill (now Act) 2010 para 71 and the evidence of the then Solicitor General Vera Baird to the Joint Committee on Human Rights: JCHR Twenty-Sixth Report of 2008–09, 'Legislative Scrutiny: Equality Bill', www.publications.Parliament.uk/pa/jt200809jtselect/jtrights/169/169.pdf, ev 67 at Q 15. *cf* the decision (under the DDA) of the EAT in *Aitken v Commissioner of Police of the Metropolis* [2011] 1 CMLR 58, [2010] All ER (D) 107 (Aug)), upheld on different grounds by the Court of Appeal at [2011] EWCA Civ 582, [2011] All ER (D) 165 (May).

[82] See J Scales-Trent, *Notes of a White Black Woman* (University Park, PA: Pennsylvania State University Press, 1995).

[83] L Outlaw, 'Towards a Critical Theory of Race' in D Goldberg (ed), *Anatomy of Racism* (Minneapolis: University of Minnesota Press, 1990) 58, 68. See also A Harris, 'Equality Trouble: Sameness and Difference in Twentieth-Century Race Law' (2000) 88 *California Law Review* 1923. At 1923 Harris highlights the role of law in the US in regulating the 'formation, recognition, and maintenance of racial groups, as well as . . . the relationships among these groups'. For more general discussion of the role of social construction, see S Haslanger, 'What Are We Talking About? The Semantics and Politics of Social Kinds' (2005) 20(4) *Hypatia* 10, 'Gender and Race: (What) Are They? (What) Do We Want Them To Be?' (2000) 34 *Noûs* 31.

[84] AK Wing, 'Brief Reflections Toward a Multiplicative Theory and Praxis of Being' (1990–91) 6 *Berkley Women's Law Journal* 181. See also N Ignatiev, *How the Irish Became White* (New York: Routledge, 1995).

that provide us with distinctions to trace the ways in which some peoples are marked as more or less civilized and more or less alien than others in order to justify differences in treatment. Irishness operates as a racial category because the Irish have been constructed as racially inferior under British colonialism, represented as being prone to violence and liable to terrorism in post-colonial efforts to deny the political causes of conflict, and discriminated against as immigrants. Yet Irishness can also be a marker of racial privilege and an agent of racism. Travellers, Jews, and new immigrants have all been subjected to racism on the basis of their exclusion from Irishness . . . To acknowledge that Irishness is racial and that the Irish have been victims of racism in different ways at different moments does not in itself negate the fact that the Irish can also be racist in using Whiteness against others or the actuality that Irishness could be Black in skin colour as well as cultural experience.[85]

The ascription of 'race' can have profound significance. But this significance is not the consequence of any 'truth' it captures about the essential 'nature' of those who fall into the category;[86] Jean Charles de Menezes, who was shot in London in July 2005 by police who apparently mistook him for an Islamist bomber, was not saved from death by the fact that he was, in fact, a Brazilian Catholic, rather than a Muslim (or even, by proxy, an 'Arab' or an 'Asian'[87]).

Gender, as well as race, is a social construct, in part because it is significantly the product of learned behaviours and societal expectation.[88] So too is disability, both in the sense that it is, for many, the failure of the built environment and others to accommodate difference which transforms mental or physical impairment into 'disability', and also because much of the disablement associated with a condition such as HIV is the product of societal prejudice, rather than bodily infirmity. Sex is subject to alteration and sexual orientation frequently far less rigid in nature than is generally supposed. Age is fixed only at any given moment in time, and religious and other beliefs subject to fluctuation.

CHALLENGING A GROUNDS-BASED APPROACH

It could be argued that we should eschew grounds altogether in reconstructing a legal approach to discrimination. Such an approach has its advocates. In *Egan v*

---

[85] R Fletcher, 'Reproducing Irishness: Race, Gender and Abortion' (2005) 11 *Canadian Journal of Women and the Law* 365, 374–75, footnotes omitted.

[86] This has been recognised by the European Union (see recital 6 of Council Directive 2000/43). According to the European Network of Independent Experts in the non-discrimination field, (*Developing Anti-Discrimination Law in Europe*: 2005, 19–20), some Member States have avoided using the words 'race' or 'racial' in transposing the Directive on the basis that their use 'reinforces the perception that humans can be distinguished according to "race", whereas there is no scientific foundation for such categorisation'.

[87] This being the category his assumed membership of which caused him to be suspected of being a terrorist. See P Currah, 'Defending Genders: Sex and Gender Non-Conformity in the Civil Rights Strategies of Sexual Minorities' (1997) 48 *Hastings Law Journal* 1363, 1365–66.

[88] See for discussion, S Haslanger, 'Ontology and Social Construction' (1995) 23 *Philosophical Topics* 95.

Canada (1995), Madame Justice L'Heureux-Dubé, dissenting, suggested that the Supreme Court should abandon the grounds-based approach to the Charter's equality provision in favour of a focus on the *effects*, rather than *constituent elements*, of discrimination.[89] As above, section 15(1) of the Charter provides that 'Every individual is [1] equal before and [2] under the law and has the right to [3] the equal protection and [4] equal benefit of the law without discrimination' and, in particular, without discrimination based on race, national or ethnic origin, colour, religion, sex, age or mental or physical disability' L'Heureux-Dubé J took the view that section 15 of Canada's Charter should be interpreted as being breached by (1) a legislative distinction which (2) resulted in a denial of one of the four equality rights on the basis of the claimant's membership in an identifiable group, in circumstances such that (3) the distinction was 'discriminatory'. This in turn required that the distinction (direct or impact related) was capable of either promoting or perpetuating the view that the individual adversely affected by it was less capable, or less worthy of recognition or value as a human being or as a member of Canadian society, equally deserving of concern, respect and consideration.

For L'Heureux-Dubé J, 'the social context of the distinction', rather than the 'grounds' upon which it operated, were 'dispositive of the question of whether discrimination exists' and an a priori limitation on the grounds of discrimination 'marks the introduction of the same sort of counter-productive, formalistic and artificial debates that have been conducted under anti-discrimination legislation' on issues such as whether 'sex' discrimination included discrimination in connection with pregnancy and sexual orientation.[90] Using the example of discrimination against domestic workers, L'Heureux-Dubé J criticised the fact that the court would, under the grounds-based approach adopted by the Court, 'have to ask whether legislation involving differential treatment of domestic workers differentiates on the basis of sex because most domestic workers are women . . . rather than facing squarely the issue of differential treatment of domestic workers'.[91] She went on to state that 'categories of discrimination cannot be reduced to watertight compartments, but rather will often overlap in significant measure' and that, accordingly, the fact that most domestic workers were immigrant women, 'a subgroup that has historically been both exploited and marginalized in our society', was relevant to the assessment of 'the social context of the impugned distinction'.

There is much to be said for the approach advocated by L'Heureux-Dubé J, not least because it would facilitate the handling of claims of 'multiple discrimination', that is, discrimination arising from combination or intersection of

---

[89] *Egan v Canada* [1995] 2 SCR 513.

[90] ibid, 521.

[91] ibid, 562, citing AF Bayefsky, 'A Case Comment on the First Three Equality Rights Cases Under the Canadian Charter of Rights and Freedoms' (1990) 1 *Supreme Court Law Review* (2d) 503, 518–19.

characteristics such as (for example) gender and ethnicity.[92] The courts have struggled to deal with such claims, regarding them as stretching the boundaries of legitimacy.[93] Thus, for example, in *Degraffenreid v General Motors* (1976),[94] a US district court summarily dismissed a discrimination claim arising from the application of a 'last in first out' policy which had resulted in the dismissal of all black women working at the car plant. For the court, the claim depended on the creation of 'a new classification of "black women" who would have greater standing than, for example, a black male'[95] and 'The prospect of the creation of new classes of protected minorities, governed only by the mathematical principles of permutation and combination, clearly raises the prospect of opening the hackneyed Pandora's box'.[96]

The effect of *Degraffenreid* was to deny protection to black women from intersectional discrimination which was unique to them.[97] Although the case was directed at a claim by black women *as black women*, its logical conclusion would appear to be that black women could not demand parity of treatment with white men. They could, it would appear, challenge sex discrimination if they were treated less favourably than a black man would have been. They could challenge race discrimination if they were treated less favourably than a white woman would have been. Under the *Degraffenreid* analysis, however, it would appear that they had no claim to 'special treatment' in the form of 'race plus sex' protection vis-à-vis white male comparators.

This apparent implication of *Degraffenreid* was not tested, that decision being overtaken by that of the Fifth Circuit Court of Appeals in *Jefferies v Harris County Community Action Association* (1980) in which a 'sex plus race'

---

[92] See S Hannett, 'Equality at the Intersections: the Legislative and Judicial Failure to Tackle Multiple Discrimination' (2003) 23 *Oxford Journal of Legal Studies* 65; A McColgan, 'Reconfiguring Discrimination Law' (2007) *Public Law*, 74–94; E W Shoben 'Compound Discrimination: The Interaction of Race and Sex in Employment Discrimination' (1980) 55 *New York University Law Review* 793, 794; M Eaton 'Patently Confused: Complex Inequality and *Canada v Mossop*' (1994) 1 *Review of Constitutional Studies* 203, 229. For an analysis of the dangers of an undue concern with intersectionality see J Conaghan, 'Intersectionality and UK Equality Initiatives' (2007) *South African Journal of Human Rights* 317–54. See also Chapter 4.

[93] See McColgan (n 92) in particular, the discussions of *Degraffenreid v General Motors* 413 F Supp 142 (1976); *Jefferies v Harris County Community Action Association* 615 F2d 1025 (1980); *Moore v Hughes Helicopter Inc* 708 F 2d 475 (1983); and *Bahl v Law Society* [2004] IRLR 799.

[94] *Degraffenreid v General Motors*, ibid.

[95] As P Smith points out ('Part II: Romantic Paternalism – The Ties that Bind' (1999) 3 *Journal of Gender, Race & Justice* 181, 217) 'Black women as a class already existed . . . The question was whether the court would preclude discrimination that was targeted at this class'.

[96] The appeal was rejected by the Eighth Circuit Court of Appeals on different grounds (558 F 2d 480, 1977).

[97] This is not to say that black men (or, in some circumstances) white women, might not suffer from particular, intersectional discrimination, though as Kimberly Crenshaw points out in 'Demarginalizing the Intersection of Race and Sex' (1989) *University of Chicago Legal Forum* 139, 145, white women's 'race does not contribute to the disadvantage for which they seek redress'. Hannett (n 92) distinguishes between 'additive' and 'intersectional' discrimination, citing Shoben (n 94) 794 and Eaton (n 92) 229.

claim by a black woman was permitted.[98] Closer to home, however, the Court of Appeal insisted in *Bahl v Law Society* that the claimant, an Asian woman whose claim to have been discriminated against *as a black woman* had been accepted by a tribunal, established in relation to each incident complained of 'what evidence goes to support a finding of race discrimination and what evidence goes to support a finding of sex discrimination'.[99] More recently the Equality Act 2010 (s 14) provides for claims of 'combined discrimination' where discrimination is alleged to have taken place on two (but not more) combined grounds. In March 2011 Chancellor George Osborne announced that section 14 would not be brought into effect. Meanwhile the Employment Appeal Tribunal has accepted a claim of intersectional discrimination outside section 14, although this approach has yet to be confirmed by the higher courts.[100]

There is also the difficulty, as Nitya Iyer has pointed out, that a grounds-based approach inevitably 'obscures the complexity of social identity in ways that are damaging both to particular rights claimants, and to the larger goal of redressing relations of inequality'.[101] Thus, for example, by characterising discrimination related to childbearing as an aspect of sex discrimination, we may entrench the notion that childcare is the responsibility of women and deny protection to men who subvert gender stereotypes in this context. Women who are not directly affected by childcare issues may be in danger of being marginalised as women, while men who undertake more than their traditional share of childcare risk having their masculinity undermined by the association between sex discrimination (specifically, discrimination against women) and the protection of those with childcare responsibilities.

In his preface to *The Order of Things* Michel Foucault cites a 1942 essay by Jorge Luis Borges in which the latter quotes a classification system said to appear in a Chinese encyclopaedia entitled *Celestial Emporium of Benevolent Knowledge*. The classification system is said to categorise all animals as follows: 'belonging to the Emperor', 'embalmed‛, 'tame', 'suckling pigs'; 'sirens', 'fabulous', 'stray dogs', 'included in the present classification'; 'frenzied'; 'innumerable', 'drawn with a very fine camel hair brush', '*et cetera*'; 'having just broken the water pitcher', 'that from a long way off look like flies'.[102] Fanciful or otherwise, the list demonstrates the essential arbitrariness of categorisation. The groups of people who find themselves classified together by virtue of their

---

[98] *Jefferies v Harris County Community Action Association* 615 F2d 1025 (1980). In *Judge v Marsh* 649 F Supp 770 (1986) the US District Court for the District of Columbia limited 'sex-plus' cases to those featuring a single other factor only, taking the view that allowing 'sex plus' claims 'turns employment discrimination into a many-headed Hydra', resulting in 'protected subgroups . . . for every possible combination of race, color, sex, national origin and religion'.

[99] *Bahl v Law Society* [2004] IRLR 799.

[100] *Ministry of Defence v Debique* [2010] IRLR 471.

[101] N Iyer, 'Categorical Denials: Equality Rights and the Shaping of Social Identity' (1993) 19 *Queen's Law Journal* 179, 181.

[102] M Foucault, *The Order of Things: An Archaeology of the Human Sciences* (New York: Vintage, 1994) xiv.

shared possession (actual or perceived) of a characteristic which is protected by any particular system of anti-discrimination/equality law may be no more 'natural' than the groups of animals in one or other of Borges's categories. The very act of categorisation, however, 'tends to suppress differences and emphasize similarities among [the elements in each category] . . . heighten[] differences between members and non-members of a category [and] suppress[] any similarities that some members might share with non-members'.[103] Further, grounds-based approaches tend to essentialise the groups which they create:

> Once a characteristic is created as intrinsic to a group, and becomes its identifier, it is regarded as wholly constitutive of that group's social identity. . . [and] the social identity constructed on the basis of this now 'intrinsic' difference is *exactly the same* for every member of the group . . . In this cartoon drawn from the perspective of the categorizer not from that of the subject of categorization, one social characteristic assumes gigantic proportions.[104]

This is not to say that the 'protected characteristics' (to use domestic terminology) by reference to which discrimination is regulated are unimportant in some contexts to those who share them. If, for example, the protected characteristic is pregnancy and the context the sphere of employment, there may be significant overlaps between the needs and interests of the women within the pregnant group. But those overlaps are the product of the particular characteristic and context, rather than being inherent in the fact of group membership. Where the context is access to goods and services and the protected characteristic religion, there may be very little by way of overlap between Anglicans and Mormons, or between Quakers and Muslims. The very creation of groups by virtue of categorisation may, however, *produce* a form of likeness within the group. Where, as in Borges' classification, a group of animals exist which have 'just broken the water pitcher', the fact of having done so will readily take on the quality of being the most significant, or one of the most significant, attributes of those within the group.

It is striking that, although the Equality Act 2010 (like its predecessor legislation), deals with protected characteristics rather than protected groups (ie, except in the case of disability, it prohibits discrimination because of sex, race, sexual orientation, rather than discrimination against women, African Caribbeans, or lesbians), it is very often referred to as creating protected groups. The creation of religious 'groups' by the prohibition of discrimination on particular grounds may then encourage the members of such groups to define themselves, and outsiders to define them, significantly by reference to those grounds, which in turn may strengthen the role of one or more protected grounds in the constitution of identity.

---

[103] ibid, 183.
[104] ibid, 191–92. *cf* the sensory homonculous which represents body parts in proportion to the area of the cortex of the brain concerned with the movement of each: see www.sciencephoto.com/media/114471/view.

The grounds-based approach tends in practice to produce one-dimensional, 'flattened' claimants who are identified by reference to a single characteristic for the purposes of making a discrimination claim. Reference to more than one ground may threaten to 'muddy the waters' and jeopardise the chances of success in litigation by making it more difficult to convince factfinders that the treatment complained of was causally related to any one or more *particular* ground(s). And even where multiple grounds are permitted, Angela Harris remarks that the 'essentialism' inherent in the grounds-based approach serves 'to reduce the lives of people who experience multiple forms of oppression to additional problems: "racism + sexism = straight black women's experience," or "racism + sexism + homophobia = black lesbian experience". Thus, in an essentiality world, black women's experience will always be forcibly fragmented before being subjected to analysis, as those who are "only interested in race" and those who are "only interested in gender" take their separate slices of our lives'.[105]

The approach suggested by L'Heureux-Dubé J in *Egan* would facilitate the articulation of complex claims under an asymmetrical constitutional equality/anti-discrimination provision such as section 15 of Canada's Charter. And where prohibitions on discrimination are concerned, in Christopher McCrudden's schema, with the protection of 'prized public goods', they may not require the identification of grounds, much less a closed list thereof.[106] Where, on the other hand, the focus is on the 'proactive promotion of equality of opportunity between particular groups', it may be difficult to avoid an *ex ante* identification of those groups. And the grounds-based approach, however problematic, is inevitable where discrimination is addressed by a detailed statutory scheme such as the Equality Act 2010. That statute simply could not operate otherwise than by reference to a closed list of 'protected characteristics'.[107] In order to function fairly as between employers and employees, for example, or service providers and their customers/clients, there must be a degree of clarity as to whether requirements for reasonable adjustment and prohibitions on less favourable or disparately impacting treatment apply, or do not apply, in connection with (for example) caring responsibilities or political belief. Nor could any other detailed scheme provide sufficient certainty to those falling within its scope without specifying the characteristics by reference to which distinctions may not be drawn or disparate impact imposed absent justification. Further, as Joanne Conaghan has pointed out, 'Grounds still provide the primary lens and filter through which inequalities are detected and redressed . . . Grounds are the bulwark of any anti-discrimination framework . . . how can we identify

---

[105] A Harris, 'Race and Essentialism in Feminist Legal Theory' (1989) 42 *Stanford Law Review* 581, 588–9.

[106] ibid, 582–83 and C McCrudden, 'Theorising European Law' in C Costello and E Barry (eds), *Equality in Diversity: The New Equality Directives* (Dublin: Irish Centre for European Law, 2003) 1.

[107] It is the case that countries such as Romania have broad-ranging statutory prohibitions on discrimination in relation to an open-ended list of grounds. I would suggest, however, that this approach is not workable in the absence of a broad justification defence.

inequality without recourse to grounds?'.[108] I turn now to consider how we might determine the grounds on which discrimination ought to be regulated or equality guaranteed.

'STATUS' AND INEQUALITY

Joel Balkin argues that immutability is not the key to understanding suspect discrimination, preferring instead to consider status:

> Focusing on immutability per se confuses biological with sociological considerations. It confuses the physical existence of the trait with what the trait means in a social system . . . The question is not whether a trait is immutable, but whether there has been a history of using the trait to create a system of social meanings, or define a social hierarchy, that helps dominate and oppress people. Any conclusions about the importance of immutability already presuppose a view about background social structure.[109]

Eschewing any demand for immutability as a criterion for protection not only sidesteps entanglement in sterile and (at least currently) unwinnable arguments about the extent to which, for example, sexual preference is the product of nature or nurture, or religion a question of choice, but also helps to avoids the essentialist trap.

Balkin suggests that the US Constitution, properly understood, 'does not oppose all status hierarchies' which would include, for example, 'social disapproval of gamblers, sluggards, gossips, opticians, and MTV watchers', such people not constituting 'groups who suffer overlapping and reinforcing forms of subordination and social disadvantage due to their place in that social hierarchy. This is not due to any physical property of these groups but a contingent fact of social history'.[110] Thus, while any status hierarchy between snowboarders and skiers

> is not something that affects many overlapping aspects of one's everyday interactions with others, or that has ripple effects in various parts of one's life, including wealth, social connections, political power, employment prospects, the ability to have intimate relationships and form families, and so on . . . being a black person as opposed to a white person, or being female as opposed to being male, is a central feature of one's identity, at least in contemporary America. It does affect a large percentage of one's personal interactions with others, and it has many mutually supporting and overlapping effects.[111]

---

[108]   Hannett (n 92) 324.

[109]   JM Balkin, 'The Constitution of Status' (1997) 106 *Yale Law Journal* 2313, 2366. See also MR Shapiro, 'Treading the Supreme Court's Murky Immutability Waters' (2002) 38 *Gonzaga Law Review* 409.

[110]   Balkin (n 109) 2359.

[111]   ibid, 2360.

Similar conclusions to those drawn by Balkin in respect of snowboarders and skiers could be applied, in the UK, to smokers and non-smokers and, arguably, to those who are more or less clever and more or less attractive (leaving out of account those whose appearance or intelligence is such as to bring them within the range of disability).[112]

Michael Walzer also recognises the significance of status inequalities in his theory of justice, devising a theory of 'complex equality' whereby inequalities of, for example, wealth, power and reputation, which he regards as individually acceptable, are unacceptable when they generate broader classes of (dis)advantage: where, for example, advantage in terms of income results in an expectation of social deference and a disproportionate share of political power.[113] Building on Walzer, Iris Marion Young suggests that:

> The sort of status inequality that ought to worry us . . . is that experienced systematically by certain *groups* of people. Diverse social structures and practices conspire to locate some people in positions where they repeatedly suffer disadvantage in access to benefits, or they are stigmatized in many situations, or they are regarded as suspect or inferior by others who are more advantaged. It is the systematic character of this status inequality that raises issues of justice, for at least two reasons. The relative disadvantage of those presumed lower status spreads across many aspects of their lives, limiting their options for improvement in many reinforcing ways. Second, those in the lower status positions often find themselves placed there by social meanings, attitudes and behavior of others in ways they can little control and from which exit is often difficult.[114]

Groups and the problems associated with them are returned to in subsequent chapters, the focus here being on the types of identifying factor which might require broad protection from discrimination. Balkin goes on to suggest that the status hierarchy which privileges heterosexual over homosexual is *'unjust'* in part because it derives from the 'systematic privileging of things associated with being male over those associated with being female', formal rejections of sex discrimination having left in place 'the set of social meanings that privilege masculinity over femininity', and which departures from gender norms transgress.[115] 'Racial discrimination is wrong because of the historical creation of a status hierarchy organized around the meaning of skin color'.[116] By contrast, societal disapproval of paedophilia (and discrimination against those who

---

[112] The Equality Act 2010 and its predecessor legislation include as 'disabled' those whose intellectual functioning is substantially impaired and those who have 'disfigurements', in the latter case whether or not they cause or are accompanied by any functional impairment. 'Disability' would also extend to substantial functional impairments caused by obesity, as well as those caused by alcoholism, smoking or other addictions (though not to the addictions themselves). On smoking see D Cooper, *Challenging Diversity: Rethinking Equality and the Value of Difference* (Cambridge: Cambridge University Press, 2004) Chapter 3.

[113] M Walzer, *Spheres of Justice* (New York: Basic Books, 1983) 277.

[114] IM Young, 'Equality of Whom? Social Groups and Judgments of Injustice' (2001) 9 *The Journal of Political Philosophy* 1–18, 2.

[115] Balkin (n 109) 2361–62.

[116] ibid, 2365–66.

practise it) serves to 'preserve [neither] unjust traditional gender roles [nor] an unjust set of social meanings about gender', while 'sexual relationships with children are inherently exploitative, or so likely to be exploitative that society has good reasons for forbidding them as a class'.[117] Rather than avoiding moral judgments, Balkin argues that 'because people use moral arguments to justify existing status hierarchies, we must try to be morally critical about claims of morality. The question is whether moral condemnations are linked to the preservation of an unjust form of status hierarchy'.[118]

Unjust status hierarchies are associated with group-based oppression. Iris Marion Young suggests that such oppression occurs when the group suffers any of the following forms of subordination: exploitation, marginalisation, powerlessness, cultural imperialism and/or systematic violence.[119] And, as Sally Haslanger points out, whereas *agent oppression* takes the form of individual acts of wrongdoing, *structural oppression* consists of unjust practices or institutions.[120] Such structural oppression can result from formally discriminatory laws and from laws and widespread practices whose effect is systematically to disadvantage particular groups, also from 'Cultural norms and informal practices that impose unfair burdens on or create disproportionate opportunities for members of one group as opposed to another [such as g]ender norms concerning child care, elder care, housework, appearance, dress, education, careers and so forth' and from 'Cultural practices and products that foster negative stereotypes of particular groups . . . [which] are insulting to members of those groups or foster contempt or hatred towards them . . . also because they can have a distorting effect on the judgment of those who are asked to apply discretionary policies . . .'.[121] Haslanger goes on to suggest that structural oppression can exist without individual acts of wrongdoing by those who are privileged within oppressive systems, which systems may not have been intentionally created:

> [T]he question is whether the structure (the policy, practice, institution, discursive framing, cultural norm) is unjust and creates or perpetuates illegitimate power relations. . . A structure may cause unjustified harm to a group without this having been anticipated in advance or even recognized after the fact; those responsible for the structure may even be acting benevolently and with the best information available . . .
>
> . . . individuals play a role in creating and maintaining the social world, but most of the practices and institutions that structure our lives, although made up of individuals and influenced by individuals, are not designed and controlled by anyone individually.[122]

---

[117]   ibid, 2364.

[118]   ibid, 2364.

[119]   IM Young, *Justice and the Politics of Difference* (Princeton: Princeton University Press, 1990) Chapter 2.

[120]   See for example S Haslanger, 'Oppressions Racial and Other' in MP Levine and T Pataki (eds), *Racism in Mind* (Ithaca: Cornell University Press, 2004) 97, 100.

[121]   ibid, 101–02.

[122]   ibid, 103–04.

In an observation returned to in Chapter 3 Haslanger points out that, whereas

> to show that a group suffers from agent oppression, we must establish that there is an agent(s) morally responsible for causing them unjust harm . . . to say that a group suffers from structural oppression, we must establish that power is misallocated in such a way that members of the group are unjustly disadvantaged.[123]

AVOIDING OVER-STRETCH

What grounds should, then, qualify for protection against discrimination? The answer turns in part on the nature of the protection. Where broad constitutional or international prohibitions on discrimination are at issue, a finding of differential treatment on a protected ground is only the starting point for the analysis of the discrimination/equality claim. As is the case under Article 14 of the EC HR, even direct discrimination is capable of justification. In the US, as discussed above, differential standards of justification have been formalised, while in Canada and South Africa the level of justification varies less rigidly according to the ground and nature of the discrimination at issue (though the threshold for qualifying for protection is higher[124]). The ECtHR has also, as we saw above, established a hierarchy of justification which in its case is coupled with a very broad approach to protected grounds.

That is not to say that there are no dangers in over-broad approaches to (quasi) constitutionally protected grounds. In *Corbiere*, Canada's Supreme Court rationalised its relatively narrow approach to 'analogous grounds' by reference to the need to 'avoid trivializing the s. 15 equality guarantee and promote the efficient use of judicial resources'. The very breadth of grounds subject to 'rational review' in the US has no doubt contributed to the extreme level of deference which generally characterises such review.[125] So there is reason to be cautious about the grounds which are protected even at constitutional level.

Competing Private Interests

There is all the more reason to ration the protection provided by detailed statutory provisions. Such provisions are horizontally as well as vertically binding and, as a result, impact on the liberty of private individuals rather than simply

---

[123] ibid, 105.

[124] See for example the speech of L'Heureux-Dubé J in Canada's Supreme Court in *Sauvé v Canada (Chief Electoral Officer)* [2002] 3 SCR 519.

[125] Such is the general level of deference accorded by rational review that the suggestion has been made that *Romer* actually signals a move towards intermediate review (see for example Goldberg (n 25) fn 121, a suggestion made in relation to pre-*Craig v Boren* case law on gender discrimination by G Gunther, 'Foreword: In Search of Evolving Doctrine on a Changing Court: A Model for a Newer Equal Protection' (1972) 86 *Harvard Law Review* 1, 33–37.

constraining the power of the state to act. John Hasnas suggests that the Kantian categorical imperative prohibits the imposition of over-broad anti-discrimination legislation on individuals, as distinct from the state,[126] that 'Neither the principle of respect for persons nor any other readily identifiable moral principle generates a moral obligation to evaluate individuals strictly on the basis of their qualifications and abilities and no such obligation can be derived from a utilitarian moral perspective'. In his view, treating people as ends rather than means 'requires us to respect their autonomy . . .'[127] A decision to hire a worker on the basis of his ability to play softball rather than his qualifications does, Hasnas thinks, entail a failure to recognise the unchosen, better qualified, candidate 'as an autonomous agent' or an 'attempt[] to denigrate his or her humanity', does not in fact entail any 'use' of that other at all:

> Denying an applicant a position he or she desires and is qualified for may disappoint that person, but it implies nothing more than that one would prefer to associate with someone else. It is not oppression and it does not indicate that the person lacks intrinsic moral value or is a mere tool for the advancement of one's own ends. It certainly does not imply that one regards the applicant as less than fully human. Hence, it does not violate the principle of respect for persons. [128]

This being the case, Hasnas suggests that restricting the hirer's freedom to select on the basis he or she chooses itself breaches the categorical imperative by treating (private) employers as means rather than ends, such persons being entitled to have their autonomy valued.[129]

I do not seek to defend Hasnas's approach to the regulation of discrimination in the private sector. His analysis does, however, serve to underline that anti-discrimination legislation may impinge on significant other rights, and ought not to be lightly imposed. A prohibition on discrimination on grounds of political opinion may, as in the *Lee v ASLEF* litigation, for example, amount to an undue interference with freedom of association (the case concerned a ban on trade unions (alone) from discriminating on grounds of political party membership, in that case active membership of the British National Party).[130] A ban on discrimination on grounds of religious or other belief may prevent the lesbian feminist collective from refusing to recruit, for a job in their bookshop, a

---

[126] J Hasnas, 'Equal Opportunity, Affirmative Action, and the Anti-Discrimination Principle: The Philosophical Basis for the Legal Prohibition of Discrimination' (2009) 71 *Fordham law Review* 423, 430–31, footnotes omitted. Hasnas's particular argument concerns the appropriate interpretation of the US Civil Rights Act, which prohibits discrimination on various grounds by employers and others.

[127] ibid, 494–95.

[128] ibid.

[129] ibid.

[130] The EAT decision is at *Lee v ASLEF* [2004] All ER (D) 209 (Mar). The outcome of the subsequent employment tribunal case was that the union was not entitled to expel Mr Lee for membership of the BNP as a result of s 174 of the Trade Union and Labour Relations (Consolidation) Act 1992, which at the time prohibited trade unions from excluding or expelling a person on the ground of political party membership. The ECtHR subsequently decided (*ASLEF v UK* (2007) 45 EHRR 793) that the legislation breached Art 11 ECHR (freedom of association).

militant anti-feminist activist; equally, it may prevent a religious organisation from refusing to recruit a militant secularist for a customer-facing, or even a policy-development, role.

John Gardner also regards as problematic the prohibition of discrimination by non-state actors, suggesting that 'the liberal state cannot properly require us to desist from discriminating merely because, by discriminating, we fail to treat fellow citizens with equal respect', this because such 'would be wholly inconsistent with any commitment to allowing [individuals'] personal preferences and projects to prevail'.[131] He suggests that the harm principle might permit the regulation of direct discrimination where the quality of the stigmatisation concerned was sufficient,[132] though he warns that a symmetrical approach to the regulation of discrimination poses 'a serious risk to liberalism' (a warning further discussed in Chapter 3). Gardner further suggests that the regulation of indirect discrimination by private actors, though capable of being justified in terms of distributional justice,[133] is problematic given the disproportionate burden it imposes on those private actors who happen to be caught (as prospective employers, for example) by the anti-discrimination legislation. While liberals can, Gardner concedes, accommodate these and other tensions, he warns that assuming 'that we can extend indefinitely the coverage or application of an argument (responding to changes in social meaning) while leaving the nature of the argument intact' is akin to believing that 'one could change indefinitely the rules of chess while leaving the game the same'.[134]

Recognition of the ways in which disadvantage is entrenched and perpetuated by institutionalised practices of public and private actors makes it impossible to regard as adequate any legal approach to discrimination/equality which fails to challenge private sector activities, and discrimination in its indirect as well as its direct forms. But while it may be entirely appropriate to place obligations on public authorities to act rationally, and in so doing not to discriminate on all or any grounds without adequate justification, Gardner's warnings serve as a reminder that there are limits to the defensible coverage of anti-discrimination legislation in terms of the grounds regulated (which is the subject matter of this chapter), the definition of the prohibited conduct and/or the material scope of such regulation.

By way of alternative to the infinite stretching of harm and redistribution principles in this context Gardner discusses Joseph Raz's wide approach to the harm principle, which permits

> governments 'to use coercion both in order to stop people from actions which would diminish people's autonomy and in order to force them to take actions which are required to improve people's options and opportunities' [such that] . . . distributive

---

[131] J Gardner, 'Liberals and Unlawful Discrimination' (1989) 9 *OJLS* 1, 3.
[132] ibid, 7.
[133] ibid, 11.
[134] ibid, 16.

justice is not a principle which *competes* with the harm principle, but is rather a concomitant of it.[135]

Raz suggests that in the UK 'the right not to suffer intentional discrimination "is meant to foster a public culture which enables people to take pride in their identity as members of . . . groups" '[136] and in which personal autonomy is central. 'The government has an obligation to create an environment providing individuals with an adequate range of options *and the opportunities to choose them*'[137] and (as Gardner puts it) 'We are all involved in a participative enterprise of protecting autonomy, an enterprise which carries with it obligations of mutual life-enhancement'.[138]

Raz is returned to in Chapter 6 in which I consider the tensions which may arise between equality and the accommodation of group difference. Here it is sufficient to note that his wide approach to the harm principle is equally compatible with an understanding of the prohibitions on direct (and indirect) discrimination as intended to foster a public culture which seeks to eliminate identity-based oppression and/or unjust status hierarchies. The justification of anti-discrimination provisions by reference to such ends requires, however, that the grounds upon which discrimination is regulated are closely connected to those ends.

RECONSIDERING 'PROTECTED CHARACTERISTICS'

The question then arises whether the grounds upon which statutory protection from discrimination is currently provided are over broad, or over narrow. Adopting Balkin's concept of status hierarchies, it is evident that perceived or 'actual' sex, race, sexual orientation and disability have repercussions which extend across numerous aspects of life including (*per* Balkin) 'wealth, social connections, political power, employment prospects, the ability to have intimate relationships and form families, and so on'.[139] Similarly (Young) such identifying factors 'locate some people in positions where they repeatedly suffer disadvantage in access to benefits, or they are stigmatized in many situations, or they are regarded as suspect or inferior by others who are more advantaged'. And taking Haslanger's indicia of oppression, women, LGBT people, BME and disabled people have historically been subject to legal disadvantage (whether formally or in practice), and are disadvantaged by cultural norms, informal and/ or cultural practices which impose on them unfair burdens/deny them advantages and/or foster negative stereotypes of them.

---

[135]   ibid, 18 citing J Raz, *The Morality of Freedom* (Oxford: Clarendon Press, 1986) 416.
[136]   Raz, ibid, 254 cited by Gardner (n 131) 18.
[137]   Raz (n 135) 418 cited by Gardner (n 131) 19, his emphasis.
[138]   Gardner (n 131) 19.
[139]   Balkin (n 109) 2360.

The characteristics associated with entrenched disadvantage/structural oppression are not all universal. Women, those with disabilities, those who do not conform to gender norms and some minority ethnic groups tend to be relatively disadvantaged politically, economically and socially across the globe. In mainland China, those who migrate from rural to urban areas take on many of the disadvantages associated with minority ethnicity elsewhere, while in parts of the Middle East this is true of non-citizens. These characteristics are significantly less mapped onto disadvantage in the UK, for example, though immigrant and refugee status are.

The relationship between religious affiliation, belief or (inevitably amorphous) age is more complex. In Northern Ireland, actual or perceived status as Catholic has traditionally been associated with systemic disadvantage and oppression as a result of the creation of a Protestant state in the early part of the twentieth century and a robust approach to its maintenance at least until the mid 1970s. Elsewhere in the UK, identification with particular religions, especially those associated with some minority ethnic groups (the most obvious example being Muslim/Asian), is synonymous with disadvantage across multiple spheres of life. There is, further, no doubt that those who insist that the earth is flat or that humans are descended from Martians might have difficulty securing positions in the field of science, but generally speaking religious adherence (or non-adherence) cannot be characterised in Britain as correlated with disadvantage, much less systematic oppression.

Such is the nature of 'age' that it can be difficult to characterise particular groups as generally disadvantaged, rather than advantaged, by their chronological years. It is the case that relatively older people (and the young) face particular difficulties in the employment market, and that many elderly people (in particular, elderly women) suffer severe economic disadvantage and social exclusion, and are vulnerable to abuse by virtue of their frailty. But it is also the case that older people benefit from a variety of state supports unavailable to others, and that total household wealth increases with the age of the household head until age 55–64 before declining, households whose heads are aged 65 to 74 being the second wealthiest group and those headed by persons aged 25 to 34 and 16 to 24 the poorest.[140] Neither the young nor the elderly, much less those in other age categories, are oppressed by reason of their age.

This is not to say that freedom of religious or other belief ought not to be protected, or that the young or elderly ought to be left vulnerable to ill-treatment on grounds of their age. It is, however, to suggest that prohibitions on discrimination on grounds of age, religion or belief may not be identical to those which apply to (for example) sex or ethnicity. Further, for the reasons Balkin puts forward, religion and belief cannot coherently be treated like characteristics such as sex, race, disability or sexual orientation. Leaving aside cases in which actual or perceived membership of faith groups functions as a proxy

---

[140] Office for National Statistics, Wealth in Great Britain: Main results, 2006/08, fig 2.8.

for ethnicity, the question whether or not particular religious or other beliefs are worthy of protection must depend, absent acceptance that the mere holding of (any) beliefs is a moral good sufficiently strong to defeat other claims (such as claims to gender equality, freedom of association etc), on the particulars of the belief in question. An additional problem with treating 'religion' and/or 'belief' in like manner to sexual orientation, ethnicity etc as regards protection from discrimination is that equality claims can be made by those who would seek, on the grounds of their own religious or other beliefs, to discriminate against others. This is further considered in Chapter 5. As we there see, the treatment of religion/belief as a protected characteristic akin to ethnicity or sex, for example, gives rise to intractable problems resulting from the implication of (in particular) religious beliefs in the creation and maintenance of structures which discriminate according to characteristics including, in particular, sex and sexual orientation.

Even if it were to be argued that religion was an intrinsic good,[141] it is incoherent to posit the same for 'belief' which is, in the domestic and EU framework, subject to the same protection (as, in the UK, is the absence of belief/religious belief). Freedom of belief, whether religious or not, should be protected at the constitutional level. But protecting beliefs (and, to a limited degree, their manifestation) from *state* interference is qualitatively different to including them within a framework of anti-discrimination provisions. The accommodation of particular religious or other beliefs (a commitment to female subordination, for example, white supremacy, anti-Semitism or a belief in the evils of homosexuality) hinders rather than promotes the pursuit of equality on grounds of sex, race, sexual orientation and even religion characterised in terms of group membership rather than individual belief. The protection of other beliefs (a commitment to securing full equality in practice for people with disabilities, for example, antiracism, feminism or, possibly, some religious beliefs) might well promote equality, but this will be the product of the *nature* of those religious or other beliefs rather than the bare *fact* of them.

The regulation of discrimination connected with religion or belief is considered in some detail in Chapters 5 and 6. As to age, being of any particular age works positively as well as negatively at most life stages, the overall package of advantages and disadvantages in terms of work, health, welfare and access to cultural goods turning very significantly on questions of class and economic status. It is difficult to say, therefore, that age operates in like fashion to protected characteristics such as ethnicity, disability, sex or sexual orientation. Again, as above, this is not to say that age should necessarily be unprotected. There is a case for recognising that age, like generally advantageous characteristics such as maleness, can exacerbate disadvantage associated with (for example), femaleness and minority ethnicity characteristics respectively, and can otherwise interact in complex ways to produce particular types of disadvantage.

---

[141] See, for example, T Macklem, 'Faith as a Secular Value' (2000) 45 *McGill Law Journal* 1–63.

And being old or young also renders people vulnerable to particular types of wrong from which they may require specific legal protection.

The other point which can be made here is that, where a characteristic such as ('actual' or perceived) race, sex/gender,[142] sexual orientation or disability is associated with status/oppression, the status is necessarily part of a hierarchy. Men tend to be advantaged and women disadvantaged by virtue of their sex, similarly people of majority and minority ethnicity, those who do not and those who do challenge norms of gender-appropriate behaviour by virtue of their sexual orientation(s) and/or identity. The leap from recognising status disadvantage associated with particular characteristics, to prohibiting (all) discrimination on grounds of that characteristic, ought to be recognised as a leap. We might instead move from acknowledging the disadvantage associated with sex to dealing with that disadvantage, as has been done in the UK and elsewhere in the case of disability, rather than to prohibiting sex discrimination in a symmetrical fashion. The question of symmetry is considered further in Chapter 3.

---

[142] Sex to include pregnancy and gender to include gender reassignment.

3

'Equality' and '(A)symmetry'

INTRODUCTION

DOMESTIC DISCRIMINATION LAW has, at least until recently, been characterised by a strong preference for what might be termed a symmetrical approach to discrimination. The Race Relations Acts of 1965, 1968 and 1976 and the Sex Discrimination Act 1975 (SDA), passed in order to counter asymmetrical problems of discrimination against, respectively, those from minority ethnic groups and women, prohibited discrimination on grounds of race and sex. Subsequent legislation adopted similarly symmetrical approaches to what is, for the most part, discrimination against those characterised as 'other' by their sexual identity or religious or other beliefs, and to age discrimination.[1]

The Race Relations Act 1976 (RRA), SDA and other discrimination provisions have now been consolidated into the Equality Act 2010 which, except as discussed below, regulates discrimination related to particular *characteristics*, rather than discrimination against particular persons or groups. The major exception to the general rule of symmetry concerns disability, the Disability Discrimination Act 1995 (DDA) and (now) the Equality Act protecting from disability discrimination only those categorised as 'disabled' by the legislation.[2] Exceptions apply also to discrimination related to pregnancy (of which men cannot complain) or gender reassignment (of which only those 'proposing to undergo . . . undergoing or [who have] undergone a process (or part of a process) for the purpose of reassigning . . . sex by changing physiological or other attributes of sex' can complain), and discrimination against married persons or civil partners (but not the single) in the context of employment.[3] The general pattern of legislative protection in the UK, however, is a symmetrical one.

The symmetrical model adopted by the legislature has been reinforced by the judicial interpretation of direct discrimination in particular. The early decision

---

[1] The Employment Equality (Sexual Orientation) Regulations 2003, Employment Equality (Religion or Belief) Regulations 2003, Employment Equality (Age) Regulations 2006 and Equality Act 2006 (Sexual Orientation) Regulations 2007, subsequently absorbed into the Equality Act 2010.

[2] And, as a result of the decision of the ECJ in *Coleman v Attridge Law* [2008] ELR I-05603, those discriminated against by virtue of their association with a person or persons recognised as 'disabled' though not, according to the decision of the EAT in *Aitken v Commissioner of Police of the Metropolis* (UKEAT/0226/09/ZT, 21 June 2010), to discrimination on the basis of *perceived* disability.

[3] Sections 7, 13(6)(b), 13(4), 17 and 18 Equality Act 2010.

of the Court of Appeal in *Peake v Automotive Products* (1978) insulated from scrutiny under the SDA 'the chivalry and courtesy which we expect mankind to give womankind [and t]he natural differences of sex' (*per* Lord Denning MR), Shaw LJ suggesting that the term 'discrimination against' one sex 'involves an element of something which is inherently adverse or hostile to the interests of the persons of the sex which is said to be discriminated against'.[4] This false start was abandoned in *Ministry of Defence v Jeremiah* (1980) in which Lord Denning MR stated that 'What is sauce for the goose is sauce for the gander – nowadays' and accepted that his conclusions in *Peake* '(about chivalry and administrative practice) should no longer be relied upon'.[5] And in *R v Birmingham ex p EOC* (1989) the House of Lords ruled that no intention or motive to discriminate against members of one sex was required in order to establish direct discrimination, as long as there was less favourable treatment on the ground of sex.[6]

It was clear as a result of the *Birmingham* case that malign motivation was not a necessary ingredient of direct discrimination, but yet to be addressed was the specific question whether an intention to ameliorate existing disadvantage, or the impact of past discrimination, could render differential treatment on protected grounds lawful. In *James v Eastleigh* (1990), the House of Lords confirmed the approach in the *Birmingham* decision in a case which involved discrimination in favour of women resulting from their earlier pensionable age and greater economic need.[7] According to the majority (Lords Lowry and Griffiths dissenting), direct discrimination was established wherever it could be shown that, 'but for' the fact of his or her sex, the claimant would have been more favourably treated.

The combination of the decision in *James v Eastleigh* and the absence of any general justification defence for direct discrimination (other than in the case of age), or of a justification defence permitting discrimination in favour of those disadvantaged by sex, race, etc, had the effect of making positive action very difficult to justify under the UK's statutory regime.[8] Prior to the implementation of the Equality Act 2010, and except in the case of disability and (because of the general justification defence applicable thereto) age, most differential treatment intended to ameliorate disadvantage was unlawful. The main exceptions concerned the provision of training for, and the encouragement of job applications from, those in groups under-represented in the particular occupation and/or

[4] *Peake v Automotive Products* [1978] 1 QB 233, 238C (Lord Denning) and 240F (Shaw LJ).
[5] *Ministry of Defence v Jeremiah* [1980] QB 87, 98A and G.
[6] *R v Birmingham ex p EOC* [1989] AC 1155.
[7] *James v Eastleigh* [1990] 2 AC 751.
[8] That is not to say that all measures which would fall within, for example, McCrudden's five-type typology of positive action (1) eradicating discrimination; (2) facially neutral but purposefully inclusionary policies; (3) outreach programmes; (4) preferential treatment in employment and (5) redefining 'merit': see Rethinking Positive Action' (1986) 15 *Industrial Law Journal* 219–43) would have been unlawful (see following text), rather that any departures from (formally) 'equal' treatment were legally problematic except in the case of disability.

workplace.[9] In addition, and outside the employment field, section 35 of the Race Relations Act 1976 (RRA) permitted the provision of access to facilities or services to persons of a particular racial group where the facilities or services 'meet the special needs of persons of that group in regard to their education, training or welfare, or any ancillary benefits', similar provision being made by the Equality Act 2006 and the Equality Act 2006 (Sexual Orientation) Regulations 2007 in respect of 'special needs for education, training or welfare' of persons of particular religions, beliefs and sexual orientations. The SDA, further, permitted 'special provision[s] for persons of one sex only in the constitution, organisation or administration of' political parties,[10] and exempted from section 21A (which prohibited discrimination in the exercise of public functions) 'Action taken for the purpose of assisting one sex to overcome: (a) a disadvantage (as compared with the other sex), or (b) the effects of discrimination'.

Section 35 RRA was recognised as a provision intended to further equality, Moses LJ declaring in the Administrative Court, in *R (Kaur & Shah) v London Borough of Ealing* (2008),[11] that the provision 'is not an exception to the [RRA]. It does not derogate from it in any way. It is a manifestation of the important principle of anti discrimination and equality measures that not only must like cases be treated alike but that unlike cases but must be treated differently'. It should be said, however, that this decision, reached over 30 years after the enactment of the 1976 Act, is one of very few examples of cases in which section 35 fell to be judicially considered, much less determined the outcome.[12]

Prior to the implementation of the Equality Act 2010, the scope for lawful positive action (in the sense of differential treatment designed to ameliorate disadvantage or address specific need) remained narrow. Leaving aside the specific statutory provisions above, which largely correspond to McCrudden's second and third classifications of positive action ((2) facially neutral but purposefully inclusionary policies and (3) outreach programmes),[13] asymmetrical action designed to redress inequality was generally unlawful. So, for example, while the recognition of the disparate impact of work practices on women might lead to the disapplication of those practices from those with childcare responsibili-

---

[9] Race Relations Act 1976 ss 37–38 and SDA ss 47–48. For discussion see A McColgan, *Discrimination: Text, Cases and Materials*, 2nd edn (Oxford: Hart Publishing, 1995) 133–36.

[10] Section 35 SDA. While gender-neutral in its expression and applicable in its terms equally to provisions intended to exacerbate as to reduce the over-representation of men in political life, in practice this provision was designed to allow all-women shortlists and similar.

[11] *R (Kaur & Shah) v London Borough of Ealing* [2008] EWHC 2062 (Admin), [2008] All ER (D) 08 (Oct) para 23.

[12] The provision was referred to in *Stephenson v Stockton-on-Tees Borough Council* [2005] 1 FCR 165, para 28 but, any discrimination there at issue being indirect, was unnecessary (a justification defence being available). In *R (E) v Governing Body of the Jews Free School* [2008] ELR 445, para 176, Munby J advocated a narrow approach to s 35, though his remarks were *obiter*. The provision was mentioned in *Conwell v Newham London Borough Council* [2000] 1 WLR 1 and in *Lambeth London Borough Council v Commission for Racial Equality* [1990] ICR 768 but in neither case was it substantively considered.

[13] Above n 8.

ties, it would not result in formally different treatment for men and women. This is not necessarily to complain – such developments might be regarded as falling within McCrudden's fifth classification of positive action: the redefinition of merit.[14] It is simply to underline the point that the preferred approach was a symmetrical one.

Section 158 of the Equality Act, which does not apply to recruitment or promotion, now permits 'proportionate' action to be taken to 'enabl[e] or encourag[e] persons who share [a] protected characteristic to overcome or minimise' disadvantages, or to participate in activities which are connected with that protected characteristic, or in which participation by those with that characteristic is disproportionately low, or to meet needs which differ from the needs of others.[15] In addition, section 159 permits the more favourable treatment of the disadvantaged or underrepresented (A) in relation to recruitment or promotion where (s 159(4)) the action is proportionate, 'A is as qualified as B to be recruited or promoted' and the person seeking to rely on the defence 'does not have a policy of treating persons who share the protected characteristic more favourably in connection with recruitment or promotion than persons who do not share it'.

The Parliamentary discussions of these provisions illustrate some of the confusion and anxiety that characterises any move away from symmetry in the UK. The then Solicitor General, Vera Baird, stated at the Bill's Committee Stage that the 'positive action' permitted under (now) section 158 did not include 'positive discrimination' which she defined as 'favour[ing] a person from a particular under-represented or disadvantaged group *solely* because they come from that particular group irrespective of merit' (emphasis added).[16] She went on to state that section 159(4)'s requirement that the person taking positive action 'does not have a policy of treating persons who share the protected characteristic more favourably in connection with recruitment or promotion than persons who do not share it' was

> there to ensure that there is not a blanket policy of favouring candidates because they have a protected characteristic, even if they are disadvantaged and under-represented as a consequence. An employer has to ensure that the candidate that she wishes to prefer is as qualified for the job or promotion as another person . . . [a] person can use positive action as long as they use positive action only and do not have a policy of positive discrimination.[17]

Conservative MP Mark Harper distinguished between 'positive action' and 'positive discrimination', confining the former to the type of action permitted

---

[14] The point is more obvious if the disparately impacting factor is a demand for a particular qualification (a maths degree) or attribute (experience as a rugby player) in applicants for applicants for accountancy or management consultancy jobs but the ability to work extended hours can also be seen as a form of 'merit' which may have to be reconsidered where its impact cannot be justified.

[15] In each case the requirement is the reasonable belief of the actor that the threshold of need, disadvantage etc is met.

[16] HC Debs 1 July 2009, col 603.

[17] ibid, cols 609, 617.

under the RRA and SDA and defining as 'positive discrimination' 'where an organisation was trying to widen its diversity, but it was doing so by specifically discriminating'.[18] He went on to state his satisfaction, however, with discrimination in favour of a person from an under-represented group in a 'tie-break' case in which the candidates were 'equally qualified'.[19]

The contrast typically drawn between 'positive' or 'reverse discrimination' or 'affirmative action', on the one hand, and the reward of 'merit', on the other, presupposes that the notion of merit is itself uncontested and capable of objective measurement. This is far from being the case, however, a point well made by Labour MP Diane Abbott at the Committee stage of the Equality Bill 2009:

> [T]he notion of less qualified and better qualified candidates can be highly subjective. Years ago, before I came to the House, I worked for the big London television company, which was called Thames Television. When I first went to work for that company, the head of news and current affairs was a tall, thin, cerebral man with a Cambridge degree. He systematically promoted to the editorship of programmes and to head of department tall, thin, cerebral men with Oxbridge degrees. When that man left and his post was taken over by a rotund, northern, beery ex-tabloid journalist, lo and behold – the people he thought were better qualified were people in his image . . . the propensity of people to promote in their own image and justify it by some subjective notion of qualifications is one of the big issues when it comes to diversity.[20]

It is also noteworthy that in the US, where university affirmative action programmes have proven both controversial and legally difficult to tailor within the Constitution, most prestigious universities grant preference to the children of alumni. According to an article in the *Wall Street Journal* in 2003:

> Sons and daughters of graduates make up 10% to 15% of students at most Ivy League schools and enjoy sharply higher rates of acceptance. Harvard accepts 40% of legacy applicants, compared with an 11% overall acceptance rate. Princeton took 35% of alumni children who applied last year, and 11% of overall applicants. The University of Pennsylvania accepts 41% of legacy applicants, compared with 21% overall.
>
> At Notre Dame, about 23% of all students are children of graduates . . .

The *Wall Street Journal* went on to point out that the 'legacy preference' took effect in the early twentieth century 'in some cases partly to limit enrollment of Jews' and that its impact is now to disadvantage a number of minority ethnic groups:

> At the University of Virginia, 91% of legacy applicants accepted on an early-decision basis for next fall are white; 1.6% are black, 0.5% are Hispanic, and 1.6% are Asian. Among applicants with no alumni parents, the pool of those accepted is more diverse: 73% white, 5.6% black, 9.3% Asian and 3.5% Hispanic . . .[21]

---

[18] ibid, col 602.

[19] ibid, cols 604–05. The Bill then used the rubric 'as qualified as' each other.

[20] ibid, col 615.

[21] *Wall Street Journal*, 'Aiding Mainly Whites, Legacy Policy Gets Embroiled in Debate Over Affirmative Action' 15 January 2003. For discussion of the legality of 'legacy preferences' see SD Shadowen, SP Tulante and SL Alpern, 'No Distinctions Except Those Which Merit Originates: The

'Legacy preferences', while subject to occasional critical comment, generate only a fraction of the controversy associated with 'racial preferences', notwithstanding the fact that (or, perhaps, because) the latter are designed to ameliorate disadvantage while the former serve to entrench advantage.

INTERNATIONAL COMPARISONS

Canada

We return below to consider the US. Canada's Charter of Rights makes specific provision for positive action. Section 15(1) provides that:

> Every individual is equal before and under the law and has the right to the equal protection and equal benefit of the law without discrimination and, in particular, without discrimination based on race, national or ethnic origin, colour, religion, sex, age or mental or physical disability.

Section 15(2) goes on to state that the provision 'does not preclude any law, program or activity that has as its object the amelioration of conditions of disadvantaged individuals or groups including those that are disadvantaged because of' any of the protected grounds.

In *R v Turpin* (1989), Canada's Supreme Court stated that the overall purpose of section 15 was to remedy or prevent discrimination against groups suffering social, political and legal disadvantage in Canadian society, and ruled that a breach of section 15 would generally require 'disadvantage that exists apart from and independent of the particular legal distinction being challenged'.[22] The '1995 Trilogy'[23] of cases saw a three-way split between the justices of the Supreme Court as to the proper approach to section 15, which gave way in 1999 to the unanimous decision in *Law v Canada (Minister of Employment and Immigration)*.[24] There the Court ruled that the purpose of section 15(1) was to prevent the violation of essential human dignity and freedom through the imposition of disadvantage, stereotyping, or political or social

Unlawfulness of Legacy Preferences in Public and Private Universities' (2009) 49 *Santa Clara Law Review* 51; CFW Larson, 'Titles of Nobility, Hereditary Privilege, and the Unconstitutionality of Legacy Preferences in Public School Admissions' (2006) 84 *Washington University Law Review* 1375.

[22] *R v Turpin* [1989] 1 SCR 1296. See also *McKinney v University of Guelph* [1990] 3 SCR 229, 391; *R v Swain* [1991] 1 SCR 933; H Lessard, 'Equality and Access to Justice in the Work of Bertha Wilson' (1992) 15 *Dalhousie Law Journal* 35; J Fudge, 'What do we Mean by Law and Social Transformation?' (1990) 5 *Canadian Journal of Women and the Law* 47, 58; G Brodsky and S Day, *Canadian Charter Equality Rights for Women: One Step Forward or Two Steps Back?* (Ottawa: Canadian Advisory Council on the Status of Women, 1989).

[23] *Thibaudeau v Canada* [1995] 2 SCR 627; *Egan v Canada* [1995] 2 SCR 513; and *Miron v Trudel* [1995] 2 SCR 418.

[24] *Law v Canada (Minister of Employment and Immigration)* [1999] 1 SCR 497. For discussion see D Majury, 'The *Charter*, Equality Rights and Women: Equivocation and Celebration' (2002) 40 *Osgoode Hall Law Journal* 297.

prejudice, and to promote a society in which all persons enjoyed equal recognition at law as human beings or as members of Canadian society, equally capable and equally deserving of concern, respect and consideration.

That aspect of the judgment, and its overruling in *R v Kapp* (2008),[25] is considered in Chapter 1. Unaffected by the decision in *Kapp*, however, are the factors which the Court in *Law* emphasised would be important in determining whether section 15(1) had been breached. One of these was whether the claimant had been subject to differential treatment on the basis of one or more personal characteristics, or whether there had been a failure to take into account his or her already disadvantaged position within Canadian society, in either case resulting in the claimant's subjection to substantively different treatment amounting to 'discrimination'. This involved determining whether a burden had been imposed upon, or a benefit withheld from, the claimant

> in a manner which reflects the stereotypical application of presumed group or personal characteristics, or which otherwise has the effect of perpetuating or promoting the view that the individual is less capable or worthy of recognition or value as a human being or as a member of Canadian society, equally deserving of concern, respect, and consideration.

In *Law* the Court ruled that the existence of historical disadvantage was 'probably the most compelling factor favouring a conclusion that differential treatment imposed by legislation is truly discriminatory', although it was not essential.[26] This approach to section 15(1) rendered section 15(2) largely superfluous,[27] and in *Lovelace v Ontario* the Court declared that section 15(2) did not provide a 'defence or exemption' to section 15(1) but was, rather, 'confirmatory of' it, and that section 15(1) 'can embrace ameliorative programs of the kind that are contemplated by s. 15(2)'.[28] This is not to say that section 15 protects only those disadvantaged by reference to the protected characteristic; in *R v Hess*, a challenge (successful on other grounds) to the criminalisation of sexual intercourse with girls (but not boys) aged under 14, McLachlin J explicitly rejected the argument put by Canada's Attorney General that section 15's prohibition of sex discrimination protected only women.[29] Differential treatment which does not serve to exacerbate existing disadvantage will, however, be

---

[25] *R v Kapp* [2008] 2 SCR 483.

[26] See also *Withler v Canada (Attorney General)* (2011) SCC 12, also discussed in Chapter 1, in which the Supreme court emphasised the significance of pre-existing disadvantage, though it ruled at [36] that 's. 15 may be found to be violated even in the absence of proof of historic disadvantage'.

[27] W Tarnopolsky, 'The Equality Rights in the Canadian Charter of Rights and Freedoms' (1983) 61 *Canadian Bar Review* 242, 257–59, suggested that the provision was added out of 'excessive caution' in an attempt to safeguard affirmative action programmes from possible judicial activism. In 'The New Canadian Charter of Rights and Freedoms as Compared and Contrasted with the American Bill of Rights' (1983) 5 *Human Rights Quarterly* 227, 247, he further suggested that s 15(1) 'may seem to be the camel that a committee produces when attempting to design a horse'. See generally H Orton, 'Section 15, Benefits Programs and Other Benefits at Law: The Interpretation of Section 15 of the Charter since Andrews' (1990) 19 *Manitoba Law Journal* 288, 299.

[28] *Lovelace v Ontario* [2000] 1 SCR 950, 105, 108.

[29] *R v Hess* [1990] 2 SCR 906, 943–44, and see *Withler* (n 26).

readily justifiable under the Charter's general justification provision (s 1) even if it is categorised as discrimination under section 15(1).[30]

Canada's asymmetric constitutional equality guarantee is coupled with statutory prohibitions on discrimination at the federal and provincial level, as well as 'employment equity' legislation, again at provincial and federal level, which requires the adoption and implementation of special programmes to address workforce under-representation of women, people with disabilities, Aboriginal people and visible minorities. The statutory prohibitions on discrimination typically include provisions to the effect that 'special programs' designed to remedy disadvantage do not amount to actionable discrimination.[31] Some provincial human rights legislation imposes upon 'special programs' an effectiveness requirement,[32] or a requirement for pre-authorisation by the provincial Human Rights Commission.[33] Others are more permissive, Yukon's Human Rights Act, for example, stating simply that 'Special programs and affirmative action programs are not discrimination'.[34] Guidance issued by Canada's Human Rights Commission on 'Special Programs' emphasises that such programmes 'are not a limit or exception to equality' rather 'a means of advancing the achievement of equality',[35] though it states that 'Special Programs must be temporary', 'must address genuine disadvantage', 'must be tailored to meet the actual needs of the disadvantaged group' and 'must be proportional to the degree of under-representation or disadvantage'.

South Africa

Canada is not alone in adopting a clearly asymmetrical approach to the prohibition on discrimination. South Africa's constitutional equality provision (s 9), for example, prohibits only 'unfair discrimination' and specifically provides (s 9(2)) that 'To promote the achievement of equality, legislative and other measures

---

[30] As in *Hess* itself. The discussion of s 15 and asymmetry is not intended to suggest that the jurisprudence is unproblematic. See Chapter 1 and Majury (n 24) for a critique of the case law to that date including *Law* and *Gosselin v Quebec (Attorney General)* [2002] 4 SCR 429 in particular.

[31] See eg s 16(1) of the federal Human Rights Act, s 42 of British Columbia's Human Rights Code, s 67 of the North West Territories Human Rights Act and s 6 of the Nova Scotia Human Rights Act.

[32] See eg s 11(b)(ii) of Manitoba's Human Rights Code.

[33] Section 19 Newfoundland and Labrador Human Rights Code. British Columbia, Saskatchewan, Quebec and Prince Edward Island also require approval by the relevant Commission while s 13 of New Brunswick's Human Rights Act and s 67 of the North West Territories Human Rights Act permit but do not require Commission approval as a precondition of lawfulness.

[34] Section 13. The terms are defined, respectively, as 'programs designed to prevent disadvantages that are likely to be suffered by any group identified by reference to a prohibited ground of discrimination' and 'programs designed to reduce disadvantages resulting from discrimination suffered by a group identified by reference to a prohibited ground of discrimination'.

[35] See also the 1995 Commission Consultation Document, *Promoting Equality: A New Vision*, Chapter 3, (www.collectionscanada.gc.ca/webarchives/20071124203042/http://www.justice.gc.ca/chra/en/frp-c3.html).

designed to protect or advance persons, or categories of persons, disadvantaged by unfair discrimination may be taken'. Perhaps most strikingly, in *Hugo v President of the Republic of South Africa* (1997), the Constitutional Court upheld the legality of a Presidential grant of amnesty to women, but not men, prisoners who were parents of young children.[36] The Court did not accept that discrimination was unfair *only* where it affected historically disadvantaged groups, but emphasised the 'particularly vulnerable' status of the mothers of young children in concluding that the restriction of the amnesty to mothers rather than fathers could not be said 'fundamentally [to] impair [. . . fathers'] rights of dignity or sense of equal worth'. [37] Justice O'Regan, with whom a majority of the Justices concurred, stated that 'The more vulnerable the group adversely affected by the discrimination, the more likely the discrimination will be held to be unfair'.[38]

In *Minister of Finance and Other v Van Heerden* (2004), Mosenke J, with whom Sachs J and Skweyiya J agreed, stated:

> [O]ur constitutional understanding of equality includes . . . remedial or restitutionary equality. Such measures are not in themselves a deviation from, or invasive of, the right to equality guaranteed by the Constitution. They are not 'reverse discrimination' or 'positive discrimination' . . . They are integral to the reach of our equality protection.[39]

The constitutional commitment in section 9(1) to 'equal[ity] before the law and . . . the right to equal protection and benefit of the law' was 'complementary' to the measures envisaged in section 9(2): 'both contribute to the constitutional goal of achieving equality to ensure "full and equal enjoyment of all rights"'.

The particular provisions there under challenge provided for differential pension contributions payable over a five-year period in respect of (but not by) MPs who had previously been MPs in apartheid South Africa, and who benefited from membership of a (closed) pension fund which had only been open to whites. Sachs J went on to state that:

> The necessary reconciliation between the different interests of those positively and negatively affected by affirmative action should, I believe, be done in a manner that takes simultaneous and due account both of the severe degree of structured inequality with which we still live, and of the constitutional goal of achieving an egalitarian society based on non-racism and non-sexism. In this context, redress is not simply an option, it is an imperative.[40]

---

[36] *Hugo v President of the Republic of South Africa* (1997) (4) SA 1 (CC). The case concerned the interim Constitution whose equality provision was materially identical to s 9 of the final Constitution.

[37] ibid, para 47.

[38] ibid, para 112.

[39] *Minister of Finance and Other v Van Heerden* [2004] ZACC 3; 2004 (6) SA 121 (CC), citing Ackermann J in *National Coalition for Gay and Lesbian Equality & Anor v Minister of Justice & Anor* 1999 (1) SA 6 (CC); 1998 (12) BCLR 1517 (CC), para 60.

[40] ibid, paras 136–37.

Further:

> [P]roperly designed race-conscious and gender-conscious measures are not automatically suspect, and certainly not presumptively unfair . . .
>
> Remedial action by its nature has to take specific account of race, gender and the other factors which have been used to inhibit people from enjoying their rights. In pursuance of a powerful governmental purpose it inevitably disturbs, rather than freezes, the status quo. It destabilises the existing state of affairs, often to the disadvantage of those who belong to the classes of society that have benefited from past discrimination . . .
>
> Even if section 9(2) had not existed, I believe that section 9 should have been interpreted so as to promote substantive equality and race-conscious remedial action.[41]

The EU

The EU approach to discrimination is more symmetrical than that characteristic of Canada and South Africa, the early case law firm in its conclusions that Article 2(4) of the then Equal Treatment Directive, which provided that the Directive 'shall be without prejudice to measures to promote equal opportunity for men and women, in particular by removing existing inequalities which affect women's opportunities', was 'a derogation to th[e] principle [of equal treatment]'[42] and, as such, 'must be interpreted strictly'.[43] The Treaty of Amsterdam, which entered into force on 1 May 1999, provided (Art 141(4)) that:

> With a view to ensuring full equality in practice between men and women in working life, the principle of equal treatment shall not prevent any Member State from maintaining or adopting measures providing for specific advantages in order to make it easier for the underrepresented sex to pursue a vocational activity or to prevent or compensate for disadvantages in professional careers.

This provision, which is now Article 157(4) of the TFEU, had a markedly more permissive tone than Article 2(4) of the Equal Treatment Directive, previously the only EC provision on positive action. This did not, however, prevent the ECJ in *Abrahamsson & Anderson v Fogelqvist*,[44] a case concerned with Article 2(4) of the Equal Treatment Directive, from suggesting that Article 141(4) did not extend to allowing the selection of a less (but adequately) qualified woman over a more qualified man under conditions of significant female under-representation (this on the basis that such action was disproportionate).

Colm O'Cinneide suggested in 2006 that 'a lingering attachment to "formal"

---

[41] ibid, paras 143–44, 147.

[42] According to Advocate General Tesauro in Case C-450/93 *Kalanke v Freie Hansestadt Bremen* [1995] ECR I-3051, para 6.

[43] Decision of the Court in *Kalanke v Freie Hansestadt Bremen*, ibid, para 21. See also Case C-409/95 *Marschall v Land Nordrhein-Westfalen* [1997] ECR I-6363, para 32; Case C-476/99 *Lommers v Minister van Landbouw, Natuurbeheer en Visserij* [2002] ECR 1-2891, para 39; Case C-158/97 *Re Badeck* [2000] ECR I-1875, para 22.

[44] Case C-407/98 *Abrahamsson & Anderson v Fogelqvist* [2000] ECR I-05539.

equality concepts has resulted in a confusing, incoherent and complex case-law that has a "chilling effect" on the use of positive action'.[45] But notwithstanding the apparent lack of enthusiasm at ECJ (now CJEU[46]) level for positive measures, the EU has included fairly strong provisions along the lines of Article 141(4) EC in the anti-discrimination Directives adopted subsequent to the Treaty of Amsterdam. Thus Article 5 of Directive 2000/43 (the Race Directive) provides that 'with a view to ensuring full equality in practice, the principle of equal treatment shall not prevent any Member State from maintaining or adopting specific measures to prevent or compensate for disadvantages linked to racial or ethnic origin'. Article 7 of Directive 2000/78 (the Employment Equality Directive) is in materially identical terms as is Article 6 of Directive 2004/113, while Article 3 of Directive 2006/54 (the Recast Gender Directive) provides that 'Member States may maintain or adopt measures within the meaning of Art 141(4) of the Treaty with a view to ensuring full equality in practice between men and women in working life'.[47]

The Treaty of Lisbon, by which the Charter entered into force, committed the EU to accede to the ECHR while Protocol No 14 to the ECHR provides for the possibility of EU accession.[48] That Protocol entered into force on 1 June 2010 with Russia's ratification, and official talks between the Council of Europe's Steering Committee for Human Rights and the European Commission on the EU's accession to the Convention began the following month. The Steering Committee's October 2011 report to the Committee of Ministers of the Council of Europe included a draft agreement on accession.[49] Such accession may result in an increased enthusiasm for positive action on the part of the CJEU, the emerging signs being that the Strasbourg Court may require, as distinct from merely permitting, ameliorative action under Article 14 of the Convention.[50] And whatever uncertainties there are as to the exact parameters of lawful positive action under EU law as it is interpreted by the CJEU, most EU states provide for positive action broadly in line with the approach now typical of EU legislation, though the exact parameters of that approach remain uncertain pending further CJEU guidance.

---

[45]   C O'Cinneide, 'Positive Action and the Limits of Existing Law' (2006) 13 *Maastricht Journal of European & Comparative Law* 351–64, 351.

[46]   Court of Justice of the European Union.

[47]   Other than in the case of gender, these positive action provisions are not underpinned by any particular Treaty base. It is perhaps also worthy of note that the Charter of Fundamental Rights of the EU expressly permits positive action only in relation to gender, Art 23 providing that 'The principle of equality [which 'must be ensured' between men and women 'in all areas, including employment, work and pay'] shall not prevent the maintenance or adoption of measures providing for specific advantages in favour of the under-represented sex'.

[48]   Article 17 amending Art 59 of the Convention to provide that '2. The European Union may accede to this Convention'.

[49]   CDDH(2011)009, available at www.coe.int/t/dghl/standardsetting/hrpolicy/CDDH-UE/CDDH-UE_documents_en.asp.

[50]   See Chapter 4.

The United States

Contrasted with the approach taken in Canada and South Africa, in particular, the UK's traditional approach to positive action appears almost eccentrically narrow. And even in the United States, in which the parameters of lawful positive action have been strongly contested, there has been much more scope for lawful positive action than in the UK, at least prior to the implementation of the Equality Act 2010.

The jurisprudence of the US Supreme Court in this area has fluctuated with the political complexion of that Court. Before turning to consider this jurisprudence, however, it is important to point out the long history of 'affirmative action' obligations imposed by the State, notably by Presidential Executive Order, on Federal contractors and subcontractors. As early as 1961, President Kennedy's Executive Order 10925 required all government contracting agencies to take 'affirmative action to ensure that applicants are employed, and that employees are treated during employment, without regard to their race, creed, color, or national origin'. And in 1965 President Johnson's Executive Orders required the taking of positive measures by State contractors and subcontractors, including the adoption of goals and timetables to increase participation by women and minority ethnic workers.[51] The use of affirmative action measures in university admissions with a view to creating or maintaining a more diverse range of students than might otherwise be the case has also been relatively common over the years.

In 1978, in *Regents of the University of California v Bakke*, the Court ruled that the use of quotas by the university's medical school to ensure that African American students were awarded at least 16 per cent of the available places breached the Constitution's Equal Protection Clause.[52] However unwelcome to the university, the decision did not involve a blanket ban on 'affirmative action'. Four of the justices made their decision on a reading of Title VI of the Civil Rights Act 1965, which prohibited exclusion from federally financed programmes 'on the ground of race', stating expressly that 'the question whether race can ever be used as a factor in an admissions decision is not an issue in this case'.[53] The dissenters would have allowed race to be taken into consideration in order to remedy substantial chronic minority ethnic under-representation in the medical profession.[54] And Justice Powell, whose opinion was decisive in the case, ruled that race could not be *the* basis for a refusal to admit, though it could be one of multiple factors in an admissions process.

---

[51] Executive Orders 11246 and 11375. President Nixon also imposed affirmative action obligations in 1969 and 1971 and President Carter did so in 1979.
[52] *Regents of the University of California v Bakke* 438 US 265 (1978).
[53] ibid, 411, *per* Burger CJ and Stewart and Rehnquist JJ.
[54] Brennan, White, Marshall and Blackmun JJ.

The decision in *Bakke* was generally taken to prohibit *quotas* while allowing some race-conscious decision making of a remedial nature. In 2003 the Supreme Court, in a pair of university admissions cases (*Grutter v Bollinger* and *Gratz v Bollinger*[55]), reiterated this approach after a quarter of a century of fluctuating jurisprudence further considered below. In the *Grutter* case O'Connor CJ, delivering the opinion of the Court, remarked that:

> It has been 25 years since Justice Powell first approved the use of race to further an interest in student body diversity in the context of public higher education . . . We expect that 25 years from now, the use of racial preferences will no longer be necessary to further the interest approved today.[56]

In June 2013 the Supreme Court issued judgment in a challenge to an affirmative action programme run by the University of Texas. The case was widely regarded as calling into question the future legality of affirmative action programmes,[57] though the Court resisted the urgings of many to bring the curtains down on affirmative action in favour of a further 'nip and tuck' approach which continues to raise the bar to be met by such programmes without prohibiting them entirely.[58] The following month it was reported that the Court had agreed to hear an appeal from a ruling by the US Court of Appeals for the Sixth Circuit that an amendment to Michigan's constitution which banned affirmative action on grounds of race and sex in the State was unconstitutional.[59]

Whatever the outcome of the Michigan challenge, the scope for positive action in the US has actually been broad by comparison to the domestic position. *Bakke* confirmed that the goal of achieving a diverse student body was a compelling State interest such that the use of appropriately tailored racial classifications to achieve it would pass 'strict scrutiny'. The following year (1979) the Court ruled in *United Steelworkers of America v Weber* that voluntary and temporary racial employment quotas in the private sector did not breach the prohibition on race discrimination in Title VII of the 1964 Civil Rights Act.[60] The majority suggested that the purpose of the Act was to open to ethnic minorities positions from which they had previously been excluded, and interpreted the Act's prohibition on 'discriminat[ion] because of . . . race' consistent with that purpose.[61]

In *Fullilove v Klutznick* (1980) the Court upheld the constitutionality of a 10 per cent 'minority business enterprise' set-aside in a Federal public works pro-

---

[55] *Grutter v Bollinger* 539 US 306 and *Gratz v Bollinger* 539 US 244.

[56] *Grutter*, ibid, paras 20–21.

[57] And see www.newyorker.com/online/blogs/comment/2012/05/the-other-big-supreme-court-case.html.

[58] *Fisher v University of Texas* 24 June 2013.

[59] www.upi.com/Top_News/US/2013/07/14/Under-the-US-Supreme-Court-Affirmative-action-living-on-the-edge/UPI-84841373787000. The case is *Schuette v Coalition to Defend Affirmative Action*.

[60] *United Steelworkers of America v Weber* 443 US 193 (1979).

[61] Rehnquist and Burger JJ dissented while Justices Stevens and Powell took no part in consideration.

gramme.[62] At the relevant time less than 1 per cent of all federal procurement was concluded with minority business enterprises, although minorities comprised 15–18 per cent of the population. Three Supreme Court Justices, led by Chief Justice Burger, ruled in *Fullilove* that 'in the . . . remedial context, there is no requirement that Congress act in a wholly "color-blind" fashion', and that 'When effectuating a limited and properly tailored remedy to cure the effects of prior discrimination . . . "a sharing of the burden" by innocent parties is not impermissible'. Justice Marshall, with Justices Brennan and Blackmun, concurred on the wider grounds that:

> [T]he proper inquiry for determining the constitutionality of racial classifications that provide benefits to minorities for the purpose of remedying the present effects of past racial discrimination is whether the classifications serve important governmental objectives and are substantially related to achievement of those objectives . . . and that, judged under this standard, the . . . set-aside provision . . . is plainly constitutional.

Justices Stewart and Rehnquist cited the dissenting opinion in *Plessy v Ferguson* (1896),[63] in which Harlan J had protested that the US Constitution was 'color-blind, and neither knows nor tolerates classes among citizens', and condemned the decision of the majority in *Fullilove* as 'wrong for the same reason that *Plessy v. Ferguson* was wrong'.[64] They insisted that the use of any racial classifications breached the Equal Protection Clause unless it survived strict scrutiny, an identical approach being required of the Court 'whatever the race may be of those who are its victims'.[65] 'The equal protection standard of the Constitution has one clear and central meaning – it absolutely prohibits invidious discrimination by government . . .[and] racial discrimination is by definition invidious discrimination'. Justice Stevens, who joined Justices Stewart and Rehnquist in the dissent, was 'not convinced that the [Equal Protection] Clause contains an absolute prohibition against any statutory classification based on race' but was 'persuaded that it does impose a special obligation to scrutinize any governmental decision making process that draws nationwide distinctions between citizens on the basis of their race and incidentally also discriminates against noncitizens in the preferred racial classes'. In his view the set-aside was 'a perverse form of reparation'.[66]

Despite the strong contrary views of some Supreme Court Justices, affirmative action programmes were generally upheld between 1978 and 1989.[67] The

---

[62] *Fullilove v Klutznick* 448 US 448 (1980).

[63] *Plessy v Ferguson* 167 US 537 (1896), in which a majority of the Court had embraced the notorious 'separate but equal' approach to uphold the constitutionality of apartheid in the US.

[64] Note that Justice Stewart had agreed with the decision of the majority in *Weber*, which concerned Title VII rather than the Equal Protection Clause.

[65] Citing, inter alia, *Loving v Virginia* 388 US 1, 11 (1967) and *Brown v Board of Education* 347 US 483 (1954).

[66] Although he, too, was to uphold a species of affirmative action in *Metro Broadcasting v FCC* (1990) 497 US 547.

[67] Though *cf Wygant v Jackson Board of Education* 476 US 267 (1986) in which Justice Stevens dissented.

routine defenders of affirmative action took the view that the normal standard of 'strict scrutiny' by which race-conscious decision making was to be judged was not applicable where affirmative action was concerned: 'while racial distinctions are irrelevant to nearly all legitimate State objectives and are properly subjected to the most rigorous judicial scrutiny in most instances, they are highly relevant to the one legitimate State objective of eliminating the pernicious vestiges of past discrimination' and that 'because whites have none of the immutable characteristics of a suspect class, the so-called "strict scrutiny" [standard is] not applicable'.[68] Opponents of affirmative action generally coupled a demand for 'strict scrutiny' in Equal Protection Clause cases with a narrow approach to those interests which might be regarded as 'compelling'.[69] Those, such as Stevens J, who sided with the defenders on occasion, generally did so without abandoning the strict scrutiny approach expressly, even if on occasion they may have appeared to do so implicitly.[70]

By 1989 it appeared that race (and, presumably, sex) could form the basis for ameliorative programmes where it was established that the institution involved had itself been guilty of discrimination in the past; and that educational establishments could pursue a policy of race-based diversity, at least where this did not consist of rigid quotas for ethnic minority students. Private and public sector employers could adopt voluntary and temporary training quotas or other race-conscious methods in hiring and promotion 'to eliminate conspicuous racial imbalance in traditionally segregated job categories'.[71] In addition, affirmative action programmes could be imposed by the courts as well as being embraced voluntarily by employers, and federal programmes could operate race-based set-asides where severe inequality of access had been shown. These judgments were never unanimous and frequently failed even to rest on clear majorities, the level of scrutiny appropriate to remedial programmes was never settled and the issue set social liberals in the Court against each other. But, until 1989, remedial race programmes, whether carried out at federal or State level, in the public or private sector, voluntarily or at the behest of the courts, had a reasonable chance of being upheld by the Supreme Court.

With the replacement in 1989 of Justice Powell by Justice Kennedy the tide turned. In *Wards Cove Packing Co v Antonio* the Supreme Court all but overruled its decision in *Griggs v Power Duke Co*, which had formed the basis for our domestic regulation of indirect race and sex discrimination.[72] Part of the

---

[68] *cf Wygant*, ibid, *per* Justice Marshall, with whom Justices Brennan and Blackmun concurred.

[69] See, for example, the majority in *Wygant*, ibid. Note that in *Fullilove* Burger and Powell JJ, together with White J, declined to specify the standard of review under which they upheld the racial classifications there applied.

[70] See *Metro Broadcasting* (n 66) (dissenting).

[71] *Weber* (n 60) applied (though without express consideration of the position under the Equal Protection Clause, or a reasoned decision) in *Bushey v New York State Civil Service Commission* 469 US 1117 (1985).

[72] *Wards Cove Packing Co v Antonio* 490 US 642 (1989) and *Griggs v Power Duke Co* 401 US 424 (1971).

Wards Cove decision was reversed by Congress in the 1991 Civil Rights Act but the change of approach the decision signalled was felt in the affirmative action context almost immediately when, in *Martin v Wilks* (1989), the Court ruled that non-minorities who suffered as a result of court-approved affirmative action programmes without having agreed to the programmes could sue under the Constitution's Equal Protection Clause.[73] The programme challenged in *Wilks* had been adopted in the wake of a finding that the fire department involved had discriminated against minority candidates in contravention of Title VII, and in advance of a finding on discrimination in promotion practices, the issuing court expressing the view, however, that the department would probably be found to have discriminated in this area also. The majority decision did not refer to the historical context of the case.[74]

Also in 1989, in *Croson v City of Richmond*, the Supreme Court invalidated Richmond's 30 per cent set-aside of public works funds for minority-owned businesses and, for the first time, ruled that all State and local use of racial classifications to benefit minorities must meet strict scrutiny.[75] In *Metro Broadcasting v FCC* (1990) a majority ruled that 'race-conscious classifications adopted by Congress to address racial and ethnic discrimination are subject to a different standard than such classifications prescribed by state and local governments', and upheld minority ethnic preferences in the award of broadcasting licences.[76] But the post-1989 approach to affirmative action was generally hostile and in 1995, in *Adarand Constructors v Peña*, the Court overruled *Metro Broadcasting* and demanded that federal, as well as State and local, affirmative action programmes meet strict scrutiny where they operated on the basis of racial or ethnic classifications.[77]

The application across the board of the 'strict scrutiny' standard did not amount to a blanket prohibition on affirmative action.[78] In *Adarand*, Justice Stevens castigated the majority for its 'disregard [of] the difference between a "No Trespassing" sign and a welcome mat' and insisted that there was 'no moral or constitutional equivalence between a policy that is designed to perpetuate a caste system and one that seeks to eradicate racial subordination'.[79] He accepted, however, that 'Nothing is inherently wrong with applying a single

---

[73] *Martin v Wilk* 490 US 755 (1989). These suits could be made without time limit, although on the same day in a sex discrimination case the Supreme Court required in *Lorance v AT&T Technologies Inc* 490 US 900 (1989) that women who wished to challenge an allegedly discriminatory seniority system must do so within 300 days of its adoption.

[74] Rehnquist CJ delivered the opinion of the Court in which White, O'Connor, Scalia and Kennedy JJ joined.

[75] *Croson v City of Richmond* 488 US 469.

[76] *Metro Broadcasting v FCC* 497 US 597 (1990), Justice Brennan for the majority declaring that 'benign race conscious measures mandated by congress – even if those measures are not 'remedial' in the sense of being designed to compensate victims of past governmental or societal discrimination – are constitutionally permissible'.

[77] *Adarand Constructors v Peña* 512 US 200.

[78] Though *cf* the view of Ginsberg J, dissenting, that it did precisely this.

[79] A proposition with which Justice Thomas expressly disagreed.

standard to fundamentally different situations, as long as that standard takes relevant differences into account'. And Justice O'Connor, who delivered the Opinion of the Court, stated that 'The principle of consistency simply means that whenever the government treats any person unequally because of his or her race, that person has suffered an injury that falls squarely within the language and spirit of the Constitution's guarantee of equal protection' and that the determination of 'the ultimate validity of any particular law . . . is the job of the court applying strict scrutiny' to decide whether 'a compelling governmental interest justifies the infliction of that injury'.

Adarand was followed by a period in which the Court declined to hear affirmative action cases, notably appeals from decisions of the Fifth and Ninth Circuit Courts of Appeal. The former court had ruled that a diversity-related affirmative action programme at Texas Law School was unconstitutional because, inter alia, the pursuit of diversity could not be regarded as a compelling interest in higher education. This ruling, by the Fifth Circuit Court of Appeals, was simply inconsistent with the earlier decision of the Supreme Court in *Bakke* in which four of the justices adopted a generous approach to affirmative action programmes and the fifth, Justice Powell, specifically accepted diversity as a compelling goal. The Ninth Circuit Court of Appeal had rejected a challenge by the American Civil Liberties Union to California's 'Civil Rights Initiative', also known as 'Proposition 209', a State constitutional amendment banning sex- and race-based public sector affirmative action even where it is necessary to remedy past discrimination, unless the action is adopted by court order. Then in 2003 it handed down decisions in the *Gruter v Bollinger* and *Grantz v Bollinger* cases which confirmed both that race-based affirmative action programmes had to satisfy 'strict scrutiny' in order to pass constitutional muster and also that, at least in the context of higher education, 'obtaining the educational benefits that flow from a diverse student body' amounted to a 'compelling state interest' the pursuit of which by appropriately tailored means would pass the constitutional test.[80] As in *Bakke*, the adoption of a programme which failed to take account of the individual merits of applicants would not be acceptable.

After 2003 it appeared that the legal position regarding affirmative action was relatively clear. The University of Texas reinstated its affirmative action programme which had been declared unlawful by the lower courts prior to the decisions in *Gruter* and *Grantz*. In 2007, however, affirmative action suffered a further blow when the Supreme Court decided, in *Parents Involved in Community Schools v Seattle School District No 1*[81], that the correction of racial imbalances in schools (as distinct from the dismantling of deliberate racial segregation) was not a compelling State interest. This decision was in marked contrast to those in *Gratz* and *Grutter* in which the pursuit of diversity (including, though not limited to, racial diversity) was accepted as a compelling

---

[80]   *Grutter v Bollinger* (n 55).
[81]   *Parents Involved in Community Schools v Seattle School District No 1* 551 US 701.

State interest in third level education. The Court further ruled that racial classifications could only be justified by compelling State interests if they were actually effective in achieving those interests. Justice Kennedy, who agreed with
Roberts CJ and Scalia, Thomas and Alito JJ that the pursuit of racial diversity
of itself was not a compelling State interest, would have accepted the broader
pursuit of diversity as a compelling interest but was not satisfied that it was at
issue in the instant case.

Roberts CJ concluded his opinion in *Parents Involved in Community Schools*
by stating that:

> Before *Brown [v Board of Education]*, schoolchildren were told where they could and
> could not go to school based on the color of their skin . . . For schools that never seg-
> regated on the basis of race . . . or that have removed the vestiges of past segregation
> . . . the way 'to achieve a system of determining admission to schools on a nonracial
> basis,' [citing *Brown*] is to stop assigning students on a racial basis.

Stephens J, dissenting, pointed out that the Chief Justice 'fails to note that it
was only black schoolchildren who were so ordered'. He went on to characterise
the approach of the majority to the Equal Protection Clause as 'wooden',
'fail[ing] to recognize the obvious importance' of the question whether racial
classifications burdened 'one race alone', or 'stigmatize[d] or exclude[d]', and to
declare that 'a rigid adherence to tiers of scrutiny obscures *Brown*'s clear message', referring to the Court's earlier approval of the dicta of the Supreme Court
of Massachusetts in *School Comm of Boston v Board of Education* (1967) that
'It would be the height of irony if the racial imbalance act, enacted as it was
with the laudable purpose of achieving equal educational opportunities, should,
by prescribing school pupil allocations based on race, founder on unsuspected
shoals in the Fourteenth Amendment'. [82]

Stephens J concluded by stating his 'firm conviction that no Member of the
Court that I joined in 1975 would have agreed with today's decision'. Breyer J,
with whom Stevens, Souter and Ginsburg JJ joined, declared that the plurality

> reverses course . . . distorts precedent . . . misapplies the relevant constitutional princi-
> ples . . . announces rules that will obstruct efforts . . . to deal effectively with the grow-
> ing resegregation of public schools . . . and . . . undermines *Brown*'s promise of
> integrated primary and secondary education that local communities have sought to
> make a reality.

Noting that schools had become increasingly integrated between 1968 and 1980
but that the process had reversed by 2000 (by which stage 72% of black children
were educated in predominantly black schools, up from 63% in 1980, with 37%
of black children in schools whose pupils were at least 90%, up from 33% in
1980[83]), and that 'Today, more than one in six black children attend a school that

---

[82] *School Comm of Boston v Board of Education* 352 Mass. 693, 698; 227 NE E 2d 729, 733
(1967).
[83] These figures had stood at 77% and 64% respectively in 1968.

is 99–100% minority', Breyer J concluded that the efforts made in the cases before the Court, which arose from school boards which had been 'highly segregated in fact' as a result of State laws and/or school board policies and actions, were narrowly tailored to compelling interests 'on any reasonable definition of those terms'; that 'the distinction between *de jure* segregation (caused by school systems) and *de facto* segregation (caused, *e.g.*, by housing patterns or generalized societal discrimination) is meaningless in the present context'; and that 'real-world efforts to substitute racially diverse for racially segregated schools (however caused) are complex, to the point where the Constitution cannot plausibly be interpreted to rule out categorically all local efforts to use means that are "conscious" of the race of the individuals'.

In *Fisher v Texas* a majority of the Court (Justice Ginsburg dissenting and Justice Kagan, one of the two Obama nominees who have replaced Souter and Stevens JJ, not participating[84]) ordered the Fifth Circuit Court to take a new, and apparently more demanding, look at an admissions formula which was closely modelled on that upheld by the Supreme Court in *Grutter*, and accepted by the lower Court as consistent with *Grutter*. It is clearly the case that the Supreme Court has been backing away from affirmative action for decades. It is also noteworthy that the US judicial approach to indirect discrimination, initially ground breaking,[85] has more recently been hostile to the point of sabotage.[86] Having said all this, the scope for lawful positive action has been very considerably broader than that which prevailed in the UK, at least prior to the Equality Act 2010.

A QUESTION OF PRINCIPLE?

The distinction drawn between (lawful) 'positive action' and (unlawful) 'positive discrimination' (see the comments of Vera Baird and Mark Harper above) has no real philosophical underpinning. 'Positive action' constitutes a narrow (though recently enlarged) exception to the generally symmetrical approach to 'discrimination', understood as differential treatment on a protected ground. In Chapter 2 I suggested that some of the grounds currently singled out for broad statutory protection in the UK (and the EU) ought not to be so protected. I further suggested that, where factors such as race, sex and sexual orientation are

---

[84] She disqualified herself from hearing it because she had worked on the case in her previous role as Solicitor General. Justice Kagan will not hear the Michigan affirmative action challenge either. Sotomayor J, the other Obama nominee, voted with the majority in *Fisher* despite her extra-judicial record on affirmative action.

[85] *Griggs v Power Duke* (n 72).

[86] See the decision of the US Supreme Court in *Ricci et al v DeStefano et al* 000 US 07-1428 (2009), which ruled that a refusal to promote on the basis of tests which appeared to have a very significant disadvantageous effect on African American candidates, where there were (according to the minority opinions) significant reasons to doubt that the tests were appropriate to measure the skills required, entailed direct racial discrimination against the white and Hispanic claimants who had passed the tests.

associated with significant disadvantage across multiple spheres of life, legal protection from discrimination ought perhaps not to be afforded in relation to protected characteristics, rather to those generally disadvantaged by such characteristics (as is currently the case with disability). Because men tend to be advantaged and women disadvantaged by virtue of their sex, for example, so sex itself cannot truly be seen as characteristic of disadvantage, much less of oppression.[87] The same is true of race and sexual orientation, racial characteristics advantaging some while they disadvantage others and heterosexuals being by and large the beneficiaries rather than the victims of disadvantage related to sexual orientation. Disadvantage associated with religion tends to accrue to those having particular religious beliefs, frequently linked with minority ethnicity within a geographical area, rather than being associated with the holding of (any) religious beliefs per se. And age works positively as well as negatively at most life stages, a person's overall package of advantages and disadvantages in terms of work, health, welfare and access to cultural goods at any given age turning very significantly on questions of class and economic status.

If, as I suggest in Chapter 2, discrimination law ought to be concerned with the elimination of unjust status hierarchies/group-based oppression, there may be no reason in principle to favour a symmetrical approach (and good reason to oppose it). The absence of individual wrongdoing in many cases of structural oppression (see discussion of Sally Haslanger in Chapter 1) will mean that merely prohibiting discrimination and providing a remedy to those discriminated against will be ineffective to challenge the results of such oppression. It may be necessary instead to require positive steps which, being designed to alleviate existing disadvantage suffered by *particular groups* of individuals identified by reference to personal characteristics (women, for example, BME people, gay men or disabled persons), cannot equally apply to others (in the examples above, men, non-BME people, heterosexuals or non-disabled persons).

The question arises, however, whether there is anything in the concepts of 'equality' or 'non-discrimination' themselves which militates in favour of symmetry. Whether positive action (understood, as above, as differential treatment designed to ameliorate disadvantage or address specific need) is consistent with equality depends entirely on the approach which is taken to the latter concept. If equality is understood to demand equal treatment for all, regardless of starting position or need, positive action cannot be defended. If equal treatment is to be accorded only to those who are regarded as equally meritorious, the notion of merit can be taken to include characteristics consideration of which would militate towards positive action (achievement in the face of social or personal adversity or disadvantage, for example; contribution to 'diversity'; potential as a role model for those under-represented in the relevant context). And if equality

---

[87] This is not, however, to suggest that men may never be disadvantaged for reasons related to sex. It may be appropriate, for example, to target positive educational measures towards boys, or particular categories of boys (African-Caribbean, for example, or working class white), and/or to target employment-related training towards young black men.

demands unequal treatment in proportion to inequality,[88] the fact of pre-existing disadvantage, under-representation and/or particular need can be regarded as justifying, even demanding, positive action.

'Groups', 'Discrimination' and Disadvantage

Owen Fiss suggested in 1976 that the Equal Protection Clause of the US Constitution should be interpreted in accordance not with what he termed the 'antidiscrimination principle', rather on the basis of what he called the 'group-disadvantaging principle'.[89] Fiss characterised the 'antidiscrimination' principle as 'reduc[ing] the idea of equality to the principle of equal treatment' that is, a prohibition on the drawing of arbitrary or otherwise impermissible distinctions,[90] and argued that this approach could not adequately guide judicial reasoning or explain the case law. More importantly for our purposes, he took the view that the anti-discrimination approach to the Equal Protection Clause could not accommodate the asymmetrical approach, which he strongly favoured:

> The antidiscrimination principle does not formally acknowledge social groups, such as blacks; nor does it offer any special dispensation for conduct that benefits a disadvantaged group. It only knows criteria or classifications; and the color black is as much a racial criterion as the color white . . . Reverse discrimination, so the argument is made, is a form of discrimination and is equally arbitrary since it is based on race . . . the anti-discrimination principle does not supply any basis or standards for determining what is 'reform' and what is 'regression' . . .[91]

Fiss's interpretation of the 'antidiscrimination principle' is not representative of any general understanding of the meaning of 'antidiscrimination'. His view was, for example, that the principle could not even adequately address indirect discrimination,[92] this because the recognition of de facto or adverse impact discrimination 'involves a basic modification of the anti-discrimination principle. The trigger is no longer classification, but rather group-impact'. Fiss suggested that the anti-discrimination principle 'roughly corresponds to the lay concept of equal treatment',[93] but acknowledged that his understanding of it as 'a theory

---

[88] See discussion in Chapter 1.

[89] O Fiss, 'Groups and the Equal Protection Clause' (1976) 5 *Philosophy & Public Affairs* 107, 108.

[90] 'Impermissible' here means related only to an illegitimate State purpose.

[91] Fiss (n 89) 129–30, 135–36. Fiss's article pre-dated the decision in *Regents of the University of California v Bakke* (n 52), in which the Supreme Court affirmed the legality of affirmative action based on race.

[92] Fiss (n 89) 140–46. At the time of his writing the US Supreme Court had allowed a disparate impact claim in *Griggs v Power Duke* (n 72), a case decided under the Civil Rights Act. It subsequently declined to recognise disparate impact discrimination under the Equal Protection Clause (*Washington v Davis* 426 US 229 (1976)).

[93] Fiss (n 89) 173.

about ill-fit' is not required by any dictionary definition.[94] Under his analysis, the principle would not prohibit the physical separation of black and white students during a graduation ceremony where this was 'based solely on aesthetics'.[95]

Whether or not Fiss was correct in his view that the Equal Protection Clause jurisprudence corresponded to the 'anti-discrimination principle' as he described it,[96] that principle is the manifestation of the 'treat like cases alike' mantra, indistinguishable in effect from Westen's 'empty vessel' of equality.[97] It does not exhaust the meaning which could be ascribed to the concept of 'anti-discrimination'. So while, for Fiss, an asymmetric approach to the Equal Protection Clause required the jettisoning of the 'antidiscrimination principle' *as he interpreted it*, this is not to say that anti-discrimination provisions are *by their nature* symmetrical, much less (as is clear in the European and international context) that they cannot accommodate disparate impact (otherwise known as indirect discrimination) claims.

Turning to questions of substance, Fiss proposed a shift to what he terms the 'group-disadvantaging principle' as the basis for Equal Protection Clause analysis. This would entail the recognition of social groups characterised by group identity and the interdependence of group members. Where groups are subordinated and politically disempowered, Fiss suggested that the Equal Protection Clause ought to be interpreted to prohibit the infliction of 'status-harms' on the group, that is, the taking of actions which aggravated the subordinated position of group members. Whereas '[t]he antidiscrimination principle, with its individualistic, means-focussed, and symmetrical character, would tend towards prohibiting' preferential treatment based on disadvantaged-group membership, 'the group-disadvantaging principle . . . would tend towards permitting it (and indeed might even provide the foundation for the fourth-order claim that may lie around the corner – that of requiring the preferential treatment)'.[98]

Fiss suggested that a social group is a group of people that 'has a distinct existence apart from its members, and also . . . has an identity' and that 'the

---

[94] See M Dorf, 'A Partial Defense of an Anti-Discrimination Principle' (2002) *Cornell Law Faculty Publications* Paper 116, and J Balkin and R Siegel, 'The American Civil Rights Tradition: Anticlassification or Antisubordination' (Yale Faculty Scholarship Series, 2004). The latter suggest (p 2) that, while Fiss's 'choice of words was quite unfortunate . . . [b]oth antisubordination and anticlassification might be understood as possible ways of fleshing out the meaning of the antidiscrimination principle, and thus as candidates for the "true" principle underlying antidiscrimination law'.

[95] Fiss (n 89) 116.

[96] John Hasnas ('Equal Opportunity, Affirmative Action, and the Anti-Discrimination Principle: The Philosophical Basis for the Legal Prohibition of Discrimination' (2002) 71 *Fordham Law Review* 423) suggests (at 441–42) that the 'anti-discrimination principle' of the Equal Protection Clause was 'at the time of [its] adoption . . . understood as an anti-oppression principle, that over the ensuing century, [it] gradually came to be understood as an anti-differentiation principle, and that over the past three and half decades, this understanding shattered into a confused amalgam of anti-differentiation, anti-oppression, and anti-subordination interpretations of the principle'. Balkin and Siegel suggest (n 94, 2) that American civil rights jurisprudence vindicates both anticlassification and antisubordination commitments'.

[97] See further Chapter 1, 15, Chapter 4, 106.

[98] Fiss (n 89) 171–72.

identity and well-being of the members of the group and the identity and well-being of the group are linked'.[99] His ascription of significance to social groups which are not readily definable or identifiable, and to the 'status' of such groups, has been subject to criticism. Lawrence Alexander, for example, insists that *individual*, rather than *group*, disadvantage is the proper subject of concern, and questions whether it is possible to rank 'group' disadvantage in any satisfactory way.[100] Iris Marion Young agrees that status is central to equality, and that 'conceptualizing status inequality as a kind of injustice entails thinking about harm in terms of social groups', but challenges Fiss's 'articulation of social groups [as] too naturalistic and reifying'. She accepts that individuals 'often bring to . . . interactions . . . stereotyped or group generalized assumptions, attitudes and feelings about the individuals they deal with, which often condition these interactions'; that, therefore, 'To the extent that they implicitly or explicitly locate others in groups, a group based orientation motivates action' and that 'Both as motivators for action and as observable effects, then, social groups are *real*'.[101] But:

> Contrary to Fiss's formulation, . . . groups do not exist independently of individuals; nor are they 'natural classes.' Groups are entirely constituted by social norms and interaction . . . the situation of groups can be observed over time and we can say that we are talking about the same group. It is also true that you can talk about the situation of the group in relation to other groups along certain parameters of comparison without referring to any particular members of the group. Ultimately, however, these generalizations derive from knowledge of circumstances of many of the individuals associated with the group. When theorists and activists call on others to improve the situation of groups, moreover, they rarely mean that the well being of the group is something independent of the well-being of its individual members.[102]

Young insists that consideration of the 'normative ideals of equality' (whether these are conceived in terms of welfare, resources or otherwise) must take account of groups as well as individuals, the 'assessment of inequality solely by comparing the situation of individuals provid[ing] little or no basis for making claims about social justice'.[103] She further argues that, in situations in which the basic needs of all are satisfied, inequalities would indicate injustice only when considered at the level of the group, defined

> by reference to [shared] attributes or affinities [of their members] or generalized social relations in which they stand. . . if we simply identify some inequality of condition or situation between individuals at a particular time we have no account of the causes of

---

[99] ibid, 148.

[100] L Alexander, 'Equal Protection and the Irrelevance of "Groups"' (2002) 2(1) *Issues in Legal Scholarship*.

[101] IM Young, 'Status Inequality and Social Groups' (2002) 2(1) *Issues in Legal Scholarship*.

[102] ibid.

[103] IM Young, 'Equality of Whom? Social Groups and Judgments of Injustice' (2001) 9 *The Journal of Political Philosophy* 1–18, 2. It is precisely the failure to take this into account which leads to the ultimate vacuity of luck egalitarianism.

this unequal condition. It is the causes and consequences of some pattern of inequality, rather than the pattern itself, that raises issues of justice. If the causes of an inequality lie in the uncoerced and considered decisions of the less well-off persons, for example, then the inequality is probably not unjust [this the central belief of luck egalitarians] . . . A large set of the causes of an unequal distribution of resources or unequal opportunities between individuals, however, is attributable neither to individual preferences and choices nor to luck or accident [but to] . . . social institutions, their rules and relations, and the decisions others make within them that affect the lives of the individuals compared.[104]

Structural factors including 'the legal system's definition of basic rights and duties, market relations, the system of property in the means of production[,] . . . family organization [and] the basic kinds of positions in the social division of labor . . . condition [people's] opportunities and life chances' and 'Structural social groups are constituted through the social organization of labor and production, the organization of desire and sexuality, the institutionalized rules of authority and subordination and the constitution of prestige'.[105] This is not to suggest that social structures exist 'independent of social actors'.[106] Nor is it to deny individual agency. It is, rather, to point out that life choices are constrained by social and economic contexts. Recognition of this means that patterns of difference in the outcomes experienced by those in different social groups, whether those differences concern resources, access to political or other forms of power, health and well-being or other forms of flourishing, have ethical significance which is not so readily attributable to differences which may be identified between individuals considered in abstraction from their membership of relevant social groups.

In Chapter 2 I made reference to Michael Walzer's theory of 'complex equality', and to Young's use of that theory to suggest that the groups to which inequality analysis ought to have regard are those whose members experience systemic or structural disadvantage. Young goes on to posit that:

If some individuals command more respect or deference than others because of their class or ethnic background, their occupational position, their gender behavior, and so on, institutions and interactions are grouping them as different from others in relevant respects. When these differentiations align with several axes of privilege, we have broad social groups.[107]

When a person complains of being the victim of/arbitrary search because he is Black, we do not need to know very much about how this person defines his Black identity, or whether he does so at all. A person does not even need to identify herself as a lesbian, to take another example, to find her identity diminished or her person threatened by other people who so identify her.

---

[104] ibid, 8.
[105] ibid, 12.
[106] ibid, 13.
[107] ibid, 4.

Acknowledging the relevance of social groups to questions of equality thus does not entail the reification of such groups or the reduction of individuals identified by reference to membership of them to a single facet of their identity. Recognition of the importance of religious affiliation to life chances in Northern Ireland, at least until the very recent past, does not, for example, require the treatment of those of Northern Irish Catholic descent as a disadvantaged group in Britain today in the context of employment, for example, housing or education, any more than recognising the disadvantage, relative to male colleagues, that a female merchant banker may suffer requires her to be regarded as generally disadvantaged in the employment market or elsewhere. As Young points out, '[c]omparison of groups is [nonetheless] necessary to judge inequalities unjust because doing so helps show that different individuals have different opportunities and inhibitions related to their structural social positions',[108] this being as true where the inequality at issue consists in a gender pay gap between highly paid bankers as where it consists in differences in life expectancy between groups defined by reference to ethnicity.

The pragmatic approach to groups advocated by Young avoids the problem highlighted by Richard Thompson Ford, that 'the idea of the natural group and its associated practices too often functions to discipline and regulate individuals' by encouraging members of the 'group' to adopt practices or behaviour associated with the group, 'and only slightly more subtly to censure [members] who fail to exhibit the prescribed behavior'.[109] Ford cites the example of Anita Hill, whose accusations of sexual harassment against then Supreme Court nominee Clarence Thomas were characterised by sociologist Orlando Patterson as

'unfair and disingenuous' because although the comments were 'completely out of the *cultural* frame of his white, upper-middle-class/work world' they were 'immediately recognizable to Hill and most women of southern working-class backgrounds, especially the latter' . . . 'as a way of affirming their common origins'.[110]

As Ford points out:

Not only is Hill told that she must forbear Thomas's behavior because it is *his* culture – she is also told she must embrace it because it is *her* culture as well . . . she is told that she *does* in fact embrace it; that she 'perfectly understands' it and that her objections to it and disclaimers of it are therefore 'disingenuous'.[111]

[108] ibid, 17.

[109] RT Ford, 'Unnatural Groups: A Reaction to Owen Fiss's 'Groups and the Equal Protection Clause' (2002) 2(1) *Issues in Legal Scholarship*. Thus 'those concerned about the authenticity of cultural practices might best serve their cause by resisting the natural group idea and the positivistic description of group culture it reflects'.

[110] ibid, 9–10, citing *St Petersburg Times* 22 October 1991, 11A 'Thomas hearings can help us reassess views of race and sex'.

[111] Ford (n 109) 10, emphasis in original.

ANTI-ESSENTIALIST ASYMMETRY

It is possible on the one hand to reject the reification of 'groups' and on the other hand to make strategic use of the concept in the context of equality/non-discrimination. To use an example put forward by Kenneth Karst, while 'The idea of a binary system dividing the world into 'gay' and 'straight' persons is ludicrous . . . the Boy Scouts has no trouble in drawing just such a line'[112] (this a reference to the *Boy Scouts of America v Dale*,[113] in which the organisation's right to discriminate on grounds of sexual orientation was affirmed by the Supreme Court). In other words, discrimination connected with minority sexual orientation can be addressed regardless of whether sexual orientation is fixed, immutable or even particularly meaningful as a concept. Difficulties can arise in defining groups for the purposes of (for example) carving out religious exemptions to the application of laws (whether, controversially, anti-discrimination laws or, perhaps less so, requirements for the wearing of motor cycle helmets or hard hats on construction sites).[114] But for the purposes of considering asymmetric approaches to discrimination, the contingent recognition of groups does not require the ossification of individuals into fixed, homogeneous and/or immutable collectives. It can, rather, provide a counterweight to classifications which serve in practice to disadvantage those characterised, whether by themselves or others, by reference to particular factors ('actual' or perceived). One does not have to share the racist ideology of the South African apartheid system to suggest that those categorised as 'Black', 'Indian' or 'Coloured' by that system can be recognised as such,[115] for example for the purposes of 'remedial or restitutionary equality'.[116]

The question of groups is returned to in Chapter 5, in which I consider the tensions which may arise between individual rights, equality and the recognition of group membership. Here it is sufficient to say, however, that the adoption of an asymmetric approach to the regulation of discrimination does not require the recognition of bounded groups, much less the provision of rights to such groups (or to their members in virtue of their membership). Recognition, for example, that discrimination against women is endemic in the workplace, or that many people regarded as ethnically 'other' by the majority are disadvantaged in work, access to goods and services, housing and education, does not depend on essentialising women or those of minority ethnicity, much less on seeing them as inhabiting only (particular) 'group' identity. The same is true of recognising that gay men and lesbian women often find themselves viewed

---

[112] K Karst, 'Sources of Status-harm and Group Disadvantage in Private Behavior' (2002) 2(1) *Issues in Legal Scholarship*.

[113] *Boy Scouts of America v Dale* 530 US 640 (2000).

[114] See further Chapter 5.

[115] Or at any rate as having been classified as such.

[116] See discussion above of *Minister of Finance and Other v Van Heerden* (n 39).

uni-dimensionally, by reference solely or predominantly to their sexual orientation rather than, for example, their family status and/or their religious or political beliefs and, by reason of this, are denied recognition as fully human. These
acts of recognition, however, permit an approach to equality/discrimination
which allows, and may require, such elements of disadvantage to be addressed
without requiring equivalent attention to be paid to the 'me too' protests of
those who are, in the particular context, advantaged by their ethnicity, sexual
orientation, gender or other relevant characteristic.

CONCLUSION

All this is not to say that there is no room for symmetry, even for a predisposi-
tion towards symmetry, in the context of a detailed statutory scheme such as
that exemplified by the Equality Act 2010. There is much to be said, for the most
part, for attempting to remove consideration of characteristics such as sex, race
and sexual orientation from decisions about recruitment, promotion, bank
loans, tenancies, access to public services, membership of golf clubs and so on.
And preferential treatment intended to ameliorate existing disadvantage may, if
carelessly designed or thoughtlessly pursued, trigger resentment and devalue the
achievements of those identifiable by reference to characteristics associated with
disadvantage, whether or not they are the beneficiaries of such treatment. It is
also obviously the case that the elimination of patterns of discrimination within
organisations against persons with particular characteristics is a logically prior
step to targeting preferential recruitment measures at others with those characteristics. There was an air of absurdity in the Metropolitan Police's lobbying in
2004 to be permitted to 'fast track' BME recruits into the force in order to meet
the government target of 25 per cent BME officers by 2009,[117] a mere seven
months after a protest at Scotland Yard by hundreds of BME police officers and
civilian workers about alleged race discrimination within the Met[118] and eight
months before Sir Bill Morris's investigation into professional standards and
employment matters in the Met reported, inter alia, that BME officers were disproportionately likely to be subjected to conduct investigations and formal disciplinary procedures.[119]

---

[117] 'Met plan to fast track black recruits' *Guardian*, 17 April 2004. According to the Home Office
Annual Statistics, BME strength in the Met had increased to only 10.1% by 31 March 2012 (www.
homeoffice.gov.uk/publications/science-research-statistics/research-statistics/police-research/
hosb0912/).

[118] 'Black police to march on Yard in protest at alleged discrimination' *Guardian*, 29 September
2003.

[119] *The Case for Change: People in the Metropolitan Police Service* (available at www.policeau-
thority.org/Metropolitan/downloads/scrutinites/morris/morris-report.pdf), para 5.67. In May 2005,
a report released under the Freedom of Information Act noted that, within the Met, 'Black and
minority ethnic recruit retention rates continue to improve, increasing this month by 2.35% to
88.80%'. This compared with a retention rate of non-black and minority ethnic recruits of 96.4%:
www.met.police.uk/foi/pdfs/priorities_and_how_we_are_doing/archive/2005/hr_scorecard_

Positive discrimination is capable of misuse. But it also has the potential to assist real social change. One generally accepted success story is the US military, which was segregated on racial lines until 1948, with all-black units continuing to exist until 1954, and which by 1989 boasted African American Colin Powell as Chairman of the Joint Chiefs of Staff. A group of retired US military generals and admirals filed an *amicus* brief in the *University of Texas* case, arguing that any overruling of *Grutter* would put at risk the diverse military leadership which they said was necessary to national security.[120] And in Northern Ireland, where the pre-2000 police force (the Royal Ulster Constabulary) was over 90 per cent Protestant/Unionist, and was seen by many as a 'Protestant police force for a Protestant people', positive discrimination has been successfully used to ensure that the RUC's successor, the Police Service of Northern Ireland, is more broadly reflective of the community (which was about 40 per cent Catholic in 2000). The Police (Northern Ireland) Act 2000, by which the Police Service of Northern Ireland (PSNI) was established, provided that 50 per cent of trainee officers recruited were to be from a Catholic background (and 50 per cent from a non-Catholic background), this to continue until the service was 35 per cent Catholic. While this approach was not universally popular, and required the negotiation of a special exception in Council Directive 2000/78 (Art 15), it had the effect of increasing Catholic participation to just under 30 per cent in 2011 (among support staff, where affirmative action measures were used only in larger recruitment exercises, Catholics accounted for 18 per cent).[121]

My purpose in this chapter has been to challenge the tendency to assume that anything other than a symmetrical approach represents (at least in relation to protected characteristics other than disability) a departure from the ideal. If it is such a departure, it is one required and justified by the inequalities in starting positions which characterise the competition for many of life's advantages. Recognition of those inequalities, and of the tendency for equal treatment of the unequally situated to exacerbate, rather than challenge, inequality ought to do much to defuse the unease which characterises domestic discussions of 'positive discrimination'.

Having said all of this, the implementation of the PSED in Great Britain has begun to initiate some movement away from a rigidly symmetrical approach to equality/discrimination even where what is statutorily framed as 'positive action' (ss 158 and 159) is not at issue. The PSED is contained, with the 'positive action' provisions, in Part 11 of the Act, which is entitled 'Advancement of Equality'. The decision of Moses LJ in *Kaur & Shah*, a PSED case brought under the RRA, was mentioned above. His Lordship's approach to the concept

---

may_2005.pdf. The scorecard rated retention rates as amber, and recorded a red ('progress is behind schedule or high risk that objective/target will not be achieved within the given timescale') against BME to non-BME officer resignations.

[120] Mark Thompson, 'Military Affirming College Affirmative Action' *Time US*, 22 August 2012.

[121] www.psni.police.uk/directory/updates/updates_statistics.htm. The figures on this page are updated regularly so at the time of writing the reported statistics are from May 2013.

of equality was focused in that case on section 35 RRA rather than the PSED. More recently, there have been a number of other examples of judicial movement away from a fixation on symmetrical treatment. Section 149(1), which imposes the PSED, provides that each public authority 'must, in the exercise of its functions, have due regard to' three distinct statutory needs, that is:

(a) the need to 'eliminate discrimination, harassment, victimisation and any other conduct that is prohibited by or under this Act';
(b) the need to 'advance equality of opportunity between persons who share a relevant protected characteristic and persons who do not share it'; and
(c) the need to 'foster good relations between persons who share a relevant protected characteristic and persons who do not share it'.

Section 149(3) goes on to provide in terms that:

Having due regard to the need to advance equality of opportunity between persons who share a relevant protected characteristic and persons who do not share it involves having due regard, in particular, to the need to –

(a) remove or minimise disadvantages suffered by persons who share a relevant protected characteristic that are connected to that characteristic;
(b) take steps to meet the needs of persons who share a relevant protected characteristic that are different from the needs of persons who do not share it;
(c) encourage persons who share a relevant protected characteristic to participate in public life or in any other activity in which participation by such persons is disproportionately low.

Section 149(3) reflects the predecessor disability duty which required (s 49A DDA) that:

(1) Every public authority shall in carrying out its functions have due regard to –
(a) the need to eliminate discrimination that is unlawful under this Act
. . .
(c) the need to promote equality of opportunity between disabled persons and other persons; [and]
(d) the need to take steps to take account of disabled persons disabilities, even where that involves treating disabled persons more favourably that other persons . . .

In R (Brown) v Secretary of State for Work and Pensions (2009) the High Court stated that, in order to satisfy section 49A, an authority 'will, in our view, have to have due regard to the need to take steps to gather relevant information in order that it can properly take steps to take into account disabled persons' disabilities in the context of the particular function under consideration'.[122] That dictum has been followed in a number of cases including R (JM) v Isle of Wight Council (2011) in which Laing J ruled that 'When carrying out their functions, public authorities must have "due regard" to six "needs" identified in [s 49A

---

[122] R (Brown) v Secretary of State for Work and Pensions [2009] PTSR 1506, para 85.

DDA]. Each "need" represents a particular goal, which if achieved, would further the overall goal of the disability legislation'. [123] It follows from section 149(3) that public authorities may breach the PSED by failing to pay due regard to the statutory needs to remove or minimise disadvantage, address unduly low levels of participation and meet needs associated with protected characteristics other than disability.

Of particular significance here are a couple of recent decisions in Article 14 challenges in the domestic courts. The cases, *Burnip v Birmingham City Council* (2012) and *R (Knowles) v SSWP* (2013), are discussed in Chapter 4.[124] Their significance in the present context lies in their application in domestic law of the ECtHR decision in *Thlimmenos v Greece* in which (see further Chapter 4) that Court ruled that Article 14 ECHR was breached not only by the unjustified differential treatment of those in similar situations, but also by the unjustified *failure* to treat differently those whose situations were relevantly dissimilar.[125]

In *Burnip* this approach was applied to a case in which the claimants, who were disabled, challenged a failure by the state to recognise their disability-related additional needs concerning accommodation in imposing a 'bedroom tax' (that is, penalising those in receipt of housing benefit for occupying accommodation larger than was regarded as necessary on the basis of family size). That decision was significant, in particular, for its recognition of the domestic effect of the UN Convention on the Rights of Persons with Disabilities. As far as positive discrimination is concerned it is of less note given the asymmetric approach of domestic law to disability discrimination and the well-recognised duties to treat persons with disabilities *more* favourably than others (in particular, by making reasonable adjustments).[126] In *Knowles*, however, the *Thlimmenos* analysis was applied in a case in which it was argued that a failure to treat Gypsies/Travellers differently (and more favourably) than others breached Article 14 read in the light of the *Thlimmenos* decision. The claim failed, because the claimants failed to establish that they were significantly disadvantaged, as Gypsies/Travellers, by being treated the same as others, and because the failure by the state to ameliorate such disadvantage as was established was regarded as justified on the facts. Had the decision on justification gone the other way, however, what would have been required would have been tantamount to positive discrimination in favour of Gypsies/Travellers.

The PSED was not argued in *Burnip* or in *Knowles*. In *R (Bracking) v SSWP* (2013), however, Blake J accepted that the terms of the UN Convention on the Rights of People with Disabilities might require to be considered as part of the PSED.[127] This entailed reading the PSED in light of Article 14, and Article 14 in

---

[123] *R (JM) v Isle of Wight Council* [2011] EWHC 2911 (Admin), para 96.

[124] *Burnip v Birmingham City Council* [2012] LGR 954; *R (Knowles) v SSWP* [2013] EWHC 19 (Admin).

[125] *Thlimmenos v Greece* (2001) 31 EHRR 411, para 44.

[126] Equality Act 2010, s 20 and see also DDA, s 49A(3)(d).

[127] *R (Bracking) v SSWP* [2013] EWHC 897 (Admin), paras 54–55.

light of the Convention (see further the discussion of *Burnip* in Chapter 4). And in *R (MA & Ors) v SSWP* (2013) the Divisional Court accepted, in a case in which *Thlimmenos* discrimination and a breach of the PSED were pleaded, that (similar treatment of different cases having been established) the question of justification was bound up with the question whether the PSED had been fulfilled.[128] The particular focus of the PSED argument in that case was on the statutory duty to pay due regard to the need to eliminate discrimination. There is no reason why, in another case, however, a failure to pay due regard to the second PSED limb (the need to promote equality of opportunity by, in a particular case, 'remov[ing] or minimis[ing] disadvantages suffered by persons who share a relevant protected characteristic that are connected to that characteristic', or 'tak[ing] steps to meet the needs of persons who share a relevant protected characteristic that are different from the needs of persons who do not share it').[129] If this were the case, a failure by a public authority at least to consider positive discrimination may result in a breach of the PSED as well as of Article 14.

---

[128] *R (MA & Ors) v SSWP* [2013] EWHC 2213 (Admin).
[129] Equality Act 2010, s 149(3)(a)–(b).

4

The Evolution of Equality Law[1]

INTRODUCTION

IN CHAPTER 2 I SUGGESTED that one of the barriers to an adequate legal response to multiple discrimination (that is, to discrimination resulting from the combination or intersection of protected characteristics) is the identification of the comparator on which successful discrimination claims frequently depend. The concept of equality is of its nature concerned to some extent with comparison; consideration of whether persons have been treated equally, or with equal concern and respect, whether they have been provided with equal opportunities, or with equal access to human flourishing, all require some comparative evaluation. The business of comparison, however, generates its own conceptual and practical difficulties. As to the former, it is difficult to do comparison without explicitly or implicitly accepting one of the persons or things compared as the 'norm', and assessing the other's entitlement to equal treatment, respect, outcomes etc, on the basis of the degree of fit they exhibit to the norm, that is, their measure of Aristotelian 'likeness'. This is the problem identified by Catherine MacKinnon who has criticised (in the context of sex) 'the white male standard in neutral disguise, the fist of dominance in the glove of equality . . .'[2] 'Why,' MacKinnon demands, 'should anyone have to be like white men to get what they have, given that white men do not have to be like anyone except each other to have it?'[3] Further, since 'women' have been defined by men

> as different to the extent that they are female, can women be entitled to equal treatment only to the extent that they are not women? Why is equality as consistent with systematic advantage as with systematic disadvantage, so long as both correlate with differences?[4]

[1] Elements of this Chapter were previously published in A McColgan, 'Cracking the Comparator Problem, "Equal" Treatment and the Role of Comparisons' [2006] *European Human Rights Law Review* 650–77.

[2] C MacKinnon, 'Reflections on Sex Equality Under the Law' (1990–91) 100 *Yale Law Journal* 1281, 1297 and see Lucinda Finley, 'Transcending Equality Theory: A Way Out of the Maternity and the Workplace Debate' (1986) 86 *Columbia Law Review* 1118, 1154–6: 'In our society, that power has always been held by white men [who] . . . have defined desirable human traits in their own image, according to their own world view.. The role of men in defining the standard of normalcy and in assigning significance to female differences, means that the whole premise of our equality jurisprudence is whatever is male is the norm'.

[3] ibid (MacKinnon) 1287.

[4] ibid.

Among the practical problems in which the comparison-based approach to equality results is the difficulty the judiciary has had in the UK, as well as in Canada and the US, in recognising gender-specific disadvantages imposed on women as 'equality' issues. As MacKinnon puts it:

> Because the 'similarly situated' requirement continues to control access to equality claims, the laws of sexual assault and reproductive control – areas as crucial in the social construction of women's inferior status as they are laden with misogyny – have not been seen as amenable to constitutional sex equality attack . . . gender comparisons are . . . unavailable or strained. So sexuality and procreation become happy differences or unhappy differences but never imposed inequalities.[5]

Conditioning equal treatment on 'likeness', however defined, functions so as to grant less privileged actors access to the benefits enjoyed by the more privileged only to the extent that the former can prove 'sameness' with the latter. Domestic equal pay legislation and the Part-time Workers Regulations 2000, for example, require that women (who constitute the bulk of equal pay claimants and the large majority of part-time workers) are treated like men to the extent that they are similar in terms of the nature (or at least value) of the jobs they perform, and the workplaces in which and the employers for whom they work.[6] But much of the disadvantage suffered by women, and by part-time workers in particular, stems precisely from the fact that they are *not* like men in the relevant respects. And to the extent that that lack of likeness is associated with discriminatory treatment (in the sense of treatment related to sex), it is immune from challenge under legislation which adopts this comparator requirement. Such legislation has little to offer to women who are subject to disadvantage by virtue of uniquely, predominantly or stereotypically 'female' characteristics or behaviour.[7]

Questions of comparison have loomed large in the domestic case law concerning both the interpretation of the statutory discrimination provisions and, more recently, Article 14 of the ECHR, bedevilling early attempts to fit pregnancy discrimination within the statutorily prohibited 'sex discrimination',[8] and threatening to straitjacket judicial approaches to Article 14.[9] The 'comparator question' has also, on occasion, troubled the CJEU (formerly the ECJ) and the ECtHR.

In *Hlozek v Roche Austria Gesellschaft mbH* (2004), for example, the ECJ held that a 54-year-old man was not comparably situated with a 54-year-old woman for the purposes of a challenge to a bridging allowance paid to dismissed workers who had reached the age of 50 (in the case of women) or 55 (in

---

[5] ibid, 1297.

[6] Though the Equality Act 2010 allows a narrow challenge to directly discriminatory pay and contractual terms even absent an actual comparator.

[7] The Equality Act requires an indirect pay discrimination challenge to be made by reference to an actual male comparator.

[8] See discussion in A McColgan, *Discrimination: Text, Cases and Materials*, 2nd edn (Oxford: Hart Publishing, 1995) 491–500.

[9] See *Wandsworth London Borough Council v Michalak* [2003] 1 WLR 617.

the case of men), where the domestic state pension age was 65 in the case of men and 60 for women.[10] Article 141 TEC (now Article 157 TFEU), which prohibited sex discrimination in pay (including pensions), did not permit an overt ruling of justified differential payment on grounds of sex but the ECJ declared that 'the principle of equal pay, like the general principle of non-discrimination which it embodies in a specific form, presupposes that the men and women to whom it applies are in identical or comparable situations', and ruled that men who were dismissed aged 50–54 were 'not in a situation that is identical or comparable to that of women in the same age group' because of their different proximity to state retirement age and associated risks of long-term unemployment.[11] In *James v Eastleigh* (1990), by contrast, the House of Lords had ruled that a local authority policy of providing free access to its leisure facilities to those of state pensionable age discriminated directly on grounds of sex against the claimant, a man aged 61, because he was charged for entry to the authority's swimming pool whereas his wife, also aged 61, was not.[12] In response to the local authority's argument that the claimant and his wife were not similarly situated because she had, and he had not, reached state pensionable age (then 60 in the case of women and 65 for men) Lord Bridge, with whom Lords Goff and Ackner agreed, ruled that:

> Because pensionable age is itself discriminatory it cannot be treated as a relevant circumstance in making a comparison . . . the relevant circumstance which was the same here for the purpose of comparing the treatment of the plaintiff and his wife was that they were both aged 61.[13]

The comparator question has presented occasional difficulties for those challenging discrimination under Article 14 ECHR. In *Shackell v United Kingdom* (2000), for example, the ECtHR rejected a complaint that British social security legislation discriminated against an unmarried surviving partner by denying her entitlement to widows' benefits on her partner's death on the basis that unmarried and married couples were not in analogous situations because of 'in particular, differences in legal status and legal effects'.[14]

David Feldman has pointed out that

> The way the court approaches it is not to look for identity of position between different cases, but to ask whether the applicant and the people who are treated differently are in 'analogous' situations. This will to some extent depend on whether there is an objective and reasonable justification for the difference in treatment, which overlaps

---

[10] Case C-19/02 *Hlozek v Roche Austria Gesellschaft mbH* [2004] ECR I-11491.

[11] Similarly see Case 342/93 *Gillespie v Northern Health and Social Services Board* [1996] ECR I-475 and Case 218/98, *Abdoulaye v Régie Nationale des Usines Renault* [1999] ECR I-5723. A similar approach has on occasion been adopted by the domestic courts (see in particular *Dhatt v MacDonalds Hamburgers Ltd* [1991] 1 WLR 527) despite its rejection by the House of Lords in *James v Eastleigh BC* [1990] 2 AC 751, discussed below.

[12] *James v Eastleigh* [1990] 2 AC 751.

[13] ibid, para 13.

[14] *Shackell v United Kingdom* App no 45851/99, citing the Commission's decision in *Lindsay v UK* (1986) DR 49.

with the questions about the acceptability of the ground and the justifiability of the difference in treatment. That is why, as van Dijk and van Hoof observe, and 'in most instances of the Strasbourg case law . . . the comparability test is glossed over, and the emphasis is (almost) completely on the justification test'.[15]

In *AL (Serbia) v SSHD*, in which Lady Hale declared that 'in only a handful of cases has the court found that the persons with whom the complainant wishes to compare himself are not in a relevantly similar or analogous position (around 4.5%)',[16] she suggested that 'the classic Strasbourg statements of the law do not place any emphasis on the identification of an exact comparator [but] ask whether differences in otherwise similar situations justify a different treatment'.[17] There have, nevertheless, been a number of ECtHR decisions, including the Grand Chamber decisions in *Burden v United Kingdom* and *Carson v United Kingdom*,[18] which have explicitly turned on the (lack of) similarity between the applicants and relevant comparators.

The tendency of courts faced with questions of discrimination/equality to demand 'likeness' as a threshold criterion is unsurprising,[19] though it tends to overlook the second limb of Aristotle's approach to equality: that 'things that are unalike should be treated unalike in proportion to their unalikeness'.[20] But the shortcomings of what is frequently described as the 'formal' approach to equality have long been clear, as is clear from the discussion in Chapter 1 of *Powell v Pennsylvania* (1888)[21] in which the US Supreme Court rejected a challenge to the differential treatment of margarine and butter sellers on the basis that the sellers of margarine and butter were different.[22] Tussman and tenBroek criticised the decision on the basis that 'like' 'cannot mean simply 'similar in the possession of the classifying trait'. 'All members of any class are similarly situated in this respect and consequently any classification whatsoever would be reasonable by this test' (as in *Powell*). This approach ignored the very substance of the complaint: that the manufacturers of margarine were subject to restrictions that manufacturers of butter were not. As Tussman and tenBroek went on to point out, 'By the same token a law applying to red-haired makers of margarine would satisfy the requirements of equality'.[23]

---

[15] D Feldman, *Civil Liberties and Human Rights in England and Wales*, 2nd edn (Oxford: Oxford University Press, 2002) 144, cited by Lord Walker in *Carson v SSWP* [2006] 1 AC 173, para 65.

[16] *AL (Serbia) v SSHD* [2008] 1 WLR 1434, para 25.

[17] ibid, paras 23–24.

[18] The decisions of the section and Grand Chamber respectively in *Burden v UK* and in *Carson v UK* are at (2007) 44 EHRR 51 and (2008) 47 EHRR 38, (2009) 48 EHRR 41 and (2010) 51 EHRR 13.

[19] For an indication of the strength of this tendency see *LB Lewisham v Malcolm* [2008] 1 AC 1399 in which the House of Lords insisted on applying a 'similarly situated' approach to a form of discrimination expressly designed to operate other than by way of such a comparator requirement.

[20] *Ethica Nicomachea* V.3 1131a–b (W Ross trans, 1925). Also his recognition that the 'difficult problem' posed by the 'like cases alike' question is 'Equals and unequals in *what*?': see Elisa Holmes, 'Anti-Discrimination Rights Without Equality' (2005) 68 *Modern Law Review* 175, 179.

[21] *Powell v Pennsylvania* (1888) 127 US 678.

[22] J Tussman and J tenBroek, 'The Equal Protection of the Laws' (1949) 37 *California Law Review* 341.

[23] ibid, 345.

Distinguishing between the manufacturers of margarine and those of butter may or may not be defensible. The difficulty with the 'like cases alike' approach, as it was applied in *Powell*, is that it operates to prevent any substantive engagement with the justifiability of distinctions drawn between such manufacturers (or, indeed, between red-haired and other makers of margarine).[24] In *Andrews v Law Society of British Columbia*, in which the Supreme Court of Canada first considered the approach to be taken to section 15 of Canada's Charter of Rights, the Court stated that equality was a comparative concept which could 'only be attained or discerned by comparison with the condition of others in the social and political setting in which the question arises',[25] but that the interpretation of section 15 to require only that 'persons who are "similarly situated be similarly treated" and conversely, that persons who are "differently situated be differently treated"[26] [was] . . . seriously deficient in that it excludes any consideration of the nature of the law'. As Oddný Mjöll Arnardóttir has put it:

> [T]he questions of comparability formulated in the question: 'who are equal/unequal?' are really posed at the level where the value judgments governing equality analysis take place. Otherwise they can only be answered with reference to the equality maxim as: 'those who should receive equal/unequal treatment'. . .[27]

The observation of McIntyre J of the Canadian Supreme Court that the ' "similarly situated" test applied literally . . . could be used to justify the Nuremberg laws of Adolf Hitler' which contemplated 'Similar treatment . . . for all Jews' was mentioned in Chapter 1. That test would also 'have justified the formalistic separate but equal doctrine of *Plessy v Ferguson*' (1896), in which the US Supreme Court provided the imprimatur of judicial approval to racial segregation in the US, and which was relied upon by the British Columbia Court of Appeal in *R v Gonzales* (1962) to uphold a legislative provision criminalising the possession, other than within reserves, by Indians of intoxicants against challenge under the equality provision of the Charter of Right's predecessor Bill of Rights.[28] McIntyre J went on in *Andrews* to agree with the statement of Kerans JA in *Mahe v Government of Alberta* (1987) that the 'like cases alike' approach

> accepts an idea of equality which is almost mechanical, with no scope for considering the *reason* for the distinction. In consequence, subtleties are found to justify a finding of dissimilarity which reduces the test to a categorization game. Moreover, the test is not helpful. After all, most laws are enacted for the specific purpose of offering a benefit or imposing a burden on some persons and not on others. The test catches every conceivable difference in legal treatment (emphasis added).[29]

---

[24] See similarly the criticism made by the Court of Appeal in *Aston Cantlow v Wallbank* [2002] Ch 51 of the High Court's reasoning in that case (para 50, *per* Sir Andrew Morritt VC).

[25] [1989] 1 SCR 143, 164.

[26] Citing McLachlin J (as she then was) in the Court of Appeal.

[27] O Arnardóttir, *Equality and Non-discrimination under the European Convention on Human Rights* (Leiden: Martinus Nijhoff Publishers, 2003) 84–85.

[28] *Plessy v Ferguson* 163 US 637 (1896); *R v Gonzales* 132 CCC 237 (1962).

[29] *Mahe v Government of Alberta* (1987) 54 Alta LR (2d) 212, 244, cited by McIntyre J.

Peter Westen claimed, in a much-cited 1982 article[30], that the idea of treating like alike was vacuous because it did not contain any basis on which to determine 'likeness' and that 'equality is entirely "Circular" . . . an empty vessel with no substantive moral content of its own . . .':

> Once one determines that two people are alike for purposes of the equality principle, one knows how they ought to be treated . . . [But] categories of morally alike people do not exist in nature; moral alikeness is established only when people define categories. To say that people are morally alike is therefore to articulate a moral standard of treatment – a standard or rule specifying certain treatment for certain people – by reference to which they are, and thus are to be treated, alike.[31]

Others have attempted to rescue the 'like cases alike' principle by suggesting that the 'more plausible interpretation of the principle of formal equality . . . is that legislative distinctions must be relevant to the purposes of the law'. [32] The requirement for 'legislative rationality (if not reasonableness) . . . combined with constitutional principles that impose limits on the purposes legislation might legitimately pursue' [33] would impose limits on discriminatory legislation, many advocates of the 'relevance' test appearing to assume that some differences will never (or almost never) prevent a finding of 'likeness', whether as a matter of policy or because (perhaps in turn as a matter of policy) they are deemed to be never (or almost never) relevant to treatment,[34] with the effect that those who are marked only by these differences must nevertheless be regarded as 'like' for the purposes of equality comparisons. There is at present, for example, a general presumption that bare differences of 'race' will almost never make people relevantly different for the purposes of the entitlement to be treated in like fashion. The same assumption is probably made about differences of sex *as such* (though not, as we see below from the relevant litigation on the matter, sex-specific differences associated with pregnancy). Other grounds of distinction are seen as largely or entirely unproblematic, and therefore as potentially relevant to the determination of (un)'like'ness.[35]

DOMESTIC LAW

A requirement for a 'similarly situated' comparator may be hard-wired into a statutory provision, as in the case of the Equal Pay Act 1970 which required, as

[30] P Westen, 'The Empty Idea of Equality' (1982) 95 *Harvard Law Review* 537, 547–51, footnotes omitted.

[31] ibid, 543–45.

[32] See M Gold, 'The Canadian Concept of Equality' (1996) 46 *University of Toronto Law Journal* 349, 352.

[33] ibid. See also D Gibson, 'Equality for Some' (1991) 40 *University of British Columbia Law Journal* 2, 10–11.

[34] See *McLaughlin v Florida* 379 US 184, 192 (1964); *Cleburne Living Ctr* 473 US 432, 440 (1985); Tussman and tenBroek (n 22) 355–56; S Goldberg, 'Equality without Tiers' (2003–04) 77 *Southern California Law Review* 481, 538.

[35] See further discussion at 110–17 below.

a condition of success in a challenge to sex-based pay disparities, that the claimant point to a person of the opposite sex who was engaged in comparable work (like work, work rated as equivalent by a job evaluation scheme or work of equal value), and who was (contemporaneously) employed by the same or an associated employer at the same establishment as the claimant or at a different establishment at which similar terms and conditions apply.[36] The role of the comparator was there, as it is today in the Part-time Workers Regulations and the Fixed Term Employee Regulations, to limit the application of the principle of non-discrimination/equal treatment, permitting a successful claim only by reference to strictly defined 'others' regardless of whether a claimant has in a broader sense been the victim even of malign and deliberate mistreatment related to his or her sex, part-time or fixed-term status.[37]

Other than in its 'equal pay' provisions the Equality Act 2010, like its predecessor statutes, makes no express reference to the role of comparators in establishing discrimination, requiring instead (in the case of direct discrimination other than in the case of pregnancy) less favourable treatment (which implies a comparison) and providing that comparisons must be such that 'there must be no material difference between the circumstances relating to each case'.[38] In the case of indirect discrimination the pools by reference to which the impact of a disputed provision criterion or practice are to be measured must be selected according to the same criteria.

The comparator requirement in the 2010 Act is materially identical to that which was found in the Act's predecessor provisions. At least prior to the decision of the House of Lords in *Shamoon v Chief Constable of the Royal Ulster Constabulary* (2003),[39] the courts frequently adopted a two-stage approach to determining whether actionable discrimination had occurred, considering first whether the claimant had received less favourable treatment than an appropriate comparator (real or hypothetical) and, second, whether the less favourable treatment was on the relevant protected ground. As Lord Nicholls pointed out in *Shamoon*, although this approach could be useful it was not required by statute and could produce unnecessary complications where the identity of the relevant comparator was a matter of dispute.

Examples of such complications have included the characteristics to be ascribed to a male comparator for a sex discrimination claim based on pregnancy,[40] and to a non-Indian comparator for the purposes of a race discrimination claim by a person of Indian nationality, who was entitled by virtue

---

[36] Section 1(2) and (6) Equal Pay Act 1970. The Equality Act 2010 preserves this type of claim but, as mentioned, also allows direct sex discrimination in pay to be challenged without reference to an actual comparator

[37] The regulations *in addition* require that the claimant establish that the less favourable treatment complained of is on the ground that the claimant is a part-time worker or fixed-term employee (Regs 5(2) and 3(3) respectively).

[38] Equality Act 2010, s 23.

[39] *Shamoon v Chief Constable of the Royal Ulster Constabulary* [2003] ICR 337.

[40] No longer necessary as a result of statutory amendments necessary to comply with EU law.

of his immigration status to work without restriction in the UK.[41] Lord Nicholls stated in *Shamoon* that the single question which the court was in fact required to answer in a claim of direct discrimination was whether the claimant was treated less favourably on the protected ground,[42] and that 'arid and confusing' disputes about the identification of the appropriate comparator might be avoided by a primary focus on the reason for the treatment complained of, consideration of whether this treatment was 'less favourable' being held over until after the reason for the treatment had been determined. If treatment was on grounds (now because) of a protected characteristic there will usually be no difficulty in deciding whether such treatment was less favourable than that which was or would have been afforded to others. If it was not, no question of comparators would arise.

Comparators may of course play a useful role in assisting to establish the reason for the less favourable treatment complained of, any differences between the claimant and comparator suggesting a possible explanation other than the protected characteristic for the treatment complained of. In the *Shamoon* case itself, the actual comparators relied upon were flawed by the absence of any complaints against them: the removal from the claimant of her appraisal role might have been the result of the complaints against her rather than the fact of her sex. This is not to say, however, that any difference between the claimant and her comparator must be fatal to the claim.

As Lord Scott recognised in *Shamoon*, evidential comparators 'are no more than tools which may or may not justify an inference of discrimination on the relevant prohibited ground . . . The more significant the difference or differences, the less cogent will be the case for drawing the requisite inference'.[43] The treatment accorded to a comparator whose material circumstances differed from those of the claimant could still, however, 'in conjunction with other material, justify the tribunal in drawing the inference that the victim was treated less favourably than she would have been treated if she had been' a man. If, for example, a local authority denied planning permission to a Muslim applicant who wished to extend his house, and did so *because* he was Muslim,[44] it would be no answer to a race discrimination claim that the unsuccessful applicant and his neighbour, to whom planning permission for a similar extension had been granted, were 'unlike' in terms of other factors, even where the authority could in principle have based a planning decision on them. The existence of differ-

---

[41] *Dhatt v McDonalds Hamburgers Ltd* (n 11) .

[42] Post-Equality Act 2010, 'because of' the protected characteristic.

[43] *Shamoon v Chief Constable of the Royal Ulster Constabulary* (n 39), para 109. See also SR Moreau, 'The Wrongs of Unequal Treatment' (2004) 54 *University of Toronto Law Review* 291, who states at 318 that comparators can 'serve a valuable evidentiary function'. More recently, the Supreme Court in *Hewage v Grampian Health Board* [2012] UKSC 37, [2012] ICR 1054 rejected the argument that the Employment Tribunal was entitled to find a prima facie case of discrimination only if there was (para 18) a 'like for like comparison' between claimant and comparator(s).

[44] And, for example, this caused the decision makers to assume that the extension would be used to house extended family members currently resident abroad, in circumstances in which it wanted to preserve the ethnic 'balance' of a council ward.

ences other than that of religion between the unsuccessful applicant and his neighbour will erect hurdles to his establishing that he was subjected to discrimination because of his religion but, in a case in which religion was *in fact* the reason for the impugned decision, these differences would be irrelevant to the question whether the comparator is an appropriate one.

The *Shamoon* approach has obvious advantages where multiple/intersectional discrimination is at issue. Leaving aside for the moment whether and how such discrimination is capable of recognition in domestic law,[45] a comparator-driven approach to discrimination would quite obviously generate difficulties for someone who (for example) claims that she has been subject to discrimination because she is a Muslim woman of Asian ethnicity, or that he has been discriminated against because he is a young black man of African-Caribbean ethnicity. Would the first of these claimants have to establish less favourable treatment than a real or hypothetical non-Muslim man of non-Asian ethnicity? A non-Muslim woman of non-Asian identity? A Muslim woman of non-Asian ethnicity? Or a non-Muslim man of Asian ethnicity?

The decision of the House of Lords in *Shamoon* heralded a change in the approach of the appellate courts at least to the statutory prohibitions on discrimination. In *Islington LBC v Ladele* Elias J (as he then was) remarked, for the EAT, that:

> By establishing that the reason for the detrimental treatment is the [protected characteristic], the claimant *necessarily* establishes at one and the same time that he or she is less favourably treated than the comparator who did not share the [protected] characteristic. Accordingly, although [EU and domestic provisions] . . . both identify the need for a tribunal to determine how a comparator was or would have been treated, that conclusion is necessarily encompassed in the finding that the claimant suffered the detriment on the prohibited ground. So a finding of discrimination can be made without the tribunal needing specifically to identify the precise characteristics of the comparator at all.[46]

Having echoed Lord Nicholls' observation in *Shamoon* that 'The determination of the comparator depends upon the reason for the difference in treatment',[47] Elias J went on to state that 'a focus on how the comparator was or would have been treated can be positively misleading' where the protected characteristic 'contributes to an act or decision even though it is not the sole or principal reason for the act or decision'.[48] It was 'well established that there will be unlawful

---

[45] See *Bahl v Law Society* [2004] IRLR 799. *cf Ministry of Defence v DeBique* [2010] IRLR 471 and see s 14 Equality Act 2010 (as yet unimplemented) which would allow claims of 'combined discrimination' on two (but not more) grounds. The Coalition Government has indicated that s 14 will not be implemented so the development in *DeBique* is significant, though see Joanne Conaghan, 'Intersectionality and UK Equality Initiatives' (2007) *South African Journal of Human Rights* 317–54 for a warning on the perils of identity politics in this context.

[46] *Islington LBC v Ladele* [2009] LGR 305, para 32, emphasis added.

[47] ibid, para 37 citing Lord Nicholls at paras 7–11.

[48] ibid, para 39.

discrimination where the prohibited ground contributes to an act or decision' without being the sole or principal reason for it, but in such a case:

> [A]n employee [would have] a claim for unlawful discrimination even though he would have been subject to precisely the same treatment even if there had been no discrimination, because the prohibited ground merely reinforces a decision that would have been taken for lawful reasons. In these circumstances the statutory comparator would have been treated in the same way as the claimant was treated. Therefore if a tribunal seeks to determine whether there is liability by asking whether the claimant was less favourably treated than the statutory comparator would have been, that will give the wrong answer . . .[49]

More recently, in *Cordell v FCO*, Underhill P remarked, in the EAT, that the emphasis in *Shamoon* on the 'reason why', 'has been repeatedly emphasised since, both in this tribunal and in the Court of Appeal . . . though still too often too little heeded by tribunals'.[50] And an emphasis on the role of comparators has also characterised the domestic judicial approach to Article 14 in the wake of its incorporation by the Human Rights Act 1998. Thus in *Michalak v London Borough of Wandsworth* (2003), one of the early post-Human Rights Act decisions, the Court of Appeal suggested that whether 'the chosen comparators [were] in an analogous situation to the complainant's situation' was one of four critical questions in an Article 14 claim.[51] The *Michalak* claim was dismissed on the basis that the claimant (a person subject to the Rent Act 1977) was not sufficiently similar to his comparators (those whose tenancies were subject to the Housing Act 1985) to compare his treatment with theirs under Article 14. And in *R (Carson) v Secretary of State for Work and Pensions* (2005),[52] in which the House of Lords disapproved the *Michalak* approach, that Court placed even greater emphasis on the comparator in dismissing the Article 14 challenge of a British woman living in South Africa to the failure of the British government to pay an annual uprate to her state pension. Having declared that there was 'nothing unfair or irrational about according different treatment to people who live abroad', Lord Hoffmann continued:

> Discrimination means a failure to treat like cases alike. There is obviously no discrimination when the cases are relevantly different . . . There is discrimination only if the cases are not sufficiently different to justify the difference in treatment . . . Whether cases are sufficiently different is partly a matter of values and partly a question of rationality. Article 14 expresses the Enlightenment value that every human being is entitled to equal respect and to be treated as an end and not a means. Characteristics such as race, caste, noble birth, membership of a political party and (here a change in

---

[49] ibid.

[50] *Cordell v FCO* [2012] ICR 280, para 18, citing *D'Silva v NATFHE* [2008] IRLR 412, para 30; *Ladele* (n 46); *Stockton on Tees Borough Council v Aylott* [2011] ICR 1278, paras 43–45 and *JP Morgan Europe Ltd v Chweidan* [2011] IRLR 673, para 5.

[51] *Michalak v London Borough of Wandsworth* (n 9). The others related to the other Convention right engaged, differential treatment and justifiability.

[52] *R (Carson) v Secretary of State for Work and Pensions* [2006] 1 AC 173.

values since the Enlightenment) gender, are seldom, if ever, acceptable grounds for differences in treatment. In some constitutions, the prohibition on discrimination is confined to grounds of this kind and I rather suspect that article 14 was also intended to be so limited. But the Strasbourg court has given it a wide interpretation, approaching that of the 14th Amendment, and it is therefore necessary, as in the United States, to distinguish between those grounds of discrimination which prima facie appear to offend our notions of the respect due to the individual and those which merely require some rational justification.

Lord Hoffmann stated that, as regards 'suspect grounds', discrimination could not be justified 'merely on utilitarian grounds', whereas 'differences in treatment in the second category . . . usually depend upon considerations of the general public interest'. And:

> [W]hile the courts, as guardians of the right of the individual to equal respect, will carefully examine the reasons offered for any discrimination in the first category, decisions about the general public interest which underpin differences in treatment in the second category are very much a matter for the democratically elected branches of government.

His Lordship accepted that 'there may be borderline cases in which it is not easy to allocate the ground of discrimination to one category or the other and . . . there are shifts in the values of society on these matters', but 'there is usually no difficulty about deciding whether one is dealing with a case in which the right to respect for the individuality of a human being is at stake or merely a question of general social policy', and the answer in *Carson* was 'clear'. Having stated that entitlement to a pension relied not only on contributions but also on other factors such as 'whether one lives in the United Kingdom and participates in the rest of its arrangements for taxation and social security', Lord Hoffmann declared that 'the position of a non-resident is materially and relevantly different from that of a UK resident', that Ms Carson 'therefore cannot claim equality of treatment, [and that] the amount (if any) which she receives must be a matter for Parliament'.[53] In other words, place of residence prevented scrutiny of a challenge to discrimination based on place of residence.

Lords Rodger, Nicholls and Walker agreed with Lord Hoffmann, Lord Carswell alone dissenting on the basis that it was 'fallacious' to argue that variations in exchange rates and cost of living prevented a comparison being made between the claimant and those who lived in the UK or in other countries in which uprates were paid, and from whom she was 'unquestionably treated differently'. Such differences no more blocked a comparison between those in the UK and outside for his Lordship than would differences in additional income or spending habits between UK pensioners: 'The common factor for purposes of comparison is that all of the pensioners, in whichever country they may reside, have duly paid the contributions required to qualify for their pensions'. For Lord Carswell, the appeal 'turn[ed] on the question whether the difference made

---

[53] ibid, para 25.

between the two classes, uprated and not uprated, is justified' by economic considerations and the answer, in his view was that it was not 'the selection of this class for less favourable treatment as [not] a matter of high state policy or an exercise in macro-economics. It has the appearance rather of the selection of a convenient target for saving money'.

The Grand Chamber of the ECtHR rejected Ms Carson's appeal, the majority ruling that she was not in a relevantly similar situation either with pensioners resident in the UK nor with those resident abroad in states with which the UK had reciprocal arrangements to win her Article 14 claim.[54] Judges Tulkens, Vajic, Spielmann, Jaeger, Jociene and Lopez Guerra dissented on the basis that, having accepted (as the majority did) that 'residence' was a prohibited ground under Article 14, relying upon it 'as the main reason for distinguishing between the two groups of pensioners . . . seems self-contradictory and inconsistent with the spirit of this provision'.[55] The dissenters went on to draw attention to the characteristics which the applicant and her putative comparators had in common (in particular, equal payment of National Insurance contributions and entitlement to pensions according to the rules) and concluded that their differential treatment was not justified.

More recently, in *Burden v United Kingdom*[56] the Grand Chamber rejected a claim from two elderly cohabiting sisters that the UK's failure to provide them with the same inheritance tax exemption as was available to civil partners breached their rights under Article 1 Protocol 1 and Article 14. The Court ruled that the women were not analogously situated to civil partners, this because (para 62) their

> relationship [was] . . . qualitatively of a different nature to that between married couples and homosexual civil partners under the United Kingdom's Civil Partnership Act. The very essence of the connection between siblings is consanguinity, whereas one of the defining characteristics of a marriage or Civil Partnership Act union is that it is forbidden to close family members.

Again, this contrasts with the approach taken in *James v Eastleigh* and, more recently, by Baroness Hale for the House of Lords in *AL (Serbia)* in which, commenting on the decision in *Burden*, she warned of the

> dangers in regarding differences between two people, which are inherent in a prohibited ground and cannot or should not be changed, as meaning that the situations are not analogous. For example, it would be no answer to a claim of sex discrimination to say that a man and a woman are not in an analogous situation because one can get pregnant and the other cannot. This is something that neither can be expected to change. If it is wrong to discriminate between them as individuals, it is wrong to focus on the personal characteristics which are inherent in their protected status to argue that their situations are not analogous. That is the essential reason why, in *Ghaidan v*

---

[54]　*Carson v UK* (2010) 51 EHRR 369, paras 85–87.
[55]　ibid, para 5.
[56]　*Burden v United Kingdom* (n 18).

Godin-Mendoza [2004] UKHL 30, [2004] 2 AC 557, the argument that same sex couples were not in an analogous position to opposite sex couples, because they could not have children together, did not succeed.[57]

As was made clear above, the ECtHR does not invariably adopt a comparator-driven approach to Article 14.[58] But that such an approach continues on occasion to defeat Art 14 claims is evident from the decision in *Burden v United Kingdom*[59] and, more recently again, in *Efe v Austria* in which the First Section rejected a challenge brought under Article 1 Protocol 1 and Article 14 by a Turkish national resident in Austria to the latter's refusal to provide him with family allowance in respect of his children, who were resident in Turkey.[60] Such allowance had been paid to him prior to 30 September 2006, when a bilateral agreement between Turkey and Austria which provided for its payment had been terminated. Having accepted that the claim fell within the scope of Article 1 Protocol 1 and Article 14 and that 'country of residence' was 'an aspect of personal status for the purposes of Article 14', the Court relied on *Carson* to reject his claim on the ground that 'family allowance was . . . primarily designed to cater for the needs of the resident population and that it . . . [did] not consider that the applicant . . . was in a relevantly similar position to persons claiming family allowance for children living in Austria'.[61]

A Critique

The difficulty with the *Carson* approach, as applied subsequently in cases including *Burden* and *Efe*, is not that the majority in the House of Lords or Grand Chamber accepted that it was justifiable to treat pensioners differently according to their place of residence, rather that what amounted to an instinctive decision on justification took place in the absence of analysis. It is noteworthy, then, that the judges in both courts who actually addressed the question of justification found it to be lacking. Lord Hoffmann's easy distinction between

---

[57] *AL (Serbia) v SSHD* (n 16) para 27, citing Lord Walker in *Carson*.

[58] And even where it does, as in *Hode & Abdi v UK* (2013) 56 EHRR 27, Fourth Section, it does not invariably apply it narrowly. In that case the Court rejected the argument put for the UK government that refugees who married prior to and after leaving their country of permanent residence were not analogously situated, as regards the entry into the UK of their spouses, for the purposes of an Art 14 claim. According to the Court (para 50): 'the requirement to demonstrate an "analogous situation" does not require that the comparator groups be identical [, r]ather . . . that, having regard to the particular nature of their complaints, [that] they had been in a relevantly similar situation to others treated differently'. At para 51: 'refugees who married before leaving their country of permanent residence were in an analogous position as they were also in receipt of a grant of refugee status and a limited period of leave to remain in the United Kingdom'. Similarly in *Smallwood v UK* (App no 29779/96); *McMichael v UK* (24 Feb 1995); *PM v UK* App no 6638/03 and *Sidabras and Džiautas v Lithuania* (2004) 42 EHRR 104, arguments based on alleged unlikeness failed.

[59] The decisions of the section and Grand Chamber are at (2007) 44 EHRR 51 and (2008) 47 EHRR 38 respectively.

[60] App no 9134/06, 8 January 2013, First Section.

[61] ibid, paras 48, 52–53.

'case[s] in which the right to respect for the individuality of a human being is at stake' and 'mere[]. . . question[s] of general social policy', and his application of it in the *Carson* case, are also open to challenge. We saw in Chapter 1 the criticism which has been levelled at a dignity-based approach to 'discrimination', which Lord Hoffmann appeared to adopt, not least because of the tendency of those who adopt it to overlook (as Lord Hoffmann did in *Carson*) the relationship between dignity and access to material resources.

The reason why a lack of 'likeness' defeated Ms Carson's claim was that the majority of the judges who considered the case reduced the discrimination question to an inquiry as to whether the ground upon which she and her comparators were distinguished was relevant to the asserted purpose of the legislation. It appears that this approach is to be applied by the domestic courts only where the grounds on which discrimination is alleged are not regarded as 'suspect',[62] Lord Hoffmann adopting an approach in relation to 'race, caste, noble birth, membership of a political party and . . . gender' which would permit substantive scrutiny of legislation which taxed married men and married women differently in order to encourage married partners to conform to the traditional gendered division of labour, or to an anti-miscegenation statute such as that struck down by the US Supreme Court in *Loving v Virginia*.[63] But the classification of grounds is assumed by Lord Hoffmann to be an exercise in common sense which does not require analysis, much less justification. As Arnardóttir points out, the effect of a comparator-driven approach is to place the burden of justification on the applicant by requiring her to establish that she should have been treated the same as her comparator (because they are relevantly similar), rather than requiring the alleged discriminator to justify the differential treatment (whether on public policy grounds or because they are relevantly different).[64]

The effect of insisting on 'likeness' as a threshold condition of a discrimination case may be, as in *Shackell* or *Carson*, to cede a great deal of control to the legislator to draw distinctions along certain lines. This problem was not lost on the House of Lords in 2004 in the *Belmarsh* case, in which it rejected the government's argument that, as persons subject to immigration control, non-national suspected terrorists were not analogously situated to national terrorist suspects for the purposes of determining whether the subjection of the former, but not the latter, to internment involved unlawful discrimination. Lord Bingham, with whom the majority agreed, declared that the 'Secretary of State's choice of immigration control as a means to address the Al-Qaeda security problem' was

---

[62] This accords with the decision in *A v SSHD* [2005] 2 AC 68, and with the suggestion made in the Canadian context by Gold (n 32) 1066, that the 'like cases alike' approach could be applied where discrimination was alleged to have occurred on grounds other than those listed or analogous to those listed in s 15. In the event the Supreme Court declined to read s 15 as reaching discrimination on these wider grounds at all.

[63] *Loving v Virginia* 388 US 1 (1967).

[64] Arnardóttir (n 27) 84–85.

not conclusive, and that national and non-national terrorists were in fact relevantly similar.[65]

In the *Belmarsh* case, which concerned traditional civil liberties rather than questions of resource distribution, the House of Lords determined for itself the relevance of the protected characteristic to the underlying purpose of the legislation (the control of suspected terrorists rather than, as the government would have had it, immigration control). And in *AL (Serbia) v SSHD* Lady Hale suggested that the domestic focus on comparators was the product of the legislative distinction drawn between 'direct' and 'indirect' discrimination and the absence of a defence for the former:[66] 'unless there are very obvious relevant differences between the two situations, it is better to concentrate on the reasons for the difference in treatment and whether they amount to an objective and reasonable justification'.[67] It is clear from above that this approach, redolent as it is of that of the House of Lords in *Shamoon*, is not invariably adopted in relation to Article 14.

Under the *Carson* approach the hair colour of a maker of margarine is unlikely to be regarded as relevant to the regulations applicable to her margarine-making activities. But the crucial question of what differences between people may properly be regarded as giving rise to defensible differences in the distribution of benefits and/or burdens is buried in a hidden step (the determination of relevance) which forms part of the question whether the cases are 'alike' for the purposes of an equality comparison. This has the effect that only patently absurd or offensive grounds of distinction are likely to be subject to further scrutiny. To adopt McCrudden's suggestion that equality may be seen in terms of (1) 'rationality', (2) the protection of 'prized public goods', (3) the prevention of 'status harms' resulting from discrimination on particular grounds' (4) requiring the 'proactive promotion of equality of opportunity between particular groups' and/or (5) ensuring the 'participation' of excluded groups,[68] the *Carson* approach substitutes the first version of equality for the second version and undercuts the principle that 'in the distribution of "prized public goods", equals should be treated equally, except where differences can be justified'. It is particularly inappropriate when it is applied to statutory discrimination provisions which are concerned with McCrudden's third category of equality.[69]

---

[65] *A v SSHD* (n 62) para 53.

[66] ibid, paras 23–24.

[67] ibid, para 25.

[68] C McCrudden, 'Equality and Non-Discrimination' in D Feldman (ed), *English Public Law* (Oxford, Oxford University Press, 2004) 582, 582–83 and, by the same author, 'Theorising European Law' in C Costello and E Barry (eds), *Equality in Diversity: The New Equality Directives* (Dublin: Irish Centre for European Law, 2003) 1.

[69] For an example of this see *Dhatt v McDonalds* (n 11). Note that, in connection with 'equality as rationality', comparisons actually serve to broaden the reach of equality analysis by bringing within the scope for challenge any differences between the (relevantly) similar. Thus, for example, David Beatty and Marc Gold, who have defended the 'like cases alike' approach, have adopted it as an *expansive* mechanism to encourage scrutiny of *all* legislative classifications, rather than only those (in the Canadian context) listed in s 15 of the Charter. Gold (n 32) acknowledges that the acceptance of relevance is problematic in the case of (listed and analogous) presumptively suspect grounds. See also Gibson (n 33) 10–11.

Even if it were confined to cases concerned with McCrudden's first category of equality, the *Carson* approach so emphasises the comparative exercise[70] that Lord Hoffman concluded that there was little room for consideration of the question of justification as an independent head, except perhaps where positive discrimination was at issue.[71] Everything is reduced to the question whether the ground on which the challenged distinction is based is 'relevant' to the legislative distinction. But there are real difficulties in ascertaining legislative purpose absent a single human source of legislation, and the early focus on 'relevance' can amount to an invitation to the discriminator (or, indeed, the court itself[72]) to pluck one out of the air.

Ascertaining purpose will always give rise to difficulties. But placing this question at the centre of the discrimination analysis itself (rather than taking it into account in determining whether discrimination is *justified*) is particularly problematic. Further, as McLachlin J recognised in *Egan v Canada*,[73] in which four of the nine judges on Canada's Supreme Court rejected a challenge to legislation which made pensioner dependents' benefits available only to heterosexual partners on the basis that the distinction drawn was relevant to the intention of the legislation by which, they found, Parliament intended 'to accord support to married couples who were aged and elderly', that marriage (including 'common law' marriage) was characterised essentially by the ability to procreate, and that this ability to procreate was not shared by same-sex partners:[74]

> To require the claimant to prove that the unequal treatment suffered is irrational or unreasonable or founded on irrelevant considerations[75] would be to require the claimant to lead evidence on state goals, and often to put proof of discrimination beyond the reach of the ordinary person.

It is not obviously defensible to require a claimant first to guess and second to disprove the relevance of an impugned classification to a legislative or other purpose, in circumstances such that the alleged discriminator can then defend itself by putting forward, with scant fear of contradiction, an alternative

---

[70] The 'single question,' Lord Hoffman suggested, was whether there was 'enough of a relevant difference between X and Y to justify different treatment?'

[71] Lord Walker thought this was the 'clearest case' for separate consideration of the justification question.

[72] David Beatty, for example, charges that the La Forest group 'simply ignored the most basic objectives of alleviating poverty and economic dislocation that motivated the enactment' of the laws at issue in *Egan v Canada* [1995] 2 SCR 513 and in *Miron v Trudel* [1995] 2 SCR 418 ('The Canadian Concept of Equality' (1996) 46 *University of Toronto Law Journal* 349). See more generally Note, 'Legislative Purpose, Rationality, and Equal Protection' (1972) 82 *Yale Law Journal* 123.

[73] *Egan v Canada* (n 72). The case was one of a trilogy (with *Miron* (n 72) and *Thibaudeau v Canada* [1995] 2 SCR 627) in which four Supreme Court Justices adopted an approach which, as McLachlin J pointed out in *Miron*, simply reintroduced the 'like cases alike' approach by the back door.

[74] The four did not appear to question whether the pursuit of a legislative aim which itself privileged differently sexed over same-sex couples was legitimate.

[75] Which is the effect of taking 'relevance' into account at the stage of ascertaining whether discrimination has *occurred*, as distinct from whether it is *justifiable*.

purpose to which the classification will be accepted as relevant. Nor does an approach which simply focuses on 'relevance' to legislative aim permit challenge to discrimination which is of *effect* as distinct from purpose,[76] thus leaving out of account the concept of indirect discrimination.

The demand for 'likeness' here serves in effect to convert what is a potentially challengeable ground of discrimination into one which is immune from scrutiny. So, for example, in *Hlozek v Roche Austria Gesellschaft mbH* (2004)[77] the ECJ avoided a finding of discrimination in a way which ceded control over the types of difference which could block a discrimination claim, save possibly for an implicit requirement that the difference at issue be 'relevant' to the benefit sought.[78] This approach would appear to apply equally to a case in which the claimant and his or her comparator are differently situated because of the defendant's actions (as distinct from, as in *Hlozek*, from those of a third party), and to a case in which the defendant's actions exacerbate, rather than (as in *Hlozek*) ameliorate, disadvantage. In *R (Purja) v Ministry of Defence*,[79] for example, the Court of Appeal ruled that Gurkhas and British troops were not analogously situated, and that Gurkhas could not therefore challenge less favourable treatment in relation to pay and various conditions of service because (at least in part) of the different regimes applied to Gurkhas and British troops by the defendant itself. And in the UK, prior to the decision in *Webb v EMO Air Cargo (UK) Ltd (No 2)*, the differences in terms of absence requirements, etc, between a pregnant woman and a fit male comparator would have blocked a sex discrimination claim arising from pregnancy discrimination notwithstanding the fact that, by contrast with *Hlozek*, the differential treatment of the pregnant woman would have served to disadvantage rather than benefit those in the claimant's position.[80]

An alternative approach to that adopted by the ECJ in *Hlozek* had been suggested by the European Commission in *Roberts v Birds Eye Walls*,[81] whose facts were similar to those in *Hlozek*. There the Commission had argued that it was 'inherent' in the concept of discrimination that differential treatment on protected grounds was unlawful only if unjustified. Thus, and notwithstanding the absence of any express justification defence in Article 119 EC (now Art 157

---

[76] See Beatty (n 72) 356; McLachlin J in *Miron* (n 72).

[77] Case C-19/02 *Hlozek v Roche Austria Gesellschaft mbH* [2004] ECR I-11491.

[78] The sex-related pensionable age difference was clearly relevant to the benefits at issue in *Hlozek* as the different regimes applied to Gurkhas (see *R (Purja) v Ministry of Defence* [2004] 1 WLR 289) and the unavailability of the claimant in *Webb v EMO Air Cargo (UK) Ltd* [1993] 1 WLR 49 were relevant to their perceived entitlement to the conditions of service sought by the Gurkhas and the utility to the employer of the Claimant in *Webb* – see comments immediately below.

[79] ibid.

[80] In *Webb (No 2)* [1995] 1 WLR 1454 the House of Lords, bound by the ECJ's ruling (Case C-32/93 [1994] ECR I-03567) that pregnancy discrimination per se was sex discrimination contrary to the Equal Treatment Directive, suddenly found itself able (*cf Webb*, n 78) to exclude from the 'relevant circumstances' within s 5(3) SDA the consequences of pregnancy (there impending maternity-related absence).

[81] Case C-132/92 *Roberts v Birds Eye Walls* [1993] ECR I-5579.

TFEU), the Commission would have read one in. The Commission suggested that any initiative in favour of substantive equal treatment should benefit from a presumption of legality and that, in the instant case, the fact that the aim and effect of the different payments made by the employer was to achieve equality between the sexes by compensating for the difference in state pensionable ages was enough to justify the difference.[82] Advocate General Van Gerven's opinion was broadly supportive of the Commission's approach but the ECJ did not accept the invitation to deal with the *Roberts* case as one of justified discrimination, stating instead that 'the principle of equal treatment' established in Article 119 'presupposes that the men and women to whom it applies are in identical situations' before concluding that the differences in this case meant that the differential treatment of the claimant and his comparators 'cannot be considered discriminatory'.

The reading into (the then) Article 119 of a justification defence would not have been without difficulty, not least because that provision, unlike Article 14 of the Convention, partly defines the 'discrimination' which it prohibits.[83] But the *Hlozek* approach, unlike a principled analysis of justification, provides no basis for distinguishing between the protected ground-related factors which ought and those which ought not to block comparison for the purposes of a discrimination claim. It simply functions, as discussed above, so as to restrict access to the benefits enjoyed by more privileged groups to those of the less privileged groups who can prove 'sameness' with the latter.[84] The objection to it is particularly acute where the very ground on which discriminatory treatment is alleged is the basis on which their putative comparators are found to be insufficiently similar to permit comparison.

'LIKENESS' AS A METHOD OF RATIONING: A CANADIAN ALTERNATIVE?

Underlying the use of the comparator-driven approach as a 'closure' mechanism is most likely a judicial desire for economy of reasoning as regards distinctions which are not obviously offensive to reason. There are a number of ways in which litigation arising from the drawing of such distinctions can be closed down with minimal costly engagement. The first, which is particularly charac-

---

[82] In an approach which would resurface in the aftermath of the decision in Case 450/93 *Kalanke v Freie Hansestadt Bremen* [1995] ECR I-03051: see the 'Proposal for a Council Directive amending Directive 76/207/EEC on the implementation of the principle of equal treatment for men and women as regards access to employment, vocational training and promotion, and working conditions', OJ 1996 C179, 8.

[83] 'Equal pay without discrimination based on sex means: a. that pay for the same work at piece rates shall be calculated on the basis of the same unit of measurement; b. that pay for work at time rates shall be the same for the same job'.

[84] Note that the ECJ has expressly rejected this type of analysis in the pregnancy context, though not in relation to treatment as beneficiaries of maternity leave, rather than as workers: see *Gillespie* (n 11), Case C-411/96 *Boyle v EOC* [1998] ECR I-06401.

teristic of the application by Canada's courts of section 15 of the Charter, is to interpret the grounds on which discrimination may be challenged narrowly. This had had the effect of miring much section 15 litigation in arguments about whether the ground of distinction (or disparate impact) alleged either is or is analogous to 'race, national or ethnic origin, colour, religion, sex, age or mental or physical disability'.[85] The second is the *Carson* technique of finding that the claimant and comparator are not 'alike' because they differ from each other on the basis of the very ground upon which discrimination is alleged. The alternative to these relatively economical, but crude, approaches requires explicit consideration of whether differential treatment is justified.

In *Andrews v Law Society of British Columbia*, Canada's Supreme Court categorised 'discrimination', for the purposes of section 15, as a distinction[86] which had the effect of 'imposing burdens, obligations, or disadvantages' not imposed on others, or of withholding 'access to opportunities, benefits and advantages' available to others.[87] In *Egan* and two other cases decided in 1995, four of the nine judges of the Supreme Court would have replaced the *Andrews* approach with one, discussed above, in which section 15 would only have been breached by a distinction which was, inter alia, irrelevant to the burden or disadvantage challenged.[88] This test was not in fact adopted, and in *Law v Canada* (1998) an uneasy unanimity was achieved, the Supreme Court ruling that the purpose of section 15 was to prevent the violation of human dignity and freedom by the imposition of disadvantage, stereotyping or prejudice, and to promote equal recognition at law of all persons as equally deserving and that a distinction which did not conflict with this purpose would not be 'discriminatory' for the purposes of section 15.[89]

The *Law* test and the emphasis it placed on the concept of human dignity has been the subject of much criticism, considered in Chapter 1. Of particular relevance here, however, was the Court's reference in *Law* to 'relevant comparators'[90] although the decision in that case rested on the conclusion of the Court that the differential treatment there at issue neither perpetuated disadvantage

---

[85] L'Heureux-Dubé J was particularly critical of this approach and sought, in *Egan* (n 72) to do away with the 'grounds' emphasis but neither her criticism nor those of Canadian commentators managed to persuade her colleagues on the Supreme Court, and she threw her lot in with a compromise approach in *Law*. In *Gosselin v Quebec* [2002] 4 SCR 429 she was to reiterate her *Egan* approach, see D Gilbert, 'Unequaled: Justice Claire L'Heureux-Dubé's Vision of Equality and Section 15 of the *Charter*' (2003) 15 *Canadian Journal of Women and the Law* 1. See also Nitya Iyer, 'Categorical Denials: Equality Rights and the Shaping of Social Identity' (1993–94) 19 *Queen's Law Journal* 179 for a discussion of the problem of essentialism in this context.

[86] This can be a distinction of treatment or impact, although it must be on grounds included in or recognised as 'analogous' to those in s 15.

[87] *Andrews v Law Society of British Columbia* [1989] 1 SCR 143.

[88] See *Egan* (n 72), *Miron* (n 72) and *Thibaudeau v Canada* (n 73).

[89] *Law v Canada* [1999] 1 SCR 497.

[90] At para 56, *per* Iocobucci J: '. . . the equality guarantee is a comparative concept. Ultimately, a court must identify differential treatment *as compared* to one or more other persons or groups. Locating the appropriate comparator is necessary in identifying differential treatment and the grounds of the distinction' (emphasis in the original).

nor stereotyped or stigmatised young persons as such. In the wake of *Law*, and notwithstanding the clear rejection of the comparator test in *Andrews*, the section 15 jurisprudence paid increasing attention to questions of comparisons and comparators. In *Lovelace v Ontario* (2000), for example, Iacobucci J ruled, for the Court, that 'the s. 15(1) inquiry must proceed on the basis of comparing band and non-band aboriginal communities', though he also stated that 'we must ask whether the impugned law, program or activity has a purpose or effect that is substantively discriminatory'.[91]

Judy Fudge stated in 2007 that 'simply broadening the Court's conception of dignity will not necessarily expand the redistributive potential of substantive equality', this because of the Court's emphasis on a comparative approach.[92] By 2004, and notwithstanding the warnings issued by McIntyre J in *Andrews*, the Supreme Court had come full circle to embrace the 'similarly situated' test in *Hodge v Canada*.[93] The claim was brought by a woman who had, five months before his death, terminated a 22-year relationship 'common law' relationship with a man on the basis of whose pension contributions she then sought a survivor's pension. Had they been married she would have been entitled to the pension even if she had not been living with him at the date of his death. The Court did not accept that Ms Hodge was entitled to compare her treatment with that of a married spouse who had ceased to cohabit with her husband at the date of his death, insisting instead that the correct comparator for the purpose of a claim based on marital status was a married person who had divorced prior to the date of death and who would not have qualified for a survivor's pension. Binnie J, for the Court, demanded that the comparator 'mirror[ed] the characteristics of the claimant . . . relevant to the benefit or advantage sought except that the statutory definition includes a personal characteristic that is offensive to the *Charter* or omits a personal characteristic in a way that is offensive to the *Charter*'.[94] He accepted that distinctions based on sex and sexual orientation would not render comparators unsuitable for the purposes of section 15 comparison but did not accept that the same applied to marital status.[95]

As we saw in Chapter 1, the Supreme Court resiled from the *Law* dignity-based approach in *R v Kapp* (2008) in which the Court referred to the criticism which had 'accrued for the way *Law* has allowed the formalism of some of the

---

[91] *Lovelace v Ontario* [2000] 1 SCR 950, paras 64, 54. For discussion see D Pothier, 'Connecting Grounds of Discrimination to Real People's Real Experiences' (2001) 13 *Canadian Journal of Women and the Law* 37. See also G Brodsky, '*Gosselin v Quebec (Attorney General)*: Autonomy with a Vengeance' (2003) 15 *Canadian Journal of Women and the Law* 194 and N Kim and T Piper, '*Gosselin v Quebec*; Back to the Poorhouse' (2003) 48 *McGill Law Journal* 749.

[92] J Fudge, 'Substantive Equality, the Supreme Court of Canada, and The Limits to Redistribution' (2007) 23 *South African Journal on Human Rights* 235, 243.

[93] *Hodge v Canada* [2004] 3 SCR 357.

[94] ibid, para 23.

[95] See, similarly, *Auton v British Columbia (AG)* [2004] 3 SCR 657 in which McLachlin CJ demanded, in a case in which a failure to fund a programme for autistic children was challenged as disability discrimination, that the claimant's treatment be compared with that afforded to a non-disabled person.

Court's post-*Andrews* jurisprudence to resurface in the form of an artificial comparator analysis focussed on treating likes alike'.[96] And in *Withler v Canada (AG)* the Court jettisoned the comparator requirement entirely, ruling that where a claimant established a distinction in treatment based on one or more of the enumerated or analogous grounds, the court should consider whether the distinction created a disadvantage by perpetuating prejudice or stereotyping without considering a 'mirror' comparator group such as that demanded by Binnie J in *Hodge*.[97] While it was accepted that equality was 'inherently comparative', 'Care must be taken to avoid converting the inquiry into substantive equality into a formalistic and arbitrary search for the "proper" comparator group'.[98] According to McLachlin CJ and Abella J, with whom the rest of the Court agreed, section 15 was concerned not with 'a right to identical treatment' but with 'every person's equal right to be free from discrimination':[99]

[37] Whether the s. 15 analysis focuses on perpetuating disadvantage or stereotyping, the analysis involves looking at the circumstances of members of the group and the negative impact of the law on them. The analysis is contextual, not formalistic, grounded in the actual situation of the group and the potential of the impugned law to worsen their situation . . .

[39] Both the inquiries into perpetuation of disadvantage and stereotyping are directed to ascertaining whether the law violates the requirement of substantive equality. Substantive equality, unlike formal equality, rejects the mere presence or absence of difference as an answer to differential treatment. It insists on going behind the facade of similarities and differences. It asks not only what characteristics the different treatment is predicated upon, but also whether those characteristics are relevant considerations under the circumstances. The focus of the inquiry is on the actual impact of the impugned law, taking full account of social, political, economic and historical factors concerning the group. The result may be to reveal differential treatment as discriminatory because of prejudicial impact or negative stereotyping. Or it may reveal that differential treatment is required in order to ameliorate the actual situation of the claimant group.

[40] It follows that a formal analysis based on comparison between the claimant group and a 'similarly situated' group, does not assure a result that captures the wrong to which s. 15(1) is directed – the elimination from the law of measures that impose or perpetuate substantial inequality. What is required is not formal comparison with a selected mirror comparator group, but an approach that looks at the full context, including the situation of the claimant group and whether the impact of the impugned law is to perpetuate disadvantage or negative stereotypes about that group.

McLachlin CJ and Abella J referred to *Kapp*'s rejection of the 'mirror comparator group' approach and agreed with concerns expressed that 'a comparator group approach to s. 15(1) may substitute a formal "treat likes alike" analysis

---

[96] *R v Kapp* [2008] 2 SCR 483, para 22.
[97] *Withler v Canada (AG)* [2011] 1 SCR 396.
[98] ibid, para 3.
[99] ibid, para 31.

for the substantive equality analysis that has from the beginning been the focus of s. 15(1) jurisprudence',[100] namely that:

> [T]he definition of the comparator group determines the analysis and the outcome . . . As a result, factors going to discrimination – whether the distinction creates a disadvantage or perpetuates prejudice or stereotyping – may be eliminated or marginalized.
>
> . . . the focus on a precisely corresponding, or 'like' comparator group, becomes a search for sameness, rather than a search for disadvantage, again occluding the real issue – whether the law disadvantages the claimant or perpetuates a stigmatized view of the claimant.
>
> . . . allowing a mirror comparator group to determine the outcome overlooks the fact that a claimant may be impacted by many interwoven grounds of discrimination . . .
>
> . . . finding the 'right' comparator group places an unfair burden on claimant [and] . . . may be impossible, as the essence of an individual or group's equality claim may be that, in light of their distinct needs and circumstances, no one is like them for the purposes of comparison.[101]

McLachlin CJ and Abella J pointed out that the first step of the two-stage test embraced in *Withler* involved comparison (this in finding the necessary 'distinction' drawn between the claimant and others), and ruled that it was

> unnecessary to pinpoint a particular group that precisely corresponds to the claimant group except for the personal characteristic or characteristics alleged to ground the discrimination. Provided that the claimant establishes a distinction [direct or indirect] based on one or more enumerated or analogous grounds, the claim should proceed to the second step of the analysis [ie, 'whether the law works substantive inequality, by perpetuating disadvantage or prejudice, or by stereotyping in a way that does not correspond to actual characteristics or circumstances'.[102]] This provides the flexibility required to accommodate claims based on intersecting grounds of discrimination. It also avoids the problem of eliminating claims at the outset because no precisely corresponding group can be posited.[103]

This is not to say that considerations of 'likeness' have no place in the analysis of discrimination. As Marc Gold has pointed out, questions as to the degree of similarity between claimant and comparator will inevitably reappear:

> [I]t is precisely because the principle of formal equality is so question-begging that it cannot be banished from the analysis altogether. It is like pushing in a bump on a balloon. It may be flattened, but the bump will reappear at some other place on the balloon.[104]

But the proper time for consideration of these differences is, as Lady Hale suggested in *AL (Serbia)*, at the justification stage where the burden is on the

---

[100]   *R v Kapp* (n 96) para 55.
[101]   ibid, paras 56–59.
[102]   ibid, para 65.
[103]   ibid, para 63.
[104]   Gold (n 32) 1066.

discriminator to (at least) put forward the aims pursued, rather than the claimant to second-guess them.

DEVELOPMENTS IN THE EUROPEAN COURT OF HUMAN RIGHTS

The jurisprudence of Canada's Supreme Court on section 15 is significantly more developed than that of the ECtHR on Article 14 of the Convention, touched upon above. Prior to the decision in *DH v Czech Republic* (2008) it was not even certain that Article 14 extended to the regulation of indirect discrimination, though indications had been given to this effect in *Thlimmenos v Greece* (2001).[105] In its first decision on Article 14 (*Belgian Linguistics*), itself only the third substantive case before the Court,[106] the ECtHR ruled that the justification of differential treatment under that provision 'must be assessed in relation to the aim *and effects* of the measure under consideration'.[107] Any hope that this might have been intended to indicate a concept of discrimination broader than the demand that 'like' cases be treated 'alike' was countered by the decision in the first case to deal with that point, *Abdulaziz v United Kingdom* (1985), some 17 years later.[108] There the Court, confronted with the assertion that an anti-abuse provision in the Immigration Rules operated *in practice* to disadvantage persons from the Indian subcontinent, concluded that the provision 'cannot be taken as an indication of racial discrimination [because] its main purpose was to prevent evasion of the rules by means of bogus marriages or engagements'.[109]

The underlying conception of discrimination in *Abdulaziz* was clearly limited to the direct form, the existence of a non-discriminatory rationale for disputed treatment in an indirect discrimination claim being only the first step towards its justification. Comparators then came to play an occasional role in the Article 14 jurisprudence, as we saw above, featuring recently in the Grand Chamber in *Carson* and in *Burden*.[110]

As suggested above, placing the burden of proving (relevant) 'sameness' on the complainant can avoid the requirement for the court to undertake the relatively expensive undertaking of determining justification in an equality claim which does not instinctively appeal, though it does so at the cost of placing a reverse burden of justification on discrimination claimants. It is, further, important to remember that equality/discrimination claims are not reducible merely to claims of less favourable treatment than actual or hypothetical others. The point is clearly illustrated by the decision of the ECJ in *Allonby v Accrington and Rossendale College & Ors* in which that Court simultaneously ruled that a

---

[105] *DH v Czech Republic* (2008) 47 EHRR 3; *Thlimmenos v Greece* (2001) 31 EHRR 411.
[106] *Case 'Relating To Certain Aspects Of The Laws On The Use Of Languages In Education In Belgium'* (No 2) (1968) 1 EHRR 252.
[107] ibid, para 10, emphasis added.
[108] *Abdulaziz v United Kingdom* (1985) 7 EHRR 471, para 85.
[109] ibid.
[110] *Burden* (n 18).

woman worker who supplied her labour to the respondent through an agency could not make an equal pay claim under Article 141 EC (now Art 157 TFEU) by reference to a male comparator directly employed by the college, and that no comparator was needed for a challenge to (there indirect) sex discrimination resulting from legislation (there the exclusion of agency workers from the state pension scheme for teachers).[111] And though that decision deals in terms with discriminatory legislation, there have been many other ECJ (now CJEU) decisions in which employer practices concerning, in particular, access to pension schemes have been determined other than by reference to comparators.[112]

The jurisprudence of the ECJ/CJEU, like that of Canada's Supreme Court, has been more sophisticated than that of the ECtHR. As mentioned above, prior to the 2000 decision in *Thlimmenos v Greece*,[113] it appeared that Article 14 applied only to claims of differential treatment on protected grounds, and then often only subject to an additional demand for 'likeness' with a suitable comparator.[114] *Thlimmenos* concerned the refusal of access to the chartered accountancy profession of a Jehovah's Witness who, having been convicted for insubordination arising from his refusal to wear a military uniform during conscription, was barred by a rule prohibiting felons from the profession. The Court accepted that Thlimmenos was 'treated differently from the other persons who had applied for that post on the ground of his status as a convicted person',[115] and characterised his Article 14 complaint as concerning the fact that:

> [I]n the application of the relevant law no distinction is made between persons convicted of offences committed exclusively because of their religious beliefs and persons convicted of other offences . . . he is discriminated against in the exercise of his freedom of religion, as guaranteed by art 9 of the convention, in that he was treated like any other person convicted of a felony although his own conviction resulted from the very exercise of this freedom.[116]

It continued:

> 44. The court has so far considered that the right under art 14 not to be discriminated against in the enjoyment of the rights guaranteed under the convention is violated when states treat differently persons in analogous situations without providing an objective and reasonable justification . . . However, the court considers that this is not the only facet of the prohibition of discrimination in art 14. The right not to be dis-

---

[111] Case C-256/01 *Allonby v Accrington and Rossendale College & Ors* [2004] ECR I-873.

[112] See, for example, Case 170/84 *Bilka-Kaufhaus GmbH v Karin Weber von Hartz* [1986] ECR 1607; Case 171/88 *Rinner-Kühn v FWW Spezial-Gebaudereinigung GmbH* [1989] ECR 2743; and Case 184/89 *Nimz v Freie und Hanse-Stadt Hamburg* [1991] ECR I–297.

[113] *DH v Czech Republic* (n 105).

[114] That the requirements are additive is illustrated by *Shackell* in which it was accepted that marital status could be a protected ground but also that a difference in such status prevented the claim succeeding.

[115] *DH v Czech Republic* (n 105) para 41.

[116] ibid, para 42.

criminated against in the enjoyment of the rights guaranteed under the convention is also violated when states without an objective and reasonable justification fail to treat differently persons whose situations are significantly different . . .

The decision in *Thlimmenos* involved the recognition of the second (generally neglected) limb of Aristotelian equality: the requirement to treat (relevantly) 'unlike' cases differently ('in proportion to their unalikeness'). In *DH v Czech Republic* the Grand Chamber confirmed that indirect discrimination fell within Article 14 and ruled that 'Where an applicant alleging indirect discrimination thus establishes a rebuttable presumption that the effect of a measure or practice is discriminatory, the burden then shifts to the respondent state, which must show that the difference in treatment is not discriminatory'.[117]

Thlimmenos perhaps served as a marker for the embrace by the ECtHR in *DH* of indirect discrimination. But it may go significantly further than this.[118] A mere prohibition on indirect discrimination does not fully satisfy the second limb of Aristotelian equality, that is, that 'things that are unalike should be treated unalike in proportion to their unalikeness'. The difficulty is that the prohibition on indirect discrimination is concerned only with practices which impact disadvantageously at the *collective* level. As crucifix-wearing British Christians have discovered, the fact that a prohibition on the display of religious jewellery disadvantages the *individual* Christian whose conscience might require her to display such insignia is insufficient to form the basis of an indirect discrimination challenge:[119] one of the mandatory requirements for such a challenge is that Christians[120] are more likely than others to be disadvantaged by such a rule. But if adherence to a particular belief set is sufficient to establish 'unalikeness', then it may be that this demand for group disadvantage is indefensible under Article 14.

This requirement for group disadvantage in the domestic regulation of indirect discrimination has the effect also that, whereas the impact on individuals may be taken into account in assessing whether disparately impacting practices can be justified at the macro level (this because, where a flexible or qualified rule would achieve similar ends without disadvantaging a claimant and those in the same relevant group, the adoption or maintenance of an inflexible or unqualified rule will not be justified), a challenge to the *general* rule may result in a demand for any particular accommodation (tailoring of the rule to the individual) only

---

[117] *DH v Czech Republic* (2008) 47 EHRR 3, para 189. cf *Jordan v UK* (2003) 37 EHRR 52, on which the Court in *DH* relied in applying Art 14 to indirect discrimination, in which the Court had denied that 'statistics can in themselves disclose a practice which could be classified as discriminatory within the meaning of Article 14'.

[118] Elias LJ in *AM (Somalia) v Entry Clearance Officer* [2009] EWCA Civ 634, paras 44–46 thought that indirect and *Thlimmenos* discrimination were not the same. See also Laws J in *R (M) v SSWP* [2013] EWHC 2213 (Admin), paras 45–46.

[119] See discussion of *Eweida v British Airways* [2009] ICR 303 and *Chapman v Royal Devon and Exeter NHS Trust* in Chapter 5.

[120] Or 'believers' generally.

where the refusal of that accommodation would result in *collective disadvantage*. If it is established that a rigid requirement to work long and/or (employer-determined) 'flexible' hours disadvantages women (as primary child carers), a failure to justify that rigid rule (because of its disproportionate impact on women) might result in the adoption of a less rigid rule (which, for example, provides for reasonable periods of notice of working patterns and accommodates care-related or other needs). But the degree of flexibility or qualification required of the rule will only be that which is required to avoid disadvantage to women *as a group*, rather than disadvantage to any particular woman.

The requirement, as an element of indirect discrimination, of collective disadvantage was the very reason why the Disability Discrimination Act 1995, which first prohibited disability discrimination in the UK, adopted a 'reasonable adjustment' rather than an 'indirect discrimination' model in relation to disability: that this or that practice disparately impacts on 'the disabled' at a statistically significant level is far more difficult to establish than that a practice has that effect on 'women', or on persons of a particular ethnic group. The Equality Act 2010 now prohibits indirect discrimination in relation to the 'protected characteristic' of disability, as well as the failure to make reasonable adjustments to the needs of persons with disabilities. But the duty of reasonable adjustment will continue to do most of the heavy lifting by reason of its lack of any requirement for collective disadvantage: my right, as a wheelchair user, a partially sighted person or someone with bipolar disorder to have reasonable adjustments made in order to avoid my being placed at a substantial disadvantage in comparison with others does not turn on the extent to which any other disabled person would be placed at such a disadvantage, much less whether the category of 'disabled people' generally, or any sub-category thereof, might be so disadvantaged.[121]

An interesting question then arises from *Thlimmenos* as to whether Article 14 places a duty of adjustment on employers and others in relation to *individual* disadvantage which might be experienced in connection with grounds protected by that provision. In *Eweida & Ors v United Kingdom*, in which the ECtHR considered Article 9 and 14 challenges brought by crucifix-wearing Christians,[122] the Court reiterated that the concept of discrimination under Article 14 was not limited (para 87) to differential 'treatment of persons in analogous, or relevantly similar, situation' but included the failure 'without an objective and reasonable justification . . . to treat differently persons whose situations are significantly different'. Although the Court found that there had been a violation of Article 9 in the case of Nadia Eweida, a BA employee, it did not consider her challenge under Article 14 and so missed the opportunity to clarify whether such any duty of accommodation arose under that provision. A number of other decisions of

---

[121] See s 20 Equality Act 2010.
[122] *Eweida & Ors v United Kingdom* (2013) 57 EHRR 213. The *Eweida* and *Chapman* cases were considered with those of Lillian Ladele and Gary MacFarlane, further discussed in Chapter 5.

the ECtHR have, however, hinted at developments in the analysis of Article 14 which may, over time, further isolate the rigid comparator-based approach exemplified by decisions such as *Shackell* and, more recently, *Burden* and *Carson*, to a category of grounds (those not qualifying as 'suspect') which, although within the scope of Article 14, appear to be protected by little more than rationality review.[123]

Opuz v Turkey (2009) was a claim brought under Articles 2, 3 and 14 on behalf of a woman killed by her abusive son-in-law 'for the sake of his honour and children' after she tried to help his wife escape him.[124] The ECtHR has long recognised that the provisions of the ECHR impose some positive obligations on Contracting Parties to protect individuals from the actions of private individuals which would, if carried out by state actors, breach the Convention.[125] It has also recognised the obligation to provide legal remedies for such actions.[126] But the Court in *Opuz* did not conclude its reasoning with findings of state responsibility (under Art 2) for the murder of the deceased and (under Art 3 for the domestic violence suffered by the complainant), proceeding instead to consider the application of Article 14. This itself was relatively unusual, the Court regularly declining to consider that provision when it has found breaches of other Convention rights.[127] Even more significantly, the Court ruled that:

> [W]hen considering the definition and scope of discrimination against women, in addition to the more general meaning of discrimination as determined in its case-law . . . the Court has to have regard to the provisions of more specialised legal instruments and the decisions of international legal bodies on the question of violence against women.[128]

The approach in *Opuz* involved the application of a principle first articulated in the 2009 decision in *Demir v Turkey*, in which the Court had relied on International Labour Organization Conventions and on the European Social Charter to modify its previous restrictive approach to Article 11 of the Convention in the context of trade union rights. In *Opuz* the ECtHR considered the jurisprudence developed under the Convention on the Elimination of all Forms of Violence Against Women (CEDAW), and the analysis of the UN's Special Rapporteurs on Violence against Women (VAW).

One of the key developments for which the Committee on CEDAW and the UN Special Rapporteur on VAW have been responsible has been the attribution of responsibility to the state for failures to prevent and to remedy private

---

[123] See discussion of the Equal Protection Clause of the Fourteenth Amendment to the US Constitution in Chapter 1.

[124] *Opuz v Turkey* (2010) 50 EHRR 28.

[125] See, for example, *Osman v UK* and *Z v UK* (2001) 34 EHRR 97, *X and Y v Netherlands* (1985) 8 EHRR 235.

[126] See, for example, *MC v Bulgaria* (2005) 40 EHRR 20.

[127] See, for example, *Lustig-Prean v UK* (1999) 29 EHRR 548, *Goodwin v UK* (2002) 35 EHRR 18.

[128] *Opuz v Turkey* (n 124) para 185, citing the decision in *Demir and Baykara v Turkey* (2009) 48 EHRR 54, para 85.

violence. From at least the latter part of the nineteenth century, international law has recognised that states may be held responsible not only for actions taken by and on behalf of the state itself but also, inter alia, for those of private individuals in respect of which it has 'connived . . . or failed to take adequate measures to prevent . . . or [has] . . . fail[ed] to make an adequate attempt to provide justice'.[129] This principle has been applied from time to time (by the ICJ in 1980 in the *Tehran Hostages Case*, for example,[130] and by the Inter-American Court of Human Rights in *Velasquez Rodriguez* (1988)[131]). It has also been recognised in the commentary to the 2001 International Law Commission's *Draft Articles on Responsibility of States for Internationally Wrongful Acts*.[132] But whatever the position in theory, the application of the doctrine of state responsibility to violence perpetrated against women in the 'private' sphere has been very slow.[133] Such violence is perhaps doubly insulated from the reach of international law because it is not only perpetrated by non-state actors (placing it outside the core concerns of international law) and often takes place within the 'private', domestic sphere.[134]

Instrumental in the recognition of violence against women as a human rights issue have been the activities of the Committee on CEDAW and of the UN Special Rapporteur on VAW.[135] More important for the present discussion, how-

---

[129] T Hillier, *Sourcebook on Public International Law* (London: Cavendish, 1998) 338. See also J Crawford and S Olleson, 'The Nature and Forms of International Responsibility' in M Evans et al (eds), *International Law*, 2nd edn (Oxford: Oxford University Press, 2003) 445. See also JA Hessbruegge, 'The Historical Development of the Doctrines of Attribution and Due Diligence in International Law' (2004) 36 *New York University Journal of International Law and Politics* 265; I Brownlie's discussion, in *System of the Law of Nations: State Responsibility (Part 1)* (Oxford: Oxford University Press, 1983) 161 of *Janes (US v Mexico)* 4 RIAA 82 (1926), *Youmans (US v Mexico)* 4 RIAA 110 (1926) and *Massey (US v Mexico)* 4 RIAA 155 (1927); and M Koskenniemi's discussion of the Train Smelter Arbitral Tribunal decision of 11 March 1941 in 'The Politics of International Law' (1990) 1 (1–2) *European Journal of International Law* 4–32, 19.

[130] *US Diplomatic and Consular Staff in Tehran (Hostages) (US v Iran)* 1980 ICR 1, discussed by R Barnidge, 'The Due Diligence Principle Under International Law' (2006) 8 *International Community Law Review* 81–121.

[131] *Velasquez Rodriguez*, Judgment of 29 July 1988, Inter-AmCtHR (Ser C) No 4 (1988).

[132] See J Cameron, The International Law Commission's Articles on State Responsibility: Introduction, Text and Commentary (Cambridge: Cambridge University Press, 2002) 61.

[133] See, for discussion, H Charlesworth, 'The Declaration on the Elimination of all Forms of Violence against Women', *American Society of International Law Newsletter: ASIL Insight* (June–August 1994) 1: 'The well-documented pattern of violence against women in all countries, ranging from murder and rape to domestic violence and genital mutilation, has traditionally been regarded as outside the scope of international law and a matter entirely within the domain of domestic national authorities'.

[134] See Y Ertürk, 'Third report to the UN Commission on Human Rights' (GE.06-10350 (E) 250106, available at www.coe.int) para 56.

[135] See, for example, General Recommendation 19 (1982) para 9, discussed by A Byrnes and E Bath, 'Violence against Women' (2008) 8(3) *Human Rights Law Review* 517, 519; R Coomaraswamy, 'Preliminary report on Violence against Women, its causes and consequences' UN Doc E/CN.4/195/42 (Nov 1994) pp 15–16, para 70: and E/CN.4/2000/68 (available at www2. ohchr.org) paras 51–53. In 2005 the CEDAW Committee, in *AT v Hungary* (2/2003, 26 January 2005, 12 IHRR 998) found a breach of the Convention's provisions in a case in which the complainant, who had suffered severe and regular domestic violence over a period of four years, alleged a failure on the part of the state to protect her from her former partner. And in 2006 the then Special

ever, is the characterisation of violence against women as a form of *discrimination*. In 1992 the CEDAW Committee adopted General Recommendation 19, which defined discrimination against women to include 'gender-based violence, that is, violence that is directed against a woman because she is a woman *or that affects women disproportionately*' (emphasis added).[136] This could be seen as a straightforward application of the concepts of direct and indirect discrimination but the characterisation of VAW as a form of discrimination in fact owes little to either. It is concerned far more with the nature of VAW as a form of gender-based oppression which perpetuates women's domination by men[137] than it is with questions, in particular, of whether the perpetrators of VAW would use similar techniques against men with whom they were in analogous relationships.[138] So, for example, General Recommendation 19 does not qualify the statement that 'the effect of [gender-based] violence on the physical and mental integrity of women is to deprive them of the equal enjoyment, exercise and knowledge of human rights and fundamental freedoms',[139] with any statement that this remains true only for so long as women are the primary victims of gender-based violence, or that the perpetrators of such violence employ it only against women.

Sophie Moreau's 'specific conceptions of the wrong of unequal treatment' were considered in Chapter 1. To recap, these consist of the denial of a benefit which wrongs individuals because: (i) it is based on prejudice or stereotyping; (ii) it perpetuates oppressive power relationships; or (iii) 'it leaves some individuals without access to basic goods'.[140] The definition of violence against women as a form of discrimination corresponds to Moreau's second and/or third categories. The third form of discrimination does not, in Moreau's view, require any comparative analysis.[141] The second does require such analysis, but

> the relevant comparator group is not the group that has been given the benefit in question but the group or groups who exercise oppressive amounts of power over those who have been denied the benefit . . . in order to ascertain whether the denial of a benefit genuinely perpetuates oppressive power relations, one needs to focus . . . on whether or not there is indeed some group that exercises an undue amount of power over those who are denied the benefit and on whether the denial of the benefit will perpetuate these unacceptable power relations.[142]

Rapporteur, Ertürk, suggested (Third report, para 57) that 'there is a rule of customary international law that obliges States to prevent and respond to acts of violence against women with due diligence'.

[136] Available at www.un.org/womenwatch.
[137] See for example General Recommendation 19 para 11.
[138] This being itself unlikely.
[139] General Recommendation 19 para 11.
[140] SR Moreau, 'The Wrongs of Unequal Treatment' (2004) 54 *University of Toronto Law Review* 291, 297.
[141] ibid, 308.
[142] ibid, 306.

In *Opuz v Turkey* the ECtHR relied on the CEDAW jurisprudence in concluding that the applicant's undisputed statistical evidence that 'domestic violence affected mainly women and that the general and discriminatory judicial passivity in Turkey created a climate that was conducive to domestic violence'[143] established a breach of Article 14 read with Articles 2 and 3 ECHR. It did so without any attempt to apply Article 14 in the formalistic manner exemplified by its decisions in cases such as *Carson* or *Burden*.

The question which arises is whether the decision in *Opuz* is to be regarded as a 'one off', or whether it is further confirmation (after *Thlimmenos* and *DH v Czech Republic*) of a significant movement on the part of the Court away from a formalistic approach to discrimination, which is preoccupied with questions of comparison between similarly situated individuals, to one concerned with the situations of disadvantage in which individuals or groups find themselves for reasons related to their ethnicity, sex, etc.

Early indications were not particularly promising. In *A v Croatia* the First Section found a breach of Article 8, but dismissed an Article 14 claim, in a case in which the applicant had been forced into hiding by the unsatisfactory response of the state to her multiple complaints of violence against her ex-husband.[144] The Article 14 claim was premised on the fact, inter alia, that over 75 per cent of domestic violence cases resulted in findings against both parties. The Court reiterated that:

> [A] general policy or measure which is apparently neutral but has disproportionately prejudicial effects on persons or groups of persons who, as for instance in the present case, are identifiable only on the basis of gender, may be considered discriminatory notwithstanding that it is not specifically aimed at that group . . . unless that measure is objectively justified by a legitimate aim and the means of achieving that aim are appropriate, necessary and proportionate.[145]

In the instant case, however, it found no evidence of systematic failure on the part of the state to deal with domestic violence despite the evidence that 'out of 173 sets of . . . proceedings conducted in 2007 in connection with incidents of domestic violence, in 132 . . . both spouses were found guilty'.[146]

Aksu v Turkey, decided in March 2012 by the Grand Chamber, further suggested that any development away from a formalistic 'like cases alike' approach was likely to occur in fits and starts. A challenge was brought under Articles 8 and 14 by a person of Roma origin in respect of government-funded publications which depicted Roma in a very negative light.[147] The first of these publications consisted in a book published in 2000 by the Ministry of Culture which, in the view of the applicant, characterised Roma as aggressive, polyga-

---

[143] *Opuz v Turkey* (n 124) para 198.
[144] *A v Croatia*, App no 55164/08, 14 October 2010, [2010] ECHR 55164/08, First Section.
[145] ibid, para 94.
[146] ibid, para 103.
[147] *Aksu v Turkey*, App nos 4149/04 and 41029/04, 27 July 2010 (Second Section) 15 March 2012 (Grand Chamber).

mous, 'thieves, pickpockets, swindlers, robbers, usurers, beggars, drug dealers, prostitutes and brothel keepers'.[148] The others were dictionaries, one of which was directed at school children, which were financed by the same Ministry and which contained definitions, some of which were said to be 'metaphorical' associating gypsies with miserliness, commotion, dirt, poverty, violence and vulgarity. Mr Aksu took the view that the publications violated his dignity, and complained of the state's refusal to prevent further sales of the book and to remove the offending definitions from the dictionary after he raised his complaint. His Convention challenge failed, in part because the author of the book had not expressed agreement with the views complained of, and had expressed disagreement with some,[149] and because the dictionary definitions of which Mr Aksu complained 'were based on historical and sociological reality and . . . there had been no intention to humiliate or debase an ethnic group'.[150]

Judges Tulkens, Tsotsoria and Pardalos dissented on the basis that the book contained several passages which 'convey a series of highly discriminatory prejudices and stereotypes, [and] should have given rise to serious explanation by the author, more forceful in tone than the work's concluding comments'.[151] The dissenters further took the view that 'In a [dictionary] financed by the Ministry of Culture and intended for pupils, the national authorities had an obligation to take all measures to ensure respect for Roma identity and to avoid any stigmatization'.[152] When the case came before the Grand Chamber, however, all but one of the 17 judges dismissed Mr Aksu's Article 8 claim, finding that the domestic courts had been entitled to make the findings that they did.[153]

The approach taken by the majority of Strasbourg's judges to Mr Aksu's Article 8 complaint might be rationalised by reference to the decision in *Jersild v Denmark* in which the Court upheld an Article 10 complaint by a journalist who had been prosecuted and fined for having broadcast racist remarks made by interviewees, whose comments he included in a documentary dealing with racism.[154] The decision turned in part on the significance accorded by the Court to press freedom but the Court also stressed the importance of the question 'whether the item in question, when considered as a whole, appeared from an objective point of view to have had as its purpose the propagation of racist views and ideas'.[155] While it was the case that the applicant's involvement had had the effect that racist statements which would otherwise have reached only a

---

[148] ibid (Grand Chamber) para 14. See para 12, however, for a list of the many occupations attributed to Roma, only a small number of which were disreputable.

[149] ibid, para 56.

[150] ibid, para 26 citing the Turkish court's decision with which the Grand Chamber did not disagree, ruling at para 57 that it saw no reason to disagree with the domestic courts and that 'the definitions provided by the dictionary were prefaced with the comment that the terms were of a metaphorical nature'.

[151] Dissenting opinions (ibid, Second Section), para 2.

[152] ibid, para 3.

[153] ibid, Grand Chamber, paras 69–70.

[154] *Jersild v Denmark* (1989) 13 EHRR 493.

[155] ibid, para 31.

small number of people were deliberately 'disseminated to a wide circle of people':[156]

> Taken as a whole, the feature could not objectively have appeared to have as its purpose the propagation of racist views and ideas. On the contrary, it clearly sought – by means of an interview – to expose, analyse and explain this particular group of youths, limited and frustrated by their social situation, with criminal records and violent attitudes, thus dealing with specific aspects of a matter that already then was of great public concern.[157]

More problematic for present purposes than the dismissal of Mr Aksu's Article 8 complaint, however, was the approach of the Grand Chamber to his Article 14 claim:

> 45. . . . . the Court observes that the case does not concern a difference in treatment, and in particular ethnic discrimination, as the applicant has not succeeded in producing *prima facie* evidence that the impugned publications had a discriminatory intent or effect . . .
>
> Accordingly, the main issue in the present case is whether the impugned publications, which allegedly contained racial insults, constituted interference with the applicant's right to respect for his private life and, if so, whether this interference was compatible with the said right . . .

Three months after its decision in *Aksu* the Grand Chamber reiterated, in *Kuric & Ors v Slovenia*, that 'in certain circumstances a failure to attempt to correct inequality through different treatment may, without an objective and reasonable justification, give rise to a breach of that Article'.[158] In *Makhashevy v Russia* (July 2012) the First Section found breaches of Articles 3 and 14 in a case in which the applicant ethnic Chechens were subject to physical ill-treatment and racist verbal abuse by Russian police officers. Interestingly for present purposes, the Court did not stop at its finding of a breach of the procedural aspect of Article 3 read with Article 14 arising from the state's failure 'in spite of the applicants' consistent complaints of racially motivated ill-treatment . . . to take all possible steps to investigate whether or not discrimination may have played a role in the events'.[159] It went on to find, on the evidence before it and, in the face of 'the evidence of verbal racial insults to which the applicants were subjected during the ill-treatment' and the absence of satisfactory evidence from the state, 'a violation of the substantive aspect of Article 3 of the Convention taken together with Article 14 of the Convention'.[160] And in *Eremia v Moldova* (May 2013) the Third Section found breaches of Articles 3, 8 and 14 arising from the domestic abuse by a police officer of his wife.[161] The state attempted to distin-

---

[156] ibid, para 32.
[157] ibid, para 33.
[158] *Kuric & Ors v Slovenia*, App no 26828/06, 26 June 2012, Grand Chamber, para 388, citing *Thlimmenos* para 44 and *DH* para 175.
[159] *Makhashevy v Russia* [2012] ECHR 20546/07, paras 145–46.
[160] ibid, paras 178–79.
[161] *Eremia v Moldova*, App no 3564/11, 28 May 2013, Third Section.

guish the decision in *Opuz* on the basis that the applicant's husband had in fact been subject to criminal proceedings, though he had not been prosecuted to conviction. Having referred to the fact that the authorities were aware of the violent abuse of the applicant by her husband, that the applicant's request that her divorce suit be expedited had been ignored, that an injunction designed for her protection had not been enforced and that her husband 'having confessed to beating [her] up . . . was essentially shielded from all responsibility following the prosecutor's decision to conditionally suspend proceedings'[162] the Court went on to state as follows:

> [T]he combination of the above factors clearly demonstrates that the authorities' actions were not a simple failure or delay in dealing with violence against the first applicant, but amounted to repeatedly condoning such violence and reflected a discriminatory attitude towards the first applicant as a woman . . . the authorities do not fully appreciate the seriousness and extent of the problem of domestic violence in Moldova and its discriminatory effect on women.
>
> Accordingly, in the particular circumstances of the present case, the Court finds that there has been a violation of Article 14 in conjunction with Article 3 of the Convention . . .[163]

This, like *Opuz*, might be characterised as an extreme case. The decision in *Eremia* makes clear, however, that the ECtHR is not wedded to a formalistic approach to discrimination, however much that approach may feature in the jurisprudence. There are indications that the decision in *Thlimmenos* carries at least the possibility of a radical approach on the part of the ECtHR to Article 14.

There have also been indications of a shift in the domestic case law. The tentative move away from a comparator-based approach to discrimination prohibited by the Equality Act 2010 and its predecessor provisions is discussed above. In the 2012 Court of Appeal decision in *Burnip v Birmingham City Council & Anor* Maurice Kay VP, with whom Hooper LJ agreed, suggested that 'It would be quite wrong to resort to [domestic case law] so as to produce a restrictive approach to Art 14. Indeed, one of the attractions of Art 14 is that its relatively non-technical drafting avoids some of the legalism that has affected domestic discrimination law'.[164] The Court went on to accept that a failure to make allowances for the fact that the claimants, who were in receipt of housing benefit, needed larger properties by reason of their or their children's disabilities and were therefore placed at a particular disadvantage by payment caps premised on smaller properties, breached Article 14. Perhaps of most significance was the reference made by Maurice Kay VP to the decisions of the ECtHR in *Demir* and in *Opuz*. Having remarked that the decisions did not appear to have been drawn to the attention of the judge below against whose decision the appeal was

---

[162] ibid, paras 86–88.
[163] ibid, paras 89–90.
[164] *Burnip v Birmingham City Council & Anor* [2012] EWCA Civ 629, [2012] LGR 954, para 14.

brought,[165] his Lordship declared that 'If the correct legal analysis of the meaning of art 14 discrimination in the circumstances of these appeals had been elusive or uncertain (and I have held that it is not), I would have resorted to the [UN Convention on the Rights of Persons with Disabilities]', which 'would have resolved the uncertainty in favour of the Appellants'.

More recently again, in *R (Knowles & Anor) v SSWP*, Hickinbottom J ruled (following *Burnip*) that 'the state may have a positive obligation to allocate a greater share of public resources to a particular person or group to ameliorate' what might be termed a *Thlimmenos* difference.[166] The claim there arose from the fact that housing benefit payments in respect of the costs of accommodation at caravan sites were calculated by reference to ordinary sites, and did not take account of the additional costs required to cover the infrastructure and management necessary to meet Gypsies' accommodation needs (additional site management, maintenance, clearance costs, fencing and security, education facilities for children, resolving disputes on site and with neighbours, and personal support which together were estimated to account for about a third of the costs at Gypsy sites[167]). Hickinbottom J accepted that 'Although very different on its facts, conceptually, this case appears to me indistinguishable from *Burnip*, in which the analysis was made in *Thlimmenos* terms' and that:

> Following *Burnip*, there is of course no conceptual or jurisdictional difficulty in finding a prima facie positive obligation on the state to allocate resources to remedy such a difference; and then proceeding to consider the reasons for the difference and whether they amount to an objective and reasonable justification.[168]

The claim failed, the bulk of the additional costs being ineligible to be met within the housing benefit scheme, but the case indicates that the Article 14 duty of reasonable accommodation is capable of extending beyond disability. It will be interesting to see whether the domestic courts outstrip the ECtHR in developing this approach to Article 14.

---

[165] ibid, para 21.
[166] *R (Knowles & Anor) v SSWP* [2013] EWHC 19 (Admin), para 63.
[167] ibid, paras 76, 77.
[168] ibid, para 73.

5

Competing Equalities

INTRODUCTION

IN CHAPTER 6 I consider the conflicts which may arise between the interests of minority 'groups' and those of the most vulnerable members of such groups (the 'paradox of multicultural vulnerability'[1]). Here my concern is with the conflicts which may arise between the equality claims of individuals pitted one against the other, and between the equality claims of individuals and other claims of right made by individuals or collectives. The difference between the conflicts involving collectives with which I am here concerned and those considered in the next chapter is that, whereas in Chapter 6 I discuss possible difficulties arising from the de facto allocation of power to groups over their members, the focus here is on what might be classified as *external* conflicts: those between the collective and individuals which are not located in the individual's membership of the group, or between individuals having particular religious or other beliefs and others. Such claims may arise where, for example, a religious body is permitted to reserve employment within its gift to believers, or to those defined by reference to other criteria such as sex. Individual–individual claims may arise where one person seeks to rely on her freedom of religion and/or her right not to be discriminated against because of her religion herself to discriminate on grounds, for example, of sex or sexual orientation.

Clashes between the equality claims of one party (A), and conflicting equality or other rights claims of the other (B), may be managed by means of broad justification defences such as those applicable to the prohibition of discrimination by Article 14 ECHR and (for example) section 15 of Canada's Charter of Rights.[2] The South African Constitution, further, prohibits only 'unfair' discrimination, and even that subject to a justification defence.[3] Equality claims brought by A or B under such provisions can be determined by reference to the concept of justification or unfairness or, as in Canada, by the nuanced approach to the concept of 'discrimination' itself adopted in cases such as *Andrews v Law Society of British Columbia* (1989), *Law v Canada* (1999), *R v Kapp* (2008) and

---

[1] See A Shachar, 'On Citizenship and Multicultural Vulnerability' (2000) 28 *Political Theory* 64, 65, discussed in Chapter 6.
[2] See further Chapter 1.
[3] See further Chapter 1.

Withler v Canada (Attorney General) (2011).[4] The Equality Act 2010, by contrast, in common with its predecessor provisions, does not permit the justification of direct discrimination other than in the case of age. This being so, there
is room for conflicts of rights to give rise to real legal difficulties in cases in
which no specific defence (such as the genuine occupational requirement
defence, further discussed below) applies. And whether or not the applicable
legal provisions permit equality claims to be defeated by reference to competing
equality or other rights claims, substantive questions arise concerning where the
lines should be drawn. How should my right to be free from sex discrimination
be balanced with your right to freedom of religious belief and practice, or not
to be treated less favourably because of your religious or other beliefs?

In this chapter I will consider a number of recent domestic conflict cases
involving claims of religious freedom made by individuals and organisations. It
is noteworthy that all the reported conflict claims which have arisen under the
statutory discrimination provisions have involved religion/belief. It is difficult
to conceive of situations in which my rights not to be discriminated against
because of my sex, sexual orientation or sexual identity, ethnicity, disability or
age conflict with your rights not to be discriminated against by reference to any
of these grounds.[5] The same cannot be said, as we shall see below, in the case of
religion/belief. My concern is primarily to consider whether and how conflicts
between religious freedom and equality can be reconciled within the existing
legal framework, and whether any difficulties to which such resolutions give rise
are merited by the principle of religious freedom or otherwise as a matter of
principle.

THE LEGAL FRAMEWORK: DOMESTIC

The Equality Act 2010 prohibits direct and indirect discrimination on grounds,
inter alia, of religion or belief, sex and sexual orientation, and imposes duties of
reasonable adjustment in respect of disability. Direct discrimination is now
defined as less favourable treatment 'because of' the relevant protected characteristic, indirect discrimination as formally equal treatment which unjustifiably
puts or would put the claimant, and persons of his or her relevant group,[6] at a
particular disadvantage.

---

[4] *Andrews v Law Society of British Columbia* [1989] 1 SCR 143; *Law v Canada* [1999] 1 SCR
497; *R v Kapp* [2008] 2 SCR 483; *Withler v Canada (Attorney General)* [2011] 1 SCR 396, discussed
in Chapter 1. It is not here suggested that these concepts provide the answers to the conflicts, rather
that they provide a legal mechanism through which the resolution can be reconciled with the prohibition on 'discrimination'.

[5] Leaving aside arguments arising in connection with positive action, which may result in less
favourable treatment of someone relatively advantaged by reference to a protected ground than of
someone relatively disadvantaged by reference to that ground: see Chapter 3. These conflicts, however, concern the meaning of 'discrimination' rather than the proper scope of its prohibition.

[6] ie, group defined by reference to relevant protected characteristic.

As mentioned above, direct discrimination is not (except in the case of age) subject to any general justification defence, though a number of exceptions to the prohibitions on such discrimination apply. Dealing first with the context of employment, broadly defined, the Equality Act 2010 provides a 'genuine occupational requirement' (GOR) defence which is broadly based on the 'GOR' defence permitted by the various EU directives[7] and which must be interpreted consistently therewith.[8] EU law thus permits differences in treatment where the protected characteristic is a 'genuine and determining factor' in relation to the job in question or the context in which it is carried out, 'provided that the objective is legitimate and the requirement is proportionate'.[9] Article 4(2) of Council Directive 2000/78/EC further permits national legislation which

> in the case of occupational activities within churches and other public or private organisations the ethos of which is based on religion or belief, a difference of treatment based on a person's religion or belief [but not any other ground] shall not constitute discrimination where, by reason of the nature of these activities or of the context in which they are carried out, a person's religion or belief constitute a genuine, legitimate and justified occupational requirement, having regard to the organisation's ethos.

Article 4(2) goes on to state that:

> [T]his Directive shall thus not prejudice the right of churches and other public or private organisations, the ethos of which is based on religion or belief, acting in conformity with national constitutions and laws, to require individuals working for them to act in good faith and with loyalty to the organisation's ethos.[10]

The Equality Act 2010 transposes the general GOR defence in terms which are materially similar to the EU provision.[11] Article 4(2) is given effect to by Schedule 9, paragraphs 2 and 3. The latter, which is relatively unproblematic, provides to employers 'with an ethos based on religion or belief' a GOR which is slightly more generous in that it permits them to discriminate on grounds of religion or belief where 'having regard to that ethos and to the nature or context of the work', such is an 'occupational requirement' the application of which is 'a proportionate means of achieving a legitimate aim'. More controversial is paragraph 2 which provides that employers may discriminate in relation to

---

[7] Specifically, Art 4 Council Directive 2000/78/EC, Art 4 Council Directive 2000/43/EC, Art 15(2) Council Directive 2006/54/EC.

[8] See Case C-106/89 *Marleasing v La Comercial Internacional de Alimentacion* [1990] ECR I-4135, *Webb (No 2)* [1995] 1 WLR 1454.

[9] Council Directive 2000/78/EC regulates (broadly) employment-related discrimination on grounds of sexual orientation, religion and belief, age and disability; Council Directive 2000/43/EC discrimination across a broad material scope on grounds of race, and Council Directive 2006/54/EC sex discrimination in the context of employment (broadly defined) and social security. Sex discrimination in goods and services is regulated by Council Directive 2004/113/EC.

[10] The second paragraph of Article 4(2) was a late inclusion in the Directive, not having featured in the draft Directive which was circulated as late as October 2010 (the Directive was adopted in December).

[11] Sch 9, para 1.

'employment . . . for the purposes of an organised religion' on grounds of sex, sexual orientation, gender identity, marital or civil partnership status, where such is required 'to comply with the doctrines of the religion' or 'because of the nature or context of the employment . . . to avoid conflicting with the strongly held religious convictions of a significant number of the religion's followers . . .'.

The Equality Bill in its original form required that the paragraph 2 GOR was a *proportionate* way of complying with the doctrines of the religion or of avoiding conflict with beliefs. In addition, the clause had provided that employment would only be classified as being for the purposes of an organised religion if it 'wholly or mainly involves (a) leading or assisting in the observation of liturgical or ritualistic practices of the religion, or (b) promoting or explaining the doctrine of the religion (whether to followers of the religion or to others)'. It was suggested, for the government, that the provision was intended to apply to 'senior employees with representational roles' ('the secretary-general of the General Synod and the Archbishops' Council of the Church of England . . . senior lay post[s] at the Catholic Bishops' Conference charged with acting on behalf of bishops when contributing to public policy developments' and the like),[12] also to those 'key function[s]' involving religious instruction. The government spokeswoman in the Lords went on to indicate that the exemption was unlikely to apply to a 'church youth worker who primarily organises sporting activities', 'to employees such as administrative staff, accountants, caretakers or cleaners' or 'to most staff working in press or communications offices, although senior and high-profile roles within such offices that exist to represent or promote the religion would probably be within its scope'.[13]

The current wording of Schedule 9, paragraph 2 is the result of a late amendment moved in the House of Lords by Conservative Lady O'Cathain. It was the government's view that its proposed wording would simply give express effect to the decision in the *Amicus* case, considered below, in which the High Court adopted a narrow interpretation of Regulation 7(3) of the Employment Equality (Sexual Orientation) Regulations 2003 (which was materially similar to para 2) in an attempt to make it compatible with the 2000/78 Directive.[14] The religious Right took the view, however, that the form proposed in the Equality Bill would have narrowed the scope of lawful discrimination by religious organisations considerably and Baroness Butler-Sloss suggested that the requirement for proportionality might threaten the Catholic Church's requirement that priests be celibate.[15]

As the Joint Committee on Human Rights pointed out in its Fourteenth Report of 2009–10,[16] paragraph 2 appears to be significantly more permissive

[12] HL Debs, 25 Jan 2010, cols 1215–16.

[13] Baroness Royall of Blaisdon, for the government (HL Debs, 25 Jan 2010, cols 1215–16).

[14] R *(Amicus) v Secretary of State for Trade & Industry* [2004] IRLR 430.

[15] Above n 13, col 1220.

[16] Legislative Scrutiny: Equality Bill (second report); Digital Economy Bill (www.publications. parliament.uk/pa/jt200910/jtselect/jtrights/73/73.pdf).

than Article 4 of Directive 2000/78 allows. The Committee drew attention to a reasoned opinion of the European Commission on Regulation 7(3) which, unusually, had found its way into the public domain.[17] The Commission there stated that Article 4 of Directive 2000/78 'contains a strict test which must be satisfied if a difference of treatment is to be considered non-discriminatory: there must be a genuine and determining occupational requirement, the objective must be legitimate and the requirement proportionate'; and that the wording of Regulation 7(3), which was materially similar to that of paragraph 2, 'is too broad, going beyond the definition of a genuine occupational requirement allowed under Art 4(1) of the Directive' and 'contradicts the provision under Art 4(2) of the Directive which provides that permitted differences of treatment based on religion "should not justify discrimination on another ground" '.

Notwithstanding the actual wording of paragraph 2, that provision must be interpreted, so far as possible, to be compatible with relevant EU law. The High Court in *R (Amicus) v Secretary of State for Trade & Industry* did not accept that Regulation 7(3) permitted a church's refusal to employ a gay cleaner 'in a building in which he is liable to handle religious artefacts, to avoid offending the strongly-held religious convictions of a significant number of adherents', a Catholic Order's dismissal of a science teacher for having a lesbian relationship, a religious shop's refusal to employ a lesbian shop assistant where the shop was engaged in 'selling scriptural books and tracts on behalf of an organisation formed for the purpose of upholding and promoting a fundamentalist interpretation of the Bible', or the refusal of an Islamic institute 'to employ as a librarian a man appearing to the employer to be homosexual'.[18] According to Richards J, as he then was:

> [T]he exception was intended to be very narrow; and in my view it is, on its proper construction, very narrow. It has to be construed strictly since it is a derogation from the principle of equal treatment; and it has to be construed purposively so as to ensure, so far as possible, compatibility with the Directive. When its terms are considered in the light of those interpretative principles, they can be seen to afford an exception only in very limited circumstances.[19]

I return below to the scope of the GOR defence applicable to religious organisations. The Equality Act, however, extends its prohibitions on discrimination well beyond employment, however broadly defined, to cover housing, access to goods and services and the exercise of public functions, inter alia. The GOR defence obviously has no application in these contexts, though the Act provides a number of other exceptions which may be relevant to the kinds of conflicts here under consideration. Thus Schedule 3 provides that the prohibitions on discrimination in relation to services and public functions shall not prevent the provision of single-sex services where (broadly) such is a proportionate means

[17]   ibid, para 1.9.
[18]   *R (Amicus) v Secretary of State for Trade & Industry* (n 14) para 95.
[19]   ibid, para 115.

of achieving a legitimate aim, as well as where considerations of decency or privacy apply.[20] The Act also makes generous provision for single-sex education[21] and, more generally, allows services to be provided only for persons who share a particular protected characteristic where the provider reasonably thinks that it is impracticable to provide the service to persons who do not share that characteristic.[22] Further, associations other than registered political parties may restrict membership to persons sharing any of the protected characteristics other than colour.[23]

Of more direct relevance, the Act permits religious ministers and others appointed for the purposes of religious organisations to provide single-sex services for the purposes of an organised religion, at a place which is (permanently or otherwise) occupied or used for those purposes, where 'the limited provision of the service is necessary in order to comply with the doctrines of the religion or is for the purpose of avoiding conflict with the strongly held religious convictions of a significant number of the religion's followers'.[24] Faith schools may discriminate on grounds of religion or belief in relation to admission and pupils' access to benefits, facilities or services, and the Act exempts from the prohibitions on discrimination on grounds of religion and belief in the context of education 'anything done in connection with acts of worship or other religious observance organised by or on behalf of a school'.[25]

The exceptions permitted by the Equality Act to the prohibitions on discrimination other than in the context of employment are subject to EU law only in so far as they concern sex and race, discrimination on grounds of religion or belief, age, disability and sexual orientation being regulated by EU law only in relation to employment (broadly defined). Council Directive 2000/43 (the Race Directive) permits no exceptions for race discrimination other than the GOR, discussed above. That Directive regulates discrimination on grounds of 'racial or ethnic origin' (excluding nationality discrimination) in relation to employment (broadly defined), 'social protection, including social security and healthcare', 'social advantages', 'education' and 'access to and supply of goods and services which are available to the public, including housing',[26] with the proviso that the Directive's application is 'Within the limits of the powers conferred upon the Community'. Discrimination by associations is unlikely to fall within the Directive's prohibition on discrimination in access to *publicly available*

[20] Part 7, paras 26–28.

[21] Sch 11, part 1 and Sch 12.

[22] Part 7, para 30.

[23] Also access by associates to benefits, and invitations to guests: Sch 16 Associations are regulated by the Equality Act 2010 only if they have at least 25 members (s 107).

[24] Sch 3, part 7, para 29. A religious organisation is one whose purpose is to practise or advance a religion, to teach its practice or principles, to enable persons of the religion to receive benefits, or to engage in activities, within the framework of that religion, or to foster or maintain good relations between persons of different religions, and whose sole or main purpose is not commercial.

[25] See Sch 11, part 2, para 5 for the categories of school permitted to discriminate on grounds of religion and belief.

[26] Art 3.

goods and services. And Directive 2004/113/EC, which regulates sex discrimination in access to goods and services, specifically excludes education from its scope, does 'not preclude differences in treatment, if the provision of the goods and services exclusively or primarily to members of one sex is justified by a legitimate aim and the means of achieving that aim are appropriate and necessary'.[27]

THE LEGAL FRAMEWORK:
THE EUROPEAN CONVENTION ON HUMAN RIGHTS

Also relevant to the legal analysis of conflicts which may arise, whether between individuals and individuals or individuals and collectives, are Articles 9 and 14 of the European Convention. The latter provides that:

> The enjoyment of the rights and freedoms set forth in this Convention shall be secured without discrimination on any ground such as sex, race, colour, language, religion, political or other opinion, national or social origin, association with a national minority, property, birth or other status.

The former provides that:

> 1. Everyone has the right to freedom of thought, conscience and religion; this right includes freedom to change his religion or belief, and freedom, either alone or in community with others and in public or private, to manifest his religion or belief, in worship, teaching, practice and observance.
> 2. Freedom to manifest one's religion or beliefs shall be subject only to such limitations as are prescribed by law and are necessary in a democratic society in the interests of public safety, for the protection of public order, health or morals, or the protection of the rights and freedoms of others.

Article 9 is somewhat unusual in combining an *absolute* right to *hold* beliefs with a *qualified* right to manifest them. The 'right to freedom of thought, conscience and religion . . . includ[ing] freedom to change [one's] religion or belief' is one of the very few unqualified rights recognised by the European Convention, and while the right to manifest 'religion or belief, in worship, teaching, practice and observance' is not unqualified, the right protected by Article 9 has been described by the ECtHR as:

> [O]ne of the foundations of a 'democratic society' within the meaning of the Convention [which] . . . in its religious dimension, [is] one of the most vital elements that go to make up the identity of believers and their conception of life [and] is also a precious asset for atheists, agnostics, sceptics and the unconcerned.[28]

Any interference with the 'psychic' or 'internal' aspects of Article 9 will breach that provision regardless of its aims and without consideration of any competing

---

[27] Art 4(5).
[28] *Kokkinakis v Greece* (1994) 17 EHRR 397, para 31.

interests or rights: religious freedom trumps. The same is true of direct interference with the internal affairs of religious organisations in the form, for example, of refusals to grant churches recognition required to function within a state,[29] intervention in leadership disputes,[30] and attempts to unify a divided religious community.[31] In *Metropolitan Church of Bessarabia v Moldova* the Court stressed the importance of neutrality on the part of the state in the exercise of any regulatory function and the centrality of pluralism and tolerance:

> [I]n principle the right to freedom of religion for the purposes of the Convention excludes assessment by the State of the legitimacy of religious beliefs or the ways in which those beliefs are expressed. State measures favouring a particular leader or specific organs of a divided religious community or seeking to compel the community or part of it to place itself, against its will, under a single leadership, would also constitute an infringement of the freedom of religion. In democratic societies the State does not need to take measures to ensure that religious communities remain or are brought under a unified leadership.[32]

This does not mean that the state may play no role in collective religious matters. In *Serif v Greece* the European Court regarded as 'arguable' the proposition that 'it is in the public interest for the State to take special measures in order to protect those whose legal relationships can be affected by the acts of religious ministers from deceit', though the issue did not arise on the facts of the case.[33] There the applicant had been criminalised for passing himself off as a minister in circumstances in which his election as mufti was internally contested. Had he officiated at religious weddings, to which legal effect was given, or claimed to make legally binding decisions on family or inheritance matters,[34] the outcome might well have been different. Certainly there appears to be no objection to a system of registration where the state does not involve itself in disputes of substance.[35]

Religious organisations are protected from direct state interference with their internal affairs. But there is little or no jurisprudence on the extent to which such organisations carry their protection with them when they engage in activities in the non-sacred, or secular, context. Certainly the European Commission and Court of Human Rights have been slow to recognise constraints imposed on religious individuals in their dealings with the outside world as 'interferences' for the purposes of Article 9, even where those constraints have prevented

---

[29] *Metropolitan Church of Bessarabia v Moldova* [2002] 35 EHRR 306.

[30] See for example *Hasan & Chaush v Bulgaria* (2002) 34 EHRR 55.

[31] *Supreme Holy Council of the Muslim Community v Bulgaria* (2005) 41 EHRR 43, *Holy Synod of the Bulgarian Orthodox Church (Metropolitan Inokentiy) & Ors v Bulgaria* App nos 412/03 and 35677/04, [2009] ECHR 412/03.

[32] *Metropolitan Church of Bessarabia v Moldova* [2002] 35 EHRR 306, para 117.

[33] *Serif v Greece* (2001) 31 EHRR 20, para 50.

[34] Greek law recognising such marriages and some such decisions when made by ministers of a 'known religion'.

[35] Though note that the UK prime minister appoints the Archbishop of Canterbury as head of the Anglican Church.

them from reconciling their religious convictions with their occupational or educational ambitions. Thus, for example, in *Ahmad v UK* (1982), the Commission rejected as 'manifestly ill-founded' an application from a Muslim teacher who complained that he had not been permitted to attend religious worship on a Friday afternoon. The Commission remarked that the applicant 'remained free to resign if and when he found that his teaching obligations conflicted with his religious duties'.[36] The Commission reached a similar decision in *Stedman v UK* (1997) in which the applicant had been subject to the unilateral imposition of an obligation to work on Sundays which, she argued, was incompatible with her Christian beliefs,[37] ruling that she 'was dismissed for failing to agree to work certain hours rather than for her religious belief as such and was free to resign and did in effect resign from her employment'. And in *Karaduman v Turkey* (1993) the Commission peremptorily dismissed an Article 9 challenge from a Muslim student refused permission to graduate from her university studies unless she was prepared to be photographed without her headscarf.[38]

The Commission failed in *Karaduman*, as it had in *Ahmed* and *Stedman*, to recognise any interference with the applicant's Article 9 rights. More recently, the ECtHR has begun to accept that restrictions with which members of particular religious groups find it difficult in practice to comply may interfere with the religious beliefs of individual applicants. The Court is quick, however, to find such restrictions justified within Article 9(2). In *Dahlab v Switzerland* (2001), for example, it rejected as manifestly unfounded an Article 9 challenge to a headscarf ban imposed on a Muslim primary school teacher.[39] It was, the Court suggested, 'very difficult to assess the impact that a powerful external symbol such as the wearing of a headscarf may have on the freedom of conscience and religion of very young children'; 'the wearing of a headscarf might have some kind of proselytising effect, seeing that it appears to be imposed on women by a precept which is laid down in the Koran and which . . . is hard to square with the principle of gender equality'; and it was 'difficult to reconcile the wearing of an Islamic headscarf with the message of tolerance, respect for others and, above all, equality and non-discrimination that all teachers in a democratic society must convey to their pupils'.

The justification in *Dahlab* rested significantly on the fact that the applicant was a teacher of young children. In the more recent decision of *Şahin v Turkey*,[40] however, the Grand Chamber upheld a complete headscarf ban imposed by a Turkish university, agreeing with the Fourth Section that the principles of secularism and gender equality, on which it accepted that the ban was based,

[36] *Ahmad v UK* (1982) 4 EHRR 126.

[37] *Stedman v UK* (1997) 23 EHRR CD 168.

[38] *Karaduman v Turkey* (1993) 74 DR 93, 108. See also the majority view in *Copsey v WWB Devon Clays Ltd* [2005] ICR 1789 and the views of Lords Scott, Hoffmann and Bingham in *R (B) v Headteacher and Governors of Denbigh High School* [2007] 1 AC 100.

[39] *Dahlab v Switzerland*, App no 42393/98, 15 January 2001.

[40] *Şahin v Turkey* (2007) 44 EHRR 5.

justified the interference with the applicant's Article 9 rights. The Fourth Section had expressed concern about the impact of the headscarf, 'presented or perceived as a compulsory religious duty . . . on those who choose not to wear it' in Turkey: 'a country in which the majority of the population, while professing a strong attachment to the rights of women and a secular way of life, adhere to the Islamic faith'. [41] That Court had adverted to the perceived politicisation of the headscarf in Turkey in recent years and to 'the fact that there are extremist political movements in Turkey which seek to impose on society as a whole their religious symbols and conception of a society founded on religious precepts'.[42] The Grand Chamber agreed, stating that 'the principle of secularism . . . is the paramount consideration underlying the ban on the wearing of religious insignia in universities':

> In such a context, where the values of pluralism, respect for the rights of others and, in particular, equality before the law of men and women are being taught and applied in practice, it is understandable that the relevant authorities should wish to preserve the secular nature of the institution concerned and so consider it contrary to such values to allow religious attire, including, as in the present case, the Islamic headscarf, to be worn.[43]

The Grand Chamber went so far as to suggest that, given the diversity of approaches across Europe on the issue, the extent and form of regulations concerning the wearing of religious symbols in educational institutions 'must inevitably be left up to a point to the state concerned, as it will depend on the domestic context concerned',[44] though 'this margin of appreciation goes hand in hand with a European supervision embracing both the law and the decisions applying it'.[45] It further suggested that 'An attitude which fails to respect th[e] principle [of secularism] will not necessarily be accepted as being covered by the freedom to manifest one's religion and will not enjoy the protection of art 9 of the convention'.[46]

In Chapter 6 I challenge the assumption that the imposition by the state of restrictions on women's clothing is necessarily consistent with the pursuit of gender equality. The effect on the applicants in the headscarf cases was to restrict their access to education and/or work. Further, the approach taken in *Şahin* to the perceived manifestation of 'An attitude which fails to respect th[e] principle [of secularism]' involves 'determin[ing] in a general and abstract way

---

[41] *Şahin v Turkey* (2005) 41 EHRR 8, para 108.
[42] ibid, para 109.
[43] ibid, para 116.
[44] *Şahin v Turkey* (n 40) para 109 citing *Gorzelik v Poland* (2004) 38 EHRR 4, para 7 and *Murphy v Ireland* (2004) 38 EHRR 13, para 73.
[45] ibid, para 110.
[46] ibid, para 114, citing *Refah Partisi v Turkey* (2002) 35 EHRR 3, para 93. For a critical discussion of *Şahin* see, for example, Manisuli Ssenyonjo, 'The Islamic Veil and Freedom of Religion, the Rights to Education and Work: a Survey of Recent International and National Cases' (2007) 6 *Chinese Journal of International Law* 653. cf the decision in *Eweida v UK* (2013) 57 EHRR 213, discussed in Chapter 4 and below.

the signification of wearing the headscarf [and] impos[ing] its viewpoint on the applicant', a move characterised by Judge Tulkens, dissenting, as going beyond the proper role of the Court.[47] Finally, the decision in Şahin stands in stark contrast to the decision in *Gündüz v Turkey*,[48] to take just one example, in which Article 10 provided protection in respect of explicit and extreme denouncements of the secular state by the applicant, whose critique was based on his interpretation of Islam. It may be, of course, that the difference in approach can be explained by the fact that, whereas in Article 10 cases, applicants are generally seeking bare freedom from punitive action by the state, in the Article 9 cases considered above the religious individual is seeking *accommodation* of his or her religious beliefs or practices. But the limited nature of the Article 9 protection has traditionally been such that the provision does not necessarily protect even those individuals whose religious beliefs bring them into direct conflict with the criminal law.

Cases in which accommodation is sought by believers can in practice involve interferences with the *holding* as well as the *manifestation* of beliefs,[49] as where a person's beliefs demand action which is not regarded as a matter of personal choice in circumstances in which conflict with the state cannot be avoided. Examples might include adherence to pacifism, to a particular mode of dress, or to cultural practices such as female genital cutting (FGC) and religious family law considered in Chapter 6. The prohibition by the state of FGC or of the display of religious identity at schools at which attendance is compulsory, the imposition of an obligation to perform military service, or a state override of parental refusal of blood transfusions for children, does not on its face interfere with the *holding* of religious beliefs: the relevant *beliefs* are not itself proscribed. But those *beliefs* are manifestly interfered with when the individual is prevented from acting in accordance with them, at least where there is not the opportunity to avoid the conflict even at cost. Yet not until July 2011, with the decision of the Grand Chamber in *Bayatyan v Armenia*, did the Convention organs accept, for example, that mandatory military service breached the Article 9 rights of pacifists even in the absence of civilian alternatives to armed service.[50] Prior to that decision the ECtHR had not considered the question but the Commission

---

[47] *Şahin v Turkey* (n 40) O-II12.

[48] *Gündüz v Turkey* (2005) 41 EHRR 5.

[49] This has been recognised by the US Supreme Court eg in *Wisconsin v Yoder* 406 US 205 (1972), discussed in Chapter 6, though only to the extent of recognising that interference with *action* as distinct from *belief* could require justification from the state under the first Amendment: see G Moens, 'The Action-Belief Dichotomy and Freedom of Religion' (1989–90) 12 *Sydney Law Review* 195, 207–10.

[50] *Bayatyan v Armenia* [2011] 32 BHRC 290. cf *Peters v the Netherlands* (App no 22793/93, Commission decision of 30 November 1994, unpublished); *Heudens v Belgium* (App no 24630/94, Commission decision of 22 May 1995, unpublished); *Valsamis v Greece* (1997) 24 EHRR 294 and *Bayatyan v Armenia*, 29 October 2009), [2009] ECHR 23459/03 (Third Section). Note that in *Thlimmenos v Greece* (2001) 31 EHRR 15 and *Ülke v Turkey* (App no 39437/98) the Court had found breaches of Articles 14 and 3 respectively arising from arbitrary and manifestly excessive punishment of refusal to serve.

had, on a number of occasions, concluded that conscientious objection was excluded from the scope of Article 9 by Article 4(3)(b) of the Convention, which provides that the forced or compulsory labour prohibited by Article 4(2) shall not include 'any service of a military character or, in case of conscientious objectors in countries where they are recognised, service exacted instead of compulsory military service'. In *Bayatyan* the Court ruled that this interpretive approach was no longer correct:

> [T]he *travaux preparatoires* confirm that the sole purpose of sub-para (b) of art 4(3) is to provide a further elucidation of the notion 'forced or compulsory labour'. In itself it neither recognises nor excludes a right to conscientious objection and should therefore not have a delimiting effect on the rights guaranteed by art 9.[51]

The Court went on to refer to the Convention as a 'living instrument which must be interpreted in the light of present-day conditions and of the ideas prevailing in democratic states today',[52] and to the increased recognition across European states and more broadly of a right to conscientious objection. It concluded that 'art 9 should no longer be read in conjunction with art 4(3)(b)'. [53] While

> art 9 does not explicitly refer to a right to conscientious objection . . . opposition to military service, where it is motivated by a serious and insurmountable conflict between the obligation to serve in the army and a person's conscience or his deeply and genuinely held religious or other beliefs, constitutes a conviction or belief of sufficient cogency, seriousness, cohesion and importance to attract the guarantees of art 9.[54]

The decision in *Eweida v UK*[55] is as significant in marking a change in approach on the part of the ECtHR to Article 9 as was that in *Bayatyan*. The applicant in *Eweida* was a member of British Airways check-in staff who wore a cross on a chain around her neck. This was concealed by her clothing until a uniform change replaced high-necked blouses for female staff with open-necked blouses and brought Ms Eweida into conflict with a ban on the display of non-uniform items. Approval had been given for the wearing of Sikh turbans and kara (bangles) and for hijabs worn in approved colours but Ms Eweida was refused permission to wear the cross and lost some pay as a result of being suspended before the policy was altered. Her indirect discrimination and Article 9 claims failed in the domestic courts but the ECtHR accepted that her Article 9 rights had been breached. The Court acknowledged that the Commission's case law suggested that an employee's freedom to resign meant that restrictions placed on his or her ability to observe religious practice did not amount to an interference with Article 9 rights, an approach not applied by the Court in cases arising

---

[51] *Bayatyan v Armenia*, ibid, para 100.
[52] ibid, para 102.
[53] ibid, para 109.
[54] ibid, para 110.
[55] *Eweida v UK* (n 46).

under Articles 8 or 10 (*Smith and Grady v UK*, *Vogt v Germany* and *Young, James & Webster v United Kingdom*):[56]

> Given the importance in a democratic society of freedom of religion, the Court considers that, where an individual complains of a restriction on freedom of religion in the workplace, rather than holding that the possibility of changing job would negate any interference with the right, the better approach would be to weigh that possibility in the overall balance when considering whether or not the restriction was proportionate.[57]

The Court went on to find that, in Ms Eweida's case:

> [A] fair balance was not struck. On one side of the scales was Ms Eweida's desire to manifest her religious belief . . . this is a fundamental right: because a healthy democratic society needs to tolerate and sustain pluralism and diversity; but also because of the value to an individual who has made religion a central tenet of his or her life to be able to communicate that belief to others. On the other side of the scales was the employer's wish to project a certain corporate image . . . while this aim was undoubtedly legitimate, the domestic courts accorded it too much weight. Ms Eweida's cross was discreet and cannot have detracted from her professional appearance. There was no evidence that the wearing of other, previously authorised, items of religious clothing, such as turbans and hijabs, by other employees, had any negative impact on British Airways' brand or image. Moreover, the fact that the company was able to amend the uniform code to allow for the visible wearing of religious symbolic jewellery demonstrates that the earlier prohibition was not of crucial importance.[58]

The Court found, therefore, that Ms Eweida's Article 9 rights had been breached by the UK's failure 'sufficiently to protect [her] right to manifest her religion, in breach of the positive obligation under Article 9', declining in view of this conclusion to examine her claim under Article 14 read with Article 9. It ruled, in the joined case of *Chaplin v UK*, that the imposition of a 'no necklace' rule on a nurse working in a geriatric ward, which rule prevented her from wearing a cross and chain, did not breach her Article 9 rights. In view of the health and safety reasons for the ban, the prohibition of Sikh kara and flowing hijab and the applicant's refusal of suggested compromises which would have involved wearing a cross in the form of a brooch attached to her uniform, or tucked under a high-necked top worn under her tunic (the latter having in practice been the case prior to a change in the nursing uniform rendering the cross visible, the Court accepted that the hospital authorities had not strayed beyond their margin of appreciation.

The decision in *Eweida* underlines a very significant expansion in the protection afforded by Article 9. In addition to the obvious evolution from *Dahlab* and *Şahin*, it is important to note that Ms Eweida was employed by a

---

[56] *Smith and Grady v UK* (1999) 29 EHRR 493, para 71; *Vogt v Germany* (1995) 21 EHRR 205, para 44; *James & Webster v United Kingdom* (1982) 4 EHRR 38, paras 54–55.
[57] *Eweida v UK* (n 46) para 83.
[58] ibid, para 94.

private company and not by the state. This being the case, the UK's breach of her Article 9 rights consisted not in direct action against her by the state, rather (para 95) in a 'fail[ure] sufficiently to protect [her] right to manifest her religion, in breach of the positive obligation under Article 9'. While there has been a steady march by the ECtHR since at least 1985 to impose positive obligations requiring contracting states to prevent or remedy quasi-breaches of Convention rights by private actors,[59] there were no examples of such positive obligations being imposed under or in connection with Article 9 prior to the decision in *Eweida*,[60] and scant examples of strong positive obligations being imposed in connection with other Convention provisions in the employment context. Thus, although the Court did accept in *Wilson v UK* that, in permitting employers to use financial incentives to induce employees to surrender important union rights, the United Kingdom had failed in its positive obligation to secure the enjoyment of rights under Article 11,[61] much more typical of the general approach is the decision in *Rommelfanger v Germany* (1989) in which the Commission rejected a complaint brought under Article 10 by a doctor who had been dismissed from his position at a Catholic hospital having put his name (one of 50) to a letter concerning domestic abortion legislation.[62] The Commission required only that there was a 'reasonable relation between the measures affecting freedom of expression and the nature of the employment as well as the importance of the issue for the employer' in ruling that Article 10 had not been breached.[63]

Prior to the decision in *Eweida*, and even where the employer was the state (with the effect that active interference, rather than an alleged failure to comply with positive obligations, is at issue), the competing interests of the state as employer would readily justify interference with employees' rights as in *B v UK* (1985), *X v UK* (1979) and *Morissens v Belgium* (1988), in which complaints relating to the dismissal of teachers who, respectively, complained of sexual orientation discrimination, repeated attempts to evangelise co-workers, and to the subjection to disciplinary action of a worker who spoke out about safety fears at a nuclear installation, were dismissed as 'manifestly ill founded'.[64] More

---

[59] The first example was *X & Y v Netherlands* (1985) 8 EHHR 235 which built on decisions requiring other forms of positive actions by contracting states in *Marckx v Belgium* (1979) 2 EHRR 330 and *Airey v Ireland* (1979) 2 EHRR 305. Since then positive obligations have been imposed in connection with most of the Convention provisions, the most extensive case law having developed under Articles 2, 3 and 8.

[60] *Jakóbski v Poland* (2012) 55 EHRR 8 in which the Court relied on the state's positive obligations (para 46) involved the denial to a Buddhist prisoner, by the state, of a meat free diet. Cases such as *Otto Preminger Institute v Austria* (1994) 19 EHRR 34 and *Wingrove v UK* (1996) 24 EHRR 1 para 48 in which states have been permitted to rely on Article 9 positive obligations to justify Article 10 interferences have, further, been doubted more recently by the dissenters (3/7) in *IA v Turkey* (2007) 45 EHRR 704.

[61] *Wilson v UK* (2002) 36 EHRR 1.

[62] *Rommelfanger v Germany* 62 D & R 151.

[63] ibid.

[64] *B v UK* (1985) 45 D & R 41, *X v UK* (1979) 56 D & R 127 and *Morissens v Belgium* (1988) 16 D & R 101.

recently, too, in *Pay v UK* (2009), the Court rejected, also as manifestly ill founded, complaints under Articles 8, 10 and 14 by a probation officer dismissed in connection with his merchandising of products connected with bondage, domination and sado-masochism and his performances in hedonist and fetish clubs.[65] The Court assumed, for the purposes of the case, that the applicant's rights under Articles 8 and 10 were engaged, but accepted that the interference pursued the employer's legitimate interests in protecting its reputation, the applicant's work with convicted sex offenders making it important that he retained the respect of those offenders and the confidence of the general public in general and victims of sex crime in particular. In the Court's view, the UK had not exceeded the margin of appreciation available to them in adopting a cautious approach as regards the extent to which public knowledge of the applicant's sexual activities could impair his ability to carry out his duties effectively.

Bearing all this in mind, the decision in *Eweida* that the state had breached a private employee's Article 9 rights by failing to protect her from a loss of wages caused in part by her refusal to transfer from a customer-facing role into one in which the uniform policy would not have applied (this being the compromise offered to and rejected by Ms Eweida after a month of unpaid suspension from work), is remarkable. Further, it stands in obvious contrast to that in *Şahin*, in which the Court ruled that Turkey did not breach the Article 9 rights of a university student by directly preventing her from attending university while adhering to what she regarded as her religious obligation to cover her hair. The applicant, who was by then in her fifth year of study, continued her studies in Austria though it must be assumed that many women similarly affected by the ban would not have the financial means so to do. The interference in *Şahin* appears markedly more severe than that in *Eweida*, as does the loss of employment in *Dahlab*, and the expulsion of an 11-year-old schoolgirl in *Dogru v France* (2008) because the headscarf which she insisted on wearing was regarded by her school as incompatible with her participation in PE classes.[66] The full implications of the *Eweida* decision are still to become clear but what is clear is that claims for accommodation of religious beliefs and practices in the workplace are likely to become more, rather than less, commonplace as a result of the decision. In that context, however, it is tolerably clear from *Ladele* and *MacFarlane* that the obligation imposed by Article 9 does not extend to the accommodation of beliefs which require the believer to discriminate.

---

[65] *Pay v UK* (2009) 48 EHRR SE2.
[66] *Dogru v France* App no 27058/05, 4 December 2008, [2008] ECHR 1579. See also *Kervanci v France* App no 31645/04, of the same date and the applications in *Aktas v France* (App no 43563/08); *Bayrak v France* (App no 14308/08); *Gamaleddyn v France* (App no 18527/08); *Ghazal v France* (App no 29134/08); *J Singh v France* (App no 25463/08) and *R Singh v France* (App no 27561/08), all of which concerned French school children expelled for refusing to comply with the ban on 'ostentatious' religious symbols in school, notwithstanding the willingness of most to wear a cap or (in the case of Sikh boys) an under-turban in place of the hijab and turban. The latter decisions are available only in French but are noted at (2009) EHRLR 811.

RELIGIOUS WARS? RELIGION, BELIEF AND CONFLICT

Defending the Indefensible?

I return below to the significance of Article 9, after consideration of the kinds of conflicts which may arise between equality or other claims arising in connection with religious beliefs, and the equality claims of others. Many religious beliefs share patriarchal norms which are inconsistent with gender equality (understood other than in terms of 'separate but equal'[67]) and hostile to the subversion of gender roles associated with homosexuality. Clashes between religious freedom and race equality are also possible. A number of predominantly US-based 'Christian' churches including the 'Christian Knights of the Ku Klux Klan', 'Aryan Nations' and a variety of others within the 'Christian Identity' movement advocate white supremacism and anti-Semitism while the South African Afrikaanse Protestante Kerk allows only white members.[68] And in *R (E) v Governing Body of the Jews Free School* the Supreme Court ruled that the application of schools admission criteria based on the tenets of Orthodox Judaism involved race discrimination.[69]

In 1999 the then England football coach Glen Hoddle was sacked after suggesting that people were disabled because of sins committed in a past life. His remarks appear to have been based on a muddle of evangelical Christianity and a (non-Christian) belief in reincarnation, but some disabled commentators suggested that they were reflective of more widely held opinions. Many Biblical passages also link disability to sin and the concepts of karma and reincarnation, common to Hinduism, Buddhism, Sikhism, Jainism and other Vedic belief systems, are centred around the movement of an eternal soul from life to life until it achieves ultimate liberation, and the idea that all actions will produce a reaction. The principle appears to be that suffering is rooted in mistakes made in the

[67] The 'separate but equal' doctrine characterises much thinking on gender within Christianity, Islam and Judaism. In *Plessy v Ferguson* 163 US 537 (1896) the US Supreme Court accepted that racial segregation was consistent with the Equal Protection Clause which (see Chapter 2) prohibits race discrimination. This decision legitimated the apartheid system in the US until, in *Brown v Board of Education* 347 US 483 (1954), the US Supreme Court acknowledged that 'separate' did not mean 'equal'.

[68] The Mormon Church reserved full membership to white men until the mid 1970s, when African American men were permitted for the first time to become elders, and its scriptures equate blackness to the loss of grace: Nephi 12:23 'And I beheld, after they had dwindled in unbelief they became a dark and loathsome and a filthy people, full of idleness and all manner of abominations'; Nephi 5:21 'And he had caused the cursing to come upon them, yea, even a sore cursing, because of their iniquity. For behold, they had hardened their hearts against him, that they had become like unto a flint; wherefore, as they were white, and exceedingly fair and delightsome, that they might not be enticing unto my people the Lord God did cause a skin of blackness to come upon them.' Brigham Young, the second President of the Church, wrote in his *Journal of Discourses* (10:110) 'Shall I tell you the law of God in regard to the African race? If the white man who belongs to the chosen seed mixes his blood with the seed of Cain, the penalty, under the law of God, is death on the spot. This will always be so.'

[69] *R (E) v Governing Body of the Jews Free School* [2010] 2 AC 728.

present or a former life and it is not difficult to (mis)read this to the effect that the disabled are being punished for their past misdeeds.

The scope for conflict is magnified by the fact that the Equality Act 2010 and Article 9 protect 'belief' whether or not of a religious nature. Section 10(2) of the Act states that 'Belief means any religious or philosophical belief and a reference to belief includes a reference to a lack of belief'. The Explanatory Notes state that philosophical beliefs will be protected only if they are (1) 'genuinely held', (2) 'beliefs' as distinct from 'opinion[s] or viewpoint[s] based on the present state of information available', (3) pertaining to 'a weighty and substantial aspect of human life and behavior' and (4) 'attain a certain level of cogency, seriousness, cohesion and importance [and are] worthy of respect in a democratic society, compatible with human dignity and [do] not conflict with the fundamental rights of others'.[70] The Notes suggest that 'any cult involved in illegal activities would not satisfy these criteria' and that 'Beliefs such as humanism and atheism would be beliefs for the purposes of this provision but adherence to a particular football team would not be'.

The criteria referred to in the Explanatory Notes are taken from the decision in *Grainger plc v Nicholson* (2010), in which the Employment Appeal Tribunal accepted that the 'beliefs' protected by the Employment Equality (Religion and Belief) Regulations 2003 (subsequently replaced by the Equality Act) included a belief that climate change was a result of human behaviour.[71] Beliefs that have qualified for protection under the Regulations, whose definition of 'belief' was materially identical with that in the Equality Act, included the 'belief that public service broadcasting has the higher purpose of promoting cultural interchange and social cohesion'; a 'fervent anti fox-hunting belief (and also anti hare coursing belief)'; while 'a commitment to vegetarianism and sympathy for Buddhism' and a very strong belief in personal freedom and privacy, respect for personal property, freedom from authoritarianism and respect for human rights have qualified as 'beliefs' for the purposes of the 2010 Act.[72]

The requirement that 'beliefs' protected by the Equality Act are 'worthy of respect in a democratic society, compatible with human dignity and [do] not conflict with the fundamental rights of others' attempts to avoid a situation in which a belief in white supremacy, for example, is regarded as a 'protected characteristic' for the purposes of the Act. But as attractive as this attempt may be, its inclusion in the list of qualifying criteria has no roots in the text of the Act

---

[70] www.legislation.gov.uk/ukpga/2010/15/notes/contents, para 52.

[71] *Grainger plc v Nicholson* [2010] ICR 360.

[72] *Maistry v BBC* ET Case no 1313142/2010 and *Hashman v Milton Park* ET Case no 3105555/2009; *Alexander v Farmtastic Valley Ltd & Ors* 13 October 2011, Case no ET/2513832/10 and *Nikiel-Wolski v Burton's Foods Ltd* 18 July 2012, Case no 2411204/11 [2013] EqLR 192 respectively. By contrast, in *Kelly & Ors v Unison* 28 January 2011, Case no ET/2203854/08 and *Lisk v Shield Guardian Co & Ors* 27 September 2011, Case no 3300873/11 [2011] EqLR 1290 tribunals refused to accept as protected 'beliefs', respectively, membership of the Socialist Party and the holding of views based on Marxism/Trotskyism and the belief that it necessary to show respect to those who gave their lives by wearing a poppy.

itself and results from a misunderstanding on the part of the courts as to the Article 9 jurisprudence.[73] This misunderstanding, articulated by the EAT in *Grainger*, was shared by Arden LJ in the Court of Appeal in *Williams v Secretary of State for Education and Employment*, and by the EAT in *McClintock v Department of Constitutional Affairs*.[74] But Article 9 provides absolute protection in respect of the holding of *all* beliefs, albeit that the right to *manifest* beliefs is subject to qualifications, and justifications for its limitation may turn in part on the nature of the belief (at least where its manifestation is incompatible with the Convention rights of others).[75] The requirement that beliefs must be 'worthy of respect in a democratic society' etc[76] derives from the decision of the ECtHR in *Campbell & Cosans v UK*, a case concerned with the application of Article 1 of Protocol 1 to the Convention.[77] That provision states that 'the State shall respect the right of parents to ensure . . . education and teaching in conformity with their own religious and philosophical convictions'.[78] In *Campbell & Cosans* the ECtHR ruled that 'Having regard to the Convention as a whole, including Article 17, the expression "philosophical convictions" in the present context' was limited to those 'worthy of respect in a "democratic society"' etc.

The approach adopted in *Campbell & Cosans* has limited application to Article 9 whose protection for the right to hold beliefs is, as was mentioned above, absolute. The approach taken by the Convention organs to that provision has not been to restrict the beliefs to which it affords protection.[79] Instead, Commission and Court have tended to take a narrow approach to what they accept as amounting to the 'manifestation' of a belief protected by Article 9,[80] as well as (as we saw above) being relatively slow to find interferences by the state in cases involving failures of accommodation and quick to find any such interference justifiable.[81] (The recent change in approach signalled in this context by *Eweida v UK* has been discussed above.) Similarly, in dealing with Article 10 of the Convention (freedom of expression) the ECtHR has not adopted the approach of excluding particular viewpoints from the protection of the Article

---

[73] Shared by the House of Lords in *Williamson v Secretary of State for Education and Employment* [2005] 2 AC 246 and the EAT in *McClintock v DCA* [2008] IRLR 29.

[74] *Williams v Secretary of State for Education and Employment* [2003] 1 All ER 385, para 258 and *McClintock v Department of Constitutional Affairs* (n 73).

[75] Article 17 ECHR prohibiting reliance on Convention rights to defeat the rights of others.

[76] Applied by the House of Lords in *Williamson* (n 73) as a criteria of 'beliefs' protected by Article 9, and subsequently adopted in *Grainger*.

[77] As Lord Walker there recognised.

[78] *Campbell & Cosans v UK* (1982) 4 EHRR 293.

[79] Though see *Pretty v United Kingdom* (2002) 35 EHRR 1, in which the Court stated at para 82 that 'not all opinions or convictions constitute beliefs in the sense protected by art 9(1) of the convention', ruling that Ms Pretty's views on assisted suicide did 'not involve a form of manifestation of a religion or belief, through worship, teaching, practice or observance as described in the second sentence of the first paragraph'.

[80] See, for example, *Arrowsmith v UK* App no 7050/75, Comm Rep 1978, 19 DR 5.

[81] *Şahin v Turkey* (n 40) and see also the other cases referred to in n 66.

per se. Despite statements in a number of cases that, for example, racist views 'did not enjoy the protection of Art 10',[82] closer inspection finds, invariably, a pattern whereby it is either conceded or ruled that the view falls within Article 10, but the interference is found to be justified, in particular in view of Article 17 of the Convention, which provides that:

> Nothing in this Convention may be interpreted as implying for any State, group or person any right to engage in any activity or perform any act aimed at the destruction of any of the rights and freedoms set forth herein or at their limitation to a greater extent than is provided for in the Convention.[83]

The importance of this point is that the prohibition on discrimination because of religion or belief is that the parameters of 'religion or belief' under the Equality Act 2010 and its predecessor legislation are intended, and taken, to reflect those imposed by Article 9. Whether or not 'a belief in the supreme nature of the Jedi Knights' is protected[84] is perhaps not a question of central importance, however shaky the underpinnings of this conclusion. Of much more concern is the potential of the prohibition on religion/belief discrimination to protect beliefs which are not worthy of respect in a democratic society, and/or which are incompatible with human dignity. It is only a question of time before the point is taken that the Act protects all beliefs which satisfy the first three of the criteria set out in the Explanatory Notes. Protected beliefs might then be understood to include, for example, beliefs in white supremacy, female subordination and/or the evils of homosexuality. Certainly, as mentioned above, these beliefs form part, or have previously formed part, of many mainstream religious views and would, it seems, qualify for protection on this basis regardless of any restrictions (however mistakenly imposed) on the judicial approach to (non-'religious') 'beliefs' as protected characteristics.

Yet further difficulties arise, in connection with religion in particular, because of impossibilities of classification. It may be possible to determine, on the balance of probabilities, whether an individual adheres, at least outwardly, to a certain set of religious or other beliefs (where, for example, he or she regularly attends a particular religious service, or outwardly manifests over time a commitment to pacifism, veganism or Communism). But even the model of attendance as an indicator of religious affiliation is, as was pointed out by the Administrative Court in the *JFS* case,[85] of no application to a religion such as

---

[82] *Jersild v Denmark* (1994) 19 EHRR 1, para 35.

[83] See, for example, *Jersild*, ibid, para 27 in which the Court stated that 'It is common ground that the measures giving rise to the applicant's case constituted an interference with his right to freedom of expression'. The cases cited in support of its conclusions (at para 35) also turned on the question of justification: *Kunen v Germany* App no 9235/81, 29 D & R 194 and *Glimmerveen & Hagenbeek v Netherlands* 18 D & R 187. So too did *Kuhnen v Germany* App no 12194/86 and *Remer v Germany* App no 25096/94) (1995) 82-A DR 117.

[84] It was suggested by Baroness Scotland for the government that such belief was not protected by the Religion and Belief Regulations: HL Debs 13 July 2005, col 1109.

[85] *R (E) v Governing Body of the Jews Free School* (n 69).

Orthodox Judaism in which 'attendance at the services of a synagogue has no bearing on a person's Jewish status as a matter of Jewish religious law', Judaism being exclusively a question of status. And more generally, while enquiry may be made as to whether an exemption sought by an individual from a generally applicable rule rationally relates to his or her commitment to an identifiable set of non-religious beliefs, the same is not true of an exemption sought on the basis of an asserted religious belief given the inability of secular courts to adjudicate doctrinal disputes within a religious collective as to what the religion requires, much less to determine the contents of an individual's religious belief.

In *R (Williamson) v Secretary of State for Education and Employment & Ors* the House of Lords accepted that a belief in the mandatory nature of corporal punishment in the educational setting was a religious belief for the purposes of Article 9 of the European Convention.[86] Lord Nicholls, with whom Lords Bingham, Walker and Brown agreed, stated that the court could consider, if it was at issue, whether a belief was genuinely held, but stressed that this was a 'limited inquiry . . . concerned to ensure an assertion of religious belief is made in good faith, "neither fictitious, nor capricious, and that it is not an artifice" '[87] and that the court was not entitled to judge the 'validity' of a belief relied upon by an individual, Article 9 protecting 'subjective belief'.[88] Lord Walker, who pointed out that 'Some sects claiming to be Christian' regarded polygamy as mandatory,[89] that others regarded blood transfusions as prohibited 'even if it is the only means of saving life'[90] and that 'Countless thousands' had been tortured and killed in the name of Christianity as 'apostates, heretics and witches', described as 'rather alarming' the suggestion, made below, that:

> [T]o be protected by art 9, a religious belief, like a philosophical belief, must be consistent with the ideals of a democratic society, and that it must be compatible with human dignity, serious, important, and (to the extent that a religious belief can reasonably be required so to be) cogent and coherent.[91]

---

[86] Domestic law has always been inclined to deal with accommodation cases in this way – see *Ahmed v IEA* [1978] QB 31 in which the Court of Appeal, by contrast with the Commission (in *Ahmed v UK*) accepted that there had been an interference, though the Court ruled that it was justified.

[87] *Williamson* (n 73), citing Iacobucci J in *Syndicat Northcrest v Amselem* [2004] 2 SCR 551, para 52.

[88] *Williamson* (n 73) para 22, also citing *Metropolitan Church of Bessarabia v Moldova* (2002) 35 EHRR 306, para 117: 'in principle, the right to freedom of religion as understood in the convention rules out any appreciation by the state of the legitimacy of religious beliefs or of the manner in which these are expressed'.

[89] *Williamson* (n 73) para 56, citing *Reynolds v US* 98 US 145 (1879); *Late Corp of the Church of Jesus Christ of Latter-Day Saints v US, Romney v US* 136 US 1 (1890).

[90] *Williamson* (n 73), citing *Re O (a minor) (medical treatment)* [1993] 1 FCR 925; *Re R (a minor) (medical treatment)* [1993] 2 FCR 544.

[91] *Williamson* (n 73) para 60, discussing Arden LJ in the Court of Appeal [2003] 1 All ER 385 para 258. Lord Nichols, with whom Lords Walker, Bingham and Brown agreed, suggested at para 23 that 'Everyone . . . is entitled to hold whatever beliefs he wishes', applying 'some modest, objective requirements' to beliefs whose manifestation would be protected. Lord Walker specifically agreed with this at para 64 as did Baroness Hale at para 76. Lord Brown agreed with Lord Walker and Baroness Hale and Lord Bingham also with the latter.

Lord Walker did not accept that:

> [I]t is right for the court (except in extreme cases . . .[92]) to impose an evaluative filter [in determining the existence of a belief], especially when religious beliefs are involved. For the court to adjudicate on the seriousness, cogency and coherence of theological beliefs is to take the court beyond its legitimate role . . . the court is not equipped to weigh the cogency, seriousness and coherence of theological doctrines . . . Moreover, the requirement that an opinion should be 'worthy of respect in a 'democratic society' begs too many questions . . .[93]

And in *R (Begum) v Head Teacher and Governors of Denbigh School* the House of Lords accepted that the claimant's view that, as a Muslim, she was obliged to wear a full length *jilbab* was a religious belief notwithstanding the proliferation of different views on this issue amongst Muslims, although a majority did not accept on the facts that her freedom to manifest this belief had been interfered with by the imposition upon her of a school uniform policy when she was free to attend another school.[94]

It would of course be absurd to excuse an individual from a prohibition on race, sexual orientation or sex discrimination on the basis that he or she was racist, homophobic or sexist. The question posed by law's powerlessness in the face of assertions about religious belief, as about belief more generally, is whether allowing exemptions based on religious or other beliefs to prohibitions on discrimination does not serve irreparably to undermine those prohibitions. In *Williamson* the House of Lords avoided a fatal holing of the prohibition on corporal punishment in schools by balancing the acceptance that the parents' views as to the necessity for such punishment were 'religious' with the finding that any interference with those views was justified under Article 9(2). The *Denbigh* case was decided by various members of the House of Lords on the basis that the claimant's beliefs had not been interfered with, and/or that any interference was justified on the facts. But where religious individuals assert that the imposition of a general obligation upon them amounts to discrimination against them on grounds of their religion or belief, one danger is raised that religion will trump, at least in cases where no justification is available to a direct discrimination claim. Another danger is that the courts will read prohibitions

---

[92] ibid, para 57, citing *X v UK* (1977) 11 DR 55, in which an Article 9 complaint by a prisoner of the authorities' failure to register his asserted religious affiliation was dismissed as manifestly ill-founded on the basis that the facilities for manifestation of religion to which registration entitled a prisoner were 'only conceivable if the religion to which the prisoner allegedly adheres is identifiable [whereas] . . . in the present case the applicant has not mentioned any facts making it possible to establish the existence of the Wicca religion'.

[93] *Williamson* (n 73) para 57, citing Richards J in *Amicus* (n 14), para 36, and decisions of the High Court of Australia, the Supreme Court of Canada and the United States Supreme Court in the *Church of the New Faith* case (1983) 154 CLR 120 especially 129–30, 174; *Syndicat Northcrest v Amselem* (2004) 241 DLR (4th) and *Employment Division, Department of Human Resources of Oregon v Smith* 494 US 872 (1990) respectively.

[94] *Karaduman v Turkey* (n 38) at para 21 *per* Lord Bingham and para 50 *per* Lord Hoffmann, Lord Nicholls and Baroness Hale concurring on the basis that any interference was justified on the facts.

on discrimination narrowly, and/or adopt broad interpretations to explicit justification defences, and that these interpretive steps will, over time, undermine the integrity of the discrimination provisions.

Bending the Equality Act Out of Shape?

An example of the former danger is provided by the *Azmi v Kirklees Metropolitan Borough Council* case in which a complaint of religious discrimination was brought by a Muslim teaching assistant who wished to wear a *niqab* (full-face covering) while providing language support for students for whom English was not a first language.[95] The school refused Ms Azmi's request on the evidenced basis that language support could be carried out more effectively where the teacher's face was visible. It declined her alternative suggestion that she be shielded from any contact with adult men while performing her classroom duties (this being the condition under which she was prepared to work unveiled), though it did not seek to prevent her from wearing the *niqab* outside the classroom. Ms Azmi's claim that the school's actions amounted to direct discrimination against her failed, an employment tribunal and the EAT agreeing that the discrimination at issue was of the indirect form and that it was justifiable on the facts.

Had the employers in *Azmi* allowed the claimant to teach in a *niqab* they would knowingly have been delivering sub-standard educational provision to educationally disadvantaged, minority ethnic pupils the advancement of whose language skills was the raison d'être for her presence in the school. Had they complied with her alternative suggestion, by 'protecting' her from the adult male gaze while she was teaching her pupils, they would have discriminated against male staff on grounds of their sex. The 'Catch 22' situation which would have been created by characterising the employer's approach to the *niqab* as directly discriminatory on grounds of religion may have driven the tribunal into finding that indirect, rather than direct, discrimination was at issue. The difficulty arises, however, in the fact that, leaving aside the most unusual and unlikely scenarios, the only category of persons likely to be affected by the rule was the category of Muslim women. Not all, or even a majority, of Muslim women would face difficulty in complying with a prohibition on face covering. But a significant minority of them will. In practical terms, only Muslim women will be so affected.

Analysing this as an example of indirect discrimination is of questionable consistency with the recognition of pregnancy discrimination as (always and invariably) sex discrimination. It is the case that the judicial acknowledgement of this relationship in the UK was slow, the House of Lords finally being driven to it by the decision of the ECJ in *Webb v EMO*, in which that Court ruled that

---

[95] *Azmi v Kirklees Metropolitan Borough Council* [2007] ICR 1154.

direct pregnancy discrimination was necessarily sex discrimination.[96] The reasoning was adopted from its decision in *Dekker v Stichting*:

> [O]nly women can be refused employment on the ground of pregnancy and such a refusal therefore constitutes direct discrimination on the ground of sex. A refusal of employment on account of the financial consequences of absence due to pregnancy must be regarded as based, essentially, on the fact of pregnancy.[97]

Similar reasoning might be thought to be applicable to the *niqab*,[98] such that a prohibition on its wearing would amount to direct discrimination against Muslim women.[99] The difficulty which would arise, of course, is that any such finding would place the employer between the rock of a finding that it had discriminated against the Muslim woman by refusing to allow her to wear the *niqab*, and the hard place of knowingly delivering a sub-standard level of education to already disadvantaged children. It would also, extrapolated across other 'religious' and other beliefs, threaten the conclusion that penalising race discrimination by a person whose religious or other beliefs prohibit, for example, 'miscegenation', or sex discrimination by a person whose religious or other beliefs are that married women should not work outside the home, would itself amount to direct discrimination.

THE EUROPEAN CONVENTION: A 'RELIGIOUS RIGHT' TO DISCRIMINATE?

The claimant in *Azmi* abandoned her appeal after the EAT ruled against her. By contrast, however, the claimants in *Ladele v London Borough of Islington* and *McFarlane v Relate*, as well as those in *Eweida* and *Chaplin* pursued their cases to the ECtHR.[100] The latter two cases, which did not involve conflicts save to the extent that the claimants' wishes to wear religious insignia (in each case a crucifix), clashed with their employers' uniform rules, are discussed above. *Ladele* and *McFarlane*, however, were true conflict cases in that the claimant in each sought to act in accordance with his or her own religious convictions by refusing to provide services in a non-discriminatory manner (specifically to same-sex as well as

---

[96] Case C-32/93 *Webb v EMO* [1994] ECR I-03567 and see *Webb (No 2)* (n 8).

[97] Case C-177/88 *Dekker v Stichting* [1990] ECR I-3941. See also Case 179/88 *Handels-og Kontorfunktionaerernes I Danmark v Dansk Arbejdsgiverforening* [1990] ECR I-3979 [13], and Case C-421/92 *Habermann Beltermann v Arbeiterwohlfahrt, Bezirksverband Ndb/Opf eV* [1994] ECR I-1657, para 15.

[98] Though not, I would argue, to a refusal on religious grounds to provide sexual counselling to same-sex couples such as that at issue in *McFarlane v Relate Avon Ltd* [2010] 1 WLR 955, discussed immediately below, in which the pregnancy argument was unsuccessfully deployed.

[99] Or, if the law is incapable of recognising such 'dual' discrimination, discrimination on grounds of religion and/or sex.

[100] *Ladele v London Borough of Islington* [2010] ICR 507; *McFarlane v Relate* (n 98); *Eweida v British Airways* [2010] ICR 890 and *Chaplin*, Employment Tribunal Judgment of 21 May 2010, unreported.

different-sex couples), and complained of (direct) religious discrimination when they were not permitted so to do.

Ladele concerned a Christian registrar whose refusal, on religious grounds, to accept any involvement in civil partnerships resulted in detriment including threatened disciplinary proceedings and the rejection of her application for temporary promotion. A tribunal accepted Ms Ladele's claim that she had been the victim of direct discrimination on grounds of her religion on the unusual basis that 'Applying a rule to all Registrars does not mean that the Respondent has demonstrated that it did not commit an act of discrimination'.[101] The EAT allowed the employer's appeal[102] and the Court of Appeal rejected Ms Ladele's attempt to have the tribunal decision reinstated.

Both the EAT and the Court of Appeal ruled the discrimination against Ms Ladele was at most indirect, there being no evidence on which the tribunal could properly have found that the detriment of which she complained was 'by reason of' her religion, as distinct from being the consequence of her refusal to fulfil her job functions (which included involvement in civil partnerships). The EAT ruled that any detriment imposed on Ms Ladele was proportionate to the pursuit of the council's aim of providing a civil partnership/marriage service on a non-discriminatory basis. The Court of Appeal further ruled that the council was required by the legislative prohibition on discrimination in the exercise of public functions to insist that Ms Ladele performed civil partnership functions, and that accommodation on the council's part of a refusal by her would have amounted in law to assistance in an unlawful act by her as (for these purposes) a public authority. The ECtHR in turn ruled that her claim under Articles 9 and 14 failed, the imposition by Islington of the requirement that all registrars be designated civil partnership registrars, which requirement was accepted to have had a particularly detrimental impact on her because of her religious beliefs, being a proportionate means of pursuing the legitimate aim of ensuring the provision of a non-discriminatory service by all of its employees.[103]

The *McFarlane* case concerned a religious discrimination claim by a Christian relationship counsellor employed by Relate (a secular relationship counselling organisation). Having undertaken professional training, Mr McFarlane became a sexual counsellor for Relate. He sought and was refused assurances that he could choose not to undertake such counselling with same-sex couples. Relate took the view that any such assurance would have been incompatible with equal opportunities and professional ethics policies with which he was contractually obliged to comply. Mr McFarlane was eventually dismissed, his subsequent claim of religious discrimination being rejected by a tribunal and the EAT on

---

[101] While it was suggested, above, that applying a 'no face covering' rule to all might involve direct discrimination against Muslim women, neither Christians nor, more broadly, persons holding religious beliefs could be regarded as uniquely disadvantaged by a requirement to treat same-sex couples on an equal basis with those of different sexes.

[102] *London Borough of Islington v Ladele* [2009] ICR 387.

[103] *Eweida & Ors v UK* (n 46).

the basis that he had been subject to a requirement of general application, rather than to less favourable treatment on the ground of his religion, and that Relate's approach was justifiable notwithstanding its disproportionately disadvantageous impact on Christians.

The EAT ruled that:

> [I]n some cases where an employer objects to [the] manifestation [of a religious belief] it may be impossible to see any basis for the objection other than objection to the belief which it manifests; and in such a case a claim by the employer to be acting on the grounds of the former but not the latter may be regarded as a distinction without a difference.[104]

In such cases, discrimination on grounds of manifestation would amount to direct discrimination. In other cases, however,

> there will be a clear and evidently genuine basis for differentiation between the two, and in such a case the fact that the employee's motivation for the conduct in question may be found in his wish to manifest his religious beliefs does not mean that that belief is the ground of the employer's action.[105]

The Court of Appeal refused permission to appeal, rejecting a highly unusual intervention from the former Archbishop of Canterbury who suggested that Mr McFarlane's appeal be heard before the Lord Chief Justice and a specially constituted panel of five Lords Justice who had 'a proven sensibility to religious issues' (this instead of the normal three judge panel).[106] The ECtHR dismissed his claim, which was brought under Article 9 alone and in combination with Article 14. As in the case of Ms Ladele, the Court accepted that Mr McFarlane's employer's action was necessary and proportionate in pursuit of the legitimate aim of providing a service without discrimination.

DISCRIMINATION BECAUSE OF THE BELIEFS OF OTHERS: A CONVENTION RIGHT?

The characterisation of the discrimination at issue in *McFarlane* and *Ladele* as, at most, indirect, is unproblematic. There are reasons unrelated to religion why people might object to civil partnerships or, more generally, same-sex relationships, though it may well be the case that those who characterise themselves as religious are more likely to take issue with such relationships than those who do not. Having said this, one of the questions to which the *Ladele* and *McFarlane* cases give rise concerns whether a different outcome would necessarily have been desirable (as distinct from legally required) had the discrimination there at issue been direct rather than indirect. The cases concerned a relatively mainstream, though by no means unanimously held, Christian doctrine but, as we

---

[104] *McFarlane v Relate Avon Ltd* (n 98) para 18.
[105] ibid.
[106] *McFarlane v Relate Avon Ltd* (n 98).

saw above, the Equality Act 2010, like other prohibitions on discrimination, does not apply only to *religious* beliefs, much less only to such of those beliefs as might be described as 'mainstream'. Assuming that (for example) a belief in white supremacy is a 'belief' (and there is nothing in the Equality Act, or in Article 9 of the Convention, to suggest otherwise), any less favourable treatment meted out on the basis of that belief (rather than because of behaviour based on that belief) will amount to direct discrimination and will be unlawful unless a specific exception applies. And while it is probable that an anti-racist organisation may apply a GOR relating to anti-racism in relation to at least some staff, it is by no means clear that most other employers could do likewise (the defence requiring, other than in the case of employers having 'an ethos based on religion or belief' that 'being [or not being] of a particular religion or belief is a genuine and determining occupational requirement' and that 'it is proportionate to apply that requirement in the particular case').[107]

The GOR defence would not apply to an employer whose objection to employing acknowledged white supremacists, dyed-in-the-wool sexists or homophobes was a matter of principle unrelated to the jobs for which they are employed. It is clear that 'being of a particular religion or belief' can here include *not* being of a particular religion or belief. But without robbing the GOR defence of any limitations, it is not possible to interpret it so as to permit an employer to refuse to employ such individuals on the basis that they are (for example) likely to trigger harassment complaints from other members of staff or (in a decision-making role) to act in a prejudicial way, or at least be suspected of so doing.

One of the difficulties to which this result might give rise can be extrapolated from the facts in *Redfearn v SERCO* in which an active member of the British National Party (BNP) challenged the decision to dismiss him from his job as a driver of transport for vulnerable disabled and elderly, predominantly Asian, service users.[108] Mr Redfearn lacked the qualifying service to claim unfair dismissal and the claim pre-dated any statutory prohibition on discrimination on grounds of 'belief'. He claimed that, his dismissal having involved considerations of race (albeit his own racism), it breached the prohibition on race discrimination. The EAT ruled in his favour, overturning the decision of the first instance tribunal, but sanity prevailed in the Court of Appeal whereupon Mr Redfearn petitioned the ECtHR. The Court ruled in November 2012 that, in circumstances where the one-year qualifying period for unfair dismissal claims did not apply to dismissals alleged to be related to a claimant's race, sex or religion, its application to dismissals connected with a claimant's political opinion or affiliation breached Article 11.[109]

---

[107] See above 137–38.

[108] *Redfearn v SERCO* [2006] ICR 1367.

[109] *Redfearn v UK* (2012) 33 BHRC 713. This appears to have been an error on the part of the Court in that, insofar as it was relying on the Employment Equality (Religion & Belief Regulations) 2003, as distinct from the partial coverage of religion by the Race Relations Act 1976 (see *Mandla v*

The decision in *Redfearn* was not an unqualified victory for the applicant and it did not have the effect of placing BNP membership (or other manifestations of racist beliefs) on a par with race or sex, for example, as regards entitlement to freedom from discrimination. In particular, the Court did not respond to Mr Redfearn's complaint that 'even if he had had more than one year of qualifying service, his employer would have been able to rely on his political involvement as being "some other substantial reason" to justify the termination of his employment'.[110] In finding a breach of Article 11, the Court acknowledged that 'even in the absence of specific complaints from service users, the applicant's membership of the BNP could have impacted upon [the employer's] provision of services to Bradford City Council, especially as the majority of service users were vulnerable persons of Asian origin'. It went on to note, however, that Mr Redfearn had been nominated as a 'first-class employee' by his (Asian) supervisor 'and, prior to his political affiliation becoming public knowledge, no complaints had been made against him by service users or by his colleagues'.[111] No complaints were ever made of him in relation to 'the actual exercise of his employment', and he was 'summarily dismissed without any apparent consideration being given to the possibility of transferring him to a non-customer facing role'.[112] Finally, in view of his age (56) the court thought it likely that he would struggle to find alternative employment.[113]

All this being the case, the ECtHR took the view that 'a claim for unfair dismissal under the 1996 Act would be an appropriate domestic remedy for a person dismissed on account of his political beliefs or affiliations' because it would require 'the employer to demonstrate that there was a "substantial reason" for the dismissal . . . [the tribunal] tak[ing] full account of art 11 in deciding whether or not the dismissal was, in all the circumstances of the case, justified'.[114] Interestingly, the Court dismissed as manifestly ill-founded the applicant's Article 9 claim, ruling that 'in the light of all the material in its possession and in so far as the matters complained of are within its competence . . . it does not disclose any appearance of a violation of the rights and freedoms set out in the Convention or its Protocols',[115] and found it unnecessary 'to examine whether or not there has also been a violation of art 14 of the Convention read together with arts 10 and 11'.[116]

The government chose to respond to the *Redfearn* decision by removing the qualifying period for claims of unfair dismissal where the reason or principal

---

Dowell Lee [1983] 2 AC 548 and subsequent case law discussed in A McColgan, *Discrimination Law: Text, Cases and Materials*, 2nd edn (Oxford: Hart Publishing, 2005) Chapter 7, that protection would equally have applied to 'belief'. Mr Redfearn, however, chose to rely on the RRA.

[110] *Redfearn v UK* (n 109), para 35.
[111] ibid, para 44.
[112] ibid, para 45.
[113] ibid, para 46.
[114] ibid, para 50.
[115] ibid, para 58.
[116] ibid, para 66.

reason for dismissal 'is, or relates to, the employee's political beliefs or affiliation'.[117] The effect of this is not to render such dismissals automatically unfair, just to place tribunals in a position such that they can consider them regardless of length of service. But fast-forward a number of years to the present prohibition on discrimination because of 'philosophical belief' and it is entirely possible that an employer in the situation of Mr Redfearn's might, like his employer at the time, have grave concerns about entrusting vulnerable Asian clients to the care of someone whose political activities made it clear that he was racist.

Regardless of the absence of any complaints about Mr Redfearn's behaviour, ought his employer to be required to place Redfearn's interests in retaining his employment above other concerns? The question under the Equality Act 2010 would appear to be 'yes' unless the GOR defence is stretched to accommodate the argument that not being a racist is a 'genuine and determining factor' for being a bus driver engaged in the particular context in which Mr Redfearn worked. But if the GOR defence can accommodate this it could equally be used to argue that being Catholic is a 'genuine and determining factor' for being a bus driver engaged by a Catholic organisation involved in the provision of pastoral care for the elderly, or that being heterosexual is a 'genuine and determining factor' for being a manager of a socially conservative membership club.

The question which then arises is whether the protection from employment-related or other discrimination of those with views like Mr Redfearn, as distinct from his protection from unfair dismissal in connection with those beliefs, is required by Article 9 (and/or 10/11) of the Convention? Assuming for the moment that a decision to dismiss in a case such as *Redfearn* would in principle be capable of justification by reference to, for example, the rights of others, the question which will arise is whether a dismissal based on bare knowledge on the fact of (say) white supremacist belief is an interference with the absolute right or whether, because such a belief is unlikely to be known to the employer other than through (for example) BNP membership, articulation or actions, the interference is only with the qualified right.

There is not a great deal of case law on this question but it appears from what there is that the European Court will seek to avoid a finding of breach of the absolute right to freedom of belief where it is possible to analyse the claim as involving qualified rights conferred by Article 9 or otherwise. Lester, Pannick and Herberg suggest that the Convention Organs 'have resisted the attempts of applicants to raise issues under art 9 when they may be considered as falling under some other article of the Convention'.[118] And in *Kalaç v Turkey*, in which the Court did determine the claim under Article 9, it went to some lengths to

---

[117] Section 13 of the Enterprise and Regulatory Reform Act 2013, inserting new s 108(4) Employment Rights Act 1996.

[118] *Human Rights Law and Practice* para 4.9.2, instancing cases such as *Hoffmann v Austria* (1993) 17 EHRR 293, *Zengin v Turkey* (2008) 46 EHRR 44 and *Zengin v Turkey* (1990) 13 EHRR 774.

avoid finding that an applicant's right to religious freedom was violated when he was dismissed on the basis, essentially, that he was suspected of harbouring fundamentalist Islamic views.[119]

The applicant, a military judge, had been dismissed 'for breaches of discipline and scandalous conduct' because 'his conduct and attitude "revealed that he had adopted unlawful fundamentalist opinions" '. The respondent government claimed (but Kalaç denied) that he was an active member ('as a matter of fact, if not formally') of the 'Muslim fundamentalist Suleyman sect', of whose existence the applicant claimed to have been unaware at the material time. The Commission found in the applicant's favour, in part on the basis that the evidence relied upon 'did not support the argument that Kalaç had any links with [the] sect'. The Court, however, dismissed the complaint, concluding that the action taken against Mr Kalaç was 'not based on [his] religious opinions and beliefs or the way he had performed his religious duties but on his conduct and attitude'.[120] What is striking about this decision is the fact that the Court, without expressing any conclusion as to whether Kalaç in fact belonged to the sect in question, or otherwise on what it was that he was alleged to have done, simply accepted the respondent government's bare assertion that his dismissal was based on his 'conduct and attitude' rather than his 'religious opinions and beliefs or the way he had performed his religious duties'.

The decision in *Kalaç* suggests a distinct reluctance on the part of the Court to find interferences with the absolute right conferred by Article 9. The other factor which might come into play in a case where religious conviction or other belief clashes with the equality (or other) rights of others is Article 17 ECHR, set out above, which was relied upon by the Commission in *Glimmerveen & Hagenbeek v Netherlands* to dismiss as manifestly unfounded complaints that the applicants had been convicted of distributing racist material and prevented from standing for election on a racist platform.[121] The Commission stated that 'The general purpose of Article 17 is to prevent totalitarian groups from exploiting in their own interests the principles enunciated by the Convention' and that the achievement of this purpose did not make it

> necessary to take away every one of the rights and freedoms guaranteed from persons found to be engaged in activities aimed at the destruction of any of those rights and freedoms. Art. 17 covers essentially those rights which, if invoked, will facilitate the attempt to derive therefrom a right to engage personally in activities aimed at the destruction of any of the rights and freedoms set forth in the Convention.[122]

The Commission ruled in *Glimmerveen* that the expression of racist political views 'clearly constitutes an activity within the meaning of Art 17 of the Convention' and that the applicants were attempting to use the Convention

---

[119] *Kalaç v Turkey* (1997) 27 EHRR 552.
[120] ibid, para 29.
[121] *Glimmerveen & Hagenbeek v Netherlands* 18 DR 187 (1979).
[122] Citing *Lawless v Ireland (No 3)* (1961) 1 EHRR 15, para 6.

rights 'to engage in . . . activities . . . contrary to the text and spirit of the Convention'. This being the case, Article 17 blocked their claims. As Jeremy Waldron suggests:

> To count as a genuine exercise of free speech, a person's contribution must be related to that of his opponent in a way that makes room for them both. Though they claim to be exercising that right, the Nazis' speeches do not have this character. The speeches they claim the right to make are calculated to bring an end to the form of life in relation to which the idea of free speech is conceived. We may ban their speeches, therefore, not because we think we can necessarily safeguard more rights by doing so, but because in their content and tendency the Nazis' speeches are incompatible with the very idea of the right they are asserting.[123]

More problematic, as far as the application of Article 17 is concerned, is the case where the Nazi sympathiser or white supremacist wishes to rely on the Convention to challenge decisions, such as those made by an employer, which are not aimed directly at the former's ability 'to engage personally in activities aimed at the destruction of any of the rights and freedoms set forth in the Convention'.

In *Vogt v Germany* (1996), in which the applicant had been dismissed from her position because of her active membership of the Communist Party (and therefore effectively excluded from all teaching positions within Germany), the European Court found a breach of Articles 10 and 11.[124] Vogt's membership of the party was regarded as inconsistent with the constitutional obligation imposed on civil servants (including teachers) to uphold the principle of a democracy capable of defending itself. The Court ruled that, because membership of the Communist party was not banned, because the state had known of Vogt's membership prior to her employment, because she had never been shown to have abused her position by reason of her membership and because the state was the only employer of teachers, Vogt's dismissal after ten years' service was disproportionate to the legitimate aim pursued.

It does not follow from *Vogt* that the Convention prohibits all discrimination on grounds of political or other beliefs. The Court did not there overrule its previous decisions in *Glasenapp v Germany* (1986) and *Kosiek v Germany* (1986), in which challenges to refusals to confirm the appointments of a Communist teacher and a Nazi lecturer respectively were dismissed on the basis that the applicants' political activities were inconsistent with the qualifications for the positions, which qualifications were regarded as including the ability to comply with the relevant constitutional obligation.[125] *Vogt* can be explained as a case in which the interference with the applicant's rights of expression and association was manifestly disproportionate. Further, as we saw above, at least until the decision in *Eweida*, the Convention provided relatively limited protection to

---

[123] J Waldron, 'Rights in Conflict' (1989) 99 *Ethics* 503–19, 518.
[124] *Vogt v Germany* (1996) 21 EHRR 205.
[125] *Glasenapp v Germany* (1986) 9 EHRR 25; *Kosiek v Germany* (1986) 9 EHRR 328.

employees, in particular to those employed other than by the state. Notwithstanding that decision, those in *Ladele* and *Macfarlane* make it clear that an employer is entitled to take into account its own commitments to equal opportunities, human rights and the delivery of a non-discriminatory service. At least where the beliefs at issue could reasonably be regarded as posing a risk to others by virtue of the individual's employment, the chances of a successful Convention claim in respect of a refusal to employ, or a decision to dismiss, are, it is suggested, slim.

There may, further, be a positive right to discriminate on the basis of the beliefs of others. In *Associated Society of Locomotive Engineers and Firemen (ASLEF) v UK* the ECtHR ruled that the UK had breached the union's Article 11 right to freedom of association by denying it the right to exclude from its membership a BNP activist on the grounds, inter alia, that his membership of the BNP was incompatible with membership of ASLEF, whose objects included the 'promot[ion] and develop[ment of] and enact[ment of] positive policies in regard to equality of treatment in our industries and ASLEF regardless of sex, sexual orientation, marital status, religion, creed, colour, race or ethnic origin'.[126] According to the Court:

> 39. As an employee or worker should be free to join, or not join a trade union without being sanctioned or subject to disincentives . . . so should the trade union be equally free to choose its members. Article 11 cannot be interpreted as imposing an obligation on associations or organisations to admit whosoever wishes to join. Where associations are formed by people, who, espousing particular values or ideals, intend to pursue common goals, it would run counter to the very effectiveness of the freedom at stake if they had no control over their membership. By way of example, it is uncontroversial that religious bodies and political parties can generally regulate their membership to include only those who share their beliefs and ideals. Similarly, the right to join a union 'for the protection of his interests' cannot be interpreted as conferring a general right to join the union of one's choice irrespective of the rules of the union: in the exercise of their rights under Article 11 § 1 unions must remain free to decide, in accordance with union rules, questions concerning admission to and expulsion from the union . . .

This is not, of course, to say that discrimination by unions or other organisations will necessarily be protected under the Convention: were a state to permit race discrimination by collective organisations such as trade unions to flourish unchallenged, it could well find itself in breach of Articles 8 and/or 14 of the Convention, even of Article 3.[127] It is to point out, however, that discrimination on grounds of belief, even religion, may not simply be permitted by the Convention in the sense that the latter does not require its prohibition by the state: such discrimination may attract the positive protection of the Convention.

---

[126] *ASLEF v UK* (2007) 45 EHRR 793.

[127] See *Sidabras & Džiautas v Lithuania* (2004) 42 EHRR 104 and (Art 3) the *East Asians case* (1973) 3 EHRR 76, EComHR, para 207, followed by the Court in *Cyprus v Turkey* (2002) 35 EHRR 30, paras 304–06.

DOMESTIC LAW, DISCRIMINATION AND
RELIGION/BELIEF

Whatever the Convention may require, any attempt to manage the conflicts produced by the regulation of discrimination on grounds of religion or belief by
adopting (as in *Azmi*) a narrow approach to general concepts such as direct
discrimination, or a broad approach to justification or the GOR defence, threatens to infect the whole statutory discrimination regime. Examples of the tension generated by the extension of anti-discrimination provisions to previously
unregulated territory, and the ensuing potential for damaging interpretations of
previously settled concepts, are provided by the decisions in the *Roma Rights*
case[128] (prior to that of the House of Lords) and that of the House of Lords in
R (Gillan) v Commissioner of Police of the Metropolis.[129] In these cases (though
in the latter only *obiter*) the long-established approach to direct discrimination
(that is, the 'but for' test established by the House of Lords in *James v Eastleigh
Borough Council*[130]) was abandoned in favour of one which took into account
the justifiability or otherwise of treatment differentiated on racial lines. This
happened in cases in which immigration and security (rather than the more
familiar territory of employment or the provision of goods and services) were,
respectively, at issue. What drove the decisions was the understanding of judges
not intimately acquainted with the statutory discrimination provisions of what
'common sense' required in these contexts.[131]

Prohibitions on discrimination do not inevitably accord with common sense.
Indeed it is the very commonsensical nature of much discrimination which has
resulted in its pervasiveness and tenacity. This is partly why irrationality review
at common law has been of very limited utility in challenging discrimination:
cases such as *Short v Poole* (1926) and *R (Smith) v Secretary of State for Defence*
(the 1996 'gays in the military case') make the point well.[132] This being the case,
there is always a danger that the (over-)extension of the protected characteristics will threaten to undo hard-won past gains. Where anti-discrimination provisions are well established, legal rules which may appear antithetical to
common sense are normalised to the extent that 'common sense' shifts, as arguably in the case of pregnancy discrimination (economically rational but now
legally understood to amount to unjustifiable sex discrimination). Applying

---

[128] *R (European Roma Rights Centre) v Immigration Officer, Prague Airport* [2005] 2 AC 1 (HL),
[2004] QB 811 (CA), [2002] EWHC 1989 (Admin) (QBD).

[129] *R (Gillan) v Commissioner of Police of the Metropolis* [2006] 2 AC 307.

[130] *James v Eastleigh Borough Council* [1990] 2 AC 751.

[131] See, for example, the remarks of Simon Brown LJ (with whom Mantell LJ agreed) in the
Court of Appeal in the *Roma Rights* case (n 128) paras 66, 69 and (now elevated to the House of
Lords) in the *Gillan* decision (n 129) paras 88–91.

[132] *Short v Poole* [1926] Ch 66; *R (Smith) v Secretary of State for Defence* [1996] QB 517. In *Short
v Poole* it was accepted that discrimination against red-heads would be irrational and therefore
unlawful, but dismissing a woman teacher because she was married was not).

those rules in a new context, however, opens the door once again to common sense as a trump card and the re-interpretations which result threaten to feed back into the previously established order.

The questions which then arise are (1) whether there is reason to provide, through the mechanism of anti-discrimination legislation, broader scope for the accommodation of individuals' religious or other belief than is already provided by Article 9 and other provisions of the ECHR, to which effect has been given in domestic law through the mechanism of the Human Rights Act 1998; and (2) to what extent religious organisations ought to be exempted from the scope of anti-discrimination law.

What Room for Protection of Individual Belief?

There is no coherent argument for providing protection from discrimination because of individually held beliefs in the higher purposes of public service broadcasting or the wrongness of fox hunting, such beliefs having nevertheless been granted protection under the Religion and Belief Regulations.[133] As to beliefs (religious or otherwise) which are associated with minority communities, we will see in Chapter 6 the communitarian argument that such communities are crucial to the shaping of individual identity and ought therefore to be protected.[134] Recognition of the importance of community and culture is not problematic from an equality perspective; it has long been a feminist complaint that the characterisation of persons as autonomous individuals is one which is particularly problematic for women given their disproportionate share of caring tasks.[135] But this recognition does not require the reification, much less the preservation, of static 'cultures',[136] whether those cultures are defined by reference to religion or otherwise.[137] The discussion in Chapter 6 of the hijab illustrates the complexity of cultural and/or 'religious' practices whose manifestation may be defended by their practitioners as an expression of group identity, but which may have no claim to authenticity understood in static cultural terms.

---

[133] See n 72.

[134] See, for example, C Taylor, 'Atomism' in *Philosophy and the Human Sciences: Philosophical Papers* 2 (Cambridge: Cambridge University Press, 1985); M Sandel, *Liberalism and the Limits of Justice* (Cambridge: Cambridge University Press, 1981); A Margalit and J Raz, 'National Self-Determination' in W Kymlicka (ed), *The Rights of Minority Cultures* (Oxford: Oxford University Press, 1995) 79. These arguments are frequently made in relation to 'ethnic' communities but could equally well apply to 'communities' identified by reference to religious belief, as Margalit and Raz recognise at 85.

[135] See for example S Okin, 'Equal Citizenship: Gender/Justice and Gender: An Unfinished Debate' (2004) 72 *Fordham Law Review* 1537; A Phillips, 'Defending Equality of Outcome' (2004) *Journal of Political Philosophy* 1.

[136] See generally M Sunder, 'Cultural Dissent' (2001–02) 54 *Stanford Law Review* 495.

[137] See J Waldron, 'Minority Cultures and the Cosmopolitan Alternative' (1991–92) 25 *University of Michigan Journal of Law Reform* 751, 763.

Sonu Bedi argues that, unless religion is understood as an unchosen 'immutable and fixed belief system',[138] there is no basis to differentiate 'the Jew from the Rotarian . . . the Sikh from the mere hat-wearer',[139] and no overriding reason to provide religious exemptions to rules of general application. Religion is clearly not immutable, given the shifts in doctrine which occur over time.[140] And whereas there is no strong reason to refuse to accommodate the Sikh turban which, whether or not its wearing is required as a matter of religious doctrine,[141] carries no overtones of gender inequality or subordination, and imposes on its adherents no physical harm,[142] many other practices said to be required as a matter of religious doctrine are more or less damaging for those (generally or exclusively women) subject to them.

The 'paradox of multicultural vulnerability' is discussed in Chapter 6. Here it is sufficient simply to note that, where identification of many of these practices as 'religious' as distinct from 'cultural' is strongly contested, privileging those accepted as 'religious' as distinct from merely 'cultural' increases the incentive to categorise them as 'religious' and thereby helps to perpetuate them.[143] Protecting religious beliefs through discrimination law may, further, result in the expansion of 'religious' obligation, and the reinforcement of religious hierarchies to the disadvantage of the less powerful.[144] And a further particular difficulty presented by cases concerning assertions of 'religious' belief is one of judicial competence. Secular courts may determine, as questions of fact, what beliefs an individual holds. But they cannot determine what is or is not required as a matter of religious doctrine, which interpretation of a disputed religious matter is correct.

In *R v Chief Rabbi, ex parte Wachmann*, for example, in which the High Court refused an application for judicial review of the Chief Rabbi's decision

---

[138] S Bedi, 'Debate: What is so Special about Religion? The Dilemma of the Religious Exemption' (2007) 15 *Journal of Political Philosophy* 235, 237.

[139] ibid, 234. cf L Vickers, *Religious Freedom, Religious Discrimination and the Workplace* (Oxford: Hart Publishing, 2008). Vickers argues, at 40, that religious beliefs can be distinguished from others and their protection demanded on grounds of dignity because 'it is only those . . . which feed into an individual's ability to make sense of the world, and through which they develop a sense of the good, that require protection'.

[140] Within Anglicanism, for example, as to women priests, within Catholicism as to correct punishment for heresy and the existence of 'limbo'.

[141] Bedi suggests that it is not. Contrast the letter written to Jacques Chirac arguing that the turban was cultural and not religious, this in order to seek its exemption from the French ban on 'ostentatious' religious dress in schools ('French Sikhs threaten to leave country', *Guardian*, 23 January 2004) with the Sikh Article 9 challenges to that ban (unsuccessful before the ECtHR (*Mann Singh v France* App no 24479/07, [2008] ECHR 1523), but successful before the UNHRC (*Singh v France* CCPR/C/102/D/1876/2009), which alleged breaches of freedom of *religion*.

[142] Similarly the kara (Sikh bangle) which was the issue of dispute in *R (Watkins-Singh) v Governing Body of Aberdare Girls' High School* [2008] 3 FCR 203 (a case in which the RRA was successfully relied upon).

[143] As M Sunder points out ('Piercing the Veil' (2003) 112 *Yale Law Journal* 1399, 1441, discussing the experience of the network Women Living Under Muslim Laws), 'religious claims are particularly hard to challenge, and therefore [WLUML] expends effort to deconstruct religious claims as, in part, contingent and political'.

[144] See generally Sunder ibid, and n 136.

that the applicant was 'no longer religiously and morally fit to occupy his position as rabbi' following an investigation into allegations of adultery with a member of his congregation,[145] Simon Brown J, as he then was, ruled that 'the court would never be prepared to rule on questions of Jewish law'. Nor could the claimant rely on the principles of natural justice given the difficulties inherent in 'separat[ing] out procedural complaints from consideration of substantive principles of Jewish law which may underlie them'.[146] And in *Presbyterian Church v Hull Church* (1969) the US Supreme Court refused to become involved in a property dispute between two Presbyterian factions, the resolution of which turned on 'controversies over religious doctrine and practice',[147] though it accepted that the courts could determine some property disputes involving religious organisations where this could be done 'without resolving underlying controversies over religious doctrine'.

Consideration of the difficulties generated by the prohibition of discrimination related to religion/belief points towards a movement away from treating religion/belief as materially similar, for the purposes of framing discrimination legislation, to the other protected characteristics. Even if it is accepted that religion plays a valuable, even a central, role in the lives of believers, and, arguably, that it provides benefits of a more general nature,[148] this does not require that religion be treated in like fashion to ethnicity, sexual orientation etc for the purposes of anti-discrimination legislation, much less that philosophical belief, or the absence of belief, be provided with that level of protection. Religion and belief will continue to benefit from the protection of Article 9. That provision does not, however, require the enactment of detailed statutory prohibitions on discrimination such as are currently found in the Equality Act 2010.

THE CASE FOR LIMITED STATUTORY REGULATION OF 'RELIGIOUS' DISCRIMINATION

That is not to say that religion should be excluded entirely from the protection of statutory discrimination provisions. Some such protection is merited, notwithstanding the concerns expressed above, (1) because of the overlaps between religious and ethnic categorisations and between some forms of religious hostility and racism; (2) because the state is not neutral as regards religion; and (3) in the interests of fairness. More generally, Article 9 has traditionally provided

---

[145] *R v Chief Rabbi, ex parte Wachmann* [1992] 1 WLR 1036.

[146] There have been interesting subsequent developments in the employment law sphere, previous authority to the effect that ministers of religion were outside the scope of employment law having been overruled by the House of Lords in *Percy v Board of National Mission of the Church of Scotland* [2006] 2 AC 28, discussed further below, but no doctrinal issue was at stake in that case or in *Stewart v New Testament Church of God* [2008] ICR 282 which followed it.

[147] *Presbyterian Church v Hull Church* 393 US 440 (1969).

[148] See, for example, T Macklem, 'Faith as a Secular Value' (2000) 45 *McGill Law Journal* 1. While broader than many other accounts, Macklem's approach requires the imposition of some restrictions on what counts as a 'religion'.

inadequate protection against the disadvantage suffered by persons of disadvantaged minority groups because of their religious affiliation (real or perceived).[149]

Dealing first with (1) and by way of example, discrimination between 'Catholics' and 'Protestants' in Northern Ireland has little or nothing to do with disputes as doctrine, or even with individual belief, and everything to do with ethnic affiliation (hence the logic of the apocryphal question whether someone is a 'Catholic Jew' or a 'Protestant Jew'). The overlap between race and religion was recognised in the case law which developed under the Race Relations Act 1976, extending the concept of ethnicity to accommodate claims concerning discrimination against Sikhs and Jews.[150] This understanding did not, however, stretch as far as Muslims, many of whom are among the most disadvantaged in Britain at present and are subject to vilification indistinguishable in its effects from racism.

It was suggested in Chapter 2 that 'race' is not a biological construct and racial categories are 'fundamentally social in nature'.[151] The demands for recognition and/or legal protection made by many Muslims are focused on their identity as Muslims rather than on 'racial' affiliation understood in terms of colour or national origin. This is not inconsistent, however, with a legal response which focuses on the racialised aspects of Muslim disadvantage while attempting to avoid the conflicts which arise out of the extension of protection against discrimination to religion or belief more generally. The wrong which is targeted by such a response would not extend to discrimination against Muslims, whether by Muslims or non-Muslims, by reason of disputes about the essentially religious (differences about the interpretation of the sacred text or other matters of doctrine, for example). Such disputes can, and do, occur between people who regard each other, *as people*, as equally worthy of respect, while disagreeing with each other's *views*.

This is to be distinguished from a situation where a person finds himself subject to less favourable treatment because, for example, as a Muslim Asian, he is viewed with suspicion and hostility because of his adherence to a religion regarded by some as synonymous with being a terrorist sympathiser.[152] It is equally to be distinguished from a case in which, for example, a white woman of 'European' ethnicity is regarded as having betrayed her 'race' by adopting Islam and wearing a hijab. To the extent that she finds herself subject to less favourable treatment because of her association with Muslims, who are for this

---

[149] It remains to be seen whether *Eweida* signals a lasting change in the approach of the Court to this question.

[150] See *Mandla v Dowell Lee* (n 109).

[151] L Outlaw, 'Towards a Critical Theory of Race' in D Goldberg (ed), *Anatomy of Racism* (Minneapolis: University of Minnesota Press, 1990) 58, 68. See also A Harris, 'Equality Trouble: Sameness and Difference in Twentieth-Century Race Law' (2000) 88 *California Law Review* 1923. At 1923 Harris highlights the role of law in the US in regulating the 'formation, recognition, and maintenance of racial groups, as well as . . . the relationships among these groups'.

[152] The same was true in the 1970s and 1980s of those (particularly men) perceived to be (Northern) Irish Catholics.

purpose classed as 'other', that treatment is indistinguishable from that which is based on 'racial' hostility.

Direct discrimination of these sorts may give rise to breaches of Article 9 itself or in conjunction with Article 14 of the Convention, but the limited horizontal application of those provisions justifies additional domestic legal protections. Where, by contrast, less favourable treatment is alleged to result from a doctrinal disagreement as to the proper role of women within a religious hierarchy, or different religious hierarchies, whether Christ was the Son of God or merely one of the prophets, whether the communion host *is*, or rather *represents*, the body of Christ, such discrimination is no more worthy of legal regulation than is discrimination resulting from a clash of political ideology or taste in music.

Turning to (2), working life remains organised to some extent around a Christian calendar such that working time is, for many, constructed in such a way as to permit religious observance by Christians while rendering observance by Muslims and Jews (among others) problematic. Similar observations can be made about what is regarded as 'normal' in terms of dress and practices around food and eating. To the extent that society is not neutral, reasonable accommodation should be made of those religious obligations the equivalent of which are facilitated for those of the 'favoured' faith(s). Some such accommodation may be required under Article 9 of the Convention. But the case law of the ECtHR set out above makes it clear that decisions to this effect are unlikely in practice, even where (as in *Ahmad v UK*, discussed above) Article 14 is explicitly relied upon. And if accommodation is made for the religious dress of observant Muslims and Sikhs, fairness ((3)) requires that Christians be allowed to wear crucifixes at work at least in the absence of a reason, other than the mere fact of a uniform policy, to the contrary.[153]

Suggesting this kind of accommodation does not entail granting to religion the same status as the other protected grounds, involving rather a pragmatic response to the fact that religious belief is an important organising feature of many people's lives, and that present arrangements are not even-handed in the extent to which they enable people to manage the competing demands upon them. By 'reasonable' here I mean that the accommodation is such as would be required in a case of (say) prima facie indirect race discrimination, that is, where the disparate impact is disproportionate to any legitimate need appropriately and necessarily served by the disparately impacting measures, those measures should not be applied to those disproportionately disadvantaged by them. Examples of such cases might include the existing exemptions for Sikh turbans on building sites and on motorcycles, particularly in the absence of statistical evidence of disproportionate rates of serious injuries resulting

---

[153] In *Chaplin* the crucifix was caught by a ban on jewellery worn around the neck because of concerns about such jewellery being grabbed by patients. See p 147 above.

therefrom;[154] the provision of Halal and Kosher food by prisons, and by schools where, for example, Muslim or Jewish pupils are entitled to free school meals, or attend the school in significant numbers; flexibility as regards appearance rules and early finish times for observant Jewish workers on Friday evenings where necessary to permit compliance with Sabbath restrictions; and accommodation of other religious requirements for Sabbaths and religious festivals. Such observation is not, for the most part, problematic for majority Christians given the organisation of the calendar around Christian Sabbath and holidays, but can create real difficulties for others.

Accommodating such religious requirements may create a degree of inconvenience for others, but no more so than the inconvenience of accommodating colleagues on maternity or parental leave or 'family friendly' working hours, or those with other commitments which impinge on their working time.[155] This inconvenience is quite a different cost from that associated with permitting religious individuals or collectives themselves to discriminate on grounds of sex, race, etc, at least in the public sphere, involving as it does no challenge to individuals' equality or other rights.

This approach is a modified version of that espoused by the late Brian Barry.[156] Barry himself was dismissive of equality arguments in this context, suggesting that the rule-and-exemption approach adopted in the UK in relation (for example) to humane slaughter and the requirement that motorcyclists wear helmets is neither necessary nor justifiable. His general approach was that no rules should exist as to, for example, clothing and appearance or safety requirements unless they were justifiable in the general public interest, in which case exceptions should generally not be made. Thus, if stunning was generally determined to be desirable in the case of animals about to be slaughtered, providing an exception to those whose religious beliefs forbad pre-slaughter would be analogous to allowing only those 'who could show it was part of their culture' to hunt.[157]

The shortcomings of Barry's position lay in his unwillingness to countenance that perceptions of religious obligation might be weighed in the balance at all, and in his elision of religious adherence with the 'expensive tastes' with which

---

[154] For an analysis of the increased marginal risks associated with non-use of helmets by Sikhs in British Columbia see *Dhillon v British Columbia (Ministry of Transportation and Highways, Motor Vehicle Branch)* [1999] BCHRTD No 25, British Columbia Human Rights Tribunal, 11 May 1999.

[155] This could include those who sit as magistrates, local councillors etc. Barry objects that employers should not 'be licensed to carry out intrusive investigations into their employees' religious affiliations simply in order to be able to deny permission to "rogue" headscarf-wearers' (B Barry, *Culture and Equality* (Cambridge: Polity Press, 2001) 59) and there is no dispute that the same general rule should apply to all where that rule can be made to be neutral as between religions. The issue is, however, more difficult when, as in relation to working hours, neutrality may not be possible (though it is equally possible that general flexibility around working time will accommodate many employers' as well as workers' needs).

[156] ibid.

[157] ibid, 43.

luck egalitarians are so concerned (see further Chapter 1). Barry's dismissal of complaints of disparate impact with the assertion that '[The essence of law is the protection of some interests at the expense of others when they come into conflict . . . The point is a completely general one'[158] misses the point that some people bear the burdens disproportionately while others enjoy more than a fair share of the benefits. Barry did accept that a ban imposed, in the context of employment, on the wearing of a headscarf was objectionable, this on the basis that 'there is no non-trivial reason in support of a ban on headscarves' so, because 'to abandon a long-established custom that enjoins women not to appear in public with uncovered heads is no trivial matter . . . the ban is rightly to be regarded as a denial of equal opportunity, or at the very least an unreasonable infringement of a right to make a living without having to make a gratuitous sacrifice'.[159] Where, however, the sacrifice is other than gratuitous, because the aim served by the disparately impacting rule is a legitimate and weighty one, Barry would have brooked no exceptions except, it appears, where there are strong pragmatic grounds for so doing.[160]

Barry's statement that 'special treatment for members of disadvantaged groups is justified only for so long as the inequality persists'[161] is, I think, correct. But his statement that 'the object of special treatment for members of disadvantaged groups is to make the need for that special treatment to disappear as rapidly as possible'[162] is, although apt in relation to measures designed to lift people out of poverty or ameliorate historical disadvantage, less so in this context: the accommodation of religious needs will not itself make the need for such accommodation disappear. It is at least arguable that neither will the achievement of a formally neutral state.

Remaining exceptions to formal state neutrality consist predominantly in the arrangement of conventional working hours and schooling arrangements around the Christian calendar; the role of Anglican bishops in the House of Lords and (likely of minority concern) restrictions on accession to the throne of Catholics. (Blasphemy laws, which applied to Christianity (possibly Anglicanism) alone were abolished in May 2008.[163]) The focus of those who favour religious equality should be on ridding the state of these exceptions and, in the meantime, negotiating appropriate accommodations with them for individuals who adhere to the non-'favoured' faith, rather than in ensuring to religious individuals rights to discriminate on other grounds.

---

[158] ibid, 34.

[159] ibid, 59.

[160] In the case of Sikh construction workers because their number and geographical concentration would mean that the absence of an exemption to the hard hat rule would have a very high social cost (ibid, 49–50) and in the case of school uniform which Barry sees as serving 'no interest that was worthy of protection' (at least in the case of *Mandla v Dowell Lee*, n 109).

[161] Barry (n 155) 13.

[162] ibid.

[163] By the Criminal Justice and Immigration Act 2008.

Likely to persist even in the event of formal neutrality are the difficulties thrown up by different rules or norms concerning clothing, appearance and food. It has already been suggested that these can be dealt with, by and large, by pragmatic accommodations. In many cases the result of these accommodations would not differ greatly from those which would flow from the prohibition of indirect discrimination on grounds of religion (as at present). Where the difference would be felt, however, is in those cases in which accommodation is sought by those whose religious beliefs do not place them in a disadvantaged minority group, or where such beliefs conflict with the legally protected rights of others.

In the former case there would simply be no right of accommodation over and above that provided by Article 9: absent a prohibition on religious discrimination per se no additional claim to protection arises. As to the latter type of case, an example arises from the facts of cases such as *Azmi*, where the claimant's wishes could be met only at cost to her educationally already disadvantaged pupils, or to male staff members whose freedom of movement around their workplace would have to have been curtailed to protect Ms Azmi, when she was unveiled, from their gaze. In such a case, and given the absence of a right to accommodation of religious belief *qua religious belief*, the claim fails. This is the same outcome as was actually achieved in *Azmi*, but it does not depend upon the characterisation of the discrimination at issue as indirect rather than direct, rather on the fact that *reasonable* accommodation could not require an employer to override a prohibition on direct sex discrimination or (I would argue) the obligation owed to already disadvantaged students.

Other interesting questions arise where that of which accommodation is sought is questionable in and of itself, irrespective of immediate conflicts with the rights of others. These questions are the subject matter of Chapter 6. But difficult questions as to the limits of accommodation may well be better managed by an approach which focuses on disadvantage, exclusion and alienation from 'mainstream' society, and asks how best equality might be furthered, than on one where outcomes differ according to sometimes hair-splitting distinctions between 'indirect' and 'direct' discrimination in the context of religion, and/or a wide approach to the GOR defence, particularly where such tactics threaten to reverberate across the spectrum of discrimination law.

RELIGIOUS COLLECTIVES: THE SCOPE OF EXEMPTIONS

Turning, finally, to the question of religious collectives, representatives of religious organisations regularly challenge the application to them of rules generally applicable in the context of employment, education and/or social services as inconsistent with their rights to religious freedom. Perhaps the most prominent recent examples have concerned the (unsuccessful) lobbying by the Catholic church for exemption from the prohibition on sexual orientation discrimination in the provision of adoption or fostering services, and the securing by religiously motivated peers of the extended GOR for religious organisations discussed above.

There have been a number of unsuccessful attempts by Christian hoteliers/ guest house owners to mount Article 9 claims against claims brought against them by gay couples in respect of refusals to allow them accommodation in double-bedded rooms. In *Bull & Bull v Preddy & Hall* the Court of Appeal ruled that the refusal to accommodate a same-sex couple because they were unmarried amounted to direct discrimination because of sexual orientation (this because the couple could, by definition, not get married),[164] further that Article 9 did not protect the hoteliers because any restrictions imposed on them did not impair their ability to manifest their religious beliefs outside the commercial sphere at issue. Rafferty LJ gave the leading judgment, with which Hooper LJ and Sir Andrew Morritt C agreed, the latter adding that:

> The religious beliefs of Mr and Mrs Bull do not exempt them from observing the regulations in their ownership and management of the hotel. In short, they are not obliged to provide double-bedded rooms at all, but if they do, then they must be prepared to let them to homosexual couples, at least if they are in a civil partnership, as well as to heterosexual married couples.[165]

Subsequently in *Black & Morgan v Wilkinson*, the Court of Appeal refused an appeal by a guest house owner against a finding that she had discriminated against a gay couple by refusing to allow them to share a double-bedded room in her property.[166] She claimed that she applied the same rule to all non-married couples (though it was not suggested that she demanded to examine the marriage certificates of heterosexual couples). The Court of Appeal, unconstrained by authority, would have found that the discrimination at issue was of the indirect, rather than the direct, variety. It would, however, have concluded that the discrimination was unjustified.

In November 2013 the Supreme Court reflected the appeals of the guest house owners in both cases, ruling by a majority that the discrimination was direct, with the minority being of the view that the discrimination was indirect and unjustified.[167] The *Bull* and *Black* cases concerned discrimination by religious individuals, rather than collectives but is difficult to see any principled distinction between the running of a *commercial* undertaking by a religious individual, on the one hand, and by a religious organisation on the other. If, for example, a religious order refused to accommodate same-sex couples in double-bedded rooms during a religious retreat, such refusal might well not offend section 29 of the Equality Act 2010 which is concerned only with services which are available 'to the public or a section of the public'.[168] Even if section 29 were regarded as

---

[164] *Bull & Bull v Preddy & Hall* [2012] 2 All ER 1017. The decision pre-dated the Marriage (Same Sex Couples) Act 2013.

[165] ibid, para 66.

[166] *Black & Morgan v Wilkinson* [2013] EWCA Civ 820.

[167] *Bull & Anor v Hall & Anor* [2013] UKSC 73.

[168] See *Charter & Ors v Race Relations Board* [1973] AC 868 on the materially identical provision of the RRA.

applying, Schedule 23 paragraph 2 provides that an organisation (1) the purpose of which is to practise or advance a religion or belief, teach the practice or principles of a religion or belief or 'enable persons of a religion or belief to receive any benefit, or to engage in any activity, within the framework of that religion or belief', (2) whose sole or main purpose is not commercial, and (3) which is not carrying out functions on behalf of a public authority, and under the terms of a contract with the public authority, may (consistent with the 2010 Act) restrict (inter alia):

(a) membership of the organisation;
(b) participation in activities undertaken by the organisation or on its behalf or under its auspices; [and]
(c) the provision of goods, facilities or services in the course of activities undertaken by the organisation or on its behalf or under its auspices;

for reasons related to sexual orientation because of the purpose of the organisation, or to avoid causing offence, on grounds of the religion or belief to which the organisation relates, to persons of that religion or belief.

Reasoning by analogy with the Article 9 case law on individual religious beliefs, that provision would appear to afford little by way of protection to collectives which seek to avoid rules of general application as regards, for example, discrimination on grounds of sexual orientation in the provision of adoption services. And while a religious organisation would be free to refuse women access to the higher echelons of its hierarchy, or to eject a member on the grounds that she, for example, was single and pregnant, or a lesbian, or that he was 'living in sin', Article 9 does not appear to afford such organisations carte blanche to impose their rules on those with whom they come into contact as providers of health or social services or education. The users of such services are themselves protected from discrimination by the combination of Article 14 with, for example, Articles 2, 3 and 8 of the Convention, and those provisions impose positive obligations on the state to secure some measure of protection from quasi breaches by non-state actors. This being the case, religious organisations cannot insist on their own Convention rights while interfering with or denying those of others.

This is not to say that the Convention would *prohibit* the provision of some measure of exemption from the normal rules to religious organisations operating in the public sphere, at least where potential service users had real choices between those organisations and other providers of the relevant services. But there appear to be scant grounds for asserting that the Convention *requires* the provision of such exemptions. As Lord Hope put it in *JFS*: 'it is not the business of the courts to intervene in matters of religion' and 'the court must inevitably be wary of entering so self-evidently sensitive an area, straying across the well-recognised divide between church and state'.[169] But 'It is just as well understood . . . that the divide is crossed when the parties to the dispute have deliberately

---

[169] *R (E) v Governing Body of the Jews Free School* (n 69) para 157.

left the sphere of matters spiritual over which the religious body has exclusive jurisdiction and engaged in matters that are regulated by the civil courts'.[170] In *JFS* it was

> accepted on all sides . . . that it is entirely a matter for the Chief Rabbi to adjudicate on the principles of Orthodox Judaism. But the sphere within which those principles are being applied is that of an educational establishment whose activities are regulated by the law that the civil courts must administer.[171]

The divide between 'matters spiritual over which the religious body has exclusive jurisdiction', and matters falling within the jurisdiction of the civil courts can be crossed even in matters pertaining to the relationship between religious organisations and their ministers. The suggestion of the Court in *Wachmann*, discussed above, was that questions of procedural fairness as regards the removal of a rabbi regarded as 'no longer religiously and morally fit to occupy his position as rabbi' were incapable of being disentangled from questions of doctrine such that secular adjudication of the dispute would overstep the boundary between secular and sacred. In the US, 'employment' decisions regarding ministers of religion are outside the jurisdiction of the courts, the Supreme Court ruling in January 2012 both that the First Amendment precluded the application of discrimination legislation (specifically there the Americans with Disabilities Act) to the employment relationship between a religious group and one of its ministers, and that this 'ministerial exception' was wide enough to extend to the claimant, a parochial school teacher who spent most of her work time on non-religious duties.[172] But the very fact that Schedule 9, paragraph 2 of the Equality Act provides exceptions from the normal prohibitions on discrimination to 'employment . . . for the purposes of an organised religion' suggests that the very 'hands off' approach adopted by the US Supreme Court has no application here.

Neither paragraph 2 nor paragraph 3 of Schedule 9 provide general exceptions in relation to discrimination because of sex, sexual orientation, religious belief, etc. Rather, they permit the imposition of requirements to be of a particular sex, religion etc, or more broadly, requirements 'related to sexual orientation'. Thus there would be no defence under paragraph 2 to an allegation that a spokesperson employed by a religious organisation was subject to trumped-up disciplinary charges because of a dispute as to religious matter, or under paragraph 3 to an allegation that a minister of religion was subject to harassment because of his sexual orientation, or was remunerated on a lower scale because she was a woman.

Until 2006, with the decision of the House of Lords in *Percy v Board of National Mission of the Church of Scotland* (2006),[173] the courts had ruled as a

---

[170] ibid, para 158.

[171] ibid, para 160.

[172] *Hosanna-Tabor Evangelical Lutheran Church and School v Equal Employment Opportunity Commission et al*, 565 US _ (2012), available at www.scotusblog.com/case-files/cases/hosanna-tabor-evangelical-lutheran-church-and-school-v-eeoc.

[173] *Percy v Board of National Mission of the Church of Scotland* (n 146).

matter of course that ministers of religion were not 'employed' for the purposes of employment protection legislation, including the anti-discrimination provisions.[174] This approach, which was justified on the basis that the relationships between clergy and churches were governed by God rather than by contract, applied only to ministers of religion rather than more broadly (as in the US). But in *Percy* the House of Lords ruled that a minister of the Church of Scotland was employed for the purposes of the Sex Discrimination Act 1975.

The sex discrimination alleged in *Percy* did not concern doctrine, the claimant complaining that she had been treated less favourably than a male comparator as regards alleged sexual impropriety. The House of Lords did not mention Article 9. In *New Testament Church of God v Stewart* (2008), the Court of Appeal ruled that that provision required a nuanced approach in a case in which religious practices or observance were at issue. Pill LJ ruled that Article 9 'requires that respect be given to the "faith and doctrine" . . . of the particular church, which may run counter to there being a relationship enforceable at law between the priest, curate or minister and the church'.[175] Arden LJ agreed with his conclusion that there was an enforceable contract on the facts of the case, stating that 'the fact that in an employment dispute one party to the litigation is a religious body or that the other party is a minister of religion does not of itself engage Article 9'.[176] And in *President of the Methodist Conference v Preston* (2011) the Court of Appeal suggested that Article 9 was likely to have limited relevance to the question whether a minister of religion should benefit from a contract of employment in any particular case, Maurice Kay LJ referring to 'the unattractiveness and moral poverty of the attempted invocation of Article 9 in this case' in which it had been asserted that 'the universal conviction of Methodist people that the office of the Christian ministry depends on the call of God who bestows the gifts of the Spirit the grace and the fruit which indicate those whom He has chosen' was inconsistent with the recognition of the claimant as an employee. As his Lordship observed: 'This reflects "the priesthood of all believers" but it surely does not embrace a doctrinal belief that a Minister who is treated with unfairness or discrimination must be denied common legal redress'.[177]

The Supreme Court reversed the decision of the Court of Appeal in *Preston*.[178] Lord Sumption, for the majority, read *Percy* as establishing

> that the question whether a minister of religion serves under a contract of employment can no longer be answered simply by classifying the minister's occupation by

---

[174] See *Davies v Presbyterian Church of Wales* [1986] ICR 280 which was applied in a succession of cases including *Santokh Singh v Guru Nanak Gurdwara* [1990] ICR 309; *Birmingham Mosque Trust Ltd v Alavi* [1992] ICR 435 and *Khan v Oxford City Mosque Society* (unreported, 1998).

[175] *New Testament Church of God v Stewart*, para 46. Lawrence Collins LJ agreed.

[176] ibid, para 62. Arden LJ's approach to Art 9 was regarded as narrower than that of Pill LJ by the Court of Appeal in *President of the Methodist Conference v Preston (formerly Moore)* [2011] EWCA Civ 1581, and was preferred by Maurice Kay LJ (para 32), with whom Longmore LJ and Sir David Keene agreed.

[177] *President of the Methodist Conference v Preston* [2012] 2 All ER 934, paras 33, 34.

[178] *Preston* [2013] UKSC 29.

type: office or employment, spiritual or secular. Nor, in the generality of cases, can it be answered by reference to any presumption against the contractual character of the service of ministers of religion generally.[179]

For his Lordship, 'The primary considerations are the manner in which the minister was engaged, and the character of the rules or terms governing his or her service' which 'as with all exercises in contractual construction . . . fall to be construed against their factual background [which includes] . . . the fundamentally spiritual purpose of the functions of a minister of religion'. Having concluded that Ms Preston's ministry as set out in the Church's instruments 'is a vocation, by which candidates submit themselves to the discipline of the church for life' and that absent 'some special arrangement . . . made [between the Church and] . . . a particular minister, the rights and duties of ministers arise . . . entirely from their status in the constitution of the church and not from any contract', Lord Sumption declined to find that any such 'special arrangement' arose on the facts of the case, her position in Redruth being 'simply the role for which she was stationed by the Conference'. In his Lordship's view:

> [B]oth courts below over-analysed the decision in *Percy*, and paid insufficient attention to the Deed of Union and the standing orders which were the foundation of Ms Preston's relationship with the Methodist Church. The question whether an arrangement is a legally binding contract depends on the intentions of the parties. The mere fact that the arrangement includes the payment of a stipend, the provision of accommodation and recognised duties to be performed by the minister, does not without more resolve the issue. The question is whether the parties intended these benefits and burdens of the ministry to be the subject of a legally binding agreement between them. The decision in *Percy* is authority for the proposition that the spiritual character of the ministry did not give rise to a presumption against the contractual intention. But the majority did not suggest that the spiritual character of the ministry was irrelevant. It was a significant part of the background against which the overt arrangements governing the service of ministers must be interpreted. Nor did they suggest that the only material which might be relevant for deciding whether the arrangements were contractual were the statements marking the minister's engagement, although it so happened that there was no other significant material in Ms Percy's case. Part of the vice of the earlier authorities was that many of them proceeded by way of abstract categorisation of ministers of religion generally. The correct approach is to examine the rules and practices of the particular church and any special arrangements made with the particular minister. What Lord Nicholls was saying was that the arrangements, properly examined, might well prove to be inconsistent with contractual intention, even though there was no presumption to that effect. He cited the arrangements governing the service of Methodist ministers considered in *Parfitt* as an example of this, mainly for the reasons given in that case by Dillon LJ. These were, essentially, the lifelong commitment of the minister, the exclusion of any right of unilateral resignation and the characterisation of the stipend as maintenance and support. There is nothing inconsistent between his view on these points and the more general

---

[179] ibid, para 10.

statements of principle appearing in his speech and in the speeches of those who agreed with him.[180]

Lord Hope, who had concurred with the majority in *Percy*, agreed with the majority here because, by contrast with the position in *Percy*, 'the question is whether there were any arrangements of an employment nature at all'.[181] (The very same question in fact arose in *Percy*, in which the tribunal had accepted that there was a contract but not 'having regard to the essentially religious nature of Ms Percy's duties' that it was a contract of employment[182]). Lady Hale, who had formed part of the majority in *Percy*, dissented in *Parfitt* on the basis that while 'Admission to full connexion [as an ordained minister] brings with it a life-long commitment to the church and its ministry', *assignment* as a minister was 'to a particular post, with a particular set of duties and expectations, a particular manse and a stipend which depends (at the very least) on the level of responsibility entailed, and for a defined period of time'.[183] Such would 'In any other context . . . involve a contract of employment in that post'. [184] And while there was 'a spiritual component on each side of this covenant relationship' and an obligation on the minister to 'go where Conference stations her', Lady Hale did not accept that ministers were in fact stationed absent their agreement.[185] For her:

> Everything about this arrangement looks contractual, as did everything about the relationship in the *Percy* case. It was a very specific arrangement for a particular post, at a particular time, with a particular manse and a particular stipend, and with a particular set of responsibilities. It was an arrangement negotiated at local level but made at national level. The church may well have had good reasons to be troubled about the respondent's performance. But the allegation is that, instead of addressing those directly, they reorganised the Circuits so as, in effect, to make any investigation of whether or not those complaints were justified unnecessary, thus depriving the respondent of her post by organising it out of existence, without any of the safeguards to which she would otherwise have been entitled.[186]

Whether, in fact, *Parfitt* represents an application of *Percy* or the beginning of a withdrawal from it, *Percy* does give rise to interesting questions about the limits which Article 9 might impose on the legal regulation of what might be characterised as 'internal' decisions[187] of religious and similar organisations. What seems clear, however, is that that provision does not afford such organisations the right to exemptions from rules of general application when it comes to involvement in the *external* sphere. Nor, for the reasons discussed above in rela-

---

[180] ibid, para 26.
[181] ibid, para 34.
[182] Note 146, para 4, *per* Lord Nicholls.
[183] *Preston* (n 178), para 46.
[184] ibid, para 47.
[185] ibid, para 48.
[186] ibid, para 49.
[187] Such as those which gave rise to the disputes in *Percy* and in *Preston*.

tion to individual belief, should domestic discrimination law provide such exemptions. And, whereas it has been suggested that some protection from discrimination ought to be afforded in relation to individual belief/religion/culture where there are overlaps between these characteristics and ethnicity, or where and to the extent that the absence of state neutrality or considerations of fairness require it, no equivalent arguments can be made in relation to religious collectives' exemptions from rules of general application. Any such special treatment would, by contrast with that afforded to individuals from (for example) less favourable treatment motivated by or connected with their membership (actual or perceived) of a minority religion, serve to expand the opportunities for discrimination on the basis of other characteristics (sexual orientation, sex, etc) against individuals.

It may be appropriate to permit a church-run, privately funded, marriage guidance organisation to provide its services only to members of the relevant religious group, or to those members who toe the party line on matters such as same-sex religion or adherence to doctrine. But where such an organisation enters the public sphere by (for example) providing a publicly funded service of (say) relationship counselling, it ought not to be permitted to discriminate in relation to its service users in circumstances where a non-religious body could not. It is to be hoped that *Parfitt* is not indicative of increased deference on the part of the Supreme Court to questions in respect of which claims for religious exemption are made.

6

Multiculturalism and Equality[1]

INTRODUCTION

IN CHAPTER 3 I considered the relationship between social groups and equality law, and raised the difficulty that treating 'groups' as 'natural' or fixed can facilitate the disciplining and regulation of individuals within the group by others who are advantaged by status or weight of numbers.[2] A further example of this potential is the decision in *Wisconsin v Yoder* (1972), in which the US Supreme Court ruled that requiring Old Order Amish children to attend high school (from age 14, the age of compulsory schooling in the State being 16) breached the right to religious freedom of their parents.[3] The Amish community, which believed that school attendance beyond eighth grade (by which stage children could be expected to have assimilated basic reading, writing and mathematical skills) was contrary to their religion and way of life, provided older children with informal vocational education designed to fit them for life in the rural Amish community. By a majority the Supreme Court ruled in favour of the Amish parents, thereby removing from many Amish children the right to education other than in the 'tools of the trade', with very significant repercussions for their ability to exit the Amish community in later life.

Chief Justice Berger's opinion, for the majority of the Court, placed great emphasis on the religious nature of the Amish resistance to high school education: 'A way of life, however virtuous and admirable, may not be interposed as a barrier to reasonable state regulation of education if it is based on purely secular considerations'.[4] For the Chief Justice, the relevant question was whether the education preferred by Amish parents was sufficient for 'the preparation of the child for life in the separated agrarian community that is the keystone of the Amish faith'.[5] He rejected the State's argument that Amish children's ability to leave their birth communities would be restricted by a shortened period of formal schooling as 'highly speculative'. His focus was on the question whether

---

[1] Some elements of this chapter were previously published in A McColgan, 'Equality and Multiculturalism' [2011] *Current Legal Problems* 1.

[2] See discussion of Richard Ford's 'Unnatural Groups: A Reaction to Owen Fiss's "Groups and the Equal Protection Clause"' (2003) 2(1) *Issues in Legal Scholarship*, 4, 6–7.

[3] *Wisconsin v Yoder* 406 US 205.

[4] ibid, 216.

[5] ibid, 222, citing *Meyer v Nebraska* 262 US 390, 400 (1923).

exiting Amish would burden the State, rather than upon whether such exit would be hindered by the inevitable lack of formal schooling and qualifications which would result from legal vindication of the Amish parents' refusal to have their children attend high school. He further refused to address the possible conflict between parental rights and those of children since there was no evidence that the children whose education was at stake in the *Yoder* case wished to attend high school,[6] remarking however that a ruling in favour of the state in such a case 'would, of course, call into question traditional concepts of parental control over the religious up-bringing and education of their minor children recognized in this Court's past decisions' and that 'such an intrusion by a State into family decisions in the area of religious training would give rise to grave questions of religious freedom'.[7]

The decision of the majority in *Yoder* was based in part on expert evidence that high schooling could injure Amish children by creating conflicts between their communities' beliefs and 'worldly values', including an emphasis on 'intellectual and scientific accomplishments, self-distinction, competitiveness, worldly success, and social life with other students', and because it would 'ultimately result in the destruction of the Old Order Amish church community as it exists in the United States today'. [8] The preservation of the Amish lifestyle, with its rejection of secularism, modernity and intellectualism, depended on the denial to Amish children of access to the educational and social tools which might have facilitated their exit from the Amish Community, should they have subsequently wished to leave.[9]

Mr Justice Douglas dissented from the majority in *Yoder*, complaining that Chief Justice Berger's 'analysis assumes that the only interests at stake in the case are those of the Amish parents on the one hand, and those of the State on the other'.[10] In Justice Douglas's view, the voice of the Amish child needed to be heard:

> He may want to be a pianist or an astronaut or an oceanographer. To do so he will have to break from the Amish tradition. It is the future of the student, not the future

---

[6] ibid, 231.

[7] *Wisconsin v Yoder* (n 3) 231. *cf* A Guttmann, 'Civic Education and Social Diversity' (1995) 105(3) *Ethics* 557, 570 who argues that 'Amish education is inadequate for liberal democratic citizenship just as it is for individuality or autonomy' and that the religious freedom of Amish parents 'does not extend to exercising power over their children so as to deny them the education necessary for exercising full citizenship or for choosing among diverse ways of life that lie outside the Amish community'.

[8] *Wisconsin v Yoder* (n 3) 211.

[9] R Arneson and I Shapiro suggest ('Democratic Autonomy and Religious Freedom: A Critique of *Wisconsin v Yoder*' in I Shapiro (ed), *Democracy's Place* (Ithaca: Cornell University Press, 1996) 173) that 'it is because the Amish acculturation program is explicitly designed to prevent the development of critical reason that the Amish should have lost in *Yoder*. To accept a person's choice of an Amish way of life, one must have some reasonable confidence in that person's choice-making competence. This competence . . . is developed in education for autonomy'. *cf* AK Wahlstrom, 'Liberal Democracies and Encompassing Religious Communities: A Defense of Autonomy and Accommodation' (2005) 36(1) *Journal of Social Philosophy* 31, 51.

[10] *Wisconsin v Yoder* (n 3) 241.

of the parents, that is imperiled by today's decision. If a parent keeps his child out of school beyond the grade school, then the child will be forever barred from entry into the new and amazing world of diversity that we have today . . . his entire life may be stunted and deformed.[11]

The *Yoder* case is a particularly compelling illustration of Ayelet Shachar's 'paradox of multicultural vulnerability', in which attempts to protect what are seen as minority interests end up sacrificing the rights and interests of some within minority groups.[12] This situation is to be distinguished from those in which minority interests can be safeguarded against majority compulsion without sacrifice on the part of any members of the minority group. One example of the latter might be the exemption sought by Native Americans in the US Supreme Court case of *Employment Division, Department of Human Resources of Oregon v Smith* from the general prohibition on peyote use, insofar as that use was for sacramental purposes within the Native American Church of which they were members.[13] The Supreme Court refused to permit the exemption, distinguishing *Yoder* on the dubious basis that the decision there rested not on the freedom of religion alone, but also on 'the right of parents . . . to direct the education of their children'.[14]

It would be difficult to argue that the interests of any Native American would have been threatened by an exemption such as that sought in *Employment Division v Smith*, not least because the Church forbad the use of the drug other than for sacramental purposes and further advocated abstinence from alcohol.[15] Reasonable people might argue about the rights and wrongs of creating exceptions to rules of general application, where those rules are regarded as justified in the public interest.[16] But in *Smith*, as where turban-wearing Sikh men are granted exemption from generally applicable requirements for motorcyclists to

---

[11] ibid, 244–46. See S Mazie, 'Consenting Adults? Amish *Rumspringa* and the Quandry of Exit in Liberalism' (2005) 3 *Perspectives on Politics* 745 for the impact of truncated formal education on the nature of the 'choice' made by young Amish adults.

[12] A Shachar, 'On Citizenship and Multicultural Vulnerability' (2000) 28 *Political Theory* 64, 65. See also A Shachar, 'Group Identity and Women's Rights in Family Law: the Perils of Multicultural Accommodation' (1998) 6(3) *Journal of Political Philosophy* 285. In 'The Puzzle of Interlocking Power Hierarchies: Sharing the Pieces of Jurisdictional Authority' (2000) 35 *Harvard Civil Liberties Civil Rights Law Review* 385–426, 393, Shachar specifies that the paradox 'does not refer to incidental rights violations [but to] . . . systemic intragroup practices that adversely affect a particular category of group members'.

[13] *Employment Division, Department of Human Resources of Oregon v Smith* 494 US 872 (1990). See also *Lyng v Northwestern Indian Cemetery Protective Association* (1988) 485 US 439 (1988) discussed by A Shachar, 'Two Critiques of Multiculturalism' (2001–02) 23 *Cardozo Law Review* 253, 259.

[14] *Employment Division v Smith* (n 13) 881–82. Justice Blackmun, dissenting, with whom Justices Brennan and Marshall agreed, at 907 characterised as 'distorted' the majority's reading of the authorities.

[15] ibid, 914, *per* Blackmun J who concluded that 'Far from promoting the lawless and irresponsible use of drugs, Native American Church members' spiritual code exemplifies values that Oregon's drug laws are presumably intended to foster'.

[16] See B Barry, *Culture and Inequality: an Egalitarian Critique of Multiculturalism* (Cambridge, MA: Harvard University Press, 2001).

wear helmets or construction workers to wear hard hats, no question of *intra-group injustice* arises. In other cases, however, the line may be rather difficult to draw. Thus, for example, protection of the right of members of minority religious or 'cultural' groups to adhere to the dress codes of those groups in the workplace or in school may facilitate access to the public sphere for members of those groups. It may also, however, result in pressure being placed by members of the group on some (generally, though not always, women or girls) to comply with those dress codes against their wishes. And even where adult members of minority groups express a desire to engage in practices in conformity with the 'cultures' of such groups, concern may arise as to the reality of such consent in cases where (examples would include female genital cutting, polygamy and submission to Muslim or Jewish rules governing divorce or in the former case inheritance) the costs to the women concerned appear to the outsider to be so great as to call into question the factors producing the 'consent', as well as whether it ought to be recognised in law for the purposes of founding exceptions to rules or systems of general application.

Concern about capacity to consent was one of the reasons why Baroness Hale joined the remainder of the House of Lords in *R (Begum) v Headteacher and Governors of Denbigh High School* in ruling that a school had acted proportionately in refusing to allow a 16-year-old student to wear a *jilbab* (full-length flowing robes) in place of permitted uniform (which permitted hijab and/or shalwar kemeez).[17] Her Ladyship made clear her assumption that Muslim women who choose to wear a headscarf, like Sikh men who choose to wear a turban, do so freely for reasons which might include the outward manifestation of 'defiant political identity', the 'regaining [of] control over [the] body', deference to parental wishes and the assertion of a demand for respect from male non-Muslims. And though 'the sight of a woman in full purdah may offend some people, and especially those western feminists who believe that it is a symbol of her oppression, . . . that could not be a good reason for prohibiting her from wearing it'.[18]

Outsiders' assumptions about the significance of particular dress codes can be wide of the mark. While many of us may be inclined to fear that what begins with a headscarf ends with mandatory enshroudment of women subject to peremptory punishment by religious police (as in Iran[19] and Sudan[20]) for allowing a headcovering to slip, or the deaths of Saudi schoolgirls forcibly prevented from

---

[17] *R (Begum) v Headteacher and Governors of Denbigh High School* [2007] 1 AC 100, para 97.

[18] ibid, para 96.

[19] See *Fatin v INS* 12 F 3d 1233 (3rd Cir 1993); A Graves, 'Women in Iran: Obstacles to Human Rights and Possible Solutions' (1996–97) 5 *American University Journal of Gender and the Law* 57.

[20] Iran's Islamic Punishment Law provides for 74 lashes as a punishment for women who fail to observe hijab. See also C Howland, 'The Challenge of Religious Fundamentalism to the Liberty and Equality Rights of Women: An Analysis under the United Nations Charter' (1997) 35 *Columbia Journal of Transnational Law* 271, 315–16, on Sudan, and on restrictions imposed by Iran and Saudi Arabia on women drivers, the denial of the vote to women in Kuwait and the delegation of women's votes to men in Algeria.

leaving their burning school because they were not wearing headscarves or abayas,[21] Haleh Afshar et al found that hijab wearing in the West can be a complex act of female defiance, rather than subjucation. Many hijab wearers, they found, did not come from families which insisted on it, and many young Western women wore the hijab with clothes which would be frowned upon by conservative Muslims:

> Far from an indication of submission or docility the decision to wear the *hijab* makes a public statement that places the *mohajabehs* in the full light of the public gaze; something the parents and kin groups do not necessarily wish to see. It may even be seen as a clear indication of their new radical interpretation of the faith that they define as liberating rather than constraining. These views may well make it harder for parents to marry off their newly veiled daughters in arranged marriages. An interviewee for the Muslim Diaspora research, an art student and who wears *hijab* [stated that] 'The more Islamic I become the less likely it is I will be pushed into an unwanted marriage'. This is because the parents are unable to criticise if she is following Qur'anic teaching.[22]

Whatever the precise significance to individual Muslim women of particular items of clothing, state paternalism ought not to extend to denying the choice of a Muslim woman as to her mode of dress, however motivated, any more than it should deny others the right to wear 'provocative' clothing in an attempt to 'safeguard' them from sexual danger. In either case, the sins of the man (whether the real or imagined patriarch demanding female submission to standards of modesty, or the barely tamed beast of the popular imagination, forced to break free from the restraints of civilised behaviour by the sight of an uncovered thigh) are visited upon the women whose appearance would fall to be regulated by the state.

This is not to deny that there are cases in which an individual's views as to appropriate dress may have to give way before other considerations such as, for example, the interests of the children in *Azmi v Kirklees MBC*,[23] in which a teaching assistant employed to provide language support to pupils for whom English was not a first language failed to establish her right to teach in a *niqab* (full-face veil) in the face of evidence that the ability to see the speaker's mouth and facial expressions had a significant impact on the efficacy of such language teaching. More recently, there has been wide publicity over rulings by Judge Peter Murphy, sitting at Blackfriars Crown Court in September 2013, that a defendant could appear in Court wearing a *niqab* but had to remove the face covering while giving evidence, though she could be shielded from the sight of all but the judge, lawyers and jurors. Judge Murphy ruled that the unnamed defendant's right to manifest her religious beliefs had to give way in the particu-

---

[21] See BBC News Report, 15 March 2002, http://news.bbc.co.uk/1/hi/1874471.stm.

[22] H Afshar et al, 'Feminisms, Islamophobia and Identities' (2005) 53 *Political Studies* 262. See also B Parekh, A Varied Moral World' in J Cohen, M Howard and M Nussbaum (eds), *Is Multiculturalism Bad for Women?* (Princeton: Princeton University Press, 1999) 69, 73.

[23] *Azmi v Kirklees MBC* [2007] ICR 1154.

lar case to the interests of justice, which required that those passing judgment on the defendant be able to assess her demeanour on the stand.

These examples are both far removed from blanket criminal prohibitions in place in France and Belgium on the wearing of *niqab*, and currently before the UK Parliament in the shape of the Private Member's Face Coverings (Prohibition) Bill which received its first reading in June 2013. Like all Private Members' Bills, the Face Coverings (Prohibition) Bill is most unlikely to become law. That there is some wider political appetite for regulation, however, is suggested by then Home Office Minister Jeremy Browne's call, in the wake of Judge Murphy's *niqab* rulings and the lifting of a Burqa ban at Birmingham Metropolitan College, for a national debate on face coverings.[24] Of more immediate concern for present purposes, however, are the situations in which the accommodation of religiously or culturally embedded norms by the carving of exceptions to general rules will operate against the interests of even adult women whose freedom of choice may be exceptionally constrained by their group membership.

'MULTICULTURALISM'

Debates about the accommodation of group practices are at the heart of arguments about 'multiculturalism' and 'minority rights' more generally. The concept of minority rights as they have applied, for example, to national minorities in Poland, Austria, Hungary, Czechoslovakia, Bulgaria, Romania, Greece, Albania, Lithuania, Latvia and Estonia,[25] or to indigenous peoples in Nicaragua,[26] Norway, Sweden and Finland,[27] has found purchase in the UK only in the context of Northern Ireland, whose governing structures contain representational and other guarantees for the Irish-identified (Catholic) minority. My interest here is not in the application of such minority rights,[28] rather with the

---

[24] www.telegraph.co.uk/news/politics/10311469/Jeremy-Browne-Ban-Muslim-women-from-wearing-veils-in-schools-and-public-places.html.

[25] These under League of Nations Treaties and Declarations: see S Poulter, 'The Rights of Ethnic, Religious and Linguistic Minorities' (1997) *European Human Rights Law Review* 254, 254–55.

[26] By virtue of the Political Constitution of the mid 1980s which recognised communal property and cultural rights of the indigenous peoples of the Atlantic Coast and 1987 legislation creating autonomous political regions for these peoples.

[27] In the case of the Samii whose 'immemorial' hunting, herding and fishing rights have been recognised by Norwegian and Swedish courts and who have Sami Parliaments in Norway, Sweden and Finland: see F Orton and H Beach, 'A New Era for the Saami People of Sweden' in Cynthia Price Cohen (ed), *Human Rights of Indigenous Peoples* (New York: Transnational Publishers, 1998) 91, 92.

[28] Such rights are traditionally regarded as being restricted to minorities whose members are nationals of the relevant state: see, for example, the definition proposed by Professor Caportorti (the Special Rapporteur of the UN Sub-Commission on the Prevention of Discrimination and Protection of Minorities) in relation to Article 27 ICCPR, as discussed in P Thornberry, *International Law and the Rights of Minorities* (Oxford: Clarendon Press, 1991) 878.

more diffuse measures by which the immigrant communities on which British 'multiculturalism' tends to be focused are accommodated.[29]

Britain is generally regarded as practising a form of multiculturalism, which concept can refer, descriptively, to the characteristics of a 'society consisting of a number of cultural groups, esp[ecially] in which the distinctive cultural identity of each group is maintained', and/or (normatively) to 'polic[ies] or process[es] whereby the distinctive identities of the cultural groups within such a society are maintained or supported'.[30] There is no question that the UK, in common with most developed societies, is 'multicultural' in the descriptive sense. It is, in its accommodation of diversity, to some extent 'multicultural' in the normative sense as well.

From the mid 1960s, when the first wave of British-identified Caribbean immigrants was joined by significant numbers of South Asian arrivals, until the start of the twenty-first century and the emergence of 'community cohesion', the emphasis in the UK was on the 'integration' of immigrants defined by then Home Secretary Roy Jenkins in 1966 not as 'the loss, by immigrants, of their own national characteristics and culture . . . not as a flattening process of assimilation but as equal opportunity, coupled with cultural diversity, in an atmosphere of mutual tolerance'.[31]

Multiculturalism as a normative concept has fallen out of favour in recent years in the UK with, it has been suggested, an increasing emphasis on 'community cohesion' which has a tendency to slide into being little more than a demand for assimilation, as distinct from a positive movement towards the bringing together of disparate groups in a spirit of mutual interest and respect.[32] The concern expressed by the Cantle Report into the 2001 riots about the 'parallel lives' of different communities[33] has been seized by some as a stick with which to beat minority communities accused of segregating themselves (as distinct, for example, from being isolated by 'white flight' from residential areas and schools, poverty and racism).[34] And 10 years after the publication of the Cantle report, Prime Minister David Cameron declared, in a widely reported speech to an international security conference in Munich, that Europe's terror-

---

[29] *cf* the focus of W Kymlicka's 'liberal multiculturalism' indigenous minorities: see generally *Multicultural Citizenship: A Liberal Theory of Minority Rights* (Oxford: Clarendon Press, 1995).

[30] *Oxford English Dictionary*, 2nd edn (Oxford: Oxford University Press, 1989). M Malik ('"The Branch on Which We Sit": Multiculturalism, Minority Women and Family Law' in A Diduck and K O'Donovan (eds), *Feminist Perspectives on Family Law* (London: Routledge, 2006) 211–31, 211, compares 'factual' and normative multiculturalism.

[31] Speech by the then Home Secretary Roy Jenkins, reproduced in his *Essays and Speeches* (1967) 267 and cited by S Poulter, 'Ethnic Minority Customs, English Law and Human Rights' (1987) 36 *International & Comparative Law Quarterly* 589–615, 591.

[32] A Sivanandan (Director of the Institute of Race Relations), 'Britain's shame: from multiculturalism to nativism', 22 May 2006, www.irr.org.uk/2006/may/ha000024.html.

[33] T Cantle et al, Challenging Local Communities to Change Oldham: Review of Community Cohesion in Oldham (Home Office, 2001).

[34] For an interesting rejoinder to the misuse of the Cantle report see the essays in N Johnson (ed), *Citizenship, Cohesion and Solidarity* (London: the Smith Institute, 2008), available at www.smith-institute.org.uk/file/CitizenshipCohesionandSolidarity.pdf.

ist threat comes 'overwhelmingly from young men who follow a completely perverse, warped interpretation of Islam, and who are prepared to blow themselves up and kill their fellow citizens'; and that 'an important reason so many young Muslims are drawn to ['the ideology of extremism'] comes down to a question of identity':

> Under the doctrine of state multiculturalism, we have encouraged different cultures to live separate lives, apart from each other and apart from the mainstream . . . We've even tolerated these segregated communities behaving in ways that run completely counter to our values.
>
> So, when a white person holds objectionable views, racist views for instance, we rightly condemn them. But when equally unacceptable views or practices come from someone who isn't white, we've been too cautious frankly – frankly, even fearful – to stand up to them . . .[35]

In 2007 Cameron alleged that the 'the creed of multiculturalism . . . has stopped us from strengthening our collective identity. Indeed, it has deliberately weakened it',[36] and in 2008 he had referred to the 'disastrous' and 'discredited doctrine of state multiculturalism', defined as 'the idea that different cultures should be respected to the point of encouraging them to live separately', which 'had dangerously undermined Britain's sense of identity and brought about "cultural apartheid"'.[37] But the idea that there is a unified 'creed' of multiculturalism such as that attacked by the Prime Minister does not withstand much scrutiny.[38] Steven Vertovec and Susanne Wessendorf have pointed out, for example, that the term has been applied to initiatives as varied as prohibitions on race discrimination and incitement to racial hatred, on the one hand, and the provision of 'own media facilities for minority groups'. Between these measures lie not a 'multicultural monolith' but particular, often ad hoc, measures such as the accommodation of dress codes, dietary restrictions, requirements for time off work for religious observation, religious rules concerning the slaughter of animals and diverse 'places of worship, cemeteries and funerary rites'; the adoption of inclusive curricula and the provision of language support in schools and the production of official materials in multiple languages; the creation of legal exceptions covering, for example, Sikh turban wearing; the legal recognition of

[35] https://www.gov.uk/government/speeches/pms-speech-at-munich-security-conference

[36] See S Vertovec and S Wessendorf, 'Assessing the Backlash Against Multiculturalism in Europe' (Working Paper 09-04, Max Planck Institute, 2009) 14, citing 'Bagehot: In Praise of Multiculturalism', *The Economist*, 16 June 2007.

[37] Vertovec and Wessendorf (n 36) 14–15, citing 'Sharia Law will undermine British Society', *Daily Mail* 26 February 2008. The PM's 2011 speech was welcomed by Marine Le Pen, leader of France's *Front National* and daughter of its founder, as 'exactly the type of statement that has barred us from public life [in France] for 30 years': see 'Marine Le Pen praises Cameron stance on multiculturalism', *The Guardian*, 10 February 2011.

[38] Stuart Hall remarks that 'the term "multiculturalism" has come to reference a diffuse, indeed maddeningly spongy and imprecise, discursive field: a train of false trails and misleading universalities' in *The Multicultural Question*, Pavis Papers in Social and Cultural Research no. 4 (Milton Keynes: Open University, 2001) 3; GP Freeman, 'Immigrant Incorporation in Western Democracies' (2004) 38(3) *International Migration Review* 945–69.

diverse religious beliefs in relation to the swearing of oaths; the development of 'culturally sensitive practices' by public authorities and services; the provision of 'mother tongue teaching' and 'the establishment of minority groups' own schools (usually religious, publically financed or not)'; the 'recognition of other marriage, divorce and inheritance traditions'; the provision of support to BME 'organizations, facilities, and activities' and the inclusion of BME organisations within public consultative bodies.

Vertovec and Wessendorf suggest that 'multiculturalism can at best be described as a broad set of mutually reinforcing approaches or methodologies concerning the incorporation and participation of immigrants and ethnic minorities and their modes of cultural/religious difference',[39] whereas assaults on multiculturalism typically 'describe and emphasize multiculturalism as a singular, fixed ideology or dogma' in order to facilitate its condemnation, 'paint[ing] an undemanding picture of an integrated and dominating "multicultural industry" comprised of White liberals and ethnic minority activists'.[40] Critics further argue that the alleged 'single, prevailing ideology' of 'multiculturalism' 'has created an atmosphere in which thought and speech is controlled';[41] that 'it' (this 'concrete' entity of 'multiculturalism' as its critics project it) 'has led directly to social breakdown . . . [by] promoting ethnic separatism, an explicit rejection of common national values, and a lack of interest in social integration';[42] and that 'it' 'is not interested in any form of commonality' and 'refuses to acknowledge social problems connected with immigrants and ethnic minorities';[43] 'supports reprehensible social practices'[44] and 'provides a haven for terrorists'.[45]

That the same government whose leader has been as critical as Cameron of 'multiculturalism' has also adopted, as a central plank of education policy, 'free' schools, serves to underline the fact that some forms of segregation appear to be politically acceptable,[46] also that multiculturalism in practice is far from monolithic. The *Independent* reported in March 2011 that the UK's first state-

---

[39] Vertovec and Wessendorf (n 36) 10. See also A Favell, 'Applied Political Philosophy at the Rubicon: Will Kymlicka's *Multiculturalism Citizenship*' (1998) 1 *Ethical Theory and Moral Practice* 255–78.

[40] Vertovec and Wessendorf (n 36) 13.

[41] ibid, 14.

[42] ibid.

[43] ibid, 16.

[44] ibid, 17.

[45] ibid, 19. See also A Kundnani, *Spooked: How Not to Prevent Violent Extremism* (London: Institute of Race Relations, 2009) 6, 'Key Findings' on the fact that 'Prevent' funding designed to mobilise communities to oppose the ideology of violent extremists has been provided to local areas proportionately to the number of Muslim residents and has been channelled through 'the same "community gatekeepers" which the community cohesion agenda has identified as being problematic and divisive'.

[46] According to S Burgess, D Wilson and R Lupton, *Parallel Lives & Ethnic Segregation in the Playground & the Neighbourhood*, Centre for Market & Public Organisation Working Paper no 04/094 (Bristol: CMPO, 2004) 1 'on average school segregation is greater than the segregation of the same group in the surrounding neighbourhood'.

sponsored Hindu school, approved under the 'free' school policy, was to open in Leicester in September 2011.[47] While this school would select only 50 per cent of children on religious grounds, four of the first nine 'free' schools to be given approval were faith schools (two Christian, one Jewish and one Hindu) and there was at the time a proposal from an evangelical Christian group which holds a faith in creationism as core to its beliefs to open a school in Newark. According to the *Independent* report, the group

> says it will not teach creationism through the science curriculum but that evolution will only be taught as another theory – in contradiction to the demands of the national curriculum (although the 'free' schools will have the authority to ignore the national curriculum) . . . Critics say that the weakness in the current 'free' school policy is over the policing arrangements once the school is open. They argue that a school can make a commitment to having a diverse intake but that the proof of the pudding will be in the eating.

The Newark proposal failed, in part because of concerns about the teaching of creationism, but the *Guardian* reported in March 2012 that 'Christian Family Schools', which currently run two independent schools and has applied to set up a free school in Sheffield, integrates creationist teaching across its curriculum. The inspection of the organisation's schools has been undertaken not by Ofsted itself but by the independent 'Bridge Schools Inspectorate', which the *Guardian* describes as a 'specialist faith inspectorate . . . which is made up of serving headteachers of similarly affiliated religious schools' and which has been 'commissioned by Ofsted to inspect schools "belonging to the Christian Schools' Trust and the Association of Muslim Schools throughout England"'.

There are important questions to be asked about the extent to which imaginary multicultural policies are being unjustly scapegoated for the ghettoisation of minority ethnic and religious communities which has in fact resulted from plain, old-fashioned racism (perhaps in other words, to what extent the 'backlash' against the normative multiculturalism is the manifestation of a discomfort on the part of some with 'multiculturalism' as a signifier of ethnic diversity).[48] The *Guardian* suggested in response to Cameron's speech that 'The argument that what is wrong with race in Britain today is the failure of ethnic minorities to integrate has been gaining currency for years' but that 'this view ignores . . . the numerous ways in which ethnic minorities are still discriminated against – whether it is being stopped and searched by the police or in the jobs market . . .'.[49]

---

[47] The Krishna-Avanti primary school opened in September with an initial roll of 37 students, intended to rise to 420 over time, according to the *Leicester Mercury*, 1 September 2011.

[48] See M Malik, *Muslim Legal Norms and the Integration of European Muslims* (Florence: European University Institute, 2009), EUI Working Paper RSCAS 2009/29, 5–8, and *Minority Legal Orders in the UK: Minorities, Pluralism and the Law* (London: British Academy, 2012) on the influence of Islamophobia.

[49] 'Editorial', 7 February 2011. See also S Fish, *There's No Such Thing as Free Speech and It's a Good Thing, Too* (New York: Oxford University Press, 1994) 80–88, on the characterisation by the 'the Last Liberal' (A Schlesinger, Jr, in *The Disuniting of America: Reflections on a Multicultural*

The focus of this chapter is not, however, on what has been done in the UK in the name of, and what is wrongly attributed to, multicultural accommodation, more on normative questions concerning the relationship between such accommodation and equality. My concern is not with initiatives such as prohibitions on direct discrimination or incitement to hatred, or with the regulation of indirect race/ethnicity discrimination, which will generally, I would argue, require steps to be taken to ensure that important official information is accessible to those for whom English is not a first language; that services are delivered in a way which makes them practically rather than simply theoretically available to people from minority ethnic groups;[50] that those who wish to swear a religious oath rather than to affirm may do so according to their own beliefs; that the variety of religious beliefs ought to be accommodated by rules governing the establishment and operation of places of worship and burial; that people who do not share the majority culture are permitted to reconcile religious observance as regards attendance or dress codes with work-related requirements to the extent that this is reasonably possible; and that observance of religious/cultural dietary restrictions is not rendered unreasonably difficult.

Hard-line opponents of multiculturalist policies would dispute even these kinds of accommodation. Brian Barry, for example, insists that once 'uniform rules create identical choice sets, then opportunities are equal'.[51] But this purely formal approach to 'equality' is at odds with that adopted under domestic, European and international equality law[52] and, as Ayelet Shachar points out, 'ignores power disparities that already exist in society prior to the creation of so-called "identical choice options"', and which 'may translate in practice into unequal opportunities for members of certain minority communities as they may simply not have the same access to (or knowledge about) the "choice sets" presumably open to them' and 'places the blame for failing to act on such choices entirely on the individual, regardless of the circumstances under which their decision (or non-decision) took place':

> Even more fundamentally, it assumes that all persons and cultures interpret the same choice sets in a more or less identical fashion, while failing to address the possibility that some options may be foreclosed for some people because they are deeply steeped

Society (New York: Whittle Books, 1991) 17) of multiculturalism as an 'unprecedented . . . protest against the Anglocentric culture'. Fish suggested that 'the claim that such perceived conflict is new is simply inaccurate, and [that] "the perception of the threat itself is premised upon racist ideology"', equating Schlesinger's protest against multiculturalism with racist tracts warning 'of the detrimental effects on the pure West of inferior races . . .'. See L Volpp, 'Talking "Culture": Gender, Race, Nation, and the Politics of Multiculturalism' (1996) 96 *Columbia Law Review* 1573–1617, 1610. A Schlesinger Jr was described as 'the Last Liberal' by J Nuechterlein in 'The Last Liberal (Arthur M Schlesinger, Jr.)', *First Things: A Monthly Journal of Religion and Public Life* 8 January 2001.

[50]   See for example *Kaur & Shah v London Borough of Ealing* [2008] EWHC 2062 (Admin).

[51]   Barry (n 16) 32.

[52]   See also Leti Volpp's critique of Doraine Coleman, 'Individualizing Justice Through Multiculturalism: The Liberals' Dilemma' (1996) 96 *Columbia Law Review* 1093 as an example of 'backlash politics' ('Talking 'Culture', n 49).

in a tradition that provides a 'different' normative understanding of the world. Establishing an identical 'choice set' therefore does not by itself ensure that equal opportunities are indeed offered to all.[53]

Multiculturalism and Equality

The competing models of equality/anti-discrimination are discussed in Chapter 1. In brief outline, early debates on the competing merits of 'equal' and 'special' treatment approaches to, in particular, women's gender-based disadvantage[54] have by and large given way to an understanding of 'equality' which includes, but is not limited to, a concern that 'like' cases be treated alike.[55] The jurisprudence of domestic, European and international courts and other bodies has increasingly recognised not only that the 'unlike' may have to be treated differently in order to further equality,[56] but that the 'like' treatment of all may result in the systematic disadvantaging of those who differ from the 'norm',[57] with the effect that the 'norm' itself may have to be reconfigured.[58]

When equality is understood in this broader sense, it becomes clear that some 'multicultural' initiatives will contribute to it by reducing unjustifiable indirect discrimination. This is all the more true if equality/non-discrimination is conceptualised, as I suggest, as being concerned with the eradication of unjust status hierarchies (see, in particular, Chapter 2). More difficult, however, are measures whose purpose or effect is to perpetuate the existence of minority groups (at least where national minorities are not at issue) and those (which may or may not fall within the former) which involve the facilitation of practices which may systematically operate against the interests of subcategories of

---

[53] Shachar (n 13) 279.

[54] See, for example, A Scales, 'Towards a Feminist Jurisprudence' (1980–81) 56 *Indiana Law Journal* 375; S Law, 'Rethinking Sex and the Constitution' (1984) 132 *University of Pennsylvania Law Review* 955; HH Kay, 'Models of Equality' (1985) *Illinois Law Review* 30; W Williams, 'Equality's Riddle: Pregnancy and the Equal Treatment/Special Treatment Debate' (1984–85) 13 *New York University Review of Law and Social Change* 325.

[55] See A McColgan 'Cracking the Comparator Problem: Discrimination, "Equal" Treatment and the Role of Comparisons' (2006) 11(6) *European Human Rights Law Review* 650–77.

[56] This being the second part of Aristotle's approach: not only should 'things that are alike . . . be treated alike' but 'things that are unalike should be treated unalike in proportion to their unalikeness': *Ethica Nicomachea* V.3 1131a–b (W Ross trans, 1925). See *Thlimmenos v Greece* (2001) 31 EHRR 411, in which the ECtHR stated (para 44) that 'The Court has so far considered that the right under Article 14 not to be discriminated against in the enjoyment of the rights guaranteed under the Convention is violated when States treat differently persons in analogous situations without providing an objective and reasonable justification'. Such recognition is also seen in the approach to disability discrimination (in particular, the duties of reasonable adjustment) adopted by the Disability Discrimination Act 1995 and, more recently, the Equality Act 2010.

[57] A norm which may owe more to the distribution of power within societies than it does to considerations of numerical superiority; women generally outnumber men but are disadvantaged by practices in employment and public life which are premised on a male actor.

[58] This being the result of the prohibition on indirect discrimination: practices which disproportionately disadvantage groups defined by reference to protected factors must be altered if they are not objectively justified.

those in the group.[59] The latter are problematic for obvious reasons which form much of the subject matter of this chapter. But even where they are not associated with intra-group injustice, practices such as minority group representation within public consultative bodies, the provision of separate schools and media facilities for minority groups may operate as much to *create*, and certainly to *perpetuate*, rather than simply to *recognise* and *accommodate*, already existing groups. In particular, rights of representation may result in Balkanisation where individuals are encouraged to self-identify by reference to particular characteristics in order to gain benefits associated with specific group memberships, rather than to acknowledge the multi-faceted and overlapping nature of factors which constitute individuals' identities.

Proponents of (normative) multiculturalism including Joseph Raz and Will Kymlicka emphasise the importance of 'culture' to identity.[60] Charles Taylor, too, argues that identity is formed through a process of dialogue using 'cultural scripts'.[61] One feminist liberal defence of multiculturalism is articulated by Rajoo Seodu Herr who claims that:

> We are 'strong evaluators' who make choices based not only on our desires and inclinations but also on 'hyper' goods, such as fundamental moral values or ideals [which] . . . are culturally specific and ineluctably tied to a particular form of life, bound with the vernacular language, history, and narratives of a particular locality, sustained by indigenous institutions and practices. The particular culture as inscribed in our hyper goods defines who we are and becomes constitutive of our identity. As such, it will be difficult to shed our cultural identity, especially as adults, even when we are placed, for one reason or another, in a different societal culture. [62]

Herr's argument that some protection of minority culture is necessary to avoid the case in which members of minority groups are confronted with the dilemma of being deprived of their own cultures without easy access to the 'host' culture transforms the defence of multiculturalism into a case against indirect discrimi-

---

[59] This is what is referred to by Shachar as the 'paradox of multicultural vulnerability': 'On Citizenship' (n 12) 65.

[60] J Raz, 'Multiculturalism' (1998) 11(3) *Ratio Juris* 193–205 and see J Raz, 'Multiculturalism: A Liberal Perspective' in *Ethics in the Public Domain: Essays in the Morality of Law and Freedom* (New York: Clarendon Press, 1994) 155; W Kymlicka, *Multicultural Citizenship* (n 29).

[61] C Taylor, 'The Politics of Recognition' in A Guttmann (ed), *Multiculturalism and the Politics of* Recognition (Princeton: Princeton University Press, 1994) 25, 31. See also JM Balkin, 'Ideology as Cultural Software' (1995) *Cardozo Law Review* 1221–33, 1230, who suggests a non-deterministic understanding of the constructive nature of culture to the self; C Taylor, 'Atomism', *Philosophy and the Human Sciences*, Vol 2 (Cambridge: Cambridge University Press, 1985); M Sandel, *Liberalism and the Limits of Justice* (Cambridge: Cambridge University Press, 1981) and *Democracy's Discontent* (Cambridge, MA: Harvard University Press, 1996).

[62] RS Herr, 'A Third World Feminist Defense of Multiculturalism' (2004) 30 *Social Theory and Practice* 73–103, 76, citing C Taylor, *Sources of the Self: The Making of the Modern Identity* (Cambridge, MA: Harvard University Press, 1989); 'What Is Human Agency' in *Human Agency and Language: Philosophical Papers 1* (Cambridge: Cambridge University Press, 1985) 15–44, 23–26. See also, A Margalit and J Raz, 'National Self-Determination' in W Kymlicka (ed), *The Rights of Minority Cultures* (Oxford: Oxford University Press, 1995) 79. These arguments are frequently made in relation to 'ethnic' communities but could equally well apply to 'communities' identified by reference to religious belief, as Margalit and Raz recognise at 85.

nation.[63] Such an emphasis on culture does not fall into the essentialist trap which characterises the assertion of Natan Lerner, for example, that groups identified by reference to ethnicity, religion, language or culture possess 'unifying, spontaneous . . . and permanent factors that are, as a rule, beyond the control of members of the group'.[64]

Experiments conducted by Henri Tajfel and his colleagues in the late 1960s suggest that humans are hard-wired towards group identification and intra-group preferences.[65] The researchers found that school children organised into groups on the basis of even the most minimal perceived unifying characteristic (their falsely believing that they shared a preference for a painting by Paul Klee over one by Wassily Kandinsky, or vice versa) would adopt strategies to advantage those belonging to 'their' group (the individuals being unknown personally to the decision makers) over those belonging to the 'other' group; would do so *regardless* of the absence of *personal* gain; and, further, would prefer to maximise the *relative* advantage of those in 'their' group over the 'others' even where this resulted in lower *absolute* rewards to members of 'their' group. The simple act of categorisation as group members was sufficient to provoke discrimination against 'others' in the Tajfel experiments because the individual's sense of worth became entangled with the relative success of the group.

It can be argued, on the one hand, that protecting aspects of group identity will merely exacerbate the difficulties caused by intra-group preferences such as those identified by Tajfel. Further, as Yael Tamir points out, the preservation of particular rules or practices on the assumption that they are as essential to minority groups is 'paternalistic', 'presuppos[ing] that while "we" can survive change and innovation, can endure the duality created by modernity, "they" cannot'.[66] It is equally plausible, however, that group identification is actually strengthened by perceived threats to the well-being of the group. The 'social identity theory' developed by Tajfel and his colleagues suggests that people have several levels of 'self' corresponding to widening circles of group membership (the personal, for example, the familial, the tribal, and the national), and that we feel and behave at different levels of the 'self' in different contexts,[67] and inhabit multiple 'social identities' (concepts of the self) which derive from perceived membership of social groups.[68] External factors will, however, impact on the nature and degree of our identifications at any particular time: I am a broadly secularised woman of Irish descent and origin until confronted by a

---

[63] Citing Raz, 'Multiculturalism: A Liberal Perspective' (n 60) 177.

[64] N Lerner, *Group Rights and Discrimination in International Law* (Dordrecht: Martinus Nijhoff, 1991) 29–31, cited by P Keller in 'Re-thinking Ethnic and Cultural Rights in Europe' (1998) 18 *Oxford Journal of Legal Studies* 29–59, 35. 'Groups' are also discussed in Chapter 3.

[65] For an early account of these see H Tajfel, 'Experiments in Intergroup Discrimination' (1970) *Scientific American* 96–102.

[66] Y Tamir, 'Siding With the Underdogs' in Cohen et al (eds) (n 22) 47, 49.

[67] See generally H Tajfel and JC Turner, 'The Social Identity Theory of Inter-group Behavior' in S Worchel and LW Austin (eds), *Psychology of Intergroup Relations* (Chicago: Nelson-Hall, 1986).

[68] See MA Hogg and GM Vaughan, *Social Psychology*, 3rd edn (London: Prentice Hall, 2000).

drum-beating Orangeman marching through a 'nationalist' area, whereupon I am in danger of finding myself an indignant (Northern) Irish 'Papist'. Or as Michael Walzer observed:

> When my parochialism is threatened, I am wholly, radically parochial: a Serb, a Pole, a Jew and nothing else . . . Under the conditions of security I will acquire a more complex identity than the idea of tribalism suggests. I will identify myself with more than one tribe: I will be an American, a Jew, an Easterner, an intellectual, a professor.[69]

Saskia Sassen, further, points to the 'many sources of pain and rage produced by [minority] engagements with a dominant culture which may lead in turn to the "need" (in both men and women) to take refuge in one's own culture'.[70] And Maxine Zinn et al suggest that 'Typically, Black women's vision of their situation leads them not to seek solace from Black males but to create spaces where men, women and children are relatively protected from racist cultural and physical assaults'.[71]

The late Susan Okin was a notable critic of multiculturalism which she regarded as 'bad for women',[72] complicit in practices including female genital cutting, polygamous and forced marriages and the marriage of children, and systems of property ownership 'aimed at bringing women's sexuality and reproductive capabilities under men's control'.[73] Okin acknowledged sex discrimination in 'Western cultures' including gender-based violence and the objectification and economic exploitation of women,[74] but drew attention to such societies' legal guarantees of equality and what she saw as their general movement towards acceptance of female equality, a state of affairs which she contrasted with 'women's situation in many of the world's other cultures, including many of those from which immigrants to Europe and Northern America come'.[75] Okin went so far as to conclude that:

> In the case of a more patriarchal minority culture in the context of a less patriarchal majority culture . . . the female members of the culture . . . may be much better off, from a liberal point of view, if the culture into which they were born were either gradually to become extinct (as its members became integrated into the surrounding culture) or, preferably, to be encouraged and supported to substantially alter itself so as

---

[69] M Walzer, 'The New Tribalism' in (1992) *Dissent* 164–71, 171. The late Sebastian Poulter also suggested that 'united and steadfast adherence to traditional values and practices' may be a reaction to experiences of discrimination and prejudice: n 30, 590.

[70] S Sassen, 'Culture Beyond Gender' in Cohen et al (eds) (n 22) 76, 77–78.

[71] M Zinn, L Cannon, E Higginbotham and B Dill, 'The Costs of Exclusionary Practices in Women's Studies' (1986) 11(2) *Signs* 290, 295. See also Herr (n 62) citing N Kibria, 'Migration and Vietnamese American Women: Remaking Ethnicity' in M Zinn and B Dill, *Women of Color in U.S. Society* (Philadelphia: Temple University Press, 1994) 108.

[72] See Cohen et al (eds) (n 22) Part 1.

[73] Okin (n 22) 14. See also F Raday 'Culture, Religion and Gender' [2003] 1 *International Journal of Constitutional Law* 663.

[74] Okin (n 22) and see SM Okin, 'Mistresses of the Own Destiny?: Group Rights, Gender and Realistic Rights of Exit' (2002) 112 *Ethics* 205, 219.

[75] Okin (n 22) 16–17.

to reinforce the equality, rather than the inequality, of women – at least to the degree to which this is upheld in the majority culture.[76]

Many liberals have added their support, *contra* Okin, to policies of multicultural accommodation. Joseph Raz suggests that such policies foster a sense of 'belonging' across diverse societies and can, by so doing, replace nationalism as 'the cement which bonds a political community' and 'lead to relatively harmonious coexistence of non-oppressive and tolerant communities'.[77] For Raz, 'discrimination on religious, ethnic and racial grounds, all of which are associated with membership of groups with their own distinctive culture . . . distorts [individuals'] ability to feel pride in membership in groups identification with which is an important element in their life' and prohibitions on discrimination are 'meant to foster a public culture which enables people to take pride in their identity as members of such groups'.[78] 'The government has an obligation to create an environment providing individuals with an adequate range of options and the opportunities to choose them'.[79]

Raz proposes limits on multicultural accommodation, arguing that minority groups ought not to be permitted to 'repress their own members'; that 'no community has a right to be intolerant of those who do not belong to it', and that racism and 'other manifestations of lack of respect should be discouraged by public policy, though not necessarily outlawed or criminalised'.[80] Individuals' exit from minority groups must be a 'viable option' and 'liberal multiculturalism will require all groups to allow their members access to adequate opportunities for self-expression and for participation in the economic life of the country, and the cultivation of the attitudes and skills required for effective participation in the political culture of the state'.[81] Raz remarks that Okin's

> blind[ness] . . . to the fact that the same social arrangements can have differing social meanings, and therefore differing moral significance, in the context of different cultures . . . leads her to judge other cultures more harshly than her own, for she is instinctively sensitive to the context of her culture (and mine) and is less likely to misread it . . . just as we do not cast doubt about the legitimacy of acting for the preservation of 'our' culture simply because it is unjust to women, and to many others, so we should not cast doubt on the legitimacy of acting for the preservation of other cultures just because of the injustices perpetrated by them . . .[82]

Will Kymlicka also advocates limits on the accommodation of groups, proposing that 'Liberals can and should endorse certain external protections, where they promote fairness between groups, but should reject internal restrictions which limit the right of group members to question and revise traditional

---

[76] S M Okin, 'Feminism and Multiculturalism: Some Tensions' (1998) 108 *Ethics* 661, 680.
[77] Raz, 'Multiculturalism: A Liberal Perspective' (n 60) 176.
[78] J Raz, *The Morality of Freedom* (Oxford: Clarendon Press, 1986) 254.
[79] ibid, 418.
[80] ibid.
[81] ibid.
[82] J Raz, 'How Perfect Should One Be? And Whose Culture Is?' in Cohen et al (eds) (n 22) 95, 96.

authorities and practices'.[83] Avishai Margalit and Moshe Halbertal claim that Kymlicka's approach affords too little freedom to minority groups,[84] suggesting that he restricts group rights to those groups which are essentially liberal.[85] Chandran Kukathas, by contrast, argues that the award of rights to any groups is problematic because of their fluidity and the 'danger . . . that it ties the members' interests to the views and interests of the elites who dominate' the group.[86] He goes on to assert, however, that liberalism requires that individuals be given free rein to associate in groups whose practices are a matter for the group alone, with individual freedom being safeguarded by the right to exit.[87] For Kuthakas:

> Groups will . . . be robust and independent to the extent that their *members* recognize the authority of group leaders or group institutions. All that is necessary in, and asked of, the larger society is tolerance of those who opt to live by the norms of different communities.[88]

The right of exit suffices as a safeguard against oppression even in relation to extreme cases of abuse, external demands for change to group practices amounting to 'intolerance and moral dogmatism'.[89]

Kuthakas' distinction between 'group' and 'individual' rights is a distinction without a difference. Whether or not they are characterised as 'group rights', individual rights to pursue 'minority' practices function as group rights because the parameters of these practices will be shaped largely by dominant forces within minority groups, whose relative power is enhanced by the accommodation of the practices they influence. Thus, for example, if a decision were taken to grant legal recognition to (say) Jewish or Muslim personal law; to require the public accommodation of all religious dress codes sanctioned by the relevant

---

[83] Kymlicka (n 29) 37. See also D Reaume, 'Justice Between Cultures: Autonomy and the Protection of Cultural Affiliation' (1995) 29 *University of British Columbia Law Review* 117.

[84] A Margalit and M Halbertal 'Liberalism and the Right to Culture' (1994) 61(3) *Social Research* 491–510, 507. As well as on the basis (not central to this chapter) that his distinction between national minorities and supposedly 'voluntary' others is rendered unworkable by the fact of involuntary migration including the movements of refugees, the transportations of convicts to Australia and Africans to the US for slavery, the movements of children and the difficulties of 'return' for second and subsequent generation 'immigrants': see for example C Kukathas, 'Survey Article; Multiculturalism as Fairness: Will Kymlicka's *Multicultural Citizenship* (1997) 5(4) *The Journal of Political Philosophy* 406–27, 413. Kukathas also posits the possibility of low-cost exit for some national minority individuals and points to the conceptual difficulties thrown up by those of mixed race/ethnicity.

[85] ibid. See similarly A Cassatella, 'Multicultural Justice: Will Kymlicka and Cultural Recognition' (2006) 19 *Ratio Juris* 80; W Goldstone, 'Two Concepts of Liberalism' (1995) 105(3) *Ethics* 516–34; L White, 'Liberalism, Group Rights and the Boundaries of Toleration: The Case of Minority Religious Schools in Ontario' (2003) 36 *Canadian Journal of Political Science* 975.

[86] Kukathas (n 84) 416–17. See also C Kukathas, 'Are There any Cultural Rights?' (1992) 20 *Political Theory* 105.

[87] Kukathas (n 84) 418 and Kukathas, 'Are There any Cultural Rights?' (n 86) 116–17.

[88] Kukathas (n 84) 422.

[89] C Kukathas, 'Cultural Toleration' in I Shapiro and W Kymlicka (eds), *Ethnicity and Group Rights* (New York: New York University Press, 1997) 69, 78.

religious authorities; to exempt culturally mandated FGC[90] from any criminal prohibition on the infliction of bodily harm; or to facilitate the establishment and operation of religious schools, questions would arise as to the content of the personal laws or the dress codes and as to what forms of FGC and schooling a particular 'culture' required. The answers to those questions would be provided in many cases by the leaders of the religious or 'cultural' minorities.

Kuthakas's heavy reliance on the right of exit as guarantor of individual rights is clearly incapable of protecting children (whose education, he argues, parents ought to be free to limit in pursuit of their[91] individual rights[92]). Nor does the right of exit protect those (mainly women) for whom it carries perhaps insurmountable obstacles including loss of children and impoverishment.[93] As Ayelet Shachar points out, in relation to Kukathas's suggestion that 'If an individual continues to live in a community and according to ways that (in the judgment of the wider society) treat her unjustly, even though she is free to leave, then our concern about the injustice diminishes',[94] 'the right of exit solution to the paradox of multicultural vulnerability resembles the nineteenth-century legal rhetoric that interpreted a woman's consent to marriage as implied consent to atrocities such as rape and battering by her spouse'.[95] Kuthakas's 'right of exit' also, as Henrietta Kalev remarks, ignores the fact that many who are subordinate within groups will have been socialised to fear the 'outside world';[96] assumes 'no mechanism of oppression or hegemony whereby the bonds of community are forcibly maintained'; and takes no account of the 'processes of persuasion, indoctrination, implicit or explicit threats' which may characterise life within closed communities, not least in view of Kuthakas's denial of any requirement for compliance by cultural groups with any educational norms.[97]

Kuthakas's reliance on what is likely to be a largely theoretical right of exit is not the only shortcoming in his multicultural model. Shachar suggests that 'because Kukathas promotes a noninterventionist state policy towards minority groups, he must also maintain a rigid conceptual opposition between the inside realm controlled by the minority group and the outside realm controlled by the state' and, in so doing, 'overessentializes the distance between minority group

---

[90] Also known as 'female genital mutilation' (FGM) and 'female circumcision'. See the discussions of H Lewis in 'Between *Irua* and "Female Genital Mutilation": Feminist Human Rights Discourse and the Cultural Divide' (1995) 8 *Harvard Human Rights Journal* 1–55, 7–8, and L Amede Obiora, 'Bridges and Barricades: Rethinking Polemics and Intransigence in the Campaign Against Female Circumcision' (1997) 47 *Case Western Reserve Law Review* 275–378, 290.

[91] The parents'.

[92] Kukathas, 'Are There any Cultural Rights?' (n 86) 126.

[93] HD Kalev, 'Cultural Rights or Human Rights: The Case of Female Genital Mutilation' (2004) 15 *Sex Roles* 339, 342.

[94] Kukathas, 'Are There any Cultural Rights?' (n 86) 133.

[95] Shachar, 'On Citizenship' (n 12) 79–80. See also Shachar, 'Interlocking Power Hierarchies' (n 12) 404; Shachar, 'Reshaping the Multicultural Model: Group Accommodation and Individual Rights' (1998) 8 *Windsor Review of Legal and Social Issues* 83, 107.

[96] (n 93).

[97] ibid.

cultures and the dominant state culture, thereby denying the inevitable interplay between them' and risking the reification and ossification of group identity. [98] Finally, because of the centrality of freedom of association to Kuthakas' approach, and the social fact that 'the main beneficiaries of this nonintervention-tionist policy are most likely to be cultural communities that acquire the bulk of their members by birth, rather than by explicit adult consent', Kuthakas must 'assum[e] that all adult individuals that are group members have made a conscious choice', which requires him to 'downplay the fact that even the most adherent minority group members possess multiple affiliations to their minority groups, genders, religions, families, states, and so on' thus 'reducing this richness of personal identity to a single opposition: minority group member versus citizen'. [99]

Kukathas is an easy target for feminist critics, in particular because of the centrality to his argument of the 'right of exit'. But Okin's singling out of the cultural practices of minority groups for feminist critique meant that she was accused of 'cultural imperialism' by fellow feminists, amongst others, for her broad-brush approach to (other) 'culture' and her differential treatment of Western and 'other' practices of discrimination against women. [100] Bonnie Honig warns that 'feminists ought to be careful lest they participate in the recent rise of nationalist xenophobia by projecting a rightly feared backlash . . . onto foreigners who come from somewhere else and bring their foreign, (supposedly) "backward" cultures with them'. [101] And Leti Volpp suggests that 'we equate race and culture and selectively blame culture for bad behaviour', tending to view unacceptable behaviour on the part of unfamiliar others as resulting from their 'culture' but that of those more like ourselves as aberrant, [102] citing Uma Narayan's calculation that:

> [D]eath by domestic violence in the United States is numerically as significant a social problem as dowry murders in India. But only one is used as a signifier of cultural backwardness: 'They burn their women there.' As opposed to: 'We shoot our women here'. Yet domestic violence murders in the U.S. are just as much a part of American culture as dowry death is a part of Indian culture. [103]

---

[98] Shachar, 'Interlocking Power Hierarchies' (n 12) 404.

[99] ibid, 404.

[100] See MC Lam, 'Feeling Foreign in Feminism' (1994) 19 *Signs* 865.

[101] B Honig, 'My Culture Made Me Do It' in Cohen et al (eds) (n 22) 35, 36. Note F Fanon, *Toward the African Revolution* (New York: Grove Press, 1988) Haakon Chevalier trans, 2nd edn 31–35, discussing a 'progression from vulgar to cultural racism' a 'shift from biological to cultural explanations for racial subordination' (cited in Volpp, 'Talking 'Culture' (n 49) 1061).

[102] L Volpp, 'Blaming Culture for Bad Behavior' (2000) 12 *Yale Journal of Law and the Humanities* 88–116, 89. See also L Volpp, '(Mis)identifying Culture: Asian Women and the "Cultural Defense"' (1994) 17 *Harvard Women's Law Journal* 57–80; L Volpp, 'Feminism versus Multiculturalism' (2001) 101 *Columbia Law Review* 1181–218; Herr (n 62) 73. For a defence of Okin see A Mayer, 'A "Benign" *Apartheid*: How Gender *Apartheid* Has Been Rationalized' (2000–01) 5 *UCLA Journal of International Law and Foreign Affairs* 237–338.

[103] 'Feminism versus Multiculturalism' (n 102) 1186–87, citing U Narayan, *Dislocating Cultures: Identities, Traditions, and Third-World Feminism* (New York: Routledge, 1997) 84.

Volpp goes on to argue that the ascription of 'culture' only to those without power, coupled with the liberal emphasis on agency as a condition of subject-hood, results in a 'deeply dehumanizing' characterisation of 'others' whose 'actions are [seen to be] determined only by culture'.[104] Okin's approach is to require 'other' women, as a condition of acceptance as 'a rights-bearing liberal subject [to] . . . shed the burden of difference. . . to be the compliant subjects of assimilation and to leave their minority cultures'.[105] It is Okin's approach to 'gender' and 'race' as 'oppositional, and thus mutually exclusive' which allows her to conclude that 'women of color may be better off if their cultures wither or become extinct'.[106] Further, Okin's:

'extreme focus on what is commonly conceptualized as cultural violence or subordi-nation' serves to obscure other important social, political, and economic issues affect-ing women's lives . . . such as ongoing relationships of economic inequity, development and community policies, exploitation by transnational corporations, or racism . . . The missionary impulse to save immigrant and Third World women from their subor-dination is rarely turned to uplift domestic workers from exploitative work situations . . . women in the First World . . . will not conceptualize themselves to be agents of subordinating practices. This absolution of responsibility rests on the assumption that relations between women are presumed to be non-oppressive, whereas the bonds of race are presumed to oppress women of color, ignoring class and race oppression between women.[107]

Herr suggests that 'Her good intentions notwithstanding . . . Okin's oversights and misinterpretations . . . can be traced to her uncritical adoption of two gravely problematic assumptions', the first 'that racial ethnic women are thor-oughly subjugated by their culture'[108] and the second her

highly essentialized view of minority cultures as static and backward-looking, as opposed to vibrantly changing and forward-looking Western culture. Third World cultures are seen as inveterately patriarchal beyond salvation because they are com-posites of misogynist practices and customs that are ahistorically frozen in time, closed to modifications or change toward gender equality.[109]

Also critical of what she sees as Okin's essentialising approach is Jane Flax who accuses Okin of defending 'an internally undifferentiated and conflict-free con-cept of gender' in which 'Gender is constituted through what women share, espe-cially their differences from, and domination by, men', in which 'Women are defined by the similarities of their inequalities across race, class, and geography' and in which Okin can claim that 'sexism is an identifiable form of oppression,

---

[104] 'Feminism versus Multiculturalism' (n 102), 1192.
[105] ibid, 1201.
[106] ibid, 1202. And see Volpp (n 49) 1576.
[107] 'Feminism versus Multiculturalism' n (102) 1208–12 and 1214–15 and see also Volpp (n 49) 1582.
[108] Herr (n 62) 73. Here Herr takes issue in particular with Okin's 'Gender Inequality and Cultural Differences' (1994) 22 *Political Theory* 5 and Okin (n 74).
[109] ibid (Herr) and see Volpp (n 49) 1577–81.

many of whose effects are felt by women regardless of race or class, without at all subscribing to the view that race and class oppression are insignificant'.[110] And Shachar challenges that Okin 'fails to recognize that the power dynamics at play within cultural groups are not static', that culture is malleable and that 'many religious and cultural traditions have changed over time due, in part, to women's resistance and agency'.[111] She also takes issue with Okin's identification of women in minority cultures as 'powerless victims' and her 'fail[ure] to recognize that women within nondominant communities may find their cultural membership a source of value and not only a source of oppression'.[112]

Striking a Balance? The Example of Religious Family 'Law'

Okin can be regarded as a radical critic and Kukathas as a strong proponent of multiculturalism, though the two issue similar 'your-rights-or-your-culture' ultimata to minority women who, as Shachar points out, 'may either enjoy the full spectrum of their state citizenship rights or participate in their minority communities [but] cannot have both simultaneously'.[113] The end point of both theorists' approaches is unacceptable from an equalities-driven perspective from which there is no reasonable objection to, and every reason to favour, the accommodation of some minority practices. This is particularly the case where, as in Britain, the purpose of such accommodation is not to perpetuate minorities *qua* minorities, rather to further 'the inclusion of marginal and disadvantaged groups', including those minority ethnic groups whose members define themselves predominantly in terms of their religion, 'in public life'.[114] An important question which falls to be addressed, however, is the extent to which accommodation should be extended to practices which do not appear 'benign', either because of their impact on individuals within the minority group or otherwise.

In an attempt to cast some further light on the relationship(s) between equality and multiculturalism I here consider the recognition of religious personal law. This, like the accommodation of FGC, which I have considered elsewhere, is a 'hard case' for feminists. In a paper on FGC I suggested that addressing such practices from an equality-driven perspective entails a rejection both of an unreflecting universalist and also of a crude culturally relativist approach.[115] In other words, as Bonnie Honig puts it, we must

---

[110] J Flax, 'Race/Gender and the Ethics of Difference' (1995) 23 *Political Theory* 500–10, 500, citing Okin (n 108) 7. See Okin's 'Response to Jane Flax' (1995) 23 *Political Theory* 511–16.
[111] Shachar, 'Interlocking Power Hierarchies' (n 12) 401.
[112] ibid, 402.
[113] ibid, 403.
[114] T Madood, 'Multiculturalism, Secularism and the State', 26 (available at http://the irelandinstitute.com/republic/04/pdf/modood004.pdf). See also Madood, 'Anti-Essentialism, Multiculturalism and the "Recognition" of Religious Groups' (1998) 6 *The Journal of Political Philosophy* 378.
[115] McColgan (n 1).

hold [our] own practices up to the same critical scrutiny [we] apply to Others . . . hear the plural voices of women everywhere and . . . learn from them, while also refusing to prejudge the merits of practices that are unfamiliar or threatening to those of us raised in bourgeois liberal societies.[116]

Thus avoiding 'troubling stances of arrogant perception'[117] allows us to recognise the similarities between the practices of 'others', which we may condemn as 'backward' or 'barbaric', and those we follow ourselves. In the context of FGC it allows us to draw parallels between Western female genital 'surgery' and 'third world' female genital 'mutilation', and to question the purpose of criminalising legislation under which, in the UK as elsewhere, no prosecutions have been brought.

Turning to the question of religious personal law, the Archbishop of Canterbury caused a storm when, in 2008, he was taken to suggest that religious courts might be granted jurisdiction in divorce cases.[118] Shortly thereafter Lord Phillips, then Lord Chief Justice, suggested that 'There is no reason why principles of Shari'a Law, or any other religious code should not be the basis for mediation or other forms of alternative dispute resolution . . . although when it comes to divorce this can only be effected in accordance with the civil law of this country'.[119]

A number of states cede jurisdiction over family law matters including the dissolution of marriage to religious bodies, or determine these matters in line with religious laws. In India, for example, the secular courts apply different rules concerning divorce according to whether the couples are Muslim, Hindu, Parsee or Christian, or have married under civil law. No 'opt-out' from religious marriage is offered in Israel where the regulation of family law matters is turned over by the state exclusively to the religious communities of Jews, Muslims, Christians and Druze, and where no provision is made for inter-faith or civil marriages (this despite the fact that the majority of Israelis are not religiously observant).[120] Religious courts apply religious law and, although the Supreme Court has the power of judicial review, no appeal is available to the secular

---

[116] Honig (n 101) 40.

[117] SM James, 'Shades of Othering: Reflections on Female Circumcision/Genital Mutilation' (1998) 23 *Signs* 1031–48, 1033.

[118] www.archbishopofcanterbury.org/1575 and see www.guardian.co.uk/uk/2008/feb/07/religion. world2. The full text of the Archbishop's speech is in R Williams, 'Civil and Religious Law in England: A Religious Perspective' (2008) 10 *Ecclesiastical Law Journal* 262–82 and see S Bano, 'In Pursuit of Religious and Legal Diversity: A Response' (2008) 10 *Ecclesiastical Law Journal* 285–86 for analysis of the critical response to the speech.

[119] Speech at the East London Muslim Centre on 3 July 2008. See D McGoldrick, 'Accommodating Muslims in Europe: From Adopting Sharia Law to Religiously Based Opt Outs from Generally Applicable Laws' (2009) 9 *Human Rights Law Review* 603–45, 618–19 for discussion.

[120] J Goodman, 'Divine Judgment: Judicial Review of Religious Legal Systems in India and Israel' (2009) 32 *Hastings International and Comparative Law Review* 477, 490. See also A Madera, 'Judicial Bonds of Marriage for Jewish and Islamic Women' (2009) 11 *Journal of Ecclesiastical Law* 51–64.

courts. Kenya and South Africa also provide a degree of autonomy to religious (or, in the case of South Africa, tribal) communities to regulate marriage.[121]

The ceding of control over marriage status to religious communities can have significant negative repercussions for women. Under Jewish law, for example, only men have the power to issue the *get*, the Jewish divorce:[122]

> [A] husband's refusal to grant his wife a divorce decree (or get) results not only in the wife's inability to remarry but also in severe restrictions on her sexuality and procreative activity. For example, if she were to have a sexual relationship with another man she would be considered a *moredet* (rebellious wife) and, as such, may lose her rights to child custody and spousal alimony; moreover, if she were to have a child by another man while still considered legally married to her imprisoning husband, that child would be considered a mamzer and would be doomed to exile from the Jewish community for ten generations while bearing the shameful status of a bastard.[123]

Muslim personal law does not give men the same control over divorce as Jewish law.[124] Only men can issue the *talaq*, the unilateral repudiation of the wife. But Muslim marriage is conceived as a contract the terms of which are a matter for the parties thereto, and which may include a power of divorce for the woman.[125] And while, in the absence of such a contractual safeguard, a woman cannot unilaterally divorce an unwilling husband, men may delegate the power to divorce to the woman. This type of divorce (*khul* or *khulla*) is disadvantageous to the woman at least in theory, as she is bound to return the *mahr*[126] unless her husband agrees otherwise (see further below). In addition, however, and leaving aside cases in which the woman has secured the right to divorce in the marriage contract itself, marriage can be dissolved by the *Qadi* (Islamic judge). This form

---

[121] See generally J Nichols, 'Multi-Tiered Marriage; Ideas and Influences from New York and Louisiana to the International Community' (2007) 40 *Vanderbilt Journal of Transnational Law* 135, 165–89.

[122] See generally Madera (n 120).

[123] See Shachar, 'Group Identity' (n 12) 293–94. Shacher notes (294, fn 40) that 'the threat of exclusion from the Jewish community in the case of the agunah's illegitimate children is not merely theoretical. In fact, rabbinical courts in Israel maintain "blacklists" of persons who are barred from marriage to Jews (psuley hitun), among them the mamzerim'. Men in 'limping marriages' remain free to remarry and procreate without stigma, though in defiance of rabbinic decree demanding monogamy (see Nichols (n 121)).

[124] While Islamic law is not free floating but consists of the Muslim laws which operate within particular jurisdictions (see L Carroll, 'Muslim Women and 'Islamic Divorce' in England' (1997) 17 *Journal of Muslim Minority Affairs* 97–115, 103; In SA Warraich and C Balchin, *Recognizing the Unrecognized: Inter-Country Cases and Muslim Marriages* (WLUML, 2006) www.wluml.org/section/resource/results/taxonomy%3A7%2C101, section 6.2.2), there are a number of general propositions which can be stated about its impact.

[125] See for example the new standard contract launched by the Muslim Institute in August 2008, which includes a waiver by the man of his 'right' to polygamy and an automatic delegation of the right of divorce to the wife (*talaq-i-tafweeed*), enabling the woman to initiate divorce without losing any financial rights agreed in the contract. The contract is accessible at http://www.wluml.org/node/4749.

[126] The sum settled on the woman by her husband on marriage, which may provide a degree of financial security in the event of divorce, given the absence in Muslim systems of family law of any obligation on the part of the husband to pay maintenance other than in the three-month period immediately after divorce.

of divorce (*faskh* or *tanseekh*) does not require repayment of the *mahr* by the women. It is available only on restricted grounds but among them is harm (*dhir*) done to the wife by the husband.[127] One form of such harm is the refusal to issue *talaq*, particularly in a case where a civil divorce has already been secured.[128]

The recognition of marriages contracted outside the UK generally turns on whether the marriage is formally valid under the rules applicable in the jurisdiction in which it took place,[129] and whether the parties had capacity to marry under the rules of each's *ante* nuptial domicile,[130] special rules applying to polyandrous unions.[131] In England and Wales marriages must conform to the requirements of the Marriage Act 1949 in order to be recognised as valid.[132] Marriages in registered places of religious worship may be conducted by persons authorised by the Superintendent Registrar so long as they comply with the normal requirements regarding consent, capacity etc. Such persons may also be religious officials, but a marriage which is carried out in conformity with religious requirements will not, without more, be recognised by law (as in the case, for example, of a polygamous marriage, a marriage in which one or both of the parties was under 16, or was not physically present at the marriage ceremony).[133]

What might be called 'Muslim unofficial law' has been operating in the UK for decades.[134] A 1975 proposal from the Union of Muslim Organisations for the formal recognition of Muslim family law in Britain countered strong opposition,[135] but in 1993 Walter Menski reported that many disputes arising

[127] See generally SN Shah-Kazemi, *Untying the Knot: Muslim Women, Divorce and the Shariah* (London: Nuffield Foundation, 2001) 7–9.

[128] For discussion of how this operates in practice in the UK see Shah-Kazemi's report, ibid. See Carroll (n 124) 100–103 on the roots of the misconception, common across the UK, that the power to divorce is limited to Muslim, as to Jewish, men. Shah-Kazemi, who conducted research into the experience of women using the Muslim Law (Shariah) Council UK in the 1990s, reported that many women who approached the Council were unaware that husbands did not have the monopoly on divorce.

[129] See, for example, *Wilkinson (No 2)* [2007] 1 FLR 295, *McCabe* [1994] 1 FLR 410. For exceptions see Dicey and Morris, *Conflicts of Laws*, Rule 66.

[130] Dicey and Morris (n 129) Rule 67, adopting *R v Brentwood Superintendent Registrar of Marriages ex p Arias* [1968] 2 QB 956, 968; Sir Jocelyn Simon in *Padolecchia* [1968] P 314, 336 and *Szechter* (1971) P 286, 295. This rule is not applied very strictly, the English courts favouring recognition where possible as a matter of public policy: see for example *Lawrence v Lawrence* [1985] 2 All ER 733.

[131] Dicey and Morris (n 129) Rules 72 and 73, and section 11(d) Matrimonial Causes Act 1973 as amended by the Private International Law (Miscellaneous Provisions) Act 1995.

[132] See L Blackstone, ' "Courting Islam" Practical Alternatives to a Muslim Family Court in Ontario' (2005–06) 31 *Brooke Journal of International Law* 207–52 on the unsuccessful attempts made in the 1970s to have Muslim family law recognised in England and Wales.

[133] As I Yilmaz points out ('The Challenge of Post-modern Legality and Muslim Legal Pluralism in England' (2002) 28 *Journal of Ethnic and Migration Studies*, 343–54, in 1991 civil marriages could take place in only 74 of 452 mosques because the buildings were typically used for multiple purposes. Subsequent amendments loosened the requirements with the effect that civil marriages could typically take place in mosques.

[134] See Malik (n 48) for discussion of the concept of minority legal orders and their recognition.

[135] See S Poulter, 'The Claim to a Separate Islamic System of Personal Law for British Muslims' in C Mallat and J Connors (eds), *Islamic Family Law* (London: Graham and Trotman, 1990) 147 ff.

between Muslims never came to court, instead being conciliated within the community.[136] Richard Jones and Welhengama Gnanpala suggested in 2000 that 'self-regulatory obligation systems' had developed within minority ethnic groups whose 'decisions are generally honoured and implemented through a mix of sanctions and ostracism'.[137] And David Pearl and Werner Menski coined the phrase 'angrezi shariat' to refer to a hybrid unofficial law which has emerged from the interplay between English and Muslim law and which has been administered by the Islamic Sharia Council amongst other bodies.[138]

In June 2009 a report by think tank Civitas suggested that there were at least 85 'shari'a courts' operating in the UK.[139] The report expressed concern about the issue of *fatwas* (religious rulings, some of them issued online) concerning, for example, the acceptability within Islam of polygamy and mixed marriages. The following month the *Mail on Sunday* reported in July 2009 that the Islamic Sharia Council, based in East London, has been applying Muslim personal law since 1982 'issuing fatwas . . . on matters ranging from why Islam considers homosexuality a sin to why two women are equivalent to one male witness in an Islamic court' and ruling 'on individual cases, primarily in matters of Muslim personal or civil law: divorce, marriage, inheritance and settlement of dowry payments are the most common'.[140] The newspaper reported that men had to pay £100 and women £250 to apply for a religious divorce 'because the imams say it takes more work to process a woman's application as her word has to be corroborated . . .'

The Civitas report and associated newspaper coverage were characterised by a certain hysteria of tone. Whatever view one may take about the relationship between gender equality and Islamic principles concerning divorce, the main purpose of the sharia councils is to provide women with access to religious divorce in cases in which their husbands are unwilling to issue the *talaq*,[141] men being able to effect such divorce unilaterally and informally.[142] Muslim women whose *nikah* (Muslim marriage contract) marriage is recognised in the UK because performed under the relevant conditions abroad, or who have taken

---

[136] WF Menski, 'Asians in Britain and the Question of Adaptation to a New Legal Order: Asian Laws in Britain' in M Israel and N Wagle (eds), *Ethnicity, Identity, Migration: The South Asian Context* (Toronto: University of Toronto, 1993) 238–68, 253. D Pearl and W Menski, *Muslim Family Law*, 3rd edn (London: Sweet & Maxwell, 1998) suggest, at 3-81–3-96, that Islamic Shari'a Councils have been operating in the UK since the start of the 1980s.

[137] R Jones and W Gnanpala, *Ethnic Minorities in English Law* (Stoke on Trent: Trentham Books, 2000) 103–04. Yilmaz suggests ((n 133) 343) that the use of informal Muslim mechanisms for dispute resolution is the reason why 'not many Muslim cases have appeared before the courts regarding [family law] matters in the last few years'.

[138] Pearl and Menski (n 136) 276.

[139] *Sharia Law or 'One Law for All'?* at www.civitas.org.uk/pdf/ShariaLawOrOneLawForAll.pdf, and see accompanying press release at www.civitas.org.uk/press/prcs91.php, 29 June 2009.

[140] 'Sharia law UK: Mail on Sunday gets exclusive access to a British Muslim court', *Mail on Sunday*, 4 July 2009.

[141] Bano (n 118); Carroll (n 124) 107.

[142] Though Shah-Kazemi notes (n 127, 11) that some men do approach shari'a councils to settle disputes about financial matters or children post divorce.

part in both *nikah* and civil marriage in the UK, will have to secure civil divorce according to the normal procedures if they wish to end their marriages. In addition, however, many feel it necessary to secure a certificate of 'Islamic divorce'.[143]

It has been argued that no separate step is required at least in cases in which (as is commonplace[144]) the *nikah* followed the civil ceremony, Pakistan's Supreme Court having recognised that UK civil marriage satisfied the offer and acceptance requirements of the Muslim Family Law Ordinances.[145] Lucy Carroll suggests that any *nikah* ceremony following civil marriage is of 'social and cultural significance' only insofar as it specifies the woman's *mahr*, which 'can be set or modified by mutual agreement at any time after the marriage'.[146] And a study recently carried out by Gillian Douglas and others found that the Birmingham Shariah Council regarded civil divorce as 'itself . . . proof of irretrievable breakdown and as obviating the need for a religious divorce to be pronounced'.[147] But whatever the strict legal position, and the question 'whose interests are being served by the myth that additional Islamic divorces are necessary?',[148] the practice in the UK appears to be that many Muslim women who undergo civil divorce do not regard themselves, and are not regarded by others, as free to remarry unless they secure a certificate of Muslim divorce from a sharia council.[149] Many other Muslim women undergo religious marriage alone and are

---

[143] See Shah-Kazemi, ibid.

[144] See Yilmaz (n 133) 348, who states that the civil ceremony typically precedes the *nikah* prior to consummation 'otherwise their marriage would be regarded as sinful from a religious and cultural perspective'. In Shah-Kazemi's study only 37% of those who were married in civil and religious ceremonies had the civil ceremony first, the remainder having both ceremonies on the same day (she does not disclose in which order) or the civil ceremony after the religious. 57% of the 287 women whose cases she studied had not undergone civil marriage in the UK and those women whose *nikah* marriages had taken place in the UK, and who were therefore married *only* in the religious sense, comprised 27% of the total. 55% of the women approaching the UK Muslim Law (Shariah) Council had obtained their civil divorces beforehand: n 127, 31.

[145] *Jaloi v Jaloi* PLD 1967 SC 580, Pakistan Supreme Court.

[146] Carroll (n 124).

[147] G Douglas et al, *Social Cohesion and Civil Law: Marriage, Divorce and Religious Courts* (Cardiff, Cardiff University, 2011). J Bowen, 'How Could English Courts Recognize Shariah?' (2009–10) 7 *University of St Thomas Law Journal* 411, 419, suggests that the practice at the Islamic Shariah Council in London ('the largest and oldest Council') in the UK is to 'insist that the wife who petitions for an Islamic divorce also begin proceedings to obtain a civil divorce, in cases where the marriage was registered in the United Kingdom or conducted abroad', albeit that once a civil divorce is granted 'the councilors will likely proceed quickly to grant the wife's request; they say that the marriage is over and little sense remains in prolonging its Islamic dimension' (420). Bowen reports that most of those attending the Islamic Shariah Council 'had married only in Islamic fashion' (419).

[148] This posed by Z Moosa in 'Balancing Women's Rights with Freedom of Religion' in *State of the World's Minorities and Indigenous People* (2010: Minority Rights Group International), at *www.minority*rights.org/990/state-of-the-worlds-minorities/state-of-the-worlds-minorities.html.

[149] Carroll further suggests (n 124, 106) that, under the Muslim Family Law Ordinances which apply to Muslims in Pakistan, other than the Azad Kashmir area (see *Recognizing the unrecognized*, n 125, section 4.2.2) and have extra-territorial application to all those with Pakistani sole or dual citizenship, which includes a large proportion of Muslims resident in the UK, notification to the appropriate Pakistani official of a British civil divorce would have the effect of dissolving the marriage for all purposes.

therefore dependent for 'divorce' on sharia councils in the absence of spousal consent.[150]

Leaving aside media hysteria over 'sharia courts', the research on the operation of sharia councils suggests that they do not always operate in women's best interests. Under the Hanafi school, with which most British Mosques are affiliated, women have custody of children on divorce only until boys are aged seven and girls nine,[151] and then only if they do not remarry; maintenance is generally payable for only three months post divorce and there is no provision for equitable distribution of property on divorce. Lucy Carroll reported in 1997 that the UK Shariah Council required women to comply with any 'reasonable' conditions imposed by husbands on the grant of a *talaq*, and that, if it failed to secure such agreement, would 'claim[] the right to impose a divorce by *khul*', the price of which was the return of the *mahr*, rather than using the *faskh* or *tanseekh* procedure which would leave her right to the *mahr* intact.[152] And Women Living Under Muslim Law (WLUML)[153] point out that although:

> There have been efforts to make some of the Shariah councils appear suitably moderate, innovative and critical of the rigid application of 'traditional' interpretations [154] . . . few take into account the progressive laws codified in many Muslim majority countries, and often trumpet as a sign of their modernism approaches which were codified in the sub-continent as long ago as 1939 and which have been far outstripped by for example recent reform of Morocco's family law.[155]

While, for example, the Muslim Family Law Ordinances clearly provide powers to the courts to grant women divorces irrespective of their husbands' consent on nine grounds, including on the ground that 'he makes her life miserable by cruelty of conduct even if such conduct does not amount to physical ill-treatment', WLUML cite the refusal of the Muslim Law (Shariah) Council (UK), noted in Shah-Kazemi's research for the Nuffield Foundation, 'to give a definitive answer as to whether or not a civil divorce – either uncontested after 2 years with consent, or desertion and *decree nisi* after 2 years, or contested after 5 years – was sufficient ground for the council to pronounce a Muslim marriage dissolved',

---

[150] Over half of those seeking divorce in the Douglas study were not recognised as married by English law: n 147 (Douglas), 39.

[151] In *EM (Lebanon) v Home Secretary* [2009] 1 AC 1198 the House of Lords granted asylum to a woman who was resisting return to the Lebanon on the basis that, as a divorced Muslim woman, she would lose custody of her child there to his father or father's relatives once the child reached seven (*cf* the earlier decision in *In Re S (a Minor)* (1993) 1 FLR 297), characterising the (Muslim) family law which applied in the Lebanon as 'arbitrary and discriminatory' (para 15, *per* Lord Hope with whom Lords Bingham, Carswell and Brown agreed at paras 42, 52 and 60).

[152] Carroll (n 124) 109–10.

[153] According to its website (www.wluml.org) an 'International solidarity network for women whose lives are shaped by laws and customs said to derive from Islam'.

[154] Citing I Yilmaz, 'Law as Chameleon: The Question of Incorporation of Muslim Personal Law into the English Law' (2001) 21(2) *Journal of Muslim Minority Affairs*, 297–308, which is characterised as 'right wing' commentary. See *Recognizing the unrecognized*, n 124, section 7.1 for criticism of Yilmaz's approach.

[155] (n 124) 78.

and the persistence of that Council in seeking to have ex-husbands come to give evidence before it with a view to trying to persuade them to grant *talaq*, rather than 'innovating by applying concepts of *dharar*, or *shiqauq*'[156] to grant women religious divorces[157] WLUML were also highly critical that, at the time of their report (2006):

[T]here is no female decision-making member of a Shariah council in Britain yet women are Family Court and High Court judges in both Bangladesh and Pakistan; courts in these countries will not even attempt to obtain the husband's permission for *khula* as case law firmly established as far back as 1959[158] that this is not required. When challenged at a public meeting . . . in May 2004, that the Pakistan courts indeed recognize a British civil divorce as valid between Muslims, the President of the Islamic Sharia Council, Maulana Abu Sayeed, spoke out against 'man-made law'. This could have been construed to imply that whereas the Shariah councils apply divine law and are above *man*-made patriarchal interpretations, the Pakistan courts are godless. This is a position shared by only a few on the extreme Right in Pakistan but appears more widespread in Britain. For example, Shah-Kazemi, 2001 asserts that 'jurists (*fuqaha*) do not recognize the civil divorce as ending the *nikah* contract', apparently unaware of the reality that Pakistan's courts for example do recognize British civil divorce as perfectly valid between Muslims.[159]

The Privatisation of Family Law

There does not appear at present to be any head of pressure within the UK for the state to grant exclusive authority to religious communities to determine the status, for civil as well as religious purposes, of those who marry by those community rules (as is the case in Israel), though as Maleiha Malik has pointed out, the role of women as reproducers and socialisers of future generations does result in 'a focus – sometimes an obsession' on the part of 'traditional groups concerned with the preservation and transmission of their culture or religion' on questions of family law.[160] Questions of religious versus civil approaches to

[156] Respectively meaning 'harm' and 'discord and strife'.

[157] Above n 124, 79. At 72 the report questions why 'no research to date has questioned why Shariah councils do not *automatically* issue a certificate that the marriage is also dissolved in the eyes of Muslim laws, and why instead they insist upon lengthy processes of calling husbands to "give evidence" – which often mean a woman secures her "Islamic divorce" many months after the civil process is completed. This, despite the possibility of dissolution by the courts in many Middle Eastern laws on the grounds of *dharar* [harm] or *niza'a wa shiqauq* [discord and strife] of which a civil divorce is surely ample evidence' (emphasis in the original). The report suggests that 'by insisting on a separate and complex process rather than appearing to rubber stamp the civil proceedings, the Shariah councils given themselves an opportunity to demonstrate and retain their social and political influence over the community. The net result is a process which although desired by many women is equally a means of violating their right to peace of mind and a fresh start in life'.

[158] Citing *Bilquis Fatima v Najm-ul-Ikram Qureshi* PLD 1959 WP Lahore 566. The report states that similar provisions were also recently introduced in Egypt.

[159] Above, n 124, 66–67. See section 6.3 and 6.5.2 for criticisms of Shah-Kazemi's analysis.

[160] Malik (n 30) 215. See also *Minority Legal Orders in the UK*, Malik's report for the British Academy on minorities, pluralism and the law (British Academy, 2012), available at www.britac.

marriage and its dissolution have arisen recently in the context of arbitration, in particular with the apparent suggestions by the Archbishop and Lord Phillips that faith-based arbitration ought to be recognised within family law. These interventions are perhaps of particular interest in the context of a government push towards a reduced role for the courts, and an increasing emphasis on mediation and other forms of alternative dispute resolution (ADR), in family law proceedings.

Mediation has been compulsory in publicly funded divorce cases since 2000. A consultation paper launched in November 2010 proposed the removal of legal aid from family law litigation other than that in which domestic violence, forced marriage or child abduction is alleged. And in a speech in the same month to the National Family Mediation AGM, Minister Jonathan Djanogly stated that 'this Coalition Government places great importance on [ADR]'; that the Government was 'committed to supporting mediation as a way of resolving family disputes'; that 'ADR, be it mediation, arbitration or collaborative law practices can help members of the public avoid long drawn out legal battles that can be painful as well as expensive'; and that Legal Services Commission (LSC) funding (in the princely amount of £150) would be available for family law mediation.[161] The Minister went on to say that 'The ultimate success will be when the public consider dispute resolution services such as mediation, collaborative law and arbitration to be the norm – not the alternative'.[162] The Final Report of the Family Justice Review, published in November 2011, recommended an increased role for mediation in divorce proceedings, including a requirement that any party making a court application in such proceedings have attended a 'Mediation Information and Assessment Meeting', and that such attendance should be expected, though it 'cannot be required' of respondents to proceedings.[163] A Pre-action Protocol applicable to privately paying litigants in private family law (ie

---

ac.uk/policy/Minority-legal-orders.cfm. There have been occasional interventions such as those of the Union of Muslim Organisations (UMO) in the UK and Ireland in the 1970s, 1989 and 1996 (*Recognizing the unrecognized*, n 124, section 3.3) and in 2006 (the *Independent*, 15 August 2006, 'Let us adopt Islamic family law to curb extremists, Muslims tell Kelly'). Bano (n 118) 296, suggests, however, that empirical data in her study 'found little support or enthusiasm' for any formal recognition by the state of Islamic family law. WLUML stated, in early 2006 (n 124, 33) that 'there has been no coherent demand for such an automatically applicable system' as that demanded by the UMO since 1996. B Jackson suggests (' "Transformative Accommodation" and Religious Law' (2009) 11 *Ecclesiastical Law Journal* 131–53) that the real purpose of Archbishop William's speech was 'to build a religious coalition, led by the Church of England (as the 'established' church) in favour of exemptions from secular law on grounds of religious conscience'.

[161] See subsequently Legal Aid Reform in England and Wales: the Government Response (June 2011, www.justice.gov.uk/downloads/consultations/legal-aid-reform-government-response.pdf), which states the government's view, in the face of suggestions to the contrary, that the proposed maximum £150 for 'legal help' for mediation 'is sufficient in the majority of cases' (para 38) though an additional £200 would be made available 'where legal advice is necessary to give effect to a mediated settlement to draft a court order setting out the terms of settlement in finance cases' (para 39).

[162] The final report of the Family Law Review, published in November 2011, is at http://www.familylaw.co.uk/articles/FamilyJusticeReview03112011–695.

[163] ibid, para 119.

divorce) cases gave effect to this recommendation and mediation in privately funded cases is expected to become compulsory when the Children and Families Bill, currently before Parliament, becomes law. Legal aid was withdrawn from some 255,000 per annum private family law cases from April 2013 with the implementation of the Legal Aid, Sentencing and Punishment of Offenders Act 2012, though some £10m in additional funding (less than £40 per case) was made available for mediation.

Mediation is designed to facilitate agreement between the parties to a dispute. Arbitration involves handing jurisdiction over the dispute to a third party. The Arbitration Act 1996 permits parties to contracts, or to disputes, to agree to settle their differences by reference to one or more arbitrators whose decisions will be legally binding on the parties to the arbitration agreement. Section 46(1) of the Act provides that the

arbitral tribunal shall decide the dispute –

(a) in accordance with the law chosen by the parties as applicable to the substance of the dispute, or
(b) if the parties so agree, in accordance with such other considerations as are agreed by them or determined by the tribunal.

Arbitration could proceed, therefore, on the basis of French law, or 'shari'a principles', and the arbitrator's decision would be enforceable through the domestic courts unless the disgruntled party challenged the decision on the basis, for example, of an error of law or 'serious irregularity affecting the tribunal, the proceedings or the award' which can include, inter alia, a failure on the part of the arbitrator(s) to 'act fairly and impartially as between the parties', or an award being contrary to public policy, or having been 'obtained by fraud or [in a] . . . way . . . contrary to public policy',[164] in each case where the irregularity 'has caused or will cause substantial injustice to the applicant'. A failure to challenge an alleged irregularity during the arbitration process, or within such period provided by the arbitration agreement, will result in the party losing the right to object to enforcement of the award 'unless he shows that, at the time he took part or continued to take part in the proceedings, he did not know and could not with reasonable diligence have discovered the grounds for the objection'.[165]

The Muslim Arbitration Tribunal (MAT), which was established in 2007, operates a network of tribunals in London, Birmingham, Bradford, Manchester, Nuneaton and Luton, which provide arbitration across a range of disputes including, according to its website, those arising in relation to forced marriages, domestic violence, and family and inheritance disputes.[166] The MAT website suggests that:

---

[164] Sections 68, 33 and 88(2)(a).
[165] Section 73(1).
[166] www.matribunal.com/cases.html. According to its website, MAT can bring to an end 'limping marriages': situations in which women are granted civil divorces but refused religious divorces by their husbands. The website goes on to suggest that MAT can issue 'Islamic decisions' in relation to

- 'any determination reached by MAT can be enforced through existing means of enforcement open to normal litigants';
- MAT can 'ensur[e] that all determinations reached by it are in accordance with one of the recognised Schools of Islamic Sacred Law [and] . . . will therefore, for the first time, offer the Muslim community a real and true opportunity to settle disputes in accordance with Islamic Sacred Law *with the knowledge that the outcome as determined by MAT will be binding and enforceable*' (emphasis added);[167]
- 'MAT, along with other religious organisations in the UK, can grant a talaq to finish the limping marriage' (ie, a religious marriage which survives civil divorce); and
- arbitration, by prior agreement of the parties, is legally binding and 'can be used to settle individual, family or community disputes'.[168]

In *Edgar v Edgar* (1980), the Court of Appeal ruled that the jurisdiction of the Family Courts cannot be ousted by any agreement between the parties,[169] a principle which has survived the (partial) recognition by the Supreme Court of pre-nuptial contracts in *Radmacher (formerly Granatino) v Granatino*.[170] But while MAT's website states in terms that the tribunal 'is unable to deal with criminal offences as we do not have jurisdiction to try such matters in the UK', it nowhere makes it clear that agreements reached under the Arbitration Act are not binding as regards child access and/or custody arrangements or ancillary relief arising in connection with divorce. To the contrary, the impression given is that MAT has jurisdiction in these matters as distinct from solely (in this context) in relation to the grant of *religious* divorces having no *legal* effect.

In March 2010 the *Observer* quoted Maryam Namazie, a spokeswoman for the 'One Law for All Campaign' which campaigns against sharia law in Britain, who claimed that 'women . . . are losing custody of their children in the sharia councils'[171] and complained about the informal resolution of domestic violence

allegations of forced marriages, such decisions then being evidence for the secular courts in cases brought under the Forced Marriage Act 2007. As to criminal matters, MAT 'do[es] not have jurisdiction to try such matters in the UK' but can assist the parties on request to attempt reconciliation the terms of which, it suggests, may be taken into account by the CPS in determining whether or not to prosecute.

167 www.matribunal.com/index.html.
168 www.matribunal.com/alt_dispute_res_mech.html.
169 *Edgar v Edgar* [1980] 1 WLR 1410. Then Home Secretary Jack Straw confirmed in response to a written question on 24 November 2008 that 'Arbitration is not a system of dispute resolution that may be used in family cases' and went on to state that 'Therefore no draft consent orders embodying the terms of an agreement reached by the use of a Shariah council have been enforced within the meaning of the Arbitration Act 1996 in matrimonial proceedings'. This followed shortly after Minister Bridget Prentice was reported as suggesting that the family courts could 'rubber stamp' the conclusions of sharia arbitrations embodied into consent orders.
170 *Radmacher (formerly Granatino) v Granatino* [2010] 2 FLR 1900.
171 A Hirsch, 'Fears over non-Muslim's use of Islamic law to resolve disputes', *Observer*, 14 March 2010. See One Law for All's 'Sharia Law in Britain: A Threat to One Law for All and Equal Rights' (London: One Law for All, 2010) available at www.onelawforall.org.uk. That report, at 12, states that 'One solicitor – who has assisted a number of women who have been denied their

cases such as those discussed by a MAT spokesman in an interview with the *Sunday Times* in which he recounted cases of abusive husbands being ordered to attend anger management classes and accept mentoring from community elders after which wives withdrew criminal charges against them and police terminated criminal investigations.[172] And Samia Bano, who has conducted recent empirical research on the operation of sharia councils in England, expressed concern about the fact that some of the women users she interviewed reported being placed under pressure to engage in reconciliation meetings with violent (ex)husbands, including, in four of the ten cases involving reluctant women, men against whom domestic violence-related injunctions were in place.[173] Bano further quotes an account from a woman who

> told . . . [the imam] that I left [my husband] because he was violent but he started saying things like 'Oh, how violent was that? Because in Islam a man is allowed to beat his wife!' I mean, I was so shocked. He said it depends on whether he really hurt me! I was really shocked because I thought he was there to understand but he was trying to make me admit that somehow I had done wrong.[174]

Bano remarked on the fact that some men who had already undergone civil divorce from the women who were seeking Islamic divorces from the councils used the council process to renegotiate issues relating to children and finances, in some cases securing access to children in defiance of civil injunctions prohibiting access. In the words of one interviewee:

> I couldn't understand . . . they wrote me a letter saying that there was issues to be taken into account that was about child custody, which was about the house, which was about possessions, which was about . . . all kinds of things. I thought, hold on, what jurisdiction do they have? I've already been through the courts; why do I have to go through a set of Islamic courts? Do I have to go through them again? It's all been done and what if it means I can't have custody? Who wins? English law or the Islamic Sharia Council?[175]

rights under Sharia . . . told One Law for All of cases in which women had lost child custody in Sharia Councils and felt unable to challenge such judgements in civil courts because of community pressure'.

[172] *Sunday Times*, 'Revealed: UK's first official sharia courts', 14 September 2008.

[173] See S Bano, 'Islamic Family Arbitration, Justice and Human Rights in Britain' (2007) 10(1) *Law, Social Justice and Global Development Journal*, www2.warwick.ac.uk/fac/soc/law/elj/lgd/2007_1/bano/bano.pdf, 20. See also J Bowen, 'Private Arrangements' *Boston Review*, 1 March 2009, www.bostonreview.net/john-bowen-private-arrangements-sharia-England, and 'How Could English Courts Recognize Shariah?' (n 147) on the operation of the Islamic Shariah Council, London.

[174] Bano (n 118) 303.

[175] ibid, 305. Bano saw as perhaps particularly problematic the fact that 'social workers were attending shariah council reconciliation sessions to inform their decisions in cases where access to children was contested by fathers. Therein lie, at least, the seeds of the argument that the autonomy of the women who use these services may be undermined or curtailed to some degree'. Bowen (n 147) reports at 420 that 'if the children live with the mother, and the father has indicated that he has difficulty getting access to them, the councillors [of the Islamic London Council] ask the mother to provide an affidavit stating that she will allow the father to see the children as a condition of granting the divorce'.

Bano concluded that:

> [T]he multicultural accommodation of religious family law in Britain can lead to the violation of human rights for Muslim women. In effect, this privatised form of religious arbitration may mean the shifting of state regulation to the private domain, thereby giving religious leaders greater power to dictate acceptable patterns of behaviour.[176]

The danger is that, whether or not religious arbitrations (or 'agreements' mediated in the shadow of religious rules) are given legal effect, women may find themselves caught between community pressure to conform, on the one hand, and the difficulties associated with enforcing 'Western' legal entitlements, on the other. That which is not binding in law may be binding in practice. Further, the economically driven thrust towards greater use of ADR in family law may threaten the current position that agreements reached between divorcing parties are enforceable only if given effect to by the courts in the form of a consent order between the parties.[177]

Controversy about Muslim arbitration in family law proceedings in Ontario, Canada, resulted in an announcement by Premier Dalton McGuinty in September 2005 that Islamic law could not be relied upon in family law arbitration in the province.[178] Following the failure of calls for the recognition of Muslim family and personal law in Canada in the 1990s,[179] the President of the Canadian Society of Muslims (Syed Mumtaz Ali) established the Islamic Institute of Civil Justice to 'offer' Muslim arbitration in family law disputes in 2003, declaring that 'in order to be regarded as "good Muslims," Muslims would be required as part of their faith to agree to this forum for dispute resolution'.[180] In the wake of protests, many by Muslim women, Ontario's government commissioned a report from former Attorney General Marion Boyd on the use of private arbitration in family and inheritance cases.[181] The report 'did not find any evidence to suggest that women are being systematically discriminated against as a result of arbitration of family law issues'[182] and concluded that religious arbitration could be permitted, but proposed no fewer

---

[176] ibid, 303.

[177] This is not to suggest that such consent orders are not themselves problematic, only that they at least avoid the presumptive enforceability which arises under the Arbitration Act 1996.

[178] N Bakht, 'Were Muslim Barbarians Really Knocking On the Gates of Ontario?: The Religious Arbitration Controversy – Another Perspective' (2006) 40 *Ottawa Law Review* 67–82, 67.

[179] See, in particular, A Mumtaz and A Whitehouse, *Oh! Canada. Whose Land, Whose Dream? Sovereignty, Social Contracts and Participatory Democracy: An Exploration into Constitutional Arrangements* (Toronto: Canadian Society of Muslims, 1991) http://muslimcanada.org/ocanada. pdf. See S Khan, 'Canadian Muslim Women and Shari'a Law: A Feminist Response to Oh! Canada!' (1993) 6 *Canadian Journal of Women and the Law* 52–65 for discussion.

[180] SP Chotalia, 'Arbitration Using Sharia Law in Canada: A Constitutional and Human Rights Perspective' (2006) 15(2) *Constitutional Forum/Forum Constitutionnel* 63–86, 64. See also N Bakht, 'Religious Arbitration in Canada: Protecting Women by Protecting them from Religion' (2007) 19 *Canadian Journal of Women and the Law* 119–144, 126, fn 30.

[181] M Boyd, *Dispute Resolution in Family Law: Protecting Choice, Promoting Inclusion*, December 2004, www.attorneygeneral.jus.gov.on.ca/english/about/pubs/boyd, 5.

[182] ibid, 133.

than 46 safeguards covering everything from provision for set-aside of awards which did not reflect the best interests of any children affected, or which resulted from flawed procedures, through requirements that the parties be separately screened 'about issues of power imbalance and domestic violence, prior to entering into an arbitration agreement', to arrangements for the training and education of professionals and the oversight and evaluation of arbitrations.[183]

The Boyd Report generated both praise and criticism[184] but the general public reception was hostile[185] and, in September 2005 Premier McGuinty announced his rejection of it. The Family Statute Law Amendment Act 2006 now requires that any arbitration of divorce and child custody disputes take place on the basis of Canadian law alone; that both parties receive legal advice before entering into an arbitration agreement; and that arbitrators be members of a professional arbitration organisation and be trained to detect signs of domestic violence. Notwithstanding feminist reservations about the use of arbitration, however, Natasha Bakht suggested that 'a more nuanced approach' would have been better than a complete ban on religious arbitration, and that the outcome was a ' "lost opportunity" to prevent "back-alley arbitration" through a "regime of government regulation that could have ensured a measure of transparency, accountability and competence in adjudication" '.[186] Shahnaz Khan, too, warned that 'the absence of Shari'a does not guarantee gender equality among/Muslims in Canada', pointing to informal marriages, including polygamous unions, among Muslims.[187]

The content of Hanafi rules on custody, divorce, maintenance and inheritance, mentioned above, create real difficulties, from a gender equality perspective, with any ceding of control over matters such as divorce, child custody and division of property to religious authorities or rules. It may well be the case, as Bakht suggests, that part of the 'moral panic' engendered by the prospect of 'shari'a Courts' in the UK appears to derive from 'The familiar caricature of the "imperiled Muslim woman" needing to be rescued from the "dangerous Muslim man" '.[188] Certainly the tone of the Civitas report and much contemporaneous newspaper reporting was and is shrill. Bakht and others point to the multiplicity of voices within Islam, some of them advocating equal rights for women by

---

[183] ibid, 134–41, recommendations 5 and 6, 18, 19, 26 and 26, 31–35 and 36–42.

[184] See, for example, F Bhabha, 'Between Exclusion and Assimilation: Experimentalizing Multiculturalism' (2009) 54 *McGill Law Journal* 45–90. *cf* S McGill, 'Religious Tribunals and the Ontario *Arbitration Act, 1991*: The Catalyst for Change' (2005) *Journal of Law and Social Policy* 53–66, 60, Chotalia (n 180) 66.

[185] See MS Funk, 'Representing Canadian Muslims: Media, Muslim Advocacy Organizations, and Gender in the Ontario Shari'ah Debate' (2009) 2 *Global Media Journal* 73–89.

[186] Bakht (n 178) 75, 80. See also n 180, 132. See also A Wadud, *Qur'an and Woman: Rereading the Sacred Text from a Woman's Perspective* (New York: Oxford University Press, 1999) and Bhabha who suggests that the outcome in Ontario 'did not effect the disappearance of religiously inspired dispute resolution processes from Muslim communities in Ontario. Rather, it pushed those processes back to the informal level, where people – women and children in particular – are arguably at even greater risk of being victimized by unjust rulings than in a formalized system' (n 184) 61–62.

[187] Khan (n 179) 61–62.

[188] Bakht (n 180).

reference to religious sources, and to the nature of 'Sharia . . . not simply an ancient code of rules [but] . . . [as] a process of analysis that must take into account . . . the context of the nation where it is applied'.[189] But while Amira Mashhour, in a study of Islamic family law, accepts that there are circumstances under which progressive developments in this area are possible, she warns that 'Due to the influence of patriarchal social customs, most of the mainstream interpretations are conservative . . .'.[190] And in the UK, despite the influence of Pakistani Muslims in each of the four sharia councils studied by Bano,[191] it appears from the WLUML report that the scholars in these and other councils have chosen to adopt a very conservative approach to Muslim divorce, rather than that now prevalent in (for example) Pakistan itself.

The absence of any serious pressure in the UK for the formal recognition of Muslim personal law makes it unnecessary to consider whether the common ground which may exist between Islam and gender equality is sufficient to justify the removal from Muslim women *as Muslim women* of the legal protections attendant on civil divorce, and at what point women would be required to opt in or out of such protections. This leaves the fact, however, that a significant proportion of Muslim women in the UK have undergone only religious marriage ceremonies (*nikah*), and these in circumstances (such as where they have taken place in the UK, or occurred in Pakistan but were not duly registered there) such that they are not recognised as giving rise to civil marriage in the UK. These women fall outside the jurisdiction of the family courts.[192] Further, and notwithstanding the intervention of the sharia councils, many Muslim women who undergo civil divorce regard themselves, and are regarded by others, as continuing to be married unless and until they are granted *talaq* by their (ex)husbands or dissolution by a recognised Muslim authority. Such women do not always appear to be well served by sharia councils.

The difficulties caused by 'limping marriages' are not unique to Muslim women, Jewish women also being vulnerable to ex-husbands' refusal of the *get* (Jewish religious divorce). Section 10A of the Matrimonial Causes Act 1973, inserted by the Divorce (Religious Marriages) Act 2002, provides that a party to a Jewish marriage can apply to the court for an order staying the issue of a decree absolute pending a declaration by both parties that any cooperation necessary to effect a religious divorce has been forthcoming, such an order to be

---

[189] ibid, 132, citing A Emon, 'Shades of Grey on Sharia: Counterpoint' *National Post*, 29 July 2005, A12 and A Mashour, 'Islamic Law and Gender Equality: Could There Be a Common Ground? A Study of Divorce and Polygamy in Sharia Law and Contemporary Legislation in Tunisia and Egypt' (2005) 27 *Human Rights Quarterly* 562–96, 577 and 580.

[190] Mashour (n 189) 596. See also Josh Goodman (n 120) 527–28, on the failure of secular judicial oversight in Israel or India to have significant impact on the content of religious laws.

[191] Bano (n 118) and (n 173).

[192] For a recent example see *El-Gamal Nivin v HRH Sheikh Ahmed Bin Saeed al Maktoum* [2011] EWHC B27 (Fam) in which it was ruled that the Muslim ceremony between the parties was not a valid marriage with the effect that the Claimant was not entitled under English law to any financial settlement in respect of its termination by the Respondent.

granted 'only if the court is satisfied that in all the circumstances of the case it is just and reasonable to do so'.[193] The Act can extend by regulation beyond Jewish marriages. While the Act does not bite on men unconcerned about their civil status (and therefore not seeking civil divorce), it is a powerful weapon against those who hold out against religious divorce, or who use the *get* as a bargaining tool to lever divorce terms more favourable than those which would otherwise be awarded by a civil court.[194]

Shah-Kazemi suggests that the operation of sharia councils 'clearly indicates that legislative intervention is not necessary to resolve the problem of marriage dissolution for Muslim women in the UK',[195] a conclusion at odds with that of Baroness Butler-Sloss, former head of the Family Division, who in 2008 called for judges to stop granting civil divorces to separating Muslim couples unless they had already been through a religious divorce.[196] WLUML expressed concern that the extension of the Act to Muslim marriages might make the position of Muslim women worse than at present by permitting 'husbands to use [the law] to delay the decree absolute in a woman's civil divorce and insist she go through some "religious" process' and warned that the extension of the law to Muslim women might 'open the door . . . to even greater exploitation and extortion. Moreover, it may lead to validating the role of Shariah councils within the formal system, a step which women have resisted in other contexts'.[197] The difference between Muslim and Jewish marriage would appear to be that Jewish women cannot initiate religious divorce with the effect that a stay could not properly be granted in favour of the husband whereas, at least in theory, a Muslim husband could claim that his wife should utilise the sharia councils, with their focus on conciliation, prior to being granted a civil divorce.[198]

Concerns about the activities of sharia councils resulted in an otherwise unlikely coalition of support for Baroness Cox's Private Members Arbitration and Mediation Services (Equality) Bill which would, inter alia, apply the

---

[193] Section 10A(3). New York has had similar legislation in place since 1983, when the New York Domestic Relations Law § 253 (Removal of Barriers to Remarriage 1983) was passed.

[194] Amendments made to New York's legislation in 1992 also allowed courts to take into account a refusal to issue a *get* in the distribution of property on divorce, this allowing the (civilly) divorcing women to exert pressure on the recalcitrant husband to provide her with the *get*, otherwise to bear the financial consequences of the impediment to any subsequent marriage by her.

[195] Shah-Kazemi (n 127) 70.

[196] 'Butler-Sloss Urges Courts to Recognise Sharia Divorces', *Daily Telegraph*, 27 December 2008.

[197] WLUML (n 124) 49.

[198] WLUML point out (ibid, 78) that Muslim personal law 'means all acts governed by religious law and can include economic and criminal matters' but that demands for the recognition of such law have tended to limit their horizons to family law while 'efforts to popularize [' "Islamic mortgages" and "Islamic bank accounts" '] . . . are nowhere near as visible as calls by various Shariah councils for formal state recognition of their role in family matters. Demands regarding family matters would therefore appear to be more a matter of who represents and controls the community than a question of freedom of religion'.

provisions of the Equality Act to those providing arbitration services and limit the scope for religious arbitration.[199] Clause 1(2) of the Bill provides that:

> [D]iscrimination on grounds of sex includes but is not restricted to (a) treating the evidence of a man as worth more than the evidence of a woman, or vice versa, (b) proceeding on the assumption that the division of an estate between male and female children on intestacy must be unequal, or (c) proceeding on the assumption that a woman has fewer property rights than a man, or vice versa.[200]

And clause 1(4) would amend the Equality Act 2010's Public Sector Equality Duty (PSED) to provide that:

> The steps involved in removing or minimising disadvantages suffered by persons who share a relevant protected characteristic . . . include steps to take account of the fact that those who are married according to certain religious practices or are in a polygamous household may be without legal protection

and that such steps

> should include but not necessarily be restricted to – (a) informing individuals of the need to obtain an officially recognised marriage in order to have legal protection; (b) informing individuals that a polygamous household may be without legal protection and a polygamous household may be unlawful.

If it were to become law in its present form, Baroness Cox's Bill would amend the Arbitration Act 1996 expressly to provide that criminal and family law matters cannot be settled by arbitration. It would also amend the Family Law Act 1996 to allow a family court to set aside any mediated agreement 'if it considers on evidence that one party's consent was not genuine'.[201] And:

> In assessing the genuineness of a party's consent, the court should have particular regard to whether or not – (a) all parties were informed of their legal rights, including alternatives to mediation or any other negotiation process used; (b) any party was manipulated or put under duress, including through psychological coercion, to induce participation in the mediation or negotiation process.

Finally, the Bill would make it an offence subject to a five-year maximum prison term:

> (a) falsely [to] purport[] to be exercising a judicial function or to be able to make legally binding rulings, or (b) otherwise falsely [to] purport[] to adjudicate on any matter which that person knows or ought to know is within the jurisdiction of the criminal or family courts.

The Bill will almost certainly fail to become law. It has garnered the support of a variety of groups including the Muslim Women's Network, the National

---

[199] Originally 2010–12, reintroduced in the House of Lords in 2012 and given a second reading on 19 October 2012, www.publications.parliament.uk/pa/ld201213/ldhansrd/text/121019-0001.htm, reintroduced in the 2013–14 session and due to have a second reading in February 2014.

[200] See J Eekelaar, 'The Arbitration and Mediation Services (Equality) Bill 2011' [2011] *Family Law* 1209 for discussion.

[201] Cl 5 inserting a new s 9A into the Family Law Act 1996.

Secular Society and the Kurdish and Iranian Women's Rights Organization, as well as Christians including retired bishop Michael Nazir-Ali and American evangelist Jay Smith. Potential enthusiasts might, however, be given pause for thought by the fact that Baroness Cox is a patron of the Christian Institute, a leading campaigner against gay rights, and has suggested that Christians in the UK are 'persecuted'.[202] In March 2012, at a House of Lords meeting entitled 'Islamist Resurgence: Shari'a and freedom' Cox associated the recognition of sharia law for any purposes in the UK with the legitimation of honour crimes and the introduction of child marriage and requirements that rape victims have to produce four independent Muslim witnesses.[203]

Baroness Cox is a peculiar bedfellow for those who are suspicious of special pleading for the religiously inclined. Further, an exclusive focus on the grand question whether 'shari'a law' should be recognised in the UK overlooks the very real problems that many Muslim women in the UK face in relation to marriage. WLUML reported in 2006 that 'On the whole, family law as it is interpreted and applied in Britain today in effect shunts British South Asian Muslims (and other Muslim communities) out of the legal system rather than including them in the system in a positive manner'.[204] Not only do many Muslim women mistakenly believe that religious marriage is legally recognised in the UK, but there are uncertainties as to the legal validity of many marriages contracted abroad (in countries in which Muslim marriages are recognised as legally binding), and the impact of *talaqs* issued or recognised abroad on such marriages,[205] and the situation of the many Muslims in Britain of Pakistani or Bangladeshi origin or descent is hugely complicated by the application to them of the Muslim Family Laws Ordinance 1961 which has extra-territorial effect.[206] This has the result that religious marriages which are not recognised as legally valid in the UK may nevertheless be regarded as legally binding in the countries of the parties' or their parents' origin, and that civil divorce may be insufficient to dissolve even civil marriages entered into in the UK and recognised as valid in, for example, Pakistan.[207] As WLUML point out, the women caught in the web of legal uncertainty may face the threat of being regarded as adulterers in their countries of origin/descent if they remarry without Muslim divorce, and of being subject to draconian penalties as a result. 'Add to these inadequacies indi-

---

[202] www.assistnews.net/Stories/2009/s09060037.htm.

[203] Press release from the Christian Broadcasting Council 21 March 2012 'Sharia Law UK: Threat to Women and Children' (at whose annual symposium Baroness Cox, its Vice-President, made her remarks). Interestingly, *Sun* and *Mail* online articles covering the meeting both disappeared from the web within days of the meeting. The articles had attributed to Baroness Cox warnings about stonings, amputations and whippings which she denied.

[204] ibid, vi.

[205] ibid, 2–5. See in particular the discussion at 4 of the difficulties as to definitions of 'polygamous' marriages and the concept of domicile prior to the decision of the House of lords in *Mark v Mark* [2006] 1 AC 98.

[206] ibid, 14.

[207] This because (*Jaloi v Jaloi* PLD 1967 SC 580, and see text to n 145) such marriages are recognised as valid in Pakistan.

vidual bigotry and the institutionalized racism that continues to dominate various aspects of the British system and one finds an operational context in which it is difficult to address violations of women's rights in Muslim communities'.[208]

WLUML complain that:

It was only after pressure from non-governmental organizations in Britain and abroad that action began to be taken in the late 1990s to support women in situations of forced marriage and honour crimes . . . fully five years later, a national consultation on forced marriages continues to emphasize 'community sensitivities' rather than women's human rights. Meanwhile, government reports on the specific issues facing women in Muslim communities have ignored family law matters even though these seem to rank high in the problems that support groups deal with on a daily basis.[209]

The accommodation which progressive multicultural policy might require in this context is likely to be concerned to address the difficulties faced by Muslim women as a result of the common practice of undergoing religious as well as, or rather than, civil marriage, and to achieve clarity, and avoid unnecessary legal complexity, for the many Muslim women in the UK whose marriages have been conducted, in religious form, in countries in which such marriages are legally binding. Doing justice to these women by providing for their access to the legal rights normally attendant on the dissolution of marriage may require some degree of recognition by the state of religious marriages. As to whether sharia councils ought to be permitted to engage in binding arbitration in family issues, the logically prior question concerns the advisability of allowing any 'privatisation' of law in this context.

Divorce makes women poor. In Britain in 2007, for example, women's income fell 17 per cent on divorce while men's income was boosted by 11 per cent.[210] A 2009 study of British Household Panel Surveys between 1991 and 2004 found that fathers saw their available income rising 'immediately and continuously' in the years following separation, with an average gain of around one-third, while women, whether or not they had children, 'suffer severe financial penalties' with incomes falling by around 20 per cent, 'remain[ing] low for many years' and 'rarely reach[ing] pre-split levels'.[211]

There is a long way to go in achieving equitable outcomes on family dissolution. But the strong legal trend over time has been to recognise the contribution made by women to family resources by their domestic work, as well as any material contributions, and to require redistribution of assets from relatively

---

[208] WLUML (n 124) 14.

[209] ibid, 35.

[210] M Jansen, L Snoeckx and D Mortelmans, 'Repartnering and (Re-)employment: Strategies to Cope with the Economic Consequences of Partnership Dissolution', presentation to the British Household Panel Survey 2007 conference at the Institute for Social and Economic Research (now published in (2009) 71(5) *Journal of Marriage and Family* 1271–93).

[211] A Hill, 'Men become richer after divorce', the *Observer* 25 January 2009, reporting on Stephen Jenkins, 'Marital Splits and Income Changes over the Longer Term' in M Brynin and J Ermisch (eds), *Changing Relationships* (London: Routledge, 2009).

richer to relatively poorer (ex-)spouses, ie, from men to women. The legal entitlements of women, as (typically) lower earners and primary care-givers within marriages have been granted by the state in the face of (typically male) interests in maintaining the status quo of pre-existing property rights, and most women are vulnerable in any privatisation of family law decision making, such as that which is threatened at present by the thrust towards mediation/arbitration in the resolution of family law disputes.

In the US context, Penelope Bryan warned in 1992 that 'mediation unobtrusively reduces [the] threat to patriarchy' arising from the provision of enhanced legal rights for women on divorce 'by returning men to their former dominant position'.[212] Bryan suggested that mediators' general presumption in favour of joint custody 'result[s] in custody agreements more favourable to fathers than those obtained through lawyer negotiation'[213] while 'Mediator intervention also fails to protect the divorcing wife from the husband's control over financial issues'.[214] Mary Pat Treuthart suggested in 1993 that one of the factors behind the drive in the US towards mediation was a 'Return to "privatization" after women's advocates helped strengthen laws concerning domestic abuse, division of property, enforcement of spousal and child support, and sole custody for the primary caretaking parent with whom the child is psychologically bonded'.[215] Treuthart further points out that 'The mediation process relies on good-faith bargaining between disputants who possess equal bargaining power'.[216] Mediators are neither trained nor institutionally positioned so as to be able to adjust the balance of power between the parties, 'impartiality' being central to their role. In particular, while mediators can focus on fairness of process as regards allowing both parties to speak etc, they cannot intervene in the substance of the 'agreement'. Where there are power imbalances between the parties, coupled (as is often the case in divorce) with feelings of guilt, depression and low self-esteem (particularly on the part of women), anxiety about children and a desire to avoid further conflict, the dangers of abdicating legal rule to 'voluntary' 'agreement' are stark.[217] Further, mediation may take place in the

---

[212] P Bryan, 'Killing Us Softly: Divorce Mediation and the Politics of Power' (1992) 40 *Buffalo Law Review* 441–523, 441–44.

[213] Both Bryan and MP Treuthart ('In Harm's Way? Family Mediation and the Role of the Attorney Advocate' (1993) 23 *Golden Gate University Law Review* 717–42, 734) remarked on the willingness of many fathers to 'trade' the increased custody rights that they can expect as a result of mediation for enhanced financial outcomes.

[214] Bryan (n 212) 446.

[215] Treuthart (n 213) 720.

[216] ibid, 722.

[217] See further T Grillo, 'The Mediation Alternative: Process Dangers for Women' (1991) 100 *Yale Law Journal* 1545–610; and I Ricci who points out ('Mediators Notebook: Reflections on Promoting Equal Empowerment and Entitlement for Women' in CA Everett (ed), *Divorce Mediation: Perspectives on the Field* (New York: Haworth, 1985) 49) that women are more likely to be peacemakers who 'tend to see their entitlement to custody, support and property as stemming from their ability to fulfill the role of defusing conflict rather than from legal right . . .'; R Field ('Federal Family Law Reform in 2005: The Problems and Pitfalls' (2005) 5(1) *Queensland University Technical Law and Justice Journal* 28–51, 33) states that 'women experience higher levels of depression and

absence of the full financial disclosure which is required in the context of court proceedings.[218]

In these circumstances, Bryan argued that mediation should be recognised as 'an informal process that places the low powered spouse, usually the wife, fully at the mercy of her more powerful husband'[219] while Martha Shaffer suggested that 'Removing divorce from the public realm amounts to a "re-privatization" of the family, allowing traditional patterns of inequality to flourish free from public view . . . [and] leav[ing] women subject to the prevailing values of a patriarchal culture'.[220]

The rush to mediate is driven in part by the perceived advantages in terms of efficiency and costs, without reference to the fairness of agreements resulting from mediation. While the UK's National Audit Office might have been expected to focus on the bottom line in its analysis of legal aid and mediation in family breakdown,[221] that body's conclusion that, because mediation was cheaper and quicker than other routes to settlement, its use should be encouraged by the Legal Services Commission, was reached absent any analysis of the substance of the agreements reached by the process.[222] A study commissioned by the Legal Services Commission in 2000 from Gwyn Bevan and Gwynn Davis reported that mediation did not reduce legal costs because, for many, its failure to result in resolution meant that it was simply an additional step in the divorce

distress, sometimes associated with learned helplessness and sex role identity, than men . . . [which] compromise a woman's ability to participate in consensus bargaining'.

[218] Treuthart (n 213) 740 challenges whether payments from one parent to another in respect of child maintenance can properly be mediated in the absence of a third party charged with representing the child's interests, suggesting that the level of such payments are often 'significantly less' than those achieved by lawyer-negotiated agreements or awarded by the courts.

[219] Bryan (n 212) 502. Trina Grillo further suggests (n 217) that the lack of focus on fault and rights in mediation can further disempower women and that the forward-focused nature of much mediation fails adequately to safeguard children's interests. The research carried out for the LSC in 2000 also remarked on the 'logical inconsistency' of the situation in which 'Family mediators are expected to remain impartial as between the parties and neutral as to the outcome' but 'are also supposed, as far as is possible, to redress imbalances of power between the parties'.

[220] M Shaffer, 'Divorce Mediation: A Feminist Perspective' (1988) 46(1) *University of Toronto Law Review* 162–200, 166–67.

[221] Legal Services Commission: *Legal Aid and Mediation for People Involved in Family Breakdown* (London: HMSO, 2007). See comment of R Dingwall, 'Divorce Mediation: Should We Change Our Mind?' (2010) *Journal of Social Welfare & Family Law* 107–11, 11 that the NAO report 'imposes a reading on the [Bevan & Davis report, discussed below] that has no basis in their report and recounts the traditional mantras about how mediation avoids an adversarial and acrimonious legal process, with evidence based on a survey of mediators' views. To paraphrase the immortal words of Mandy Rice-Davies, well they would say that wouldn't they!' Dingwall also takes issue with the NAO's reliance on excess capacity in the mediation sector as a reason to encourage the use of mediation: 'without ever considering whether it is the role of government to generate demand to compensate individuals who have over-optimistically invested in a particular market sector that has failed to develop as they might have hoped'.

[222] See also A Melville and K Laing, 'Closing the Gate: Family Lawyers as Gatekeepers to a Holistic Service' (2010) *International Journal of Law in Context* 167–89, 168: 'it was not until the early 1990s . . . that mediation gained much stronger policy attention [in England and Wales], especially as it was seen to be a potential solution to the growing legal aid budget required to address family law issues'.

process.[223] In what should be a cause for significant concern, Bevan and Davis reported that 'In 57% of cases in which our informant referred to fear of violence (on someone's part) mediation was nevertheless deemed to be suitable' by mediators, this notwithstanding the exemption of cases in which domestic violence was alleged from the 1996 Act's requirement to mediate.[224]

Bevan and Davis concluded that the normal methods of assessing the value of mediation by reference to 'diversion from contested legal proceedings' or the settlement of such proceedings 'are not adequate measures of value. The question: "To what extent are things now better?" tends not to be asked, although it ought to be. . .':[225]

29.2 Instead we find that family mediation has become heavily influenced by the notion of 'settlement' which is so powerful within legal proceedings. It would appear that mediators have to conform to this value if they are to attract government funding. Mediation is now judged by its capacity to reduce the demand for lawyer services, or the cost of those services. This requires mediators to devote themselves to achieving success according to standards invented by lawyers. By and large solicitor mediators (growing in number) are more comfortable with these expectations . . .

31.1 Recent government support for family mediation reflects professional enthusiasm, with little regard to the low client base. This has come about because the 'story' of mediation – its association with reasonableness and compromise – is appealing, and secondly because government has accepted the mediators' argument that spiralling legal costs can be cut through diverting cases to mediation.

It was in part on the basis of the Bevan/Davis report that the then government scrapped plans for compulsory mediation as a prerequisite to 'no fault' divorce.[226] But by 2007 the LSC was proposing to treat mediation referrals as a performance indicator for LSC funded family law solicitors 'with an implied threat that solicitors who failed to achieve LSC targets would find their

---

[223] Monitoring publicly funded family mediation: report to the legal services commission (Legal Services Commission).

[224] Para 15.2. The expression of satisfaction by many women who have been involved in mediation may be entirely unrelated to substantive outcome – many women have little idea of their legal entitlements, and may be relieved by the fact that mediation is less acrimonious than they expected (for example), or that it avoided the need for court attendance. In 'Mediation of Wife Abuse Cases: The Adverse Impact of Informal Dispute Resolution on Women' (1984) 7 *Harvard Women's Law Journal* 57–113, Lisa Lerman discusses the tendency of mediators to encourage recognition of 'mutual fault' even in cases of spousal abuse and Field (n 217) 39 states that domestic violence 'undermine[s] the fundamental core values of informal processes relating to self determination, party empowerment and party control' which are crucial to mediation: 'A history of violence creates, instead, the potential for the entrenchment and exacerbation of the perpetrator's patriarchal domination of the victim'.

[225] Legal Services Commission (n 223) para 29.1.

[226] Speech of the Lord Chancellor Lord Irvine on 16 January 2001: 'this very comprehensive research, together with other recent valuable research in the field, has shown that Part II of the Family Law Act (i.e., Mediation) is not the best way' of 'supporting marriage and . . . supporting families when relationships fail'. Dingwall (n 221) 109 states that the 2000 report 'effectively buried mandatory mediation as a proposition'.

franchise brought into question'.[227] In August 2008 the LSC was pushing mediation in family law cases on the basis that it resulted in 'cheaper, quicker and . . . less acrimonious' resolutions.[228] The withdrawal of legal aid from ordinary family law litigation has been noted above, as has the availability of (very limited) funding for mediation in such cases and the drive towards requiring mediation in privately funded cases. As Robert Dingwall, who was a member of the Bevan/Davis team, pointed out in 2010, the 2000 report had been 'airbrushed out of history'.[229]

CONCLUSIONS

If we return to consider the possible recognition of Muslim personal law in the form of an arrangement whereby institutions such as sharia councils or 'Islamic courts' would to be permitted to engage in legally binding arbitration in matters of family breakdown, or 'agreements' mediated by such institutions might be regarded as presumptively binding by the family courts, I would suggest that we might reject any such arrangements on the grounds that they are likely to be disadvantageous to women. This conclusion would be driven, however, as much by the privatising and status quo-preserving nature of *all* mediation in the context of family disputes, and the abandonment of the rights accorded by law to women on divorce which is inherent in subjection to arbitration according to principles other than those underpinning modern divorce law, as by reservations about the relationship between 'Islam' and gender equality. The suggestion that Muslim women are uniquely or particularly vulnerable to injustice if they cede their legal rights on divorce in pursuit of 'agreement', community approval or a quiet life is erroneous and Muslim men are not unique in regarding the current legal approach to divorce as unduly indulgent to their former wives.

Thinking about this example of where 'multicultural accommodation' has been proposed, whether in the UK or elsewhere, can help us begin to negotiate the relationships between such accommodation and considerations of equality. It cannot be assumed that a refusal to recognise religious personal law will further gender equality, the relationship between such recognition and questions of equality being a nuanced and complex one which turns not only on the specifics of the particular religion(s) at issue but also on wider considerations which impact on 'majority' as well as on 'minority' women, but to which our own culturally specific assumptions may blind us.

---

[227] Dingwall (n 221) 111 points out that 'If the movement for mediation has been driven by a humane aspiration for a better quality of service . . . its adoption has been driven by a desire to reduce costs to the public purse'.

[228] 'Publicly Funded Family Mediation: the Way Forward'.

[229] R Dingwall, 'Divorce Mediation: Should We Change Our Mind?' (2010) *Journal of Social Welfare & Family Law* 107–17, 107.

To say this is not to advocate cultural relativism. As Desai points out, feminism's project is not solely 'to interject the female subject or multiple female subjects where before there was only a so-called objective (read subjective male) viewpoint'; being equally concerned with 'the examination of the systemic subordination of women in male-dominated societies [with a view to] . . . eradicating the inequalities that exist between men and women'.[230] Similarly, an equality-driven engagement with practices of FGC, religious dress codes or family law ought not uncritically to accept the understandings of the parties thereto but should consider those understandings together with, and against the background of, the power relationships which operate within the particular communities, both overtly and through the constitutive effects of the cultures of those communities.[231]

Feminist theory is not, because of its refusal to vindicate existing societal norms, on all fours with cultural relativism. Nor, however, in its challenge to the asserted universality of a particular (male, white, Western[232]) viewpoint, and its demand for the affirmation of 'individual women's voices and differences',[233] is it an uncritical advocate of universalism. Unreflecting universalism can too easily metamorphose into an approach which sees subordination only in the 'other' or which too readily assumes, as Elizabeth Spelman put it, that 'the many turn out to be one, and the one that they are is me'.[234] It is vital, accordingly, never to lose sight of the constraints imposed upon us by our own cultural situatedness when seeking to pass judgment on others.

The insights gained from engaging critically with 'Shari'a law', and our own reactions thereto, can be applied to other tricky questions such as whether and how to engage with full-face veiling. There is significant evidence that the 'Arabisation' of young British Muslims of largely South Asian descent who are more, rather than less, likely than their mothers to adopt conservative dress codes, including increasingly (though still very much in the minority) the *jilbab* and *niqab*, is not the result of 'inherited community norms', much less direct parental pressure.[235] Whether and when adult women might justifiably be

---

[230] S Desai, 'Hearing Afghan Women's Voices: Feminist Theory's Re-Conceptualization of Women's Human Rights (1999) 16 *Arizona Journal of International and Comparative Law* 805–43, 812. See also TE Higgins, 'Anti-essentialism, Relativism and Human Rights' (1996) 19 *Harvard Women's Law Journal* 89–126; N Kim, 'Towards a Feminist Theory of Human Rights; Straddling the Fence between Western Imperialism and Uncritical Absolutism' (1993–94) 25 *Columbia Human Rights Law Review* 49.

[231] See M Foucault, *Power/Knowledge: Selected Interviews and Other Writings 1972–1977* (C Gordon, ed, New York: Pantheon Books, 1980); JM Balkin, 'Ideology as Cultural Software' (1995) *Cardozo Law Review* 1221.

[232] The latter two at least in the case of black and anti-racist feminist thinkers, as well as (more broadly) radical equality advocates.

[233] Desai (n 230) 814.

[234] E Spelman, *Inessential Woman: Problems of Exclusion in Feminist Thought* (Boston: Beacon Press, 1988) 159. See also J Conaghan, 'Reassessing the Feminist Theoretical Project in Law' (2000) 27 *Journal of Law and Society* 351–85, 363–74 on 'woman centredness' and a response to 'the critique of essentialism'.

[235] See Afshar et al (n 22).

prevented from covering their faces or disguising their forms is a discussion which can only be sensibly had by those who have taken the time to explore the meaning of such practices, and must take account of the variety of ways in which all women's choices about their public presentation are made within constraints imposed by culture.

7

Conclusion

A S INDICATED IN Chapter 1, the purpose of this chapter is to highlight a number of themes which have emerged from those which have preceded it and to make some suggestions as to the paths along which discrimination/equality law might best develop. Those suggestions flow from the conclusions reached in the various chapters, which are briefly recapped immediately below.

In Chapter 1 I attempted to explore the relationship between 'discrimination' and 'equality', challenging the assumption that is often made that the former is concerned primarily with distinctions in treatment whereas the latter carries a more positive or substantive heft. As I there suggested, equality can itself be viewed in formal ('treat like cases alike') or substantive terms. The former is clearly incapable of underpinning constitutional or statutory regimes which regulate indirect discrimination and provide for affirmative action etc. The latter, however, requires articulation of the values which underpin it in turn, if it is to provide guidance in the legal context (in relation to questions such as 'when is it discriminatory to treat differently situated persons similarly?', or 'when may we treat persons differently because of a protected characteristic?').

Among the candidates for this role have been, in a triumph of circularity, discrimination itself. (On this approach, differential treatment would amount to discrimination[1] if it resulted in, exacerbated or perpetuated *inequality*, such inequality itself being identified by reference to the concept of discrimination). Another is dignity, which is unsatisfactory both at a theoretical level because, as David Feldman suggests, 'dignity is a quality characteristic of human beings, so that an individual cannot have a right to it', although 'An umbrella of rights may be justified in preventing interference with . . . general human dignity' and the right to be free of discriminatory treatment has 'a particularly prominent role in upholding human dignity'.[2] More practically, too, while the concept of dignity can facilitate claims to recognition, it has proved less helpful where discrimination claims are aimed at resource redistribution,[3] being open to

---

[1] Defined by the OED as 'the unjust or prejudicial treatment of different categories of people . . .'

[2] D Feldman, 'Human Dignity as a Legal Value: Part 1' (1999) *Public Law* 682, 689, 695.

[3] See for example the discussion of the decision of Canada's Supreme Court in *Gosselin* and the commentaries of J Fudge, 'Substantive Equality, the Supreme Court of Canada, and the Limits to Redistribution' (2007) 23 *South African Journal on Human Rights* 235 and E Grabham, '*Law v*

'diverse, but usually majoritarian interpretations that do not challenge the status quo'.[4]

Equally unsatisfactory as a candidate for determining, for the purposes of discrimination/equality analysis, which cases should be treated as morally equivalent, is luck egalitarianism, tending as it does to attribute responsibility for material disadvantage to moral weakness rather than institutional factors or oppression. More promising were the insights of thinkers such as IM Young and Anne Phillips, Samuel Scheffler and Elizabeth Anderson. IM Young's concern is with the patterns of exclusion and institutionalised disadvantage which link resource distribution to social group membership, while Anne Phillips points out the dangers in 'attribut[ing] systematic differences in outcome to the different mind-sets of different groups' without taking into account the 'different conditions under which their choices were made'.[5] Samuel Scheffler regards equality as a 'a moral ideal governing the relations in which people stand to one another . . . opposed not to luck but to oppression, to heritable hierarchies of social status, to ideas of caste, to class privilege and the rigid stratification of classes, and to the undemocratic distribution of power'.[6] And Anderson insists that '[d]iversities in socially ascribed identities, distinct roles in the division of labor, or differences in personal traits, whether these be neutral biological and psychological differences, valuable talents and virtues, or unfortunate disabilities and infirmities, never justify' oppression, which she defines as the 'dominat[ion], exploit[ation], marginali[sation], demean[ing] and inflict[ion of] violence' by some groups of people upon others.[7]

The conceptualisation of discrimination/equality law as concerned with the eradication of oppression has obvious implications for the selection of protected characteristics. I conclude in Chapter 2 that a characteristic-based approach is a necessary corollary of any detailed regime: whereas broad constitutional or other equality clauses can require equal treatment or prohibit discrimination without specifying a list of grounds/characteristics, closed or otherwise, such clauses are invariably subject to express or implied justifications or qualifications such that all that is prohibited is the unfair or irrational differential treatment of persons who are accepted as being similarly situated for the purposes of the clause. Where legislation is to impose detailed statutory prohibitions and/or obligations on private actors, it will generally be necessary to specify the grounds or characteristics in respect of which such prohibitions and/or obligations apply.

Canada: New Directions for Equality Under the Canadian Charter?' (2002) 22 *Oxford Journal of Legal Studies* 641.

    [4] Grabham (n 3) 654.
    [5] A Phillips, 'Defending Equality of Outcome' (2004) 12 *Journal of Political Philosophy* 1–19, 15.
    [6] S Scheffler, What is Egalitarianism?' (2003) 31(1) *Philosophy & Public Affairs* 5–39, 17, 21–22.
    [7] ES Anderson, 'What is the Point of Equality?' (1999) 109 *Ethics* 109, 312–13, citing J Rawls, 'Kantian Constructivism in Moral Theory' (1980) 77 *Journal of Philosophy* 515–72, 525.

An excess of protected grounds leads to the danger that the level of protection against discrimination will be diluted (whether, where a justification defence is available, because of expansive interpretation of that defence or, where there is no such defence, because of narrow interpretation of the operative concepts in order to avoid perceived injustice). It also increases the potential for conflicts between equality claims and threatens unduly to restrict the rights of others (including rights to freedom of association). How, then, can the grounds be selected? It follows from the conclusion that the aim of discrimination/equality law should be the eradication of oppression, that the protected characteristics should be selected by reference to existing unjust status hierarchies and/or group oppression. Immutability, the requirement for which underpins the US approach in particular, is an unsatisfactory threshold requirement as it depends on an essentialist approach which does not map onto people's lived experience of oppression, and is as likely to be associated with advantage as disadvantage. Instead, the relevant consideration is the extent to which the characteristic in question is associated with group-based oppression and/or disadvantage (adopting Joel Balkin) across multiple aspects of life including 'wealth, social connections, political power, employment prospects, the ability to have intimate relationships and form families, and so on'.[8]

The selection of protected characteristics requires consideration not simply of whether such characteristics are associated with disadvantage but also that such disadvantage is *unjust* and, therefore, oppressive: the fact that paedophiles (or at any rate convicted paedophiles) may be disadvantaged across multiple social contexts will not entitle them to protection from discrimination[9] under this approach. More prosaically, age and religion/belief are unlikely to qualify for protection, the former because of any generalisable association between it and disadvantage/oppression and the latter in part because of this (when 'religion' and/or 'belief' are characterised in general, rather than by reference to particular religions or beliefs), and also because whether or not particular religious or other beliefs are worthy of protection must depend, absent acceptance that the mere holding of (any) belief(s) is a moral good sufficiently strong to defeat other claims (such as claims to gender equality, freedom of association etc), on the particulars of the belief in question.

Questions relating to protected characteristics re-emerge in Chapter 5 where I consider the particular difficulties raised by the regulation of discrimination on grounds of religion/belief in like fashion to that of discrimination because of sexual orientation, ethnicity etc. I consider the claims made by religious collectives and individuals for exemption from the normal prohibitions on discrimination, and the accommodation by domestic law of those claims. I explore the extent to which Articles 9 and/or 14 ECHR protect the right of religious individuals to manifest their beliefs, and the freedom of religious individuals and

---

[8] JM Balkin, 'The Constitution of Status' (1997) 106 *Yale Law Journal* 2313, 2360.
[9] As distinct, for example, from protection from criminal assault.

collectives to give effect to, as distinct from simply hold, discriminatory views. I conclude that the traditionally very thin protection of manifestation has been significantly enhanced by the recent decision of the ECtHR in *Eweida v UK*,[10] though the linked decisions in the *McFarlane* and *Ladele* cases made it clear that the Convention does not protect any right to discriminate on religious grounds.

The more difficult question concerns the extent, if any, to which the ECHR requires that individuals be protected from discrimination because of their own religious or other beliefs. The generally held view that Article 9 protects only those beliefs that are 'worthy of respect in a democratic society, compatible with human dignity and [do] not conflict with the fundamental rights of others' is wrong, that provision enshrining an absolute right to hold *any* belief, and the ECtHR's rubric about rights 'worthy of respect' relating to the right of parents protected by Article 1 Protocol 1 to the Convention to have their children educated 'in conformity with their own religious and philosophical convictions'.[11] It is also clear from the decision in *Redfearn v UK* that even those with racist views are entitled to some measure of protection from unfavourable treatment because of those views.[12] The ECtHR stopped short, however, of demanding that the BNP activist and bus driver be afforded like protection for his views (however distinct he kept them from his behaviour at work) as he would have been in connection with his sex or ethnicity. The position I put forward in Chapter 5 is that religion/belief should not be protected in like fashion to sex (gender) and race (ethnicity), disability and sexual orientation except where it serves as a proxy for ethnicity. I also leave open the possibility that age, religion/belief and, possibly, other characteristics could qualify for a lesser form of protection than that properly accorded to sex (gender) and race (ethnicity), disability and sexual orientation.

The suggestion is made in Chapter 2 that, if protected characteristics are chosen in order to challenge unjust status hierarchies and/or oppression, the obvious question arises why the law would seek to protect the beneficiaries of such hierarchies/oppression in like manner to their victims. In Chapter 3 I consider the traditional British preference for symmetry in the prohibition of discrimination, the approach taken elsewhere (Canada, the US, South Africa and the EU) and the question whether there is any principled reason to object to 'positive' or 'reverse' discrimination. Having concluded that there is no such reason of principle, I suggest that it is possible to favour an asymmetrical approach to discrimination/equality without insisting upon the identification of fixed social groups.

In Chapter 4 I consider the hold of the comparative approach to equality/discrimination, and the incompatibility of that approach with any radical challenge to unjust status hierarchies/oppression. I suggest that one of the difficul-

---

[10] *Eweida v UK* (2013) 57 EHRR 213.
[11] *Campbell & Cosans v UK* (1982) 4 EHRR 293.
[12] *Redfearn v UK* (2012) 33 BHRC 713.

ties with the comparator-based approach is that it blocks proper consideration of the justification for differential treatment. Also, and more fundamentally, it conceptualises discrimination as always consisting in *less* favourable treatment than another person, who is advantaged by the relevant protected characteristic, received or would receive. This leaves out of the account treatment which is discriminatory in the sense that it is *un*favourable for reasons that are associated with the relevant characteristic. Such treatment is now recognised as discriminatory under the Equality Act 2010 when the characteristic is pregnancy, also when it consists in the making of a protected act (this by reason of the statutory prohibition on discrimination). More fundamentally, recent decisions of both the ECtHR and the domestic courts have featured much less formalistic approaches to discrimination developed by international bodies and read across to Article 14 ECHR.

Of particular significance is the decision of the ECtHR in *Opuz v Turkey* (2009)[13] in which the Court read Article 14 in light of General Recommendation 19 of the Committee on CEDAW, which defines discrimination against women to include 'gender-based violence, that is, violence that is directed against a woman because she is a woman or that affects women disproportionately'. The characterisation by the Committee on CEDAW of violence against women as a form of discrimination results from the nature of violence against women as a form of gender-based oppression which perpetuates women's domination by men,[14] and does not turn on questions such as whether its perpetrators would use similar techniques against men with whom they were in analogous relationships.[15] More recently, while the ECtHR has continued to adopt a comparator-based approach to some cases, the domestic courts have been guided by the UN's Convention on the Rights of People with Disabilities (CRPD). This trend is consistent with the approach to discrimination law that I advocate here: that is, a concern with the eradication of group-based oppression rather than for the promotion of formally equal treatment.

It follows from my concern with oppression, and with the relationship between discrimination/equality and membership of social groups, that the question of multiculturalism, and of its relationship to equality/non-discrimination, is a subject for discussion. In the last of the book's substantive chapters, accordingly, I discuss the tensions which can exist between equality and multiculturalism from a position of concern for the interests of those who are relatively disadvantaged within minority groups. Current debates in the UK focus, not for the first time, on the acceptability of the *niqab* in public life, but other questions which are of topical interest include the role of sharia law in the context, in particular, of family disputes. The dangers of a liberal state ceding control over decisions concerning child welfare issues, family status, inheritance etc to patriarchal religious or other collectives are obvious, as exemplified by the decision in *Wisconsin v Yoder*

---

[13] *Opuz v Turkey* (2010) 50 EHRR 28.
[14] See for example General Recommendation 19 para 11.
[15] This being itself unlikely.

(1972),[16] which excluded Amish children aged 14 to 16 from the obligation of schooling, and accordingly reduced their opportunities to lead useful adult lives outside their birth communities should they later wish to do so. It is easy to point out the difficulties, from a gender equality perspective, posed by such practices as arranged marriages, FGC (female genital cutting), conservative female dress codes and the (unofficial) application in the UK of sharia law. But it is important not to adopt an orientalist perspective[17] which leads us to regard 'culture' as inhering only in those defined as 'other', and to attribute the violence and discrimination experienced by the women 'we' see as 'other' to their 'cultures' while overlooking the violence and discrimination in our own. Considering equality/discrimination as concerned with challenging unjust or oppressive status hierarchies means that the relevant question, in considering the rights and wrongs of multicultural accommodation, is not 'why should cultural "difference" be accommodated?' but rather 'how can the interests of the most vulnerable best be protected?'.

The themes which emerge from this overview include the limitations of formalistic approaches to discrimination/equality law and the potential for a more nuanced approach to allow more effective challenge to unjust status hierarchies/ group-based oppression. It is not my intention to suggest that there should be no room for a more formal 'treat like cases alike' principle of equal treatment/ non-discrimination. It would, for example, be entirely reasonable to couple statutory provisions which adopted a radically asymmetrical approach to a short list of characteristics selected by reason of their relationship to unjust status hierarchies with a general prohibition on unjustified or unfair discrimination, or a general equal treatment provision. Current front-runners in Britain for the former type of provisions would be sex/gender, ethnicity, disability and sexual orientation. The main beneficiaries would be women, LGBT, BME and disabled people. Also protected would be those who are oppressed by reason of their actual or perceived association with religions such as Islam or Judaism, which are closely associated with minority ethnicity, and membership of which may generate hostility associated with adherents' 'otherness', as distinct from doctrinal disputes. Further, and consistent with an anti-essentialist approach to the protected characteristics, the protection would apply to the disadvantaged characteristic, rather than only to those disproportionately associated with it. Thus, for example, the prohibition on gender-based discrimination should apply not only to women but also to men who are subject to unfavourable treatment in connection with their manifestation of behaviour or characteristics which are gendered 'female' (whether being too 'feminine' in appearance or mannerisms, for example, or seeking to discharge childcare obligations). (Women would be protected from being discriminated against because of inappropriately 'masculine' behaviour, since the reinforcement of gender role stereotypes is part and parcel of the maintenance of patriarchy.) The same would

---

[16] *Wisconsin v Yoder* 406 US 205 (1972).
[17] See generally E Said, *Orientalism* (London: Penguin Books, 2003).

apply in relation to ethnicity: whereas the target of protection might be characteristics/behaviour which are associated with disadvantaged racial/ethnic groups, that protection would extend to those subject to unfavourable treatment by reason of their perceived or actual rejection of 'race-appropriate' behaviour.

The list of protected characteristics I suggest above is not fixed. It may be, for example, that immigrant status requires protection other than by reference to ethnicity. (It may equally be, however, that a broad approach to race discrimination such as that suggested in the previous paragraph would in fact capture the types of unfavourable treatment that categories of immigrants, whatever their skin colour or national origin, experience.) It may also be that 'class', that is, having characteristics associated with being working class (or, perhaps more accurately, of the 'workless classes') requires specific protection. The relevant question is whether (Balkin) 'class', understood in this sense, is associated with group-based oppression and/or disadvantage across multiple aspects of life including 'wealth, social connections, political power, employment prospects, the ability to have intimate relationships and form families, and so on'.[18] The answer seems fairly clear.

The suggestion above is not a proposed blueprint for future developments in the UK, which is bound by European Union Directives to prohibit discrimination on grounds of sexual orientation, religion or belief, age and disability in relation to employment (broadly defined), and to prohibit sex and race discrimination in relation both to employment and more broadly. As we saw in Chapter 3, EU law operates on a broadly symmetrical approach, though (in common with domestic law) it requires reasonable adjustments to be made to accommodate the needs of disabled persons and it adopts a rather more generous approach to positive action than applied in Britain, at least prior to the implementation of the Equality Act 2010. The fact that radical change would be difficult or even impossible under present circumstances does not mean, however, that it is not open to discussion.

Even if, at a practical level, we work on the presumption that the EU obligations in this context are unlikely to be reduced, they do not at present require the prohibition of discrimination on grounds of age or religion/belief outside the context of employment (broadly defined). Nor do they require that heterosexuals be protected in like fashion to lesbians, gay men and bisexuals from discrimination outside that context, although EU law does impose broad prohibitions on less favourable treatment of white as well as BME people because of race, subject to (Art 5 Council Directive 2000/43) the ability of member states 'With a view to ensuring full equality in practice, the principle of equal treatment . . . [to] maintain[] or adopt[] specific measures to prevent or compensate for disadvantages linked to racial or ethnic origin'.

---

[18] JM Balkin, 'The Constitution of Status' (1997) 106 *Yale Law Journal* 2313, 2360.

Any difficulties posed by EU law could in any event be ameliorated by coupling the targeted anti-discrimination provisions outlined above with a general prohibition on unfair discrimination/requirement for equal treatment, which could apply to an open or closed long list of characteristics, or be cast without reference to specific grounds or characteristics. To apply such a provision to all private-sector decision making might reasonably be regarded as unduly restrictive of the individual freedoms of service providers, employers and the like,[19] although there is of course precedent for extensive regulation of discrimination in the context of employment at least. At present, protected characteristics include not only those listed in the Equality Act 2010 but also a wide range of others including part-time and fixed-term status; membership and non-membership of a trade union; participation in trade union duties and activities, in jury service or in health and safety-related activities; exercise of a wide range of statutory rights; whistle-blowing; the taking of various forms of leave and, in particular context, refusal to work on a Sunday.[20] Adding to these a list of other protected characteristics, however long, might serve simply to underscore what might realistically be regarded as being something close to a duty on employers to act rationally and/or fairly.[21]

A general prohibition on unfair discrimination/requirement for equal treatment might also reasonably be applied to all public-sector decision making. Such an obligation, indeed, is already significantly in place as a result of the partial implementation by the Human Rights Act 1998 of Article 14 of the ECHR. It is the case that Article 14 is parasitic on the other Convention rights, and that the UK has not signed up as yet to Protocol 12 (which includes a more comprehensive equality provision).[22] The implementation of a general equality/non-discrimination clause would not entail any radically increased burdens on public bodies given their existing obligations to act rationally and fairly.[23]

Any general prohibition on unfair discrimination/requirement for equal treatment could require that any distinctions in treatment (or distinctions based on any listed characteristics, or on these characteristics or others analogous thereto) be on grounds relevant to the legitimate aim(s) of the decision maker,

---

[19] See discussion in Chapter 2, pp 64–66.

[20] See Employment Rights Act 1996, ss 43M–47G, 98B–104G. It is the case that the prohibitions on detriment and dismissal on the protected grounds are narrower in scope than the employment-related protections provided by the Equality Act 2010 and do not apply to indirect dismissal. The general point, however, is that employers' freedom of action is already very significantly constrained.

[21] And to the extent that employers are not currently required to act rationally or fairly, there are grounds for suggesting that they ought to be in view of the central importance of work (and the economic benefits flowing therefrom) to people's lives.

[22] '1 The enjoyment of any right set forth by law shall be secured without discrimination on any ground such as sex, race, colour, language, religion, political or other opinion, national or social origin, association with a national minority, property, birth or other status.

2 No one shall be discriminated against by any public authority on any ground such as those mentioned in paragraph 1'.

[23] Or at any rate not to act with conspicuous unfairness: *R v IRC, ex p Unilever plc* [1996] STC 681, 695, *per* Simon Brown J.

and be proportionate to those aims. This would permit challenge to disproportionate treatment designed to ameliorate disadvantages associated with unjust status hierarchies such as might arise if an employer decided to offer managerial jobs exclusively to BME candidates until the proportion of BME managers equalled the proportion of BME adults in the local area, or a public authority decided to ban men from its parks in the interests of protecting women from sexual assault. The *mere fact* of unequal treatment designed to ameliorate existing racial or sexual disadvantage would not give rise to presumption of unfairness, though both of the examples provided would appear to be disproportionate to the aims pursued.

Bibliography

Books

Aristotle, *Ethica Nicomachea* V.3 1131a–b (W Ross trans, 1925)

Arnardóttir O, *Equality and Non-discrimination under the European Convention on Human Rights* (Leiden: Martinus Nijhoff Publishers, 2003)

Barry B, *Culture and Inequality: an Egalitarian Critique of Multiculturalism* (Cambridge, MA: Harvard University Press, 2001)

Benhabib S, *Democracy and Difference* (Princeton: Princeton University Press, 1996)

—— *The Claims of Culture* (Princeton: Princeton University Press, 2002)

Blackstone, *Commentaries on the Laws of England* (1765–69) (Chicago: University of Chicago Press, 1979) Book 1

Brownlie I, *System of the Law of Nations: State Responsibility (Part 1)* (Oxford: Oxford University Press, 1983)

Cameron J, *The International Law Commission's Articles on State Responsibility: Introduction, Text and Commentary* (Cambridge: Cambridge University Press, 2002)

Cooper D, *Challenging Diversity: Rethinking Equality and the Value of Difference* (Cambridge: Cambridge University Press, 2004)

Douglas G et al, *Social Cohesion and Civil Law: Marriage, Divorce and Religious Courts* (Cardiff: Cardiff University, 2011)

Dworkin R, *A Matter of Principle* (Oxford: Oxford University Press, 1985)

—— *Sovereign Virtue: The Theory and Practice of Equality* (Cambridge, MA: Harvard University Press, 2000)

Feldman D, *Civil Liberties and Human Rights in England and Wales*, 2nd edn (Oxford: Oxford University Press, 2002)

Fish S, *There's No Such Thing as Free Speech and It's a Good Thing, Too* (New York: Oxford University Press, 1994)

Foucault M, *Power/Knowledge: Selected Interviews and Other Writings 1972—1977* (C Gordon ed, New York: Pantheon Books, 1980)

—— *The Order of Things: An Archaeology of the Human Sciences* (New York: Vintage, 1994)

Frye M, *Oppression: The Politics of Reality* (Trumansburg, NY, The Crossing Press, 1983)

Hakim C, *Key Issues in Women's Work: Female Heterogeneity and the Polarisation of Women's Employment* (London: Athlone Press, 1996)

Hillier T, *Sourcebook on Public International Law* (London: Cavendish, 1998)

Hogg MA and Vaughan GM, *Social Psychology*, 3rd edn (London: Prentice Hall, 2000)

Hogg P, *Constitutional Law of Canada* (Scarborough, Ontario: Thomson Canada Limited, 2003)

Ignatiev N, *How the Irish Became White* (New York: Routledge, 1995)

Kelly P (ed), *Multiculturalism Reconsidered* (Cambridge: Polity Press, 2002)

Kundnani A, *Spooked: How Not to Prevent Violent Extremism* (London: Institute of Race Relations, 2009)

Kymlicka W, *Multicultural Citizenship: A Liberal Theory of Minority Rights* (Oxford: Clarendon Press, 1995)

—— (ed), *The Rise of Minority Cultures* (Oxford: Oxford University Press, 1995)

MacKinnon C, *Toward a Feminist Theory of the State* (Cambridge, MA: Harvard University Press, 1989)

McColgan A, *Discrimination: Text, Cases and Materials*, 2nd edn (Oxford: Hart Publishing, 1995)

—— *Pay Equity: Just Wages for Women* (Oxford: Clarendon Press, 1996)

—— *Women under the Law; the False Promise of Human Rights* (Harlow: Longman, 1999)

McCrea R, *Religion and the Public Order of the European Union* (Oxford: Oxford University Press, 2010)

Modood T, *Multicultural Politics: Racism, Ethnicity and Muslims in Britain* (Edinburgh: Edinburgh University Press, 2005)

——, Triandafyllidou A and Zapata-Barrero R (eds), *Multiculturalism, Muslims and Citizenship: A European Approach* (Abingdon: Routledge, 2006)

Narayan U, *Dislocating Cultures: Identities, Traditions, and Third-World Feminism* (1997, New York: Routledge, 1997)

Pearl D and Menski W, *Muslim Family Law*, 3rd edn (London: Sweet & Maxwell, 1998)

Raz, J, *The Morality of Freedom* (Oxford: Clarendon Press, 1986)

Rhodes S, *Incomparable Worth: Pay Equity Meets the Market* (New York: Cambridge University Press, 1993)

Said E, *Orientalism* (London: Penguin Books, 2003)

Sandel M, *Liberalism and the Limits of Justice* (Cambridge: Cambridge University Press, 1981)

—— *Democracy's Discontent* (Cambridge, MA: Harvard University Press, 1996)

Scales-Trent J, *Notes of a White Black Woman* (University Park, PA: Pennsylvania State University Press, 1995)

Shachar A, *Multicultural Jurisdictions* (Cambridge: Cambridge University Press, 2001)

Shah-Kazemi SN, *Untying the Knot: Muslim Women, Divorce and the Shariah* (London: Nuffield Foundation, 2001)

Spelman E, *Inessential Woman: Problems of Exclusion in Feminist Thought* (Boston: Beacon Press, 1988)

Taylor C, 'Atomism', *Philosophy and the Human Sciences*, Vol 2 (Cambridge: Cambridge University Press, 1985)

—— *Sources of the Self: The Making of the Modern Identity* (Cambridge, MA: Harvard University Press, 1989)

—— *Multiculturalism and 'The Politics of Recognition'* (Princeton: Princeton University Press, 1992)

—— and Gutmann A, *Multiculturalism* (Princeton: Princeton University Press, 1994)

Thornberry P, *International Law and the Rights of Minorities* (Oxford: Clarendon Press, 1991)

Van Paris P, *Real Freedom for All* (Oxford: Clarendon Press, 1995)

Vickers L, *Religious Freedom, Religious Discrimination and the Workplace* (Oxford: Hart Publishing, 2008)

Wadud A, *Qur'an and Woman: Rereading the Sacred Text from a Woman's Perspective* (New York: Oxford University Press, 1999

Walzer M, *Spheres of Justice* (New York: Basic Books, 1983)

Young IM, *Justice and the Politics of Difference* (Princeton: Princeton University Press, 1990)

—— *Intersecting Voices* (Princeton: Princeton University Press, 1997)

—— *Inclusion and Democracy* (Oxford: Oxford University Press, 2000)

Articles/Chapters

Ackerman BA, 'Beyond Carolene Products' (1985) 98 *Harvard Law Review* 713

Afshar H et al, 'Feminisms, Islamophobia and Identities' (2005) 53 *Political Studies* 262

Albertyn C and Goldblatt B, 'Facing the Challenge of Transformation: Difficulties in the Development of an Indigenous Jurisprudence of Equality' (1998) 14 *South African Journal on Human Rights* 248

Alexander L, 'Equal Protection and the Irrelevance of "Groups"' (2002) 2(1) *Issues in Legal Scholarship* (published online: http://www.degruyter.com/view/j/ils.2002.2. issue-1/issue-files/ils.2002.2.issue-1.xml),

Amede Obiora L, 'Bridges and Barricades: Rethinking Polemics and Intransigence in the Campaign Against Female Circumcision' (1997) 47 *Case Western Reserve Law Review* 275

Anderson ES, 'What is the Point of Equality?' (1999) 109 *Ethics* 109

Arneson R, 'Equality and Equality of Opportunity for Welfare' in L Pojman and R Westmoreland (eds), *Equality: Selected Readings* (New York: Oxford University Press, 1997), 229–41

—— and Shapiro I, 'Democratic Autonomy and Religious Freedom: A Critique of *Wisconsin v. Yoder*' in I Shapiro (ed), *Democracy's Place* (Ithaca: Cornell University Press, 1996) 173

Arriola E, 'Sexual Identity and the Constitution: Homosexual Persons as a Discrete and Insular Minority' (1992) 14 *Women's Rights Law Reporter* 263

Bakht N, 'Were Muslim Barbarians Really Knocking On the Gates of Ontario?: The Religious Arbitration Controversy—Another Perspective' (2006) 40 *Ottawa Law Review* 67

—— 'Religious Arbitration in Canada: Protecting Women by Protecting Them from Religion' (2007) 19 *Canadian Journal of Women and the Law* 119

Balkin JM, 'Ideology as Cultural Software' (1995) *Cardozo Law Review* 1221

—— 'The Constitution of Status' (1997) 106 *Yale Law Journal* 2313

—— and Siegel R, 'The American Civil Rights Tradition: Anticlassification or Antisubordination' (2004, Yale Faculty Scholarship Series)

Bamforth N, 'Conceptions of Anti-Discrimination Law' (2004) 24 *Oxford Journal of Legal Studies* 693

Bano S, 'Islamic Family Arbitration, Justice and Human Rights in Britain' (2007) 10(1) *Law, Social Justice and Global Development Journal*

—— 'In Pursuit of Religious and Legal Diversity: A Response' (2008) 10 *Ecclesiastical Law Journal* 285

Barnard C, 'The Principle of Equality in the Community Context' (1998) 57(2) *Cambridge Law Journal* 532

—— and Hepple B, 'Substantive Equality' (2000) 59(3) *Cambridge Law Journal* 562

Barnidge R, 'The Due Diligence Principle Under International Law' (2006) 8 *International Community Law Review* 81

Bayefsky AF, 'A Case Comment on the First Three Equality Rights Cases Under the Canadian Charter of Rights and Freedoms' (1990) 1 *Supreme Court Law Review* (2d) 503

Beatty D, 'The Canadian Concept of Equality' (1996) 46 *University of Toronto Law Journal* 349

Becker G, 'Investment in Human Capital: A Theoretical Analysis' (1962) 70(5)(II) *Journal of Political Economy* 9

Bedi S, 'Debate: What is So Special about Religion? The Dilemma of the Religious Exemption' (2007) 15 *The Journal of Political Philosophy* 235

Bhabha F, 'Between Exclusion and Assimilation: Experimentalizing Multiculturalism' (2009) 54 *McGill Law Journal* 45

Blackstone L, '"Courting Islam" Practical Alternatives to a Muslim Family Court in Ontario' (2005–06) 31 *Brooke Journal of International Law* 207

Bogdanski JA, 'Section 1981 and the Thirteenth Amendment after *Runyon v. McCrary*. On the Doorsteps of Discriminatory Private Clubs' (1977) 29 *Stanford Law Review* 747

Bowen J, 'How Could English Courts Recognize Shariah?' (2009–10) 7 *University of St Thomas Law Journal* 411

—— 'Private Arrangements' *Boston Review*, 1 March 2009

Brilmayer L, 'Carolene, Conflicts, and the Fate of the 'Insider-Outsider' (1986) 134 *University of Pennsylvania Law Review* 1291

Brodsky G, '*Gosselin v Quebec (Attorney General)*: Autonomy with a Vengeance' (2003) 15 *Canadian Journal of Women and the Law* 194

Bryan PE, 'Killing Us Softly: Divorce Mediation and the Politics of Power' (1992) 40 *Buffalo Law Review* 441

Burgess S, Wilson D and Lupton R, *Parallel Lives & Ethnic Segregation in the Playground & the Neighbourhood*, Centre for Market & Public Organisation Working Paper no 04/094 (Bristol: CMPO, 2004)

Byrnes A and Bath E, 'Violence against Women' (2008) 8(3) *Human Rights Law Review* 517

Carroll L, 'Muslim Women and "Islamic Divorce" in England' (1997) 17 *Journal of Muslim Minority Affairs* 97

Cassatella A, 'Multicultural Justice: Will Kymlicka and Cultural Recognition' (2006) 19 *Ratio Juris* 80

Charlesworth H, 'The Declaration on the Elimination of all Forms of Violence against Women', *American Society of International Law Newsletter: ASIL Insight* (June–August 1994) 1

Chotalia SP, 'Arbitration Using Sharia Law in Canada: A Constitutional and Human Rights Perspective' (2006) 15(2) *Constitutional Forum/Forum Constitutionnel* 63

Cohen GA, 'On the Currency of Egalitarian Justice' (1989) 99 *Ethics* 906

Coleman C, 'Individualizing Justice Through Multiculturalism: The Liberals' Dilemma' (1996) 96 *Columbia Law Review* 1093

Collins H, 'Discrimination, Equality and Social Inclusion' (2003) 66 *Modern Law Review* 16

—— 'Social Inclusion: A Better Approach to Equality Issues?' (2004–05) 14 *Transnational Law and Contemporary Problems* 897

Conaghan J, 'Reassessing the Feminist Theoretical Project in Law' (2000) 27 *Journal of Law and Society* 351

—— 'Intersectionality and UK Equality Initiatives' [2007] *South African Journal of Human Rights* 317

Crawford J and Olleson S, 'The Nature and Forms of International Responsibility' in M Evans et al (eds), *International Law*, 2nd edn (Oxford: Oxford University Press, 2003) 445

Crenshaw K, 'Demarginalizing the Intersection of Race and Sex' [1989] *University of Chicago Legal Forum* 139

Currah P, 'Defending Genders: Sex and Gender Non-Conformity in the Civil Rights Strategies of Sexual Minorities' (1997) 48 *Hastings Law Journal* 1363

Desai S, 'Hearing Afghan Women's Voices: Feminist Theory's Re-Conceptualization of Women's Human Rights (1999) 16 *Arizona Journal of International and Comparative Law* 805

Dingwall R, 'Divorce Mediation: Should We Change Our Mind?' (2010) *Journal of Social Welfare & Family Law* 107

Dorf M, 'A Partial Defense of an Anti-Discrimination Principle' (2002) *Cornell Law Faculty Publications* Paper 116

Dworkin R, 'What Is Equality? Part 1' (1981) 10 *Philosophy and Public Affairs* 185

—— 'What Is Equality? Part 2: Equality of Resources' (1981) 10 *Philosophy and Public Affairs* 283

—— 'Equality, Luck and Hierarchy' (2003) 31 *Philosophy & Public Affairs* 190

Eaton M, 'Patently Confused: Complex Inequality and *Canada* v *Mossop*' (1994) 1 *Review of Constitutional Studies* 203

Eekelaar J, 'The Arbitration and Mediation Services (Equality) Bill 2011' [2011] *Family Law* 1209

Favell A, 'Applied Political Philosophy at the Rubicon: Will Kymlicka's *Multiculturalism Citizenship*' (1998) 1 *Ethical Theory and Moral Practice* 255

Feldman D, 'Human Dignity as a Legal Value: Part 1' (1999) *Public Law* 682

Field R, 'Federal Family Law Reform in 2005: The Problems and Pitfalls' (2005) 5(1) *Queensland University Technical Law and Justice Journal* 28

Finley L, 'Transcending Equality Theory: A Way Out of the Maternity and the Workplace Debate' (1986) 86 *Columbia Law Review* 1118

Fiss O, 'Groups and the Equal Protection Clause' (1976) 5 *Philosophy & Public Affairs* 107

Flax J, 'Race/Gender and the Ethics of Difference' (1995) 23 *Political Theory* 500

Fletcher R, 'Reproducing Irishness: Race, Gender and Abortion' (2005) 11 *Canadian Journal of Women and the Law* 365

Ford RT, 'Unnatural Groups: A Reaction to Owen Fiss's 'Groups and the Equal Protection Clause' (2002) 2(1) *Issues in Legal Scholarship* (published online: http://www.degruyter.com/view/j/ils.2002.2.issue-1/issue-files/ils.2002.2.issue-1.xml)

Fraser N, 'From Redistribution to Recognition? Dilemmas of Justice in a "Post-Socialist" Age' (1995) 212(1) *New Left Review* 68

Fredman S, 'Equality: A New Generation?' (2001) *Acta Juridica* 214

—— 'Providing Equality: Substantive Equality and The Positive Duty to Provide' (2005) 21 *South African Journal on Human Rights* 163

Freeman GP, 'Immigrant Incorporation in Western Democracies' (2004) 38(3) *International Migration Review* 945

Fudge J, 'What Do We Mean by Law and Social Transformation?' (1990) 5 *Canadian Journal of Women and the Law* 47

Fudge J, 'Substantive Equality, the Supreme Court of Canada, and the Limits to Redistribution' (2007) 23 *South African Journal on Human Rights* 235

Funk MS, 'Representing Canadian Muslims: Media, Muslim Advocacy Organizations, and Gender in the Ontario Shari'ah Debate' (2009) 2 *Global Media Journal* 73

Gardner J, 'Liberals and Unlawful Discrimination' (1989) 9 *Oxford Journal of Legal Studies* 1

Gearey, DP 'New Protections after *Boy Scouts of America* v. *Dale*: A Private University's First Amendment Right to Pursue Diversity' (2004) 71 *University of Chicago Law Review* 1583

Gearty C, 'The Internal and External "Other" in the Union Legal Order: Racism, Religious Intolerance and Xenophobia in Europe' in P Alston, M Bustelo and J Heenan (eds), *The EU and Human Rights* (Oxford: Oxford University Press, 1999) 327

Gendelman AB, 'Equal Protection Clause, the Free Exercise Clause and Religion-Based Preemptory Challenges, The Comment' (1996) 63 *University of Chicago Law Review* 1639

Gentitjes M, 'The Equal Protection Clause and Immutability: the Chaos of Suspect Classification' (2010) 40 *University of Memphis Law Review* 507

Gibson D, 'Equality for Some' (1991) 40 *University of British Columbia Law Journal* 2

Gilbert D, 'Unequaled: Justice Claire L'Heureux-Dubé's Vision of Equality and Section 15 of the *Charter*' (2003) 15 *Canadian Journal of Women and the Law* 1

Gilreath S, 'Of Fruit Flies and Men: Rethinking Immutability in Equal Protection Analysis—with a View toward a Constitutional Moral Imperative' Wake Forest University Legal Studies Research Paper Series, April 2006

Gold M, 'The Canadian Concept of Equality' (1996) 46 *University of Toronto Law Journal* 349

Goldberg S, 'Equality without Tiers' (2003–04) 77 *Southern California Law Review* 481

Goldstone G, 'Two Concepts of Liberalism' (1995) 105(3) *Ethics* 516

Goodman J, 'Divine Judgment: Judicial Review of Religious Legal Systems in India and Israel' (2009) 32 *Hastings International and Comparative Law Review* 477

Grabham E, '*Law v Canada*: New Directions for Equality Under the Canadian Charter?' (2002) 22 *Oxford Journal of Legal Studies* 641

Grant E, 'Dignity and Equality' (2007) 7 *Human Rights Law Review* 299

Graves A, 'Women in Iran: Obstacles to Human Rights and Possible Solutions' (1996–97) 5 *American University Journal of Gender and the Law* 57

Greschner D, 'Does *Law* Advance the Cause of Equality?' (2001) 27 *Queen's Law Journal* 299

Grillo T, 'The Mediation Alternative: Process Dangers for Women' (1991) 100 *Yale Law Journal* 1545

Gunther G, 'Foreword: In Search of Evolving Doctrine on a Changing Court: A Model for a Newer Equal Protection' (1972) 86 *Harvard Law Review* 1

Guttmann A, 'Civic Education and Social Diversity' (1995) 105(3) *Ethics* 557

Hall S, *The Multicultural Question*, Pavis Papers in Social and Cultural Research no 4 (Milton Keynes: Open University, 2001)

Hannett S, 'Equality at the Intersections: the Legislative and Judicial Failure to Tackle Multiple Discrimination' (2003) 23 *Oxford Journal of Legal Studies* 65

Harris AP, 'Race and Essentialism in Feminist Legal Theory' (1989) 42 *Stanford Law Review* 581

—— 'Equality Trouble: Sameness and Difference in Twentieth-Century Race Law' (2000) 88 *California Law Review* 1923

Haslanger S, 'Ontology and Social Construction' (1995) 23 *Philosophical Topics* 95

—— 'Gender and Race: (What) Are They? (What) Do We Want Them To Be?' (2000) 34 *Noûs* 31

—— 'Oppressions Racial and Other' in MP Levine and T Pataki (eds), *Racism in Mind* (Ithaca: Cornell University Press, 2004) 97

—— 'What Are We Talking About? The Semantics and Politics of Social Kinds' (2005) 20(4) *Hypatia* 10

Hasnas J, 'Equal Opportunity, Affirmative Action, and the Anti-Discrimination Principle: The Philosophical Basis for the Legal Prohibition of Discrimination' (2009) 71 *Fordham Law Review* 423

Helfand M, 'The Usual Suspect Classifications: Criminals, Aliens and the Future of Same Sex Marriage' (2009–10) 12 *University of Pennsylvania Journal of Constitutional Law* 1

Herr RS, 'A Third World Feminist Defense of Multiculturalism' (2004) 30 *Social Theory and Practice* 73

Hessbruegge JA, 'The Historical Development of the Doctrines of Attribution and Due Diligence in International Law' (2004) 36 *New York University Journal of International Law and Politics* 265

Higgins TE, 'Anti-essentialism, Relativism and Human Rights' (1996) 19 *Harvard Women's Law Journal* 89

Holmes E, 'Anti-Discrimination Rights Without Equality' (2005) 68 *Modern Law Review* 175

Honig B, 'My Culture Made Me Do It' in J Cohen, M Howard and M Nussbaum, *Is Multiculturalism Bad for Women?* (Princeton: Princeton University Press, 1999) 35

Howland H, 'The Challenge of Religious Fundamentalism to the Liberty and Equality Rights of Women: An Analysis under the United Nations Charter' (1997) 35 *Columbia Journal of Transnational Law* 271

Huscroft G, 'Discrimination, Dignity, and the Limits of Equality' (2000) 9 *Otago Law Review* 697

Iyer N, 'Categorical Denials: Equality Rights and the Shaping of Social Identity' (1993) 19 *Queen's Law Journal* 179

Jackson B, ' "Transformative Accommodation" and Religious Law' (2009) 11 *Ecclesiastical Law Journal* 131

Jagwanth S, 'Affirmative Action in a Transformative Context: The South African Experience' (2003–04) 36 *Connecticut Law Review* 725

James SM, 'Shades of Othering: Reflections on Female Circumcision/Genital Mutilation' (1998) 23 *Signs* 1031

Jansen M, Snoeckx L and Mortelmans D, 'Repartnering and (Re-)employment: Strategies to Cope with the Economic Consequences of Partnership Dissolution' (2009) 71(5) *Journal of Marriage and Family* 1271-1293.

Jenkins S, 'Marital Splits and Income Changes over the Longer Term' in M Brynin and J Ermisch (eds), *Changing Relationships* (London: Routledge, 2009)

Jones R and Gnanpala W, *Ethnic Minorities in English Law* (Stoke on Trent: Trentham Books, 2000)

Kalev HD, 'Cultural Rights or Human Rights: The Case of Female Genital Mutilation' (2004) 15 *Sex Roles* 339

Karst K, 'Sources of Status-harm and Group Disadvantage in Private Behavior' (2002) 2(1) *Issues in Legal Scholarship* (published online: http://www.degruyter.com/view/j/ils.2002.2.issue-1/issue-files/ils.2002.2.issue-1.xml)

Kay HH, 'Models of Equality' (1985) *Illinois Law Review* 30

Kay RS, 'The Equal Protection Clause in the Supreme Court: 1873–1903'(1980) 29 *Buffalo Law Review* 667

Keller P, 'Re-thinking Ethnic and Cultural Rights in Europe' (1998) 18 *Oxford Journal of Legal Studies* 29

Khan S, 'Canadian Muslim Women and Shari'a Law: A Feminist Response to Oh! Canada!' (1993) 6 *Canadian Journal of Women and the Law* 52

Kibria N, 'Migration and Vietnamese American Women: Remaking Ethnicity' in M Zinn and B Dill (eds), *Women of Color in U.S. Society* (Philadelphia: Temple University Press, 1994) 108

Kim N, 'Towards a Feminist Theory of Human Rights; Straddling the Fence between Western Imperialism and Uncritical Absolutism' (1993–94) 25 *Columbia Human Rights Law Review* 49

—— and Piper T, '*Gosselin v Quebec*; Back to the Poorhouse' (2003) 48 *McGill Law Journal* 749

Koskenniemi M, 'The Politics of International Law' (1990) 1 (1–2) *European Journal of International Law* 4

Kukathas C, 'Are There any Cultural Rights?' (1992) 20 *Political Theory* 105

—— 'Cultural Toleration' in I Shapiro and W Kymlicka (eds), *Ethnicity and Group Rights* (New York: New York University Press, 1997) 69

—— 'Survey Article; Multiculturalism as Fairness: Will Kymlicka's *Multicultural Citizenship* (1997) 5(4) *The Journal of Political Philosophy* 406

Lam MC, 'Feeling Foreign in Feminism' (1994) 19 *Signs* 865

Larson CFW, 'Titles of Nobility, Hereditary Privilege, and the Unconstitutionality of Legacy Preferences in Public School Admissions' (2006) 84 *Washington University Law Review* 1375.

Law S, 'Rethinking Sex and the Constitution' (1984) 132 *University of Pennsylvania Law Review* 955

Lerman L, 'Mediation of Wife Abuse Cases: The Adverse Impact of Informal Dispute Resolution on Women' (1984) 7 *Harvard Women's Law Journal* 57

Lerner N, *Group Rights and Discrimination in International Law* (Dordrecht: Martinus Nijhoff, 1991)

Lessard H, 'Equality and Access to Justice in the Work of Bertha Wilson' (1992) 15 *Dalhousie Law Journal* 35

Lewis H, 'Between *Irua* and "Female Genital Mutilation": Feminist Human Rights Discourse and the Cultural Divide' (1995) 8 *Harvard Human Rights Journal* 1

Linder DO, 'Freedom of Association after *Roberts v United States Jaycees*' (1984) 82 *Michigan Law Review* 1878

Mackinnon C, 'Sex Equality: On Difference and Domination' in *Toward a Feminist Theory of the State* (Cambridge, MA: Harvard University Press, 1989)

—— 'Reflections on Sex Equality Under the Law' (1990–91) 100 *Yale Law Journal* 1281

Macklem T, 'Faith as a Secular Value' (2000) 45 *McGill Law Journal* 1

Madera A, 'Judicial Bonds of Marriage for Jewish and Islamic Women' (2009) 11 *Journal of Ecclesiastical Law* 51

Madood T, 'Anti-Essentialism, Multiculturalism and the "Recognition" of Religious Groups' (1998) 6 *The Journal of Political Philosophy* 378

Majury D, 'The *Charter*, Equality Rights and Women: Equivocation and Celebration' (2002) 40 *Osgoode Hall Law Journal* 297

Malik M ' "The Branch on Which We Sit": Multiculturalism, Minority Women and Family Law' in A Diduck and K O'Donovan (eds), *Feminist Perspectives on Family Law* (London: Routledge, 2006) 211

Margalit A and Halbertal M, 'Liberalism and the Right to Culture' (1994) 61(3) *Social Research* 491–548

—— and Raz J, 'National Self-Determination' in W Kymlicka (ed), *The Rights of Minority Cultures* (Oxford: Oxford University Press, 1995) 79

Martin S, 'Balancing Individual Rights to Equality and Social Goals' (2001) 80 *The Canadian Bar Review* 299

Mashour A, 'Islamic Law and Gender Equality: Could There Be a Common Ground? A Study of Divorce and Polygamy in Sharia Law and Contemporary Legislation in Tunisia and Egypt' (2005) 27 *Human Rights Quarterly* 562

Mathys N and Pincus L, 'Is Pay Equity Equitable? A Perspective That Looks Beyond Pay' (1993) 44 *Labor Law Journal* 351

Matravers M, 'Responsibility, Luck and the "Equality of What?" Debate' (2002) 50 *Political Studies* 558

Mayer A, 'A "Benign" *Apartheid*: How Gender *Apartheid* has been Rationalized' (2000–01) 5 *UCLA Journal of International Law and Foreign Affairs* 237

Mazie S, 'Consenting Adults? Amish *Rumspringa* and the Quandry of Exit in Liberalism' (2005) 3 *Perspectives on Politics* 745

McColgan A, 'In Defence of Battered Women Who Kill' (1993) 13 *Oxford Journal of Legal Studies* 508

—— 'Common Law and the Relevance of Sexual History Evidence' (1996) 16 *Oxford Journal of Legal Studies* 275

—— 'Cracking the Comparator Problem, "Equal" Treatment and the Role of Comparisons' [2006] *European Human Rights Law Review* 650

—— 'Reconfiguring Discrimination Law' [2007] *Public Law* 74

—— 'Equality and Multiculturalism' [2011] *Current Legal Problems* 1

McCrudden C, 'Rethinking Positive Action' (1986) 15 *Industrial Law Journal* 219

—— 'Theorising European Law' in C Costello and E Barry (eds), *Equality in Diversity: The New Equality Directives* (Dublin: Irish Centre for European Law, 2003) 1

—— 'Equality and Non-Discrimination' in D Feldman (ed), *English Public Law* (Oxford: Oxford University Press, 2004) 582

McGill S, 'Religious Tribunals and the Ontario *Arbitration Act, 1991*: The Catalyst for Change' (2005) *Journal of Law and Social Policy* 53

McGoldrick D, 'Accommodating Muslims in Europe: From Adopting Sharia Law to Religiously Based Opt Outs from Generally Applicable Laws' (2009) 9 *Human Rights Law Review* 603

Melville A and Laing K, 'Closing the Gate: Family Lawyers as Gatekeepers to a Holistic Service' [2010] *International Journal of Law in Context* 167

Menski WF, 'Asians in Britain and the Question of Adaptation to a New Legal Order: Asian Laws in Britain' in M Israel and N Wagle (eds), *Ethnicity, Identity, Migration: the South Asian Context* (Toronto: University of Toronto, 1993)

Moens G, 'The Action–Belief Dichotomy and Freedom of Religion' (1989–90) 12 *Sydney Law Review* 195

Moreau SR, 'The Wrongs of Unequal Treatment' (2004) 54 *University of Toronto Law Review* 291

Nagel T, 'The Policy of Preference' in *Mortal Questions* (Cambridge: Cambridge University Press, 1979) 91

Nichols J, 'Multi-Tiered Marriage; Ideas and Influences from New York and Louisiana to the International Community' (2007) 40 *Vanderbilt Journal of Transnational Law* 135

Note 'Legislative Purpose, Rationality, and Equal Protection' (1972) 82 *Yale Law Journal* 123

O'Cinneide C, 'Fumbling Towards Coherence: The Slow Evolution of Equality and Anti-Discrimination Law in Britain' (2006) 57 *Northern Ireland Law Quarterly* 57

—— 'Positive Action and the Limits of Existing Law' (2006) 13 *Maastricht Journal of European & Comparative Law* 351

Okin SM, 'Gender Inequality and Cultural Differences' (1994) 22 *Political Theory* 5

—— 'Response to Jane Flax' (1995) 23 *Political Theory* 511

—— 'Feminism and Multiculturalism: Some Tensions' (1998) 108 *Ethics* 661

—— 'Mistresses of Their Own Destiny?: Group Rights, Gender and Realistic Rights of Exit' (2002) 112 *Ethics* 205

—— 'Equal Citizenship: Gender/Justice and Gender: An Unfinished Debate' (2004) 72 *Fordham Law Review* 1537

Orton H, 'Section 15, Benefits Programs and Other Benefits at Law: The Interpretation of Section 15 of the Charter Since Andrews' (1990) 19 *Manitoba Law Journal* 288

—— and Beach H, 'A New Era for the Saami People of Sweden' in CP Cohen (ed), *Human Rights of Indigenous Peoples* (New York: Transnational Publishers, 1998)

Outlaw L, 'Towards a Critical Theory of Race' in D Goldberg (ed), *Anatomy of Racism* (Minneapolis: University of Minnesota Press, 1990) 58

Parekh B, 'A Varied Moral World' in J Cohen, M Howard and M Nussbaum (eds), *Is Multiculturalism Bad for Women?* (Princeton: Princeton University Press, 1999) 69

Perry K, 'Modern Equal Protection: A Conceptualization and Appraisal' (1979) 79 *Columbia Law Review* 1023

Phillips A, 'Defending Equality of Outcome' (2004) 12 *Journal of Political Philosophy* 1

Pothier D, 'Connecting Grounds of Discrimination to Real People's Real Experiences' (2001) 13 *Canadian Journal of Women and the Law* 37

Poulter S, 'Ethnic Minority Customs, English Law and Human Rights' (1987) 36 *International & Comparative Law Quarterly* 589

—— 'The Claim to a Separate Islamic System of Personal Law for British Muslims' in C Mallat and J Connors (eds), *Islamic Family Law* (London: Graham and Trotman, 1990), 147

Raday F, 'Culture, Religion and Gender' (2003) 1 *International Journal of Constitutional Law* 663

Rawls J, 'Kantian Constructivism in Moral Theory' (1980) 77 *Journal of Philosophy* 515

Raz J, 'Multiculturalism: A Liberal Perspective' in *Ethics in the Public Domain: Essays in the Morality of Law and Freedom* (New York: Clarendon Press, 1994)

—— 'Multiculturalism' (1998) 11(3) *Ratio Juris* 193

—— 'How Perfect Should One Be? And Whose Culture Is?' in J Cohen, M Howard and M Nussbaum (eds), *Is Multiculturalism Bad for Women?* (Princeton: Princeton University Press, 1999) 95

Reaume D, 'Justice Between Cultures: Autonomy and the Protection of Cultural Affiliation' (1995) 29 *University of British Columbia Law Review* 117

—— 'Dignity and Discrimination' (2002–03) 63 *Louisiana Law Review* 645

—— 'Comparing Theories of Sex Discrimination: The Role of Comparison' (2005) 25 *Oxford Journal of Legal Studies* 547

Ricci I, 'Mediators Notebook: Reflections on Promoting Equal Empowerment and Entitlement for Women' in CA Everett (ed), *Divorce Mediation: Perspectives on the Field* (New York: Haworth, 1985)

Ryder B, CC Faria and E Lawrence, 'What's Law Good for?: An Empirical Overview of Charter Equality Decisions' (2004) 24 *Supreme Court Law Review* (2d) 103

Sassen S, 'Culture Beyond Gender' in J Cohen, M Howard and M Nussbaum (eds), *Is Multiculturalism Bad for Women?* (Princeton: Princeton University Press, 1999) 76

Scales A, 'Towards a Feminist Jurisprudence' (1980–81) 56 *Indiana Law Journal* 375

Scheffler S, 'What is Egalitarianism?' (2003) 31(1) *Philosophy & Public Affairs* 5

Schmidt CW, '*Doe v. Kamehameha*: Section 1981 and the Future of Racial Preferences in Private Schools' (2007) 42 *Harvard Civil Rights-Civil Liberties Law Review* 557

Schwebel C, 'Welfare Rights in Canadian and German Constitutional Law' (2011) 12 *German Law Journal* 1901

Sedley S, 'Human Rights: A Twenty-First Century Agenda' [1995] *Public Law* 386

Seligmann M, 'Luck, Leverage, and Equality: A Bargaining Problem for Luck Egalitarians' (2007) 35 *Philosophy and Public Affairs* 266

Shachar A, 'Group Identity and Women's Rights in Family Law: the Perils of Multicultural Accommodation' (1998) 6(3) *Journal of Political Philosophy* 285

—— 'Reshaping the Multicultural Model: Group Accommodation and Individual Rights' (1998) 8 *Windsor Review of Legal and Social Issues* 83

—— 'On Citizenship and Multicultural Vulnerability' (2000) 28 *Political Theory* 64

—— 'The Puzzle of Interlocking Power Hierarchies: Sharing the Pieces of Jurisdictional Authority' (2000) 35 *Harvard Civil Liberties-Civil Rights Law Review* 385

—— 'Two Critiques of Multiculturalism' (2001–02) 23 *Cardozo Law Review* 253

Shadowen SD, Tulante SP and Alpern SL, 'No Distinctions Except Those Which Merit Originates: The Unlawfulness of Legacy Preferences in Public and Private Universities' (2009) 49 *Santa Clara Law Review* 51

Shaffer M, 'Divorce Mediation: A Feminist Perspective' (1988) 46(1) *University of Toronto Law Review* 162

Shapiro MR, 'Treading the Supreme Court's Murky Immutability Waters' (2002) 38 *Gonzaga Law Review* 409

Shoben EW, 'Compound Discrimination: The Interaction of Race and Sex in Employment Discrimination' (1980) 55 *New York University Law Review* 793

Siegel SA, 'Justice Holmes, *Buck v. Bell*, and the History of Equal Protection' (2005) 90 *Minnesota Law Review* 106

Smith N, 'A Critique of Recent Approaches to Discrimination Law' (2007) *New Zealand Law Review* 499

Smith P, 'Part II: Romantic Paternalism—The Ties that Bind' (1999) 3 *Journal of Gender, Race & Justice* 181

Ssenyonjo M, 'The Islamic Veil and Freedom of Religion, the Rights to Education and Work: a Survey of Recent International and National Cases' (2007) 6 *Chinese Journal of International Law* 653

Steyn, Lord 'Democracy through Law' (2002) 18 *European Human Rights Law Review* 723

Sunder M, 'Cultural Dissent' (2001–02) 54 *Stanford Law Review* 495
—— 'Piercing the Veil' (2003) 112 *Yale Law Journal* 1399
Tajfel H and Turner JC, 'The Social Identity Theory of Inter-group Behavior' in
    S Worchel and LW Austin (eds), *Psychology of Intergroup Relations* (Chicago: Nelson-
    Hall, 1986)
Tajfel T, 'Experiments in Intergroup Discrimination' [1970] *Scientific American* 96–102
Tamir Y, 'Siding With the Underdogs' in J Cohen, M Howard and M Nussbaum (eds), *Is
    Multiculturalism Bad for Women?* (Princeton: Princeton University Press, 1999) 47
Tarnopolsky W, 'The Equality Rights in the Canadian Charter of Rights and Freedoms'
    (1983) 61 *Canadian Bar Review* 242
—— 'The New Canadian Charter of Rights and Freedoms as Compared and Contrasted
    with the American Bill of Rights' (1983) 5 *Human Rights Quarterly* 227
Taylor C, 'What Is Human Agency' in *Human Agency and Language: Philosophical
    Papers 1* (Cambridge: Cambridge University Press, 1985) 15
—— 'The Politics of Recognition' in A Guttmann (ed), *Multiculturalism and the Politics
    of Recognition* (Princeton: Princeton University Press, 1994)
Treuthart MP, 'In Harm's Way? Family Mediation and the Role of the Attorney Advocate'
    (1993) 23 *Golden Gate University Law Review* 717
Tussman J and tenBroek J, 'The Equal Protection of the Laws' (1949) 37 *California Law
    Review* 341
Van Parijs P, 'Why Surfers Should Be Fed: The Liberal Case for an Unconditional Basic
    Income' (1991) 20 *Philosophy and Public Affairs* 101
Vickers L, 'Promoting Equality or Fostering Resentment? The Public Sector Equality
    Duty and Religion and Belief' (2011) 31(1) *Legal Studies* 135
Volpp L, '(Mis)identifying Culture: Asian Women and the "Cultural Defense"' (1994) 17
    Harvard Women's Law Journal 57
—— 'Talking "Culture": Gender, Race, Nation, and the Politics of Multiculturalism'
    (1996) 96 *Columbia Law Review* 1573
—— 'Blaming Culture for Bad Behaviour' (2000) 12 *Yale Journal of Law and the
    Humanities* 88
—— 'Feminism versus Multiculturalism' (2001) 101 *Columbia Law Review* 1181
Wahlstrom AK, 'Liberal Democracies and Encompassing Religious Communities: A
    Defense of Autonomy and Accommodation' (2005) 36(1) *Journal of Social Philosophy*
    31
Waldron J, 'Rights in Conflict' (1989) 99 *Ethics* 503
—— 'Minority Cultures and the Cosmopolitan Alternative' (1991–92) 25 *University of
    Michigan Journal of Law Reform* 751
Walzer M, 'The New Tribalism' [1992] *Dissent* 164
Westen P, 'The Empty Idea of Equality' (1982) 95 *Harvard Law Review* 537
White L, 'Liberalism, Group Rights and the Boundaries of Toleration: The Case of
    Minority Religious Schools in Ontario' (2003) 36 *Canadian Journal of Political
    Science* 975
Williams R, 'Civil and Religious Law in England: A Religious Perspective' (2008) 10
    Ecclesiastical Law Journal 262
Williams W, 'Equality's Riddle: Pregnancy and the Equal Treatment/Special Treatment
    Debate' (1984–85) 13 *New York University Review of Law and Social Change* 325
Wing K, 'Brief Reflections Toward a Multiplicative Theory and Praxis of Being' (1990–
    91) 6 *Berkley Women's Law Journal* 181

Yilmaz I, 'Law as Chameleon: The Question of Incorporation of Muslim Personal Law into the English Law' (2001) 21(2) *Journal of Muslim Minority Affairs* 297

—— 'The Challenge of Post-modern Legality and Muslim Legal Pluralism in England' (2002) 28 *Journal of Ethnic and Migration Studies* 343

Young IM, 'Equality of Whom? Social Groups and Judgments of Injustice' (2001) 9 *The Journal of Political Philosophy* 1

—— 'Status Inequality and Social Groups' (2002) 2(1) *Issues in Legal Scholarship* (published online: http://www.degruyter.com/view/j/ils.2002.2.issue-1/issue-files/ils.2002.2.issue-1.xml)

Zinn M, Cannon L, Higginbotham E and Dill B, 'The Costs of Exclusionary Practices in Women's Studies' (1986) 11(2) *Signs* 290

Reports

Boyd M, Dispute Resolution in Family Law: Protecting Choice, Promoting Inclusion, December 2004

Brodsky G and Day S, Canadian Charter Equality Rights for Women: One Step Forward or Two Steps Back? (Ottowa: Canadian Advisory Council on the Status of Women, 1989)

Cantle T et al, Challenging Local Communities to Change Oldham: Review of Community Cohesion in Oldham (Home Office, 2001)

Chopin I and Uyen Do U, 'Developing Anti-Discrimination Law in Europe' (November 2011, European Network of Legal Experts in the Non-discrimination Field)

Coomaraswamy C, 'Preliminary Report on Violence Against Women, Its causes and Consequences' UN Doc. E/CN.4/195/42 (Nov 1994)

—— 'Preliminary Report on Violence Against Women, Its Causes and Consequences' UN Doc. E/CN.4/2000/68 (Feb 2000)

Ertürk Y, 'Third Report to the UN Commission on Human Rights' (GE.06-10350 (E) 250106)

Johnson N (ed), Citizenship, Cohesion and Solidarity (London: the Smith Institute, 2008)

Legal Services Commission, Legal Aid and Mediation for People Involved in Family Breakdown (London: HMSO, 2007)

Malik M, Muslim Legal Norms and the Integration of European Muslims EUI Working Paper RSCAS 2009/29 (Florence: European University Institute, 2009)

—— Minority Legal Orders in the UK: Minorities, Pluralism and the Law (London: British Academy, 2012)

McEoin D, Sharia Law or 'One Law for All?, Civitas

Ministry of Justice, Legal Aid Reform in England and Wales: the Government Response

Moosa Z, 'Balancing Women's Rights with Freedom of Religion' in State of the World's Minorities and Indigenous People (2010: Minority Rights Group International)

Mumtaz A and Whitehouse A, Oh! Canada. Whose Land, Whose Dream? Sovereignty, Social Contracts and Participatory Democracy: An Exploration into Constitutional Arrangements (1991, Toronto: Canadian Society of Muslims, 2012)

One Law for All, Sharia Law in Britain: A Threat to One Law for All and Equal Rights (2010: One Law for All, London)

Vertovec S and Wessendorf S, 'Assessing the Backlash Against Multiculturalism in Europe' (Working Paper 09-04, Max Planck Institute, 2009)

Warraich SA and Balchin C, Recognizing the Unrecognized: Inter-Country Cases and Muslim Marriages 7 Divorces in Britain (WLUML, 2006)

Index